THE AUGUST TRIALS

THE AUGUST TRIALS

THE HOLOCAUST AND
POSTWAR JUSTICE IN POLAND

Andrew Kornbluth

 Harvard University Press

CAMBRIDGE, MASSACHUSETTS, & LONDON, ENGLAND   2021

Copyright © 2021 by the President and Fellows of Harvard College
ALL RIGHTS RESERVED
Printed in the United States of America

First printing

Library of Congress Cataloging-in-Publication Data

Names: Kornbluth, Andrew, 1982– author.
Title: The August trials : the Holocaust and postwar justice in Poland / Andrew Kornbluth.
Description: Cambridge, Massachusetts : Harvard University Press, 2021. | Includes bibliographical references and index.
Identifiers: LCCN 2020033862 | ISBN 9780674249134 (cloth)
Subjects: LCSH: Truth commissions—Poland—History—20th century. | Holocaust, Jewish (1939–1945)—Poland. | Poland—Politics and government—1945–1980. | Poland—History—Occupation, 1939–1945. | Poland—History—Occupation, 1939–1945—Collaborationists. | Soviet Union—Foreign relations—Poland. | Poland—Foreign relations—Soviet Union.
Classification: LCC JC580 .K67 2021 | DDC 341.6/90268—dc23
LC record available at https://lccn.loc.gov/2020033862

To the innocent

CONTENTS

	NOTE ON POLISH PRONUNCIATION	ix
	Introduction: The Country without a Quisling?	1
1	"There Are Many Cains among Us"	15
2	Crowdsourcing Genocide	37
3	Hearts Grown Brutal	78
4	The Special Courts	105
5	Rewriting the Narrative of the Past	132
6	Between Politics and Retribution	160
7	The District Courts	199
8	Cold War Considerations	226
9	The Principles of Socialist Humanism	248
10	The Math of Amnesty	259
	Conclusion: The Conspiracy of Memory	269
	ARCHIVAL ABBREVIATIONS	283
	NOTES	285
	ACKNOWLEDGMENTS	319
	INDEX	321

NOTE ON POLISH PRONUNCIATION

Ą	Own as in "loan"
C	Ts as in "arts"
Ć, Cz	Ch as in "chart"
Ch	H as in "hawk"
Ci	Chee as in "cheese"
Dż, Dź	"J" as in "jazz"
Dzi	"Jee" as in "jeer"
Ę	"En" as in "entry"
J	"Y" as in "young"
Ł	"W" as in "war"
Ń	soft "n" as in "train"
Ó	"Oo" as in "loose"
Rz, Ż, Ź	"Zh" as in "Zhivago"
Si	"Shee" as in "sheep"
Sz, Ś	"Sh" as in "sharp"
W	"V" as in "Victoria"

THE AUGUST TRIALS

INTRODUCTION

The Country without a Quisling?

IN 2018 the government of Poland, a member of the European Union (EU) for fourteen years, of NATO for almost twenty, and the only EU country to avoid recession in the wake of the 2008 financial meltdown—in short, a prosperous and stable member of the transatlantic politico-economic project after two centuries of war, occupation, and upheaval—precipitated the country's most serious international crisis since the end of communism in 1989 by passing a law that forbade reaching certain conclusions about historical events that took place seventy-four years prior, or before 90 percent of the current population had even been born. The ensuing backlash was so serious that the American government reportedly refused to accept any state visits by Polish leaders until the law was revised.[1]

Of course, this was no ordinary law. The legislation in question, the Amendment to the Law on the Institute of National Remembrance, prescribed up to three years in prison for anyone who "attributes to the Polish Nation or Polish State ... co-responsibility for Nazi crimes committed by the Third Reich ... or otherwise glaringly minimizes the responsibility of the real perpetrators of these crimes."[2]

Although innocent enough on the face of it, the law was immediately understood as an attempt to put a stop to increasingly unflattering revelations about Polish involvement in the Holocaust. These had begun in 2000, when the sociologist Jan Gross used newly available trial records from the late 1940s and 1950s to begin corroborating long-standing, albeit anecdotal, accusations by Holocaust survivors and Jewish historians that Polish collaboration in the genocide had been more enthusiastic, widespread, and independent of German initiative than anyone could have imagined. Criminal penalties aside, the official manifestation of an allergic reaction to any mention of a Polish role in the Holocaust was not new. In 2012 a previous administration had compelled its US counterpart to apologize for an infelicitous reference to "Polish death camps," and Jan Gross's revelations had weighed on many a Polish leader before then.

But the amendments were being introduced at the same time that the nationalist government of the Party of Law and Justice (Prawo i Sprawiedliwość, PiS) was engaged in a sweeping overhaul of the country's constitutional order, laying what critics claimed was the groundwork for an authoritarian state.[3] High-ranking military officers were dismissed, state television became openly partisan, the judicial branch was subjected to party control, and conspiracy theories were officially endorsed.[4] That PiS should expend so much political capital on what was seemingly a forgotten page of history reveals the extent to which modern Poland, and especially the nationalist conception of it, has been shaped by the Holocaust, the communist regime that followed the Holocaust, and the self-serving myth about the Holocaust that was institutionalized during the communist period.

ORIGIN MYTHS

Even before the Second World War was over, contemporary observers foresaw that the destruction of the country's entrepreneurial minorities, foremost the Jews, and the enormous property transfer that ensued—from factories and storefronts right down to wedding rings and blood-spattered linens—would clear the way for a Polish urban middle class in a society that had been mired in agrarian feudalism when Nazi Germany invaded in 1939. The communist assumption of power at war's end definitively swept away the old political and landowning elites, instituted a dictatorial welfare state eventually known as the Polish People's Republic (Polska Rzeczpospolita Ludowa, PRL), and elevated millions of peasants to previously unattainable positions of responsibility in an industrialized bureaucracy.

After the downfall of Poland's Stalinist leadership in 1956, the ascendant nationalist wing of the Polish communist party, positioning itself as a defender of memory and national honor, systematically propagandized a "radical apologetic" narrative of the Holocaust that first captured international attention during the notorious "anti-Zionist" persecutions of 1968. Scapegoated by the PRL for a wave of student protests that year, Poland's few remaining Jews were forced into exile by a massive, state-sponsored campaign that charged them with spreading falsehoods about the behavior of Polish society during the Nazi occupation.[5]

The essence of the radical apologia is that Poles were helpless to resist German commands regarding the Jews, that Jews willingly collaborated in their own oppression, that Poles nonetheless did everything they could to help Polish Jewry, that anyone who remembers or believes otherwise is anti-Polish, and that, in any event, Poles were the "true" victims of the war. This "myth of innocence" went on to become "one of the most important . . . mechanisms used for the creation of social consensus" in the PRL.[6]

Although the PRL evaporated in 1989, the version of Holocaust memory it popularized lived on in postcommunist Poland, ironically entrenched as the standard nationalist view of the war. Nor did history lose any of its power as a source of political legitimacy. Even as the debate raged around Jan Gross's discoveries in the early 2000s, the PiS movement began challenging the established interpretation of other key moments in recent Polish history, from the genesis of the Solidarity movement that brought down communism to the peaceful handover of power in 1989, which it viewed as a corrupt backroom deal benefiting communist collaborators.[7]

In this respect, the attempt in 2018 to prohibit interrogation of the nationalist Holocaust narrative under penalty of law was a logical step in a political environment where history is "not really about the past at all, but . . . a daily lived and vivid present." The fate of Poland's Jews, however, is extremely sensitive not just because it complicates the purely heroic view of the past, but because it raises questions about the foundations of modern Poland. As the Polish sociologist Andrzej Leder has written, the dispossession of the Jews and the industrialization of the communists were the key events in a "stolen revolution," so called because it was initiated by foreign invaders, the reality of which was "obliterated" from the memory of the society it created.[8]

It is also true that the official contestation of evidence of anti-Semitic violence in Poland has been a recurring phenomenon for over a century. The interwar Polish state vigorously defended itself on the international stage against accusations of involvement in pogroms and massacres committed by Polish soldiers and civilians during the confused warfare in Poland's eastern borderlands from 1918 to 1921. And it was the government-in-exile in London, which, "embarrassed" by reports of the enthusiastic reception of

Nazi anti-Semitism by the local populace in occupied Poland, first engaged in systematic denial about what was happening in the occupied territories.[9]

But in 1944 it was Poland's fledgling Stalinist government, not the superannuated government-in-exile, that was forced to plunge headlong into the unenviable task of cobbling together a "useable past" from the rubble of the Second World War. And within the Soviet-backed state, no institution was closer to the cutting edge than the postwar courts. It was the courts, made up of prewar judges and prosecutors who were determined not to surrender their independence, that would have to delve into the most sordid details of the crimes committed against Jews by their Polish neighbors and, in the process, make sense of acts society at large would rather pretend had never happened. It was the courts that would have to figure out how the law could encompass crimes no jurist had ever anticipated. Faced with sorting out crimes both deeply damaging to national self-image and unprecedented in their scope, the courts would have to work with the evolving Stalinist state and a recalcitrant society to broker a version of the past amenable to all. Ironically, even as they authored a mythology that has remained the backbone of Polish nationalism to the present day, they would undermine its foundations by entering into evidence a damning portrait of a society under occupation.

TWO WARS

To speak of "memory culture" is to conjure connotations of decades-long social and political ferment. But in the case of Poland, the work of the postwar courts would be enormously complicated by the fact that Jewish and Polish views of what was happening radically diverged during the war, before the events in question had even concluded.

There was general agreement among ethnic Poles that wartime collaboration had been a marginal phenomenon. Alone among the nations of Europe, Poland heroically fought the Germans from the war's first day to its very last. Alone among the occupied nations of Europe, Poland never had a collaborationist government or a collaborationist military formation. Never capitulating, the government went into exile, and an underground para-state, complete with its own university system, press office, and conspiratorial "Home Army," continued functioning inside the country in its stead. The costs of this uncompromising resistance were staggering: almost three million ethnic Poles dead; the country's intellectual, military, and political elite decimated; the capital city razed to the ground; 60 percent of industrial capacity destroyed. To a certain extent, the Poles did not have much choice in the matter. Their government's refusal to cede to German demands in 1939 had been taken as an unforgivable insult by Hitler, who slated them for extraordinarily brutal treatment. Nevertheless, the breadth and depth of Polish resistance was without parallel in wartime Europe.

Amid the destruction, many felt that collaboration had been incidental and therefore forgivable. A letter sent in early 1947 to one of Poland's main daily newspapers, written by a communist sympathizer who claimed to have spent a considerable amount of time among fellow Poles in displaced-persons camps abroad, called on the responsible authorities to do more to dispel the confusion and misinformation surrounding Poland's laws providing for the pursuit of suspected collaborators. Anticommunist agitators were scaring potential returnees, many of them former forced laborers, with the specter of the "Lublin law"—the first capital of the Soviet-backed government had been the eastern city of Lublin—which they claimed provided for the arrest "at any moment, of any person" who had worked in any capacity for the Germans or under their command, as a "Hitlerite fascist."

Clarification, the author underlined, was necessary not only to curb hysteria, but also to clear an air poisoned by the mutual recrimination and suspicion of the war years:

> Maybe finally people would begin to respect one another more and those incidents would be relegated to the past where one neighbor denounces another (often only out of hatred for his democratic work) for "collaboration with the occupier"—that he "drank with Germans" or "pointed out" a horse to the Germans and so on—after which it turns out that in the first case the accused was ordered to give a German soldier a cup, and in the second, that he was only responding to the question of some civilians, "where is the house of Józef so-and-so."

Noting the proliferation of "similar incidents of careless accusation," the author, who signed the letter with an English pseudonym, "Home," concluded that they had to be avoided, "since we all want very much to maintain the honorable opinion of us at home and in the world that among us there was never a Quisling."[10]

But Poland's ethnic Jewish citizens remembered collaboration very differently. Seventeen years after Home's letter, Oscar Pinkus, a Jew who survived the war as a teenager by renting a hiding place under a manure heap in the barn of a Polish farmer, where he had lived in constant danger of denunciation, capture, or murder by the farmer, his neighbors, and nationalist partisans, published his memoirs. He had the following comment about the role of the local Polish population in the Nazi extermination of the Jews:

> Many hoped for help from the farmers or, if not for their help, at least their neutrality. For it was never active support that we expected of individual Poles. We needed it, but could not ask for it, since there was the death penalty for hiding us. What we did ask for was their inactivity—absence of hostility. This they were unwilling to give. Just as we never expected individual Germans to disobey orders. Their record is fatal because, above and beyond orders, they individually and voluntarily, actively and tacitly, endorsed, enjoyed and enlarged the official program.[11]

Along with about 10 percent of Polish Jewry, Pinkus had avoided the mass deportations to the death camps only to fall victim to a Nazi experiment in social engineering that took place from 1943 to 1945 in the Polish countryside, on what historian Jan Grabowski has called the "margins of the Holocaust." While hardly untouched by the war, the countryside was a comparative haven. Outside the garrisoned cities, large swathes of rural Poland were policed only by isolated detachments of the German Gendarmerie that themselves lived under threat of partisan attack. Unable to scour the countryside for dispersed Jewish survivors, the Germans instead outsourced the workaday business of genocide—the hunting, the capture, and often the killing itself—to ordinary villagers and the countryside's long-standing institutions of rural self-government. What ensued was a wave of mass Polish-on-Jewish violence that, at a minimum, claimed tens of thousands of Jewish victims and whose lethality, premeditation, and sadism had no parallel in the misdeeds perpetrated by ethnic Poles against other ethnic Poles during the war.

THE AUGUST TRIALS

The Holocaust and the pressures of Sovietization would make for strange bedfellows. The postwar communist government, commonly known as "People's Poland," theoretically was beholden to no one except its creator,

Stalin, and yet was heavily dependent on ideologically unreliable technocrats to maintain the machinery of state. Nowhere was this starker than in the case of the prewar judiciary, which the government needed if it was to fulfill one of its only popular mandates—the punishment of the country's wartime antagonists.

Well-educated, patriotic, and conscientious regarding both their duties and their role in an underdeveloped country that had only enjoyed two decades of independence when Nazi Germany and the USSR attacked in 1939, Poland's surviving judges and prosecutors had every reason to mistrust the new government. Their sense of duty, the reality that People's Poland was here to stay, and the indisputable necessity of meting out some kind of justice in the wake of the greatest conflict in human history compelled them to work within a system that many otherwise rejected. For its part, People's Poland understood that its own reserve of support in devastated postwar Poland was so shallow that to simply exclude prewar jurists would bring about the complete collapse of the judicial system and its own discreditation. For this reason, prewar judges and prosecutors continued to make up the majority of the judiciary well into the 1950s. But even though society—and the judiciary—were in agreement that the Germans should be punished, when it came to locals who were implicated, there was confusion over the scale, severity, and necessity of postwar retribution. Within the thicket of issues that punishing collaboration posed, none was thornier than collaboration in the killing and despoliation of Jews; Polish-on-Polish crime had been fleeting, covert, and rarely fatal, but Polish-on-Jewish crime had been systematic and popularly endorsed, and almost always ended in murder.

Beginning in 1944, People's Poland held more than 32,000 trials for war crimes and collaboration under a special statute, the Decree of August 31st of 1944, better known as the "August Decree." These "August trials"—referred to interchangeably as "August crimes" or "August cases"—were heard by four successive judicial instances, and the decree itself was revised three times. Over the course of twelve years, more than 20,000 guilty verdicts were issued, including 1,835 death sentences, although fewer than half may have been carried out. Although the trials continued after 1956, changes to the law in that year marked the effective end of the large-scale pursuit of wartime offenders, reducing the number of prosecutions to a trickle. While the overall rate of conviction for crimes covered by the decree was likely around 50 percent, the conviction rates of persons accused of crimes against Jews may have ranged as low as 14 percent, depending on the venue and time period.

At its most basic level, this book is about those trials—how they functioned, who administered them, and what accounted for their disparities. Beyond that, it is about how different constituencies engaged with postwar retribution in Poland and worked together to create the popular memory of the war in the process. At the legal level, jurists sought to balance a tradition of legality with the necessity for reprisal but ended up tacitly acknowledging that law and "justice" could not be reconciled. The two concepts themselves consist of separate and sometimes contradictory imperatives: the law is a product of political negotiation and prioritization that nonetheless aspires to a certain baseline of equal protection—of property and person, for example—whereas justice can imply either the fulfillment of the will of the majority or the redress of wrongs done to individuals. The Polish judiciary, however, confronted the uncomfortable truth that the majority, itself wronged, was in turn implicated in wrongdoing against minorities.

On the political plane, the unpopular communist government sought to reap a dividend for punishing war crimes, but it was wary of trespassing on the war's darkest corners. Severe retribution against war criminals and collaborators was one of the few areas in which the government could expect the wholehearted support of the populace, but even a regime backed by the might of the Soviet Union knew its limits. Widely condemned as "Jewish" for the initial presence of several ethnic Jews in its uppermost echelons, and unsettled by partisan warfare and anti-Semitic violence in the immediate postwar years, the Stalinist government viewed justice as a political instrument and saw no value in further alienating its subjects by pressing the issue of what Poles had done to their Jewish neighbors during the war.

For the implicated communities, the trials were an opportunity to clear their names, or at least deflect blame. Most importantly, postwar retribution was also an opportunity to begin sketching out a new national identity in the wake of the war's obliteration of the prevailing social order. Judiciary, state, and population alike all had an interest in leaving their imprimatur on the collective memory of what had happened and therefore what it would mean to be Polish going forward. For the judiciary, august guardians of Polish sovereignty, and survivors of the intelligentsia, it meant conserving some continuity in Polish statehood. For the state, it meant condemning the prewar order for Poland's shortcomings. And for the population, it meant confirming them in their victimhood, free from any suggestion of ambiguity.

Casting a shadow over and threatening the success of all these processes was the widespread knowledge of popular, firsthand participation by Poles in the capture and killing of Jews during the final stage of the Holocaust in Poland from 1942 to 1945. But Poland, even in its Stalinist incarnation, was not a place where inconvenient truths could simply be dropped down a memory hole. Instead, accusations would be made, indictments would be issued, witnesses would be heard, and courts would have to rule on what had happened. For all involved, it was a procedure without precedent in living memory, in a period without precedent in living memory.

AN OVERLOOKED RECKONING

The heart of this study is the records of over 400 trials conducted between 1944 and 1952 for crimes committed against Jews by Poles during the war on the territory of the so-called Generalgouvernement, the rump administrative unit created by the Nazis out of much of eastern and central Poland.[12] The Generalgouvernement was where most Polish Jews lived before the war and, unlike western Poland, was not annexed directly to the Reich, making it into a laboratory of occupation policy. Those records are supplemented by another 400 case files of Polish-on-Polish crime, as well as postwar ministerial correspondence, personnel records, contemporary legal periodicals, press clippings, interviews, and published and unpublished memoirs.

The records of the August trials have been the source of major revelations about the role of local people in the Holocaust in Poland since Jan Gross rekindled the debate in 2000 with *Neighbors,* his study of the mass immolation of the Jews of the town of Jedwabne by their Polish neighbors in 1941, having been able to access case files that had not yet been fully unsealed. As the archives of these cases were finally opened to researchers and the general public in the ensuing years, other pathbreaking works on the occupation followed, many of them penned by scholars associated with the Center for Holocaust Research at the Polish Academy of Sciences, such as Barbara Engelking, Jan Grabowski, Dariusz Libionka, and Alina Skibińska. But up until now, the actual history of the trials themselves has gone undocumented, with the exception of a short overview in a 2011 article by Skibińska, and two legal studies, one published in 1963 by a future minister of justice in postcommunist Poland.[13]

To an extent, this omission is a practical one. Much of the internal documentation regarding the trials at both ministerial and court level appears to have been discarded, most likely not out of any malice but simply because it was not judged to be of historical value. The trial records themselves were made available only recently, and even today the lion's share is in the possession of the controversial Polish Institute of National Remembrance, where its use is strictly regulated. And finally, the research interests of the scholars who pioneered the use of these materials lie in building a more comprehensive picture of wartime behavior, rather than investigating the postwar era.

Until now, the subject of postwar retribution against collaborators has suffered from inattention because of the mistaken assumptions that all justice in People's Poland was Stalinist justice, and that history is a zero-sum game where the uncovering of unflattering events cancels out all that was heroic in the past. The illegitimacy and hated Soviet Russian origins of the government, the use of parts of the justice system to persecute members of the anti-Nazi and anticommunist resistance during the Stalinist era, and the state's unceremonious decline beginning in the late 1970s have understandably inclined people to write off anything having to do with People's Poland, much less its justice system in the late 1940s.

Each case contains two sets of records: the investigative files and the trial files. They run into hundreds of pages of denunciations, interviews with suspects and witnesses, indictments, trial transcripts, verdicts, appeals, testimonials on behalf of the defendant, requests for clemency, parole, and release documents. It should be noted that interrogations were rarely copied down verbatim. Instead, a stenographer or secretary would write a summary of the statement of the interlocutor, who would then read (or in the common event of illiteracy, have it read out loud) and sign it. While they lack the depth and color of true transcripts, these condensed statements do not lack for detail and more than suffice for the purposes of historical study.

Four successive courts had jurisdiction over the August trials—the Special Courts, the District Courts, the Appellate Courts, and finally the Regional Courts—and the organization of the book follows this chronology. Chapters 1 and 2, which examine in depth the characteristics of Polish-on-Polish crime and Polish-on-Jewish crime, are intended to demonstrate why anti-Jewish crimes were the more complicated offenses of the occupation. Chapter 3 deals with the circumstances in which the August Decree was introduced, including widespread xenophobia, a fragile government, and a reliance on the prewar judiciary. Chapter 4 addresses the introduction of the first Special Courts and their popular reception, as well as early legal, procedural, and investigative hurdles, while Chapter 5 proceeds to a detailed analysis of the rulings of the Special Court. Chapter 6 deals with the years 1946 to 1949, when jurisdiction for August crimes was transferred to the District Courts and fierce debates raged over the meaning of the August Decree, the reliability of the "old cadre," and sentencing. Chapter 7 reviews the work of the District Courts. Chapter 8 describes the sudden push and equally sudden retreat in the matter of August crimes by the high authorities in the years 1949 to 1954, when the cases were moved to the Appellate and then Regional Courts. Chapter 9 shows how sentencing under the Regional Courts came "full circle," returning to conditions much like those that had prevailed earlier. Chapter 10 looks at the end of the August trials in 1956 and the mass waves of commutation and parole that preceded it. Finally, the Conclusion compares the Polish example to postwar retribution in the other formerly occupied countries of Europe.

THE HISTORICAL BACKDROP

Wartime tenacity aside, Polish society had been very much a house divided before the war, both ethnically and politically. To a certain degree this reflected the clashing personalities and beliefs of the two founders of the Second Republic, the independent state that rose from the ashes of the First World War 123 years after its predecessor had been wiped off the map of Europe by Prussia, Austria, and Russia. Józef Piłsudski was the Polish Socialist Party leader and former revolutionary whose successful military campaigns during and immediately after the First World War won vast swathes of territory populated by ethnic minorities—Belarusians, Ukrainians, and Jews—who would make up a third of the new state's population. In principle Piłsudski believed in the creation of a federalist commonwealth, but in practice he was a man of autocratic tendencies who was quickly disillusioned by the back-and-forth of party politics and responded with repressive force to Ukrainian and Belarusian demands for self-determination.

Piłsudski's chief competitor in shaping independent Poland was Roman Dmowski, the "father of modern Polish nationalism," whose lobbying for Polish statehood in the Allied capitals during the First World War was the diplomatic counterpart to Piłsudski's military effort. A virulent racist and social Darwinist, Dmowski believed, among other things, that Jews were parasites responsible for Poland's historical underdevelopment and that the Ukrainians were a "tribe lacking a higher culture" whose lands were the "natural outlet for our excess strength." In one of his later treatises from 1934, he commented approvingly that the "Hitlerites understand that if they want to organize Germany on a national basis, they must destroy the position of the Jews and their influence on German society."[14] Troublingly, the nationalist political movement, which operated under various names but was referred to commonly as the Endecja, would be interwar Poland's single strongest political grouping.

Marked by under-industrialization, agricultural inefficiency, religious conservatism, rural overpopulation, an underdeveloped ethnic Polish middle class, and the legacy of feudal stratification, the Second Republic proved fertile ground for the propagation of ultranationalism and political anti-Semitism from its very beginning. After a sustained and vicious press campaign that blamed him for securing election with the help of the minority political blocs, Poland's first president, Gabriel Narutowicz, was shot and killed by a right-wing fanatic five days after his inauguration in 1922. Meanwhile, the distrust between left and right was such that unstable coalition governments were constantly dissolving and reforming in an atmosphere of "party anarchy." In 1926 a frustrated Piłsudski emerged from self-imposed retirement and overthrew the government, installing a semi-dictatorial regime known as the Sanacja (Cleansing) that was no more successful in finding lasting solutions to the nation's many problems, made worse by the ruinous effects of the Great Depression. Belarusian and Ukrainian demands and agitation were met with ever greater repression in the form of curtailment of minority institutions, colonization, Polonization, and military pacification, strengthening sympathies for Soviet Belarus and the Ukrainian terrorist movements and making "disloyal" minorities into a self-fulfilling prophecy.

After Piłsudski's death in 1935, the Sanacja leaders sought a rapprochement with the Endecja, which, now assisted by fascist splinter groups, was waging a vehement campaign against Jewish life in Poland—resorting to economic boycotts; *numeri clausi* in the universities, professions, and government; and numerous administrative chicaneries like restrictions on ritual slaughter and requirements for all businesses to display the name of the owner.

Matters were hardly better with the Polish Catholic Church, which was one of the two most influential institutions in interwar Poland, the other being the government. Traditionally one of the country's strongest propagators of anti-Jewish feeling, the Church too was influenced by the new racial and ethnic trend in anti-Semitic thinking during the 1930s, characterizing anti-Semitism as a "healthy reflex" and a "defensive reaction." To give but one example, the highest Church official in Poland, Primate August Hlond, endorsed the "boycott and isolation" of Jews in a 1936 pastoral letter, accusing them of "battling the Church, being mired in free thought, being the avant-garde of atheism, Bolshevism, and revolutionary action," of having a "fatal influence" on "morals," of propagating pornography, and of "engaging in fraud, usury, and human trafficking."[15]

Meanwhile, the government, in imitation of the far right, itself became increasingly demagogic and authoritarian. Parliamentary deputy Emil Sommerstein, whom we will meet again later, assailed government policy toward the Jews in 1938 as "actual civil and political inequality . . . the slander of the Jewish nation and religion with impunity . . . open legal discrimination . . . the absence of security of life, health, and property of the Jewish citizen . . . economic extermination."[16] The daily life of Polish-Jewish relations, according to two prominent historians, "increasingly resembled the reality of apartheid." By the eve of the Second World War, the official position of virtually all Polish center and right-wing groupings, as well as the government itself, was that the "Jewish problem" could be solved only via the voluntary emigration of all Jews from Poland.

Of course, that absurd scheme never had a chance to fail, because in September 1939 Nazi Germany invaded, occupied, and partitioned Poland in conjunction with its official ally, the Soviet Union. Poland's Jews were confined to ghettos in cities and towns across the Generalgouvernement and, following the invasion of the Soviet Union in June 1941, in parts of the territories annexed by the Soviets as well. Having decided on a "Final Solution" to the "Jewish problem" at the infamous Wannsee Conference in January 1942, the Nazi authorities implemented it in Poland in the form of *Aktion Reinhardt*, the mass deportation of Polish Jews to the extermination camps of Bełżec,

Sobibór, and Treblinka, where, it is estimated, 90 percent perished. The remaining one-tenth of Polish Jewry, or between 160,000 and 250,000 people, escaped to seek refuge, mostly in the countryside of what was still an overwhelmingly rural society. There, "where the representatives of the occupation government were most often absent on a daily basis," it would be the "position of the Polish peasantry"—70 percent of the country's population in 1939—that would decide their fate.[17]

1 "THERE ARE MANY CAINS AMONG US"

IN A EUROPE WHERE the minority "question" had been the single most pressing social issue before 1939, and where nationalism was the one common denominator on a continent already hopelessly at odds over the outcome and meaning of the First World War, the advent of a new war was bound to mean many things to many people, so much so that the event we know today as the Second World War is arguably better understood as an aggregate composed of numerous "parallel" wars. In each of these parallel wars, the same actors could appear in multiple guises, playing or being perceived to play wildly contrasting roles as they pursued national agendas that fell outside of the standard parameters of Axis and Allies.

Collaboration, by which we understand the aiding and abetting of German war aims, even indirectly, whether for tactical, pragmatic, or ideological reasons, was no less subject to this kaleidoscopic effect. What was inexcusable to some would be justified as a legitimate pursuit of national or communal interest by others; in the eye of the beholder, innocent civilians might appear as fifth-columnists or dangerous criminals, and partisans could be freedom fighters or executioners. No wonder, then, that collaboration was experienced completely differently by and imbued with a different meaning for different ethnic groups, and sometimes even for different factions within those groups.

In Poland, wartime collaboration is perceived and understood to mean the effects of cooperation with or concession to the Nazi occupation as experienced by ethnic Poles; the experiences of ethnic Jews do not figure in this national collective memory. But what Poles had survived was essentially the collaboration of the renegade—of marginalized or coerced individuals whose actions earned them, at best, social condemnation and, at worst, a death sentence from one of the armed resistance groups collectively referred to as the "Underground." Jews, on the other hand, contended with a broad social consensus on the value of ethnic cleansing and the consequent willingness of entire communities to join hands in their destruction.

ATOMIZING AND SOLIDARIZING CRIMES

The study of collaboration in Poland has been clouded by its presumed inscrutability—namely, the assumption that it is impossible to impose a taxonomy on a phenomenon for which there are as many motives as there are stars in the sky or, as one eyewitness put it, "like mushrooms after a rainfall."[1] Scholars have had to sort through a mountain of memoir literature and survivor testimony, which is naturally limited in what it can tell us about the character of the persecutors and the social dynamic in which they operated.

Specifically, studies of collaboration are susceptible to criticism on the grounds that it is impossible to extrapolate just how common these crimes were. This evidentiary gap is, in some cases, being filled in bit by bit. Jan Grabowski painstakingly reconstructed how 85 percent of the more than 300 Jews who escaped deportation by the Germans and went into hiding in just one rural county in the Generalgouvernement perished, mainly due to the actions of local people motivated partly by the hope of material gain and partly by German threats. Around 200 Jews died as a result of Polish action in thirty cases from the Kielce area, and a survey by Barbara Engelking of 300 court cases, most of them just from the Warsaw hinterlands, revealed that over 1,500 Jews were betrayed to the police and another 1,000 murdered directly by Poles. Based on this fragmentary data, it is estimated that "tens of thousands of Jews fell victim" to Polish perpetrators during the war.[2]

Nevertheless, rather than assume that no generalizations can be made in the absence of comprehensive statistics, we should consider what varieties of collaboration in Poland existed, how they differed in their execution, and what this can tell us about the degree of social opprobrium attached to them. As Jan Gross has pointed out, collaboration was a matter of not just action but also deliberate omission: "People or institutions can exercise their social authority in various ways, not only by actively ceding it to the occupier. By maintaining passivity in the face of drastic events—by not opposing practices which endanger values or a social interest traditionally in their sphere of responsibility—they can, by their negligence, sanction harmful activities."[3]

Postwar trial records are particularly useful here; through them we can study the perpetrators themselves, the communities they lived in, the response of neighbors, peers, and family members to their crimes—in other words, almost the entire microcosm of the crime. Despite the supposedly entropic quality of collaboration, patterns and commonalities are readily apparent in the cases tried by the Polish courts, and the picture that emerges does much to account for the diverging views of men like Home and Pinkus.

Quite simply, the crimes committed by Poles against fellow ethnic Poles and those committed by Poles against their Jewish neighbors differed in profound ways that stemmed from more than just the unequal degrees of persecution applied to the two groups by the Nazis.

Crimes of Poles against Poles were crimes of atomization, reflecting the inevitable splintering of society under the crushing weight of the occupation. By and large, they were the deeds of isolated individuals, usually acting out of desperation, under direct compulsion, or in the heat of the moment. In the pressure cooker of the war years, many a conflict between competitors, business partners, neighbors, in-laws, spouses, and tenants boiled over and ended with a denunciation to the Germans. Zofia Kossak-Szczucka, the Catholic intellectual and Underground leader, vividly described the contradictory mind-set of the denouncers:

> That same grandma or peasant, ready to tear apart the German with their bare hands, runs to him babbling about this and that, denouncing a neighbor, teacher, priest, or village headman. . . . The denunciations—about buried weapons, reading newspapers, secretly slaughtered livestock, illegally milled flour, stolen wood, dismissive comments about Germans, possible membership in secret organizations—accumulate in heaps and folders on the desks of the Gestapo. The Germans show off these files, not hiding their contempt.[4]

There were also myriad disputes connected to the hated levies of food, taxes, and forced labor, as well as the repression of smuggling, for which the Germans had made the uniformed Polish police, better known as the "Blue Police," and the skeleton local governments partially responsible. Tellingly, much of the "amateur" denunciation, and certainly all the work of the professional informers, relied on the ability to conceal the act from public view. The few Poles who dared to act openly in the interests of the Germans were usually armed police auxiliaries, like detectives from the Polish criminal investigative service or deputized translators.

Moreover, outright murder was strikingly rare in Polish-on-Polish crime. In Alina Skibińska's study of a court in the Kielce region, it was found that less than 4 percent of the trials involving non-Jewish civilian victims were for taking part in murder, whereas two-thirds of cases involving Jewish victims ended with their deaths, with half of those being killed by the Blue Police or the German Gendarmerie, and the other half by local people.[5] In my sample of hundreds of cases, the only Pole accused of directly killing another was a Blue Policeman who had shot a fleeing prisoner, while the majority of anti-Jewish crimes resulted in the deaths of the victims.

Overall, ideological affinity for the German cause or, more precisely, the desire for German victory, was negligible to nonexistent; nor were Poles involved in the killing of their ethnic compatriots. Their crimes against one another were, for the most part, the crimes of people seeking some temporary advantage in desperate straits, like shipwreck victims fighting over space in a lifeboat.

Crimes of Poles against Jews, on the other hand, bore the unmistakable hallmarks of a German-inspired, locally directed campaign of ethnic cleansing. The crimes were often discretionary, rarely originated in direct orders from the Germans, frequently served to gratify the material or sadistic aims of the perpetrators, and, where denunciation or capture were involved, not to speak of outright murder, were simultaneously intended to or did end in the death of the victims. Moreover, whereas Polish-on-Polish crime was generally atomized and furtive, Polish-on-Jewish crime, especially in the countryside, was a *solidarizing* and highly visible effort in which numerous locals and sometimes entire communities took coordinated part in full view of their neighbors. Even in the cities, where the combination of density and anonymity allowed denouncers and blackmailers to act discreetly and in small numbers, they were still typically cooperative affairs involving several offenders acting in tandem.

But it was in the rural areas and small towns, where the German security apparatus was stretched thin, that the alacrity and brazenness of villagers, partisans, and the Polish police in hunting down Jews was most apparent. There, the machinery of rural self-government was repurposed by the Germans to serve as a genocidal conveyor belt, in which villagers and institutions such as the local fire brigades, watchmen, and village headmen cooperated to capture and rob Jews, sometimes killing the victims out of hand but more commonly transporting them to the Germans or Blue Police for execution. Groups like the firemen and Blue Police, whose roles have been dismissed by some historians as ad hoc or auxiliary, were in fact directly and programmatically involved in the hunting and killing of Jews. Even members of the Polish Underground, sometimes acting independently and sometimes on the orders of their superiors, regularly preyed on Jews. The long-standing adage that it only took "one" hostile Pole to doom a Jew in hiding while it took "scores" to sustain him or her, was stood on its head in the countryside. Time and time again in the case files, groups of people worked together to capture Jews who were often betrayed by a lone farmer who had been assisting them or tolerating their presence.

The added fact that many of the perpetrators had demonstrably patriotic and anti-German bona fides only reinforces the evidence that this was an altogether different phenomenon from what was happening between Poles. Neither when acting against Poles nor when acting against Jews did local offenders give any sign of desiring a German victory or the prolonging of the occupation. While a contemporary audience can agree that the Holocaust was a key German war aim and that any contribution toward it, no matter the perpetrator's intent, was necessarily an act of collaboration, it is highly doubtful whether any of the perpetrators of anti-Jewish crimes considered themselves to be collaborators. To be sure, it was the Germans whose genocidal campaign against the Jews, minor rewards for their persecution, and standing threats in the event of noncompliance made these crimes conceivable. At the same time, the lack of sympathy for the occupiers among Polish victimizers of Jews suggests that the local offenders were pursuing their own agenda—namely, the despoliation and ethnic cleansing of the country's most hated minority.

The key specificity of collaboration in Poland was thus its selectivity. Even as collaboration in crimes against ethnic Poles appeared sporadic and unenthusiastic, crimes against ethnic Jews were remarkable for the zealous and unabashed way in which they were pursued. As hated as the German occupiers were, the "Jewish question" was—to use the words of the famous Home Army soldier and spy Jan Karski—the "narrow bridge on which the Germans and a large part of Polish society willingly meet."[6]

POLISH-ON-POLISH CRIME

To better understand what set anti-Polish collaboration apart from its anti-Jewish counterpart, let us examine the basic causes and mechanisms that drove Poles to collaborate with the Germans to the detriment of their co-ethnics. There were essentially three categories of offenders: local officials, including officeholders, levy collectors, and Blue Policemen; incidental collaborators, whose crimes were highly contingent because they were either coerced or unplanned; and persons, mostly destitute Lumpenproletariat, seeking material advantage in the turmoil of the war. What they all had in common was how alone they were with their crimes, which were usually less than lethal. They did not form part of a community of like-minded actors, their actions exposed them to danger and reproof from their peers, and they had few guarantees of safety even from the occupier.

Local Officials

OFFICEHOLDERS AND LEVY COLLECTORS

By dint of their office, Poles who were responsible for the fulfillment of quotas set by the occupier or for the maintenance of order, whether in a workplace or in public, could find themselves pitted against their communities, but their offenses were often mitigated by the simultaneous help that they rendered to fellow Poles. There was little evidence to suggest that their "collaboration" extended much further than harshness born of frustration, self-preservation, or the pocketing of something valuable in an atmosphere of general chaos.

One of the most sensitive positions was that of the village headman, often elected by popular vote, whose job could entail the collection of agricultural quotas known as "contingents," the designation of villagers for forced labor, or, as we shall see, the capture of Jews and other "strangers." But whereas the latter crime often had a highly discretionary quality, enjoyed the tacit if not active support of the community, and brought concrete benefits, the requisitioning of grain or ordering corvée labor could hardly fail to stoke the ire of locals. As one witness commented in the case of a headman accused of abuses in the selection of forced laborers, the "resentment is commonplace, as was resentment in general of headmen at that time."

In the small settlement of Wola Bukowska in 1942, Urszula Krawczyk testified that the headman and his deputy shoved her aside when she tried to prevent them from taking potatoes for the contingent from her storeroom, whereupon she shouted that they were "worse than Hitler." When they made as if to strike her, she fled and locked herself in her home. Although several other women also accused the two men of excessive force, the court accepted that the complainants were "quarrelsome" women. The postwar headman also stood by his predecessor, arguing that "just as there were arguments with the headman before, so there are today . . . [he] only did what he had to."

Within the world of the village, headmen could be parasitic or abusive, but they performed a necessary intermediate function. Leon Goławski had asked a German policeman to beat a villager who had shirked his road-laying shift, but his deputy defended him in more general terms, describing how Goławski had juggled his responsibilities: he had used his good relations with the pro-German county administrator to smooth over the village's refusal to contribute the required amount for the purchase of a bicycle for the county seat, and he himself was beaten by the Germans for hiding the town's best horses during a livestock confiscation. "The job of headman during the war was not exactly a pleasure," the deputy commented. Another stood accused of taking bribes of money and vodka to excuse villagers from forced labor, but he was nevertheless re-elected four times from 1932 to 1944, suggesting his irreplaceability.

Headmen who crossed the invisible line invited reprisal. When Jan Doliński went around to local farmers urging them to sign a petition in his favor, despite his having unfairly raised contingent levies on families he disliked, he was attacked and beaten in his home. Aleksander Belniak was shot and wounded by the Underground for drunkenly beating a local farmer and later refusing to vouch for part of his village during a German punitive expedition; his accomplices, a local administrator and an agronomist, were less fortunate.[7]

Other rural fixtures like tax collectors, agronomists, and foresters clashed easily with the local population. Taxmen had to deal with recalcitrant taxpayers, agronomists verified contingent deliveries, and foresters prevented poaching and illegal logging. Włodzimierz Majewski had retired as a decorated senior noncommissioned officer (NCO) in the Polish Army and was working as a tax collector when the war broke out. He received a public reprimand from the Underground for excessive zeal in his duties, which included summoning German and Polish police to intimidate a village into paying its taxes. His counterpart in a neighboring county, a rare university graduate, was convicted of inflating taxes, most likely to skim the excess for himself and his superior, who was assassinated by the Underground. The deputy forester Stefan Szymański defended himself successfully from charges that he had robbed local men gathering wood, claiming that local people "as a rule" were hostile to every forester, and that in retaliation for chasing off scavengers he was ambushed by unknown assailants in 1941 and his left ear cut off by an axe blow.

Once again, "collaboration" offered these individuals few guarantees, other than the temporary continuation of a tenuous existence. Majewski ended up in Auschwitz after the Warsaw Uprising, and his counterpart, who as a member of the targeted intelligentsia was living under an assumed name, ended the war as a forced laborer in Germany. The director of a dairy farm, accused of seizing goods and beating traders, lost all his property when his home was destroyed during the Uprising. An agronomist who persecuted farmers who were tardy in their deliveries was himself an escaped POW living under an assumed name who had been imprisoned first on the Seliger Islands in the Soviet Union—along with many eventual victims of the Katyń Massacre—then sent via prisoner exchange to East Prussia, whence he escaped.[8]

The German institution of the Arbeitsamt, or "work office," which maintained lists of Polish workers and carried out the notorious raids in which passersby were seized off the streets for forced labor in Germany, regularly employed Poles to help carry out its operations. As odious as the job could be, for the employees themselves it was a lifeline that helped them avoid deportation, allowed Poles to infiltrate and undermine the process, and was less abhorrent than working for the occupier's security forces.

Henryk Bandau was only sixteen when the war broke out in 1939. He worked various odd jobs—selling tickets, cleaning a German barracks, loading train wagons—to support his unemployed father until an acquaintance offered him a job at an office subordinate to the Arbeitsamt in the town of Łuków. Although his claims that he was only an office worker were contradicted by witnesses who had seen him in the company of Germans during roundups, others testified that he had released them or doctored their paperwork. After he was called up to perform labor duty in the German-run construction battalions, he surveilled rail lines for the sabotage unit of the communist People's Army partisan group. At the time of his arrest after the war, he was serving as a police officer.

For Jan Araczewski, a refugee from Toruń and a member of the outlawed Polish nationalist "Western Union" movement, stints press-ganging for the Arbeitsamt were part of a wartime odyssey in which he traveled eastern Poland under false papers, working in construction, as a butcher, and finally as a forced laborer in Vienna after the Warsaw Uprising. Given his patriotic credentials, his brief service as a "catcher" carrying out arrests, and his help rendered to Poles, the court forgave him.[9]

Poles who worked in supervisory capacities, such as workplace overseers or guards at factories and railways, regularly faced a host of issues relating to the unclear line between excessive force and the maintenance of discipline, the difference between regular crime and political crime, and the free will of offenders. But violence generally stayed within certain limits.

When sentencing railway guard Jerzy Zimnowłodzki, who had shoved, punched, and kicked various passengers at the train station in Radom, the court took it into account that the blows were an attempt to restore order among the masses of travelers crowding the trains and ticket windows. The reason Zimnowłodzki, a proletarian who had been working as a mechanic since the age of fourteen, might have volunteered at the Arbeitsamt in 1942 to work as a guard was perhaps to be found in his periodic confiscations of travelers' goods, including fifty kilos of potatoes and a package of women's stockings. Another rail guard successfully defended his arrest of several members of two families by producing witnesses to corroborate his claim that they were professional thieves who targeted freight cars. Elsewhere, the technical director of a factory in the Warsaw suburbs kicked a man who was sleeping on the job. Other rail and factory workers testified that the three defendants had helped them in various ways or turned a blind eye to resistance activities.

Some offenses seemed to have their origins in the character of the offender: Antoni Sliwiński was a deportee from western Poland who had lost two fingers and received the Iron Cross, Second Class, while serving in the German Army in the First World War. He had told his subordinates at the Siedlce train station that he expected the Germans to win the war and punished employees by beating them or forcing them to clean the latrines.

Perhaps the most serious case in my sample, in terms of a victim's fate, was that of Marian Piłatowicz, who had tossed cigarettes to inmates in a penal camp for Poles in Nasielsk. After scuffling with camp guard Szczepan Kęsicki, Piłatowicz was denounced to the German camp commandant, arrested, and deported to Germany, where he died. But Kęsicki's guilt was tempered by his contingent motives and his own life story. According to a prosecution witness, Kęsicki, an illiterate cobbler, had survived for two years as a smuggler before taking a job as a guard, most likely for material reasons. Criticized for his denunciation, Kęsicki expressed regret, explaining that he acted in the heat of the moment; shortly thereafter he quit his job and left for Germany as a laborer. In such cases there was little evidence of cold-bloodedness or premeditation; insofar as Kęsicki had shown initiative, he had been acting in his capacity as an agent of the German authorities rather than as a member of the community.[10]

IN ADDITION TO OFFENSES against person and property, it was a crime to "weaken the spirit of resistance" through unseemly displays of camaraderie with or subservience to the Germans. While the vast majority of defendants in the August trials came from the working class or peasantry, reflecting the country's demographics, several members of the upper classes, whose social prominence and function put them in comparatively influential positions vis-à-vis the occupier, found themselves in the dock on that charge.

Józef Górski's interrogation records listed his profession as "farmer," but his resemblance to the average villager ended there. Educated at universities in Wrocław and Kraków, the First World War had caught this nobleman in France, where he was receiving treatment for asthma. He spent the next four years as a cavalryman in the French Army before being transferred to London to oversee the integration of Polish returnees into the new national army, from which he retired as a major in 1922. The proprietor of an 800-acre estate 100 kilometers east of Warsaw, he escaped ahead of the advancing Red Army in July 1944 in a chauffeur-driven Mercedes-Benz. But he insisted that if he had wined and dined German officials and benefited from German sentries, it was only in the interests of preserving the estate, and that he paid monthly tribute in the tens of thousands of złotys to the local partisan group.

Dobromil-Emilian Huczkowski had an equally distinguished pedigree. A member of the Polish gentry in Galicia, he had served for eighteen years as an officer in the Austro-Hungarian Army and held no less than thirteen decorations. During his time as the "commissary mayor" of the rural county of Kąty, local people had seen him wearing a swastika on his lapel, flying a Nazi pennant on his car, and saluting the Germans. Although he claimed it was all a misunderstanding and that he only wore a swastika when it was necessary, the court punished him with a short sentence, given that such behavior by a man of his "education, social position, age, and experience" was likely to inspire "pessimism and depression."

At the trial of Edward Kłos, the town planner of Węgrów, many witnesses seemed to stop short of declaring him a criminal, but agreed that his behavior was disgraceful. A graduate of the civil engineering institute in St. Petersburg and head of the several-thousand-strong Polish refugee community in occupied Arkhangelsk during the Russian Civil War, Kłos had received a punishment of public shaming during the occupation from the Home Army, which was published in the main Underground newspaper; the investigating officer said that Kłos had been a German sympathizer, with a brother-in-law in the Gestapo, and that he personally witnessed him giving the Nazi salute and laying a wreath at the funeral of an assassinated German official. Others were more measured; one witness said that Kłos was not dangerous "but a swine," while the wartime mayor said that although Kłos had harmed no one, "I would call him a Pole without dignity."[11]

THE BLUE POLICE

The group of public servants with the greatest collaborationist potential, if only because it was the only armed Polish force of any considerable size allowed by the Germans, was the "Blue Police," so called for the navy hue of their uniforms. But these prewar Polish policemen, ordered to return to work by the Germans in October 1939 under the threat of the "most severe penalties" and heavily infiltrated by the Underground, were also among the most demoralized and least reliable collaborators, at least when it came to the persecution of other Poles. Considered unsuitable for "political" tasks by the occupier, they still had to deal with the mistrust of much of the populace due to their enforcement of criminal law at a time when many Poles relied on the black-market economy for survival or to supplement their incomes.

The former commander of one rural police post described this air of mutual recrimination:

> The end of 1939 and all of 1940 saw the intensive work of the Polish Police in the combating of ordinary banditry and all types of ordinary crime, which was carried out on the basis of Polish laws and which the German authorities rigorously oversaw. As a result, even today it can easily happen that many people who at the time were in conflict with the law have toward some former "Blue Policemen" . . . more or less justified complaints.[12]

Most of the internal files of the Blue Police were destroyed by the Germans during their withdrawal in 1944, but the few that survived testify to the apprehension, rock-bottom morale, and corruption of the force. In letters and orders from April 1942, the commander of the Blue Police in Warsaw, Lieutenant Colonel Aleksander Reszczyński, bemoaned a series of problems "testifying to the slackening of discipline, drunkenness, and increasing bribe-taking as well as poor performance of duties . . . such as smoking . . . on the job, improper saluting, and the sloppy appearance of uniforms."

Policemen were rarely seen on the streets at night, they were rarely on duty at tram stops, and traffic cops left their posts to chat with colleagues or did their jobs half-heartedly. The commander of the German Order Police (Ordnungspolizei), he warned, was threatening to arrest the city's entire police force. As if to add insult to injury, another circular from the same month informed policemen that due to a lack of supplies, officers and enlisted men would have to provide their own fabric if they wanted uniforms made.

These policemen, who had spent their careers upholding law and order in the first independent Polish republic in over a century, had, like all Poles, little or nothing to gain from the occupation and could feel no affinity for it. Their exasperation was evident in matters big and small. A policeman at a tram station had refused to help a ticket collector extract a fine from a female passenger, shouting, "I don't have time for this stupidity, I'm tired from my own work . . . it's not right to be busting people in these times. . . . I'll pay the five złotys, may you become rich," before storming off. It was only a matter of luck, the ticket collector complained, that he hadn't been assaulted by the incensed crowd.[13]

Likewise, the German appeal to drum up volunteers for an all-Polish police unit for service on the Eastern Front, the Schutzmannschaftbataillon 202, met with resounding silence. When Reszczyński issued orders that all officers claiming medical exemption would have to undergo an examination, one sergeant threatened the doctor with his pistol; other candidates with certificates of disqualification were reportedly harangued as shirkers by the commander himself. Memos from 1942 and 1943 revealed that policemen were skipping mandatory German-language classes, "explaining their absence at lectures with the most varied circumstances, which in most cases don't have sufficient justification."[14]

In the countryside, the intelligence network of the Home Army sent in reports detailing similar indifference. Although the German police were said to be putting "great pressure" on villagers to deliver their contingents in the fall of 1942, the Polish police whom they brought along "behaved generally passively, aside from some small exceptions where they had to." In 1944 in Mińsk Mazowiecki, where the Germans were conducting regular searches of visitors, taking some to the Arbeitsamt, "Polish police and ... detectives were used for this purpose on three occasions, but due to lack of enthusiasm and lack of trust, the Gendarmerie doesn't use them anymore." During a joint attack by SS, police, and German Army forces on partisans in the forest near Radomsko, a battalion of Polish policemen was included, but it was reported that they "fired mostly in the air." Of a sample of 47 policemen from the provincial town of Ostrów Mazowiecka, 25 were punished with arrest or expulsion for a variety of infractions during the war, the most common offense being public drunkenness.[15]

The corruption and brutality that flourished in this atmosphere of general decay eroded public trust. In 1941 an internal memo forbade off-duty policemen in Warsaw from being on the streets after midnight, because their drinking and dining out were angering the occupiers; "numerous" cases of "smuggling, bribery, and extortion" by the police were cited, as well as their rough treatment of citizens. "Society has a lot of complaints about the police and are dissatisfied with them, just like they were before the war." A circular from February 1944 detailed the atomizing effect of police misdeeds:

> An initially trusting society ... has been brutally rejected and treated in such a hostile manner by a part of the police ... that it has found itself often in a situation without support or help, as a result of which cracks have begun to appear which in time have turned into an ever

larger gulf. Behavior of this kind on the part of the Polish Police has given society an occasion to create a new name, "The Blue Police" ... signifying something foreign, cold, and aloof.

However, even as Warsaw's last wartime chief of police, Colonel Franciszek Przymusiński, lamented the decline of what "used to be one of the best [police forces] in the world," Home Army intelligence reported that his own lover was the associate of a notorious imprisoned black-marketeer who had bribed another senior city officer with an apartment full of looted Jewish valuables in return for her release.[16]

Police work had become a business. A 1942 intelligence assessment by the Home Army of the "Anti-Banditry Brigade" of the Warsaw Kriminalpolizei (Kripo), the reorganized Polish detective service integrated into the German security apparatus, described it as "divided into two groups, privileged and unprivileged. The privileged receive cases from the leadership which will bring in profit, whether in the form of willing bribes or forced ones. The remaining group doesn't enter in the equation, and gets those cases from which there is nothing to be had."[17]

Thus, the trespasses of the Blue Police, similar to the crimes of police everywhere, involved overstepping the limits of their authority, whether in the use of excessive force or the appropriation of private property. But once again these remained the crimes of individuals grabbing some temporary advantage or lashing out, bringing the aforementioned "gulf" between the offender and society into stark relief. Policemen typically stood accused of beating local farmers, traders, and smugglers, sometimes brutally, of stealing money and food or extorting bribes, of requisitioning contingents, and of participating in arrests of people dodging forced labor abroad or adolescent deserters from the Baudienst, the compulsory labor service set up by the Germans.

Policeman Witold Ślezak was accused of taking bribes for not reporting unregistered livestock; of stealing money, sausage, and bacon; of beating locals; and, in one instance, of shooting a common criminal who tried to escape from custody. He was faulted for not "confin[ing] himself exclusively to the execution of [his duty] in a purely lawful manner" but instead "exceeding the limits of 'acceptable zeal.'"

Policemen also showed a willingness to act against the communist partisan movement—the People's Guard, later renamed the People's Army. Of the anti-partisan actions that policemen in my sample were involved in, all were directed against the communist formations.

The most vicious exceptions, like Kripo officer Stanisław Witak, who was accused of assisting the Germans in the arrest and executions of dozens of Poles, had effectively become German auxiliaries and had arguably excommunicated themselves from the Polish community.[18]

Additionally, the infiltration of the Blue Police by the Underground was an important brake on any potential collaboration. In Reszczyński's estimation, fully half of the policemen in Warsaw were engaged in "conspiratorial work," and numerous policemen in the countryside had contacts with one Underground group or another. In the fragmentary Home Army correspondence that survives, officers were evaluated by the Underground intelligence apparatus and reprisals were undertaken. Reszczyński himself was assassinated in his flat in March 1943 under unclear circumstances by members of the People's Guard disguised as policemen.[19]

The Germans had even fewer illusions about their allegiance. In May 1944 a German colonel addressed the Warsaw Blue Police's special response battalion, telling them flatly, "We know that the Poles are preparing an uprising, but I'm informing you that the German army is so strong that no force can move it from this earth."[20]

Still, the Blue Police remained the only legal law enforcement body to which Poles could turn for redress. Defendants in postwar trials sometimes justified themselves by claiming that they had gone with their complaints to the Blue Police, rather than the Germans, and by that same token, courts faulted defendants who could have reported crimes and infractions to the Polish police, but chose to seek redress from the Germans instead.[21]

Incidental Collaborators

Quite apart from individuals whose occupation necessitated interaction with the occupiers, there were Poles who became implicated in German repression against their will or without making any long-term commitments. Such was the fate of those who suffered coercion or reached out to the Germans in the heat of the moment. Although one was involuntary and the other was not, neither type of collaboration had anything programmatic about it.

Among all the atomizing behaviors possible under the occupation, few could do more to ostracize the offender from the body politic than serving as an informer for the Gestapo or otherwise reporting "political" crimes to the German authorities. Not surprisingly, then, compulsion featured prominently in such cases.

A fairly typical example was the case of Władysław Strożek, who had been severely beaten in 1942 during an investigation into the derailment of a German train. When he was re-arrested in connection with another investigation in 1943, he immediately gave up an acquaintance suspected of conspiratorial activity. The court harshly decided that he had belonged to the "opportunists and cowards."

Intercession on behalf of family members was a predictable motive too. At the age of fourteen in 1942, Jan Garncarek was offered his mother's freedom in exchange for denouncing her colleagues at a secret print shop, while another man, in the aftermath of the defeat of the Warsaw Uprising, offered to inform in order to save his son from deportation to Germany. But such cooperation was a slippery slope from which there could be no turning back once the offenders had been publicly exposed, trapping them between the vengeance of the Underground state and the sanction of the occupier. Garncarek narrowly escaped assassination by the Underground. Jan Cybulski, an illiterate sawmill worker who agreed to work as a German police informant after being arrested on suspicion of helping partisans, eventually donned a Gendarmerie uniform and was wounded in an attempt on his life. Nor did the Germans take lightly the shirking of one's obligations: Ireneusz Wysocki, a young Underground member who had turned after being ensnared by an agent provocateur, went into hiding in 1941 to escape further service to the Gestapo, for which he was arrested and imprisoned in a concentration camp for the rest of the war.[22]

Of course, it didn't take any special occupational proximity to the Germans to set the gears of repression in motion. All that was needed was one festering dispute between acquaintances or the exchange of a few harsh words to send an aggrieved party running to the authorities. The occupation was the equivalent of having a loaded gun in the house, waiting for someone to avail him or herself of it in the heat of passion. But the evidence suggests that there were still unstated or intuited limits on the summoning of this demonic force, and that society did in fact maintain an important degree of cohesion.

Of the forty cases of denunciation in my sample that resulted from spur-of-the-moment disputes, as opposed to contractual or professional informing, only five involved charges that the victim was a member of the Underground or a partisan, and three of those accusations were false. That having been said, an accusation of possessing firearms or even smuggling could have potentially fatal consequences; what matters rather is the implication that few people willingly broke the code of silence regarding the Underground. Moreover, even in the case where an Underground member was targeted, the motive for betrayal was usually personal, not ideological, and in many of the incidents it is questionable whether the denunciation was expected, intended, or guaranteed to lead to the death of the victim. In short, these too were solitary crimes lacking any wider social endorsement.

One of the only cases in the sample involving a member of the noncommunist Underground was also one of the most banal: Helena Dudek suspected her boyfriend, a Blue Policeman, of cheating on her. When he caught her cheating on him in turn, he beat her with a belt; other residents of their apartment building heard her run from the flat, screaming that she would denounce him to the Germans, which she promptly did.[23] Perhaps it would be too pat to see a gender component in denunciation, but with women shut out of the Blue Police and public offices like the village administration, reporting an infraction directly to the German police was certainly the fastest way to make the occupation work for them. The proportion of female defendants in the denunciation sample—15 out of 40—was strikingly higher than in other types of wartime crime, indicating that men did not have a monopoly on violence.

JUST AS IN PEACETIME, family ties could become venomous, but the occupation raised the stakes. Aleksander Patoleta was an illiterate fifty-seven-year-old sharing a hut in the small village of Kamieniec with his wife, daughter, and son-in-law, who drank heavily and with whom he frequently argued. In an apparent effort to "scare" him, Patoleta accused his son-in-law of being a partisan, which resulted in his execution. Less seriously, property disputes and the refusal to pay an insurance claim on a burned outbuilding also led one woman to denounce her brother-in-law and two other men for spreading anti-Nazi rumors, as a result of which they received short prison terms.

Bringing to mind the adage about good fences and good neighbors, villagers clashed over issues important to them. Piotr Surowiec and Józef Pietrasik

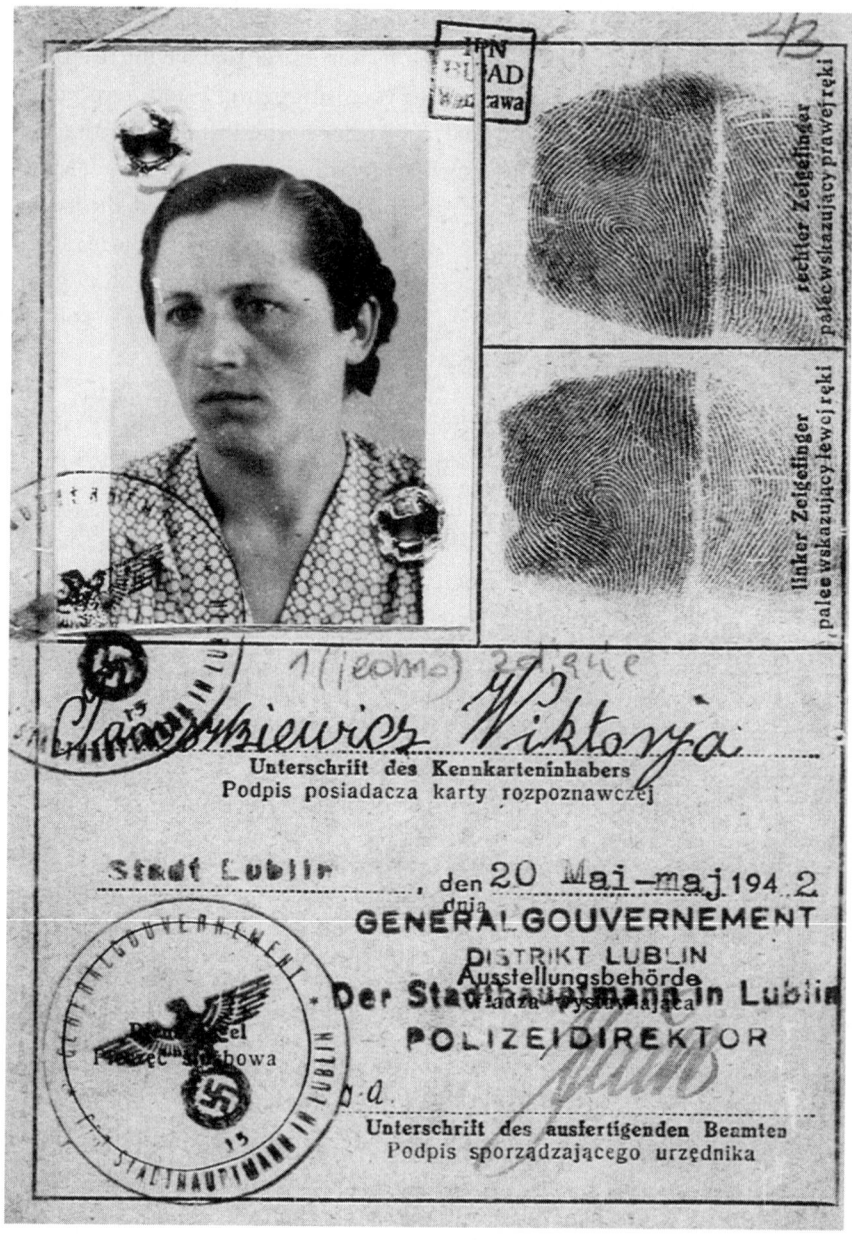

Denunciation was a weapon available to women otherwise excluded from occupation structures. Wiktoria Paruszkiewicz, shown here on her German-issued ID card, was convicted and executed in 1945 for having denounced six Jews to a lover in the Gestapo. (Photo: AIPN)

were set at odds after Surowiec disagreed with the results of a land survey in 1943 that reapportioned some of Surowiec's territory. Among other trespasses, Surowiec had torn out Pietrasik's fenceposts, shortly after which German soldiers appeared in the company of a Blue Policeman and nearly shot Surowiec's son. The prosecutor withdrew the charge, however, after the land surveyor testified that Surowiec too had earlier sought German intercession against Pietrasik.

During an argument over fodder, members of the Paczewski family brandished a knife and threw a pot of boiling water at their neighbor. He returned drunk, bringing gendarmes who searched the family's house fruitlessly for evidence of bootlegging or illegal slaughter. In two separate cases, in which locals denounced neighbors for stealing fruit and committing armed robberies, respectively, valid questions were raised as to when an appeal to the occupying security forces was legitimate.

Quarrels between neighbors in urban areas were no less acrimonious. Unraveling the case of Anna Świderska, who was accused of denouncing another resident of her apartment building, the court found that the enmity had its roots in the refusal of the complainant to extend a line of credit to Świderska at her grocery store in 1938 and involved slights as petty as the tearing up of some onion plants by one woman's small daughter.

Transactional relationships, such as those between tenants and landlords and business partners, were ideal tinder for denunciation. Marian Winerowicz and his wife were held by the Gestapo for several days after being accused of conspiratorial activity by a disgruntled former employee whose delivery services they had decided to forego; one baker extorted another in the Warsaw neighborhood of Wilanów; and neighboring store owners in Siedlce traded mutual charges, with one defending her ownership of a Germans-only restaurant with the absurd claim that it was merely a pretext for "anti-Hitler" Austrians and Silesian "resisters" in the Nazi armed forces to hold conspiratorial gatherings.[24]

Lumpenproletariat

As large as compulsion looms in the popular imagination, many more crimes seem to have resulted from an ensemble of factors, like poverty, the vagaries of wartime employment, fraternization, and simple opportunism. Still, the offenders in these cases were no less alone with their crimes.

Irena Lis was a widowed twenty-seven-year-old single mother when the small shop she had opened with money borrowed from her boyfriend's sister folded. To get rid of her creditor, she betrayed the location of the illegal press where the sister worked, and then, in order to make ends meet, she continued denouncing people who had received fake documents from the press, until a death sentence from the Underground forced her to flee to Lwów. Confronted by an acquaintance, Lis framed her choice bitterly: "If you don't have anything to eat or anywhere to live, and you turn to the Poles and no one helps you, then you too would be without conscience. And the Germans are helping me."

For some of those teetering on the brink of poverty, those who had known nothing but, or those chafing at wartime deprivation, the lure of easy riches or the acquisition of some small advantage over one's peers could be hard to resist. Fraternization frequently helped the process along, because for Poles employed in cities and towns, and on German-administered farms or rural posts, the occupiers were a constant presence; as one town-dweller on trial put it defensively, "After the invasion . . . I worked, like all Poles, in various German institutions."[25]

In a conservative, patriarchal society, afflicted by widespread unemployment and overpopulation in the interwar period, and now under the control of an explicitly racist and no less patriarchal occupying power, some women likely sought security in intimate relations with Germans. Their biographies, often recounted formulaically in their postwar interrogations, reflected lives of want, hardship, and uncertainty.

By the time Lidia Bartkowiak took a job at an airfield in 1940 and began taking visits from a German soldier working in a supply company there, she had already worked the last twenty-nine years variously as a waitress, construction worker, fruit seller, horse trader, farmhand, bootlegger, and soapmaker. Her husband, whom she had married at age sixteen, was run over by a car in 1940 and died the day before the liberation of Warsaw after drinking poisonous alcohol. And yet, she had gone from being poor to buying a plot of land, building herself a house, and dressing in furs, all apparently from goods she confiscated from Polish smugglers and Jews and resold with the assistance of "her German."

Women with husbands or family members who were known collaborators were vulnerable to guilt by association. Two teenage brides to Polish Gestapo collaborators were accused of fraternization and provoking a reprisal massacre; one had given birth to a child conceived out of wedlock at age sixteen. Another woman was criticized by the court for not breaking ties with her brother, also a Gestapo collaborator, but aside from their continued association there was no evidence of a crime.

Poles who had been forcibly resettled from the western half of the country, annexed to the Reich, often spoke German and thus could enter into contact with Germans more easily. One woman was only nineteen when she rejoined her family on a German-administered farm south of Warsaw after a stint working in Germany. Although she claimed she only washed German laundry, witnesses claimed that she was seen taking walks with Germans and that Germans would spend the night at her house. When one of her neighbors warned that such behavior did not befit a Pole, he was arrested, beaten, and sent to a concentration camp.

Whole families could be implicated in similar exchanges. In Warsaw, the jewelry businesses of a widow's two sons were said to have prospered handsomely during the war in partnership with her suitor, a Pole who had taken German nationality. On the banks of the Narew river, the Górski siblings were accused of running a racket with the sister's gendarme lover, ferrying smugglers across the river into the Reich, whereupon they were arrested and their packages confiscated.[26]

Of course, men were also susceptible to the influence of professional and personal relationships with the occupier. Shortly after the German invasion in the small town of Radzymin, a nineteen-year-old cart driver was encouraged by prewar acquaintances from the nearby settlement of ethnic German farmers to denounce several Polish men for possessing arms, three of whom were later executed; a tailor who had befriended gendarmes in another town took up spying on their behalf; and a displaced farmer was recruited as an informer by his former commanding officer in the Polish Army, an ethnic German who had joined the Gestapo.[27]

The relationships could be shallow, fleeting, and costly, however: the cart driver was wounded in an assassination attempt and spent the rest of the war in a concentration camp after being arrested by the Germans for pilfering official documents from the Arbeitsamt for resale; the tailor was beaten by his Gendarmerie contacts for sharing his denunciations with another police post and was sentenced to death by the Underground; and the farmer was imprisoned for committing armed robberies, saving him from the wrath of the Underground.

And of course there were those crimes in which no motive was discernible other than a desire for material gain or professional advancement. Stanisław Wiewiorka infiltrated an illegal radio-listening circle, in apparent return for which his father was given a smithy that had previously belonged to Jews. In the same town, Ignacy Polody was accused of overstepping social boundaries, though whether that or the jealousy he inspired was the greater offense in the eyes of his peers is open to question. Polody, a highly decorated career NCO in the Border Guards, was characterized as someone for whom the "highest value was money." He had taken over a formerly Jewish—or in the parlance of the day, a "post-Jewish" (*pożydowski*)—shop in Łuków, in which he hung a portrait of Hitler, and ran a thriving business reselling items looted from the ghetto. In their commentary on him, the postwar Polish secret police reported that the townspeople regarded his success with jealousy, which was compounded by his insolence in throwing a lavish wedding for his daughter, which the local Gestapo chief allegedly attended and for which waiters were brought in from Warsaw.[28]

LESSER COLLABORATION

If collaboration in Poland had been confined to the intra-ethnic variety, people might be forgiven for overlooking what was indeed a marginal phenomenon. When one Pole acted against another, it was generally not in a way that was sustained, lethal, or programmatic. Since they were not called on to kill their compatriots, local officials could plausibly argue that they had only done what was necessary to survive or that they had played a double game. Because the punishments meted out by the Germans to Poles for individual infractions varied widely, denouncers who had acted on impulse could plausibly claim not to have known what fate would befall their victims. And the predicament of victims of blackmail and coercion by the occupiers was readily understandable. Even those persons who, cynically and otherwise, took advantage of the occupation to eke out some material benefit, rarely rose above the level of simple opportunism. One way or another, these were all highly temporary marriages of convenience, where the overstepping of bounds exposed the offender to ostracism and the powerful vengeance of the Underground state.

2   CROWDSOURCING GENOCIDE

IN THE IMMEDIATE AFTERMATH of the Second World War, Poland was not alone in its rush to subsume Jewish victims of the Holocaust into an undifferentiated category of "national martyrs." Samuel Moyn, writing about France, could easily be referring to Italy or the Soviet Union when he describes how state and society "propagated a myth of heroic resistance, both to explain the origins of the new polity . . . and to distract attention from the potency of native fascist currents [and] collaboration with the Nazi occupation—including, of course, with the deportation and murder of [the] Jewish population."[1]

But the social consensus in France around the myth of *Résistancialisme*, as historian Henry Rousso termed it, and the accompanying conflation of the extermination of the Jews and the deportation of a variety of opponents of Nazism, began to crumble with the generational rebellion of the late 1960s and a number of controversies sparked by nonfiction films and books.[2]

In Poland, however, the "long 1968" had a very different outcome. The public protests of students and intellectuals across Poland that began in January 1968 were seized on by the nationalist wing of the Polish United Workers' Party as an opportunity to not only suppress the most active proponents of reform, but also to launch a furious, ostensibly "anti-Zionist" campaign that resulted in the emigration of the approximately 30,000 ethnic Jews still remaining in Poland.[3]

By the time the political restraints had loosened enough for the Polish intelligentsia to again discuss the issue of native involvement in the Holocaust, it was the mid-1980s, and People's Poland was in its final agonies. The "most characteristic expression of the more critical attitude toward the Polish-Jewish past" that emerged during this period was a 1987 essay, "The Poor Poles Look at the Ghetto," by the writer Jan Błoński. His article, which set the tone for scholarly approaches to the Holocaust until the early 2000s, rejected as "unfounded" the possibility that Poles took part in the Holocaust but nonetheless argued that the Polish nation "share[d] responsibility" for its "indifference" to the murder of the Jews and "for insufficient effort to resist" German plans. In essence, Błoński saw Polish "guilt" in terms of a witness to a crime who refused to intervene, taking inspiration from the famous poem "Campo di Fiori" by Czesław Miłosz, who in turn had been inspired by the disturbing sight of Poles enjoying a carousel ride outside the northeastern walls of the burning Warsaw Ghetto on Easter weekend of 1943.[4]

The idea that the fundamental problem in Polish society's coming to terms with the Holocaust was that it suffered from a "dilemma" of "passive witnessing" would also be the basic premise of the standard work in English on Polish memory culture, Michael Steinlauf's *Bondage to the Dead*. Published in 1997, the book argued that Poles were living with an "unacceptable, unmasterable substratum of guilt connected to . . . witnessing of the Holocaust." Much of what Steinlauf wrote approached the issue of witnessing from the urban perspective, with its inherently greater potential for anonymity and detachment, including the deportations, which amounted to an "'event without witness'" as Jews were transported to their extermination in discreet locations outside of metropolitan centers.

The "dilemma of witnessing" argument, though written from a critical perspective unacceptable to Polish nationalists, nevertheless dovetailed with the nationalist myth insofar as it assumed that that wartime behavior which occurred in sufficient proportion to merit condemnation was the Polish refusal to act in defense of Jewish neighbors. In its assessment of active Polish involvement in the Holocaust, it did not fundamentally diverge from the opinion of the nationalists that collaborators were "marginal elements," "dregs," and "Lumpens" who were "unequivocally condemned" by society—in other words, that the perpetrators of anti-Jewish crimes were fundamentally the same as the perpetrators of anti-Polish crimes profiled earlier.[5]

However, as the records of the August trials became widely available to researchers in the early 2000s, shedding light on what had taken place in rural Poland during the war, it became clear that many of the harshest critiques leveled by survivors had a basis in fact. Polish society, as it turns out, was not tormented by the fact of having witnessed the crimes of the occupiers or by the actions of a handful of native renegades—it was haunted by the active and popularly endorsed participation of a wide and socially prominent swath of the ethnic Polish population in the genocide and ethnic cleansing of their Jewish neighbors.

THE PRECONDITIONS FOR GENOCIDE IN RURAL POLAND

Crimes against Jews committed by their Polish neighbors were distinguished by both the motives involved and the manner in which the crimes were carried out. Their commission was marked by homicidal intent and public, collective action, which in turn indicated that something more profound was impelling the perpetrators than the petty disputes that characterized Polish-on-Polish crime. Whereas crimes against Poles drove people apart, crimes against Jews brought people together. The extermination of those who remained in hiding had a solidarizing effect on several levels. Jewish property was redistributed, villages were ethnically cleansed, and guilt was apportioned among numerous participants. The effect of witnessing, joining in, and benefiting from the destruction of Jews who had escaped the major deportations continued to resonate after the war, when the phenomenon of communities closing ranks proved critical in the legal defense of the accused.

In the towns and countryside across the Generalgouvernement, local people joined forces, in small groups, sometimes in the dozens or even hundreds, to expose, capture, and hand over Jews for execution—that is, when they themselves did not kill the victims on the spot. This collaborative aspect was no coincidence. According to established procedure, captive Jews usually passed through the hands of multiple Polish captors, from civilians to village functionaries, most often ending up in the custody of the local Blue Police or German Gendarmerie. Indeed, the empowerment of the Blue Police as executioners meant that many Jews were uncovered, captured, and executed without a single German being directly involved. In Pińczów County in southeastern Poland, for example, the local correspondent of the Home Army reported that Jews caught by locals were being executed "primarily" by the Blue Police. Not far away, in Dąbrowa Tarnowska County, more Jews in hiding were killed by the Blue Police than by the German Gendarmerie, a situation that likely obtained in "other rural areas of occupied Poland."[6]

At a time, then, when other collaborators had to camouflage their activities, and merely fraternizing with the occupiers was considered criminal behavior, the hunting of Jews took place in public, involved leading members of tightly knit village communities, and was public knowledge. Put simply, "denouncing and murdering Jews did not carry the social stigma associated with murder or denunciation of fellow Poles."[7]

Far from being outcasts, many of the perpetrators held unimpeachable patriotic credentials. There were decorated veterans of the First World War and its epilogues—the wars with the Western Ukrainians and Soviets—as well as the interwar insurrections in western Poland and Silesia, the September Campaign, and the Soviet-backed Polish Army's drive to Berlin. And contrary to the widespread belief in Poland today that the postwar communist state was a fundamentally "Jewish" creation, former killers of Jews were to be found after 1945 in all the security services and party organs, including the secret police, the regular police, the reserve police, the army officer corps, the communist youth movement, and the party itself. And for those killers who held no official position, a vast majority of them were still ordinary men and women who could count on the support and solidarity of their neighbors.

Critically, the absence of stigma was reinforced by the official silence of the two organizations that symbolized the continuation of Polish sovereignty: the Underground and the Catholic Church. After Primate August Hlond went into exile in 1939, Archbishop Adam Sapieha became the de facto head of the Church in the Generalgouvernement. Unfortunately, Sapieha was no more a friend of the Jews than Hlond had been; before the war he had referred to the Jews as a "depravity-causing race" responsible for both communism and capitalist exploitation. During his tenure, Sapieha declined to protest the Holocaust, either publicly or in his private communications with the occupation authorities.[8]

LIKEWISE, THE OFFICIAL STANCE of most of the resistance groups was marked by a *lack* of a position toward the Jews hiding in the countryside. Though some outlets of the Underground press lamented the predicament of the Jews, most remained silent altogether or refrained from issuing any directives to the populace regarding their treatment, even as they condemned other forms of collaboration. Only the media outlets of the Polish Communists and Socialists called on readers to help. Those few "leading periodicals" of the Underground press that did mention the issue of the Jews advocated, as had the prewar government, for their emigration. Among them was the official newsletter of the Peasant Battalions, the main partisan force in the countryside, which, even as it decried the brutality of the Germans in an April 1942 editorial, nevertheless condemned Poland's Jews as a "foreign body spread across our entire national organism [which] by its very presence destroys national cohesion."

Nor did the resistance forces in the countryside use their considerable moral and paramilitary authority in defense of Jews. There is only one documented instance of the most active of the Underground court systems, the "Civilian Special Courts of the Directorate of Civil Resistance" (Cywilne Sądy Specjalne Kierownictwa Walki Cywilnej, CSS KWC), executing a rural perpetrator for crimes exclusively against Jews, while an analysis of a list of 746 persons assassinated by the Home Army between April 1943 and February 1944 found only two persons involved in anti-Jewish offenses, one of them a German. Rural perpetrators "could feel totally immune from punishment."[9]

Polish partisan units operating in rural areas tended to view Jews *a priori* as communists, bandits, informers, and all-around liabilities. In the local and upper echelons of the Home Army alike, the groups of Jewish survivors in the forests, vilified as Soviet collaborators, were "linked to the plague of general banditism," and the internal correspondence of the resistance was rife with rumors that captured Jews were denouncing Poles who aided them to the Germans and that "Jewish women" figured prominently in bandit groups.[10] The antipathy was so intense that in August 1943 the central command of the Home Army refused to guarantee the safety in the countryside of a handful of survivors from the minuscule left-wing Jewish Combat Organization with whom it had previously coordinated.

Naturally, fact and fiction became easily entangled in the fog of war. One notorious incident widely reported in the Underground files, in which a group of Jewish bandits led by a woman was said to have terrorized a small town and murdered eleven Poles, was actually a communist partisan raid, led by a Polish Jewish man, that killed seven partisans from the rival far-right National Armed Forces (Narodowe Siły Zbrojne, NSZ).[11]

Nevertheless, the impression endured to such an extent that Jewish women were once again cited by General Tadeusz "Bór" Komorowski, the supreme commander of the Home Army, in the background report to the Government-in-Exile in London regarding his countrywide Order No. 116 to combat banditry, issued in September 1943. Although the order itself merely made mention of "bandits of various backgrounds," Komorowski's reference to Jews in the confidential report "was a reflection of the assessments made in the local Underground structures [i.e., at the local level]. For this reason the order . . . didn't need to contain explanations of the ethnic composition of groups recognized as criminal. For the people on the ground the matter was more than obvious."[12]

Small wonder, then, that an analysis of postwar testimonies reveals that fear of death was the "dominant feeling" among Jews in hiding in the countryside toward, for example, the Home Army, the largest and most powerful of all the Underground groups. The "decisive majority" of the few Jews who fought in its ranks lived under assumed "Aryan" identities, at constant risk of being exposed and killed by their comrades. Indeed, "no conspiratorial independence formation . . . accepted Jews into its ranks," with the exception of those aligned with the communists.[13]

As it turned out, units from the entire political spectrum of the Polish Underground would be implicated in killings of Jews; from the communist People's Guard, later redubbed the People's Army, to the small socialist Polish People's Army, through to the well-known Home Army, the Peasant Battalions, and all the way to the far-right National Armed Forces.

Crimes against Jews were also different in that they were intended to permanently eliminate the victims. Unlike Poles denounced to the authorities for various infractions, only one punishment was possible for Jews: death. An attempted capture was an attempted murder, and extortion was carried out under threat of death. Given that all that was needed to rob a Jew was to lay hands on one, the fact that crimes against Jews by ethnic Poles usually ended with the deaths of the Jews suggests that the impulse to destroy was just as important as any profit motive.

The single most-invoked postwar defense of perpetrators was submission to the standing orders of the Germans. But the gratuitous violence frequently visited on the victims belied that claim. There was precious little evidence of the horror that individuals being forced to put their neighbors to death might feel. The "zeal and the willingness of . . . participants," writes Jan Grabowski, "cannot be explained by fear of reprisals alone."[14]

Stabbed or bludgeoned to death with farming implements, thrown down wells, buried alive, shot through their genitals, beaten bloody on the way to their executions, tortured to surrender their valuables, or merely ridiculed and laughed at in their final moments, the victims who met these terrible fates were not being sacrificed with great reluctance. No less disturbing is the fact that these were often intimate crimes, taking place at close range and involving mutual acquaintances from the close-knit world of the villages and small towns. There were, quite simply, no parallels to these acts in all the variety of Polish-on-Polish crimes.

SOCIAL SANCTION FOR ETHNIC CLEANSING

Where did the social sanction for the ethnic cleansing of Jews come from? Certainly, the prospect of a massive, country-wide property transfer that had the potential to forever alter Polish society had something to do with it. The Nazi destruction of the Jews has been described as an unexpected "revolution" in Polish society that, followed immediately by the postwar Soviet-dictated "revolution" in social mobility, created the modern-day Polish middle class by first massacring the previous tenants of society's commercial rungs—the Jews—and then promoting "natives" to replace them.[15]

Virtually without exception, the perpetrators described here hastened to complete that revolution. Corpses were stripped of clothing, hiding places were emptied of rations and bedding, creditors were definitively eliminated, and hidden wealth was permanently expropriated. The prizes ranged from something as simple a dead man's pair of boots, repurposed as a Christmas gift, to a multiunit property, replete with tannery and outbuildings.

Although it was rarely admitted to after the war, the appropriation of Jewish wealth had been something of an obsession for many local people.[16] A Polish engineer, forcibly resettled in the Generalgouvernement, wrote that among the local peasants "'Scheherazade-like tales about treasures / goods buried and hidden by Jews are multiplying.... Almost daily one hears about the discovery of a dead Jew in the area.'" Ironically, this despoliation was regarded through an egalitarian lens. Feelings of "envy" toward villagers who were hiding Jews and were presumed to be "making a fortune in the process" led to many a denunciation, because "Jewish wealth ... was regarded as common property, and individual attempts at hiding Jews were considered egoistic assaults against the community."[17]

The ideological component to these crimes—namely, the enduring influence of the anti-Semitism propagated by both church and state before the war—was closely intertwined with the appreciation of the economic "benefits" derived from the Holocaust. This categorical dislike of Jews was worsened by both the occupiers' own anti-Semitic propaganda campaign and the looming specter of "Judeo-Bolshevism," which had been given new life by the widely circulated charge of Jewish "treason" during the Soviet occupation of eastern Poland between 1939 and 1941.[18] In the memoirs and testimonies of Polish Jews who survived the war, there is no shortage of bitter commentaries about the special malice directed toward Jews in hiding, but even more striking, perhaps, are the summations of public opinion in the fragmentary, surviving internal correspondence of the Underground.

General Stefan "Grot" Rowecki, the first commander in chief of the Home Army, pleaded in September 1941 with the Government-in-Exile in London to avoid any appearance of philo-Semitism: "All the [Government-in-Exile's] actions concerning Jews in Poland make a dreadful impression.... This is the case with ... the offering of good wishes for the Jewish New Year. Please take it as an established fact that the overwhelming majority of the population is anti-Semitic. Even the Socialists are no exception. There are only tactical differences about what to do."[19]

That same month—at a time when tens of thousands of Poles had already been executed in terror actions by the Germans—an Underground overview of the situation inside the country described the "'Jewish Problem'" as being perceived by the public as "'our most difficult issue,'" with people angry about the Government-in-Exile's expressions of sympathy for Jews and fixated on the retention of confiscated Jewish property in an "'utterly widespread'" atmosphere of anti-Semitism. In northeastern Poland, an intelligence dispatch reported that the Germans were still being hailed as "liberators from Soviet rule" by "all sectors of Polish society." This contrasted with the antagonism toward the Jews, which was "'so enormous'" as a result of collaboration with the Soviets that "'normal relations'" were no longer possible and any restitution of Jewish property "'would result in intense rioting.'"[20]

But virulent anti-Semitism was still a fact of life in areas that had never been under Soviet control. In Nazi-occupied western Poland, which had not previously been occupied by the Soviets, the Home Army noted "'increasing hatred for the Jews on the part of the Polish masses'" in early 1942. In the central city of Łódź, or Litzmannstadt under German rule, the Home Army analyst noted that the Polish population remained immune to all aspects of Germanization except for anti-Semitism, and that the "'the principle of Christian justice based on mercy . . . is clearly not extended to the Jews.'" Meanwhile, in the eastern region of Lublin in February 1942, Poles refused to shelter Jews "as a rule."[21]

Likewise, the repression of Polish Jews during the Soviet occupation, including the deportation of thousands to the Soviet Union and the seizure of their property, was conveniently ignored. In the summer and fall of 1942, the Home Army in the Lwów area reported that a "'huge majority of Polish society has a hostile or at least negative attitude to Jews.'"[22] But the Poles of Lwów had actually made considerable gains under the Soviet occupation, from 1939 to 1941, which they stood to lose should their Jewish neighbors survive the war: "During the Soviet occupation commerce and private industry were nationalized, causing the Jews to lose their main source of income. Almost all of Polish society is of the opinion that the accomplishments of the [Soviet] occupiers in this regard should be preserved and the return of industry and commerce into Jewish hands not be permitted." In their opinion, the Jews had received their just desserts: "Generally it is said that the 'punishment of history has descended on the Jews.' In the spirit of society there is no elemental protest against what has happened, no warm compassion . . . generally in relation to the Jews there lives a subconscious satisfaction that there will no longer be Jews in the Polish organism."[23]

In Pińczów County, near Kraków, the Home Army correspondent reported in November 1942 that "generally speaking, the Polish population gladly watches the suppression of the Jews, these attitudes having been caused in some cases by the Jews themselves, who didn't want to sell [their goods and property at fire sale prices] to the Christian population."[24]

The importance of anti-Semitism as a driver in collaboration with the Germans was emphasized, again from Pińczów in March 1943: "It is necessary to underline the growing anti-Semitism in the peasant masses. The peasants understand that the return of the Jews will block their way to the cities and commerce . . . the population is handing over [the Jews] to the Blue Police or Gendarmerie first as a result of their pronounced anti-Semitic attitude, *secundo* in fear of punishment."[25]

A report by the anticommunist section of the Home Army in early 1943 made reference to the outright killing of Jews by Poles, unbidden by the Germans, this time on the basis of combating banditry and—presumably Soviet or Jewish—partisan activity: "Many Jews from the provinces . . . are hiding in forests where they form bands that establish contact with diversionary bands operating in the area. The character of these active Jewish bands is one of robbery. . . . That is why peasants, independent of any cooperation with the German authorities . . . murder any Jews they run into."[26]

The Lublin-area Home Army in the spring and fall of 1943 reported, "The opinion is often heard that it's a blessing for us that there are no more Jews," and "The dominating slogan [in public opinion] is: down with the Jews, Ukrainians, and Germans."[27] From the Warsaw area in late 1943 came: "The most numerous minority was the Jews, but the occupier has liquidated them, which our people take satisfaction in."[28] And from Grójec County, south of Warsaw in October 1943: "The general attitude to the Jews is . . . resentful, moreover they are suspected of banditry and thefts as well as blackmail."[29]

Reports from towns west and east of Warsaw in October 1943 noted: "People predominantly feel good . . . without Jews and have no nostalgia for them whatsoever." "The largest minority . . . used to be the Jews but the occupier eliminated them. For this, our people are content."[30] From the Białystok area in December 1943 came:

> Today the population looks forward with joy to the development of artisanship [formerly dominated in many areas by Jewish craftsmen], and in particular about the possibility of apprenticing their children as craftsmen in a future reborn Poland, comparing [this with] their former state of slavery to the Jews . . . as a nightmare never to be repeated. . . . The same hopes are voiced by the people involved in trade, now controlled by Poles.[31]

And reports from Mińsk Mazowiecki, east of Warsaw, in May 1944 noted: "The fate [of] the Jews . . . has not built any sympathy whatsoever. . . . The attitude to those [Poles] who do have compassion is similarly unfavorable."

In the summer of 1944, after the Germans had annihilated most of Poland's Jews, the last head of the Delegatura (the underground civilian government of Nazi-occupied Poland) was still busy upbraiding the Government-in-Exile for its public "philo-Semitism": "It should bear in mind that inside the country Jews are disliked."[32]

In practice, however, the motives for many of these crimes intermingled to such an extent that disentangling one as the prime mover is probably impossible. One of the only surviving Polish partisans to speak openly about the killings of Jews by Home Army units, Henryk Pawelec, described his famous commander, Marian "Barabasz" Sołtysiak as an avowed anti-Semite, but also underlined the lure of supposed Jewish riches as a motive.[33] Clearly, the desire to plunder the Jews overlapped with fear or annoyance at their proximity, which overlapped with an awareness of their diminishing profitability, which overlapped with an unmistakable contempt for their persons. The outcome was the same: Jews were physically destroyed, preventing the restoration of their political and property rights and cleansing the terrain of ethnically "impure" elements.

THE MECHANICS OF GENOCIDE IN RURAL POLAND

That most of the crimes mentioned in this study could take place without the knowledge, proximity, or even involvement of the Germans was possible precisely because the local institutions that otherwise acted as a buffer between the occupiers and the population—the village self-government, the Blue Police, and the Underground—doubled as a genocidal infrastructure.

With the mass deportations of Jews complete, the evil genius of the occupier lay in outsourcing the remaining workaday business of genocide—the surveillance, arrest, detention, and conveyance of Jewish escapees—to the village headmen, who were obliged to report any strangers on their territory, and associated or subordinate village bodies like fire brigades and watchmen. The German approach to villagers holding no office differed slightly; although no occupation orders obliged civilians to denounce Jews, standing orders explicitly forbade the provision of any aid, while collaboration was encouraged in exchange for small rewards determined on a local basis—sugar, vodka, cigarettes, money, or even a bowl of soup. To borrow a word from the modern-day technological lexicon, this was the "crowdsourcing" of mass killing, in which ordinary people were invited to contribute as much or as little as they wanted to the larger project of ethnic cleansing. That this system functioned as effectively as it did, at a time when the occupiers' threats and blandishments had little effect on resistance activity or black marketeering, is itself a testament to popular attitudes to the Holocaust in the countryside.

A rough division of labor existed: villagers were to alert the headman to the presence of Jews, village watchmen or firemen would take custody of the victims, and a cart driver or escort was to be designated to convoy the Jews to the Blue Police or Gendarmerie for execution. In practice, of course, any number of permutations were possible, the essential variable being that anyone was free to take on the role of denouncer, captor, or executioner at any time. Only the Germans, who "appeared rarely, if ever, in remote areas," were generally confined to the last step in the process. For example, the combing of forests for Jews, a practice that was frequently the subject of postwar trials, could be set in motion by anyone "with the initiative and with at least some authority. The hunts were led by [headmen], forest rangers, wealthy peasants or simply by anyone who could inspire, threaten, or otherwise mobilize the village collective."[34]

The horizontal character of this "conveyor belt" was what made it effective. Although a nominal hierarchy did exist in the villages, with the headman at the top, it was not only shallow, but involved a measure of democracy. Headmen, firemen, watchmen, cart drivers, and villagers were also each other's neighbors, friends, and relatives; they were not shy about demanding action or challenging decisions they disagreed with. Before the war, the position of headman was determined by popular election. Headmen were forced to remain in their posts by the Germans, at least in some areas, but democratic elections were permitted during the occupation to fill vacant offices.[35] The similarities between the crimes of official and unofficial actors suggest how the line between them was blurred and how successful the Germans were not just in outsourcing to specific groups of officeholders but in crowdsourcing to local communities as a whole.

The offenders in these cases were not turning for help to an alien bureaucracy. Although the Blue Police, to take one example, were demoralized and degraded, they "represent[ed] continuity of familiar authority" and "belonged ... to the same 'universe of moral obligation'" as the communities they served.[36] Tellingly, witnesses in several different cases testified that the Blue Police were empowered to execute captured Jews on their own without ever notifying the Germans. In other words, the very same police force that the Germans considered unreliable in the struggle with the Polish Underground was nevertheless trusted to independently fulfill a crucial element of the occupier's racial and ideological agenda.

When villagers turned for help to their self-governing bodies, they were working with lifelong acquaintances, within the framework of familiar self-governing institutions, and toward commonly held goals. Likewise, the vil-

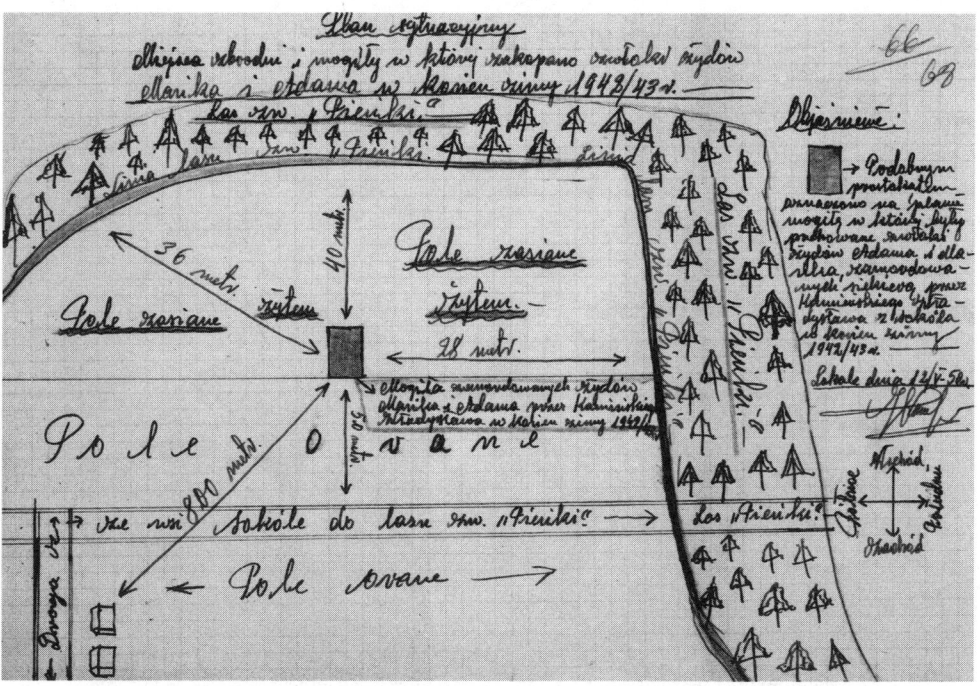

The capture and killing of Jews by their neighbors was often a coordinated effort that took place with the knowledge of local communities and without direct German involvement. A map drawn by investigators shows the rye field where two Jews, Adam and Maniek, were buried after being hacked to death by a group of seven farmers from the village of Sokóle. As was customary, the belongings of the victims were shared among the members of the raiding party. (Photo: AIPN)

lage authorities were, in many respects, doing what they had always done: responding to and resolving constituent complaints, which in this case included hastening the transfer of Jewish property to the community and completing the exterminatory process initiated by the Germans.

Though technically apart from the civilian world, which had to show a minimum of obeisance to the occupiers' rules, the Underground, in those cases in my sample where it made an appearance, followed the same logic. In addition to those of its members who became involved through their "above-ground" roles as functionaries or intervening villagers, Underground units also took on a problem-solving function where Jews in hiding were concerned, treating them as threats to the community and sources of plunder.

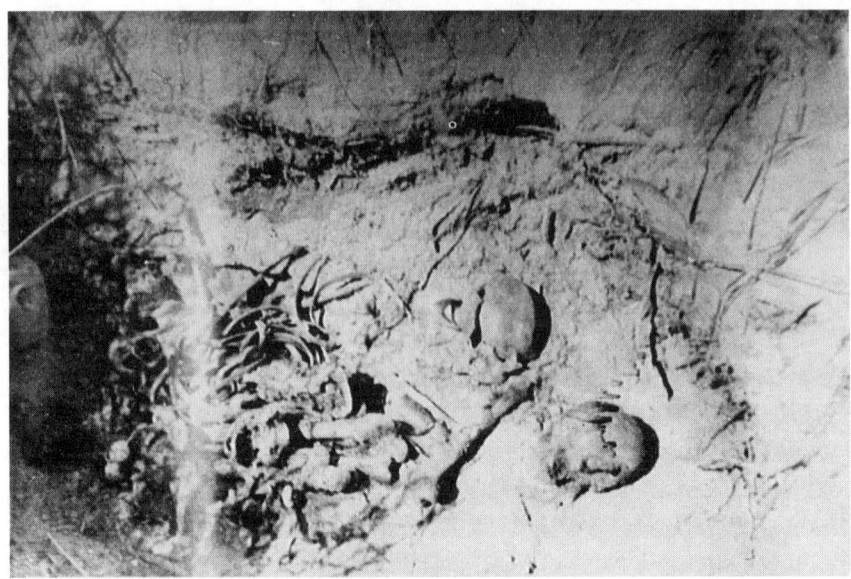

Adam and Maniek's remains were exhumed; most trials took place with no forensic evidence. Władysław Kamiński was sentenced to death in 1951 for striking the fatal blows and for denouncing other Jews, but his penalty was commuted and he was released in 1961. (Photo: AIPN)

ORDINARY MEN

The men whom the occupiers, stretched thin in the countryside, relied on to mop up Jews who evaded the mass deportations of 1942 received no special training or vetting, had no stake in the construction of a Greater Germany, and were long-standing fixtures in their communities. For them, the physical destruction of Jewry was learned behavior, initially modeled on the Nazi example and only later practiced independently on a wide scale.

Volunteer firemen, village headmen, and policemen had typically been serving in those capacities before the war. The village watch, the one innovation of the Germans, was nothing more than a rotating shift of unarmed local farmers, designated by the headman or elected by villagers to guard against "strangers" at a time when eastern Poland was being crisscrossed by Jews, escaped Soviet soldiers, and bandits.

Firemen, in particular, as a preexisting, organized source of manpower present in almost every rural community, were initially tasked with the spoliation of Jews or their transport to points of concentration in larger towns. But they could graduate rapidly to the commission of more serious and violent crimes. In the indictment of three firemen charged with taking part in the capture or murder of over thirty Jews from the village of Chrzanów, the prosecutor noted that after being employed piecemeal by the Germans in anti-Jewish actions during 1942, the fire brigade, under the leadership of Władysław Ciupak, began to show "ever more initiative."

Sława Chamit, the lead witness in the case and the mother of a rare Jewish farmer family, described how, after individual killings of Jews, including her husband, by the Germans, she sensed that the attitude of the village had "changed" and she decided to take refuge with her children and approximately 200 other Jews in a nearby forest in October 1942. Material and exterminationist motives went hand in hand: the flight of the Jews had been preceded by the German-ordered confiscation of their valuables, which were stored in the firehouse, and once in the forest, the Jews were approached by villagers demanding bribes. Shortly thereafter, a group of ten firemen swooped down on the forest, nabbing around twenty Jews and putting the rest to flight. Chamit watched from a nearby hill as one of the two Germans fetched by Ciupak passed his carbine to the firemen, who took turns shooting down their captives as they "squealed" and begged for their lives. A month later, Chamit also witnessed the capture of her youngest son, whom she had left in the care of a Polish woman, but who was seized and taken with several others to the Germans for execution. Polish witnesses said that it was rumored that the firemen had received sugar as a reward. Two male survivors who later returned to town to try and earn money threshing grain were arrested and hacked to death with fire axes, and another Jewish witness described how Rubin Af, who left the forest to recover some of the property he had entrusted to a Polish family, was chased down by Ciupak and others, who slashed his throat. Of note is the fact that this violence was not being visited on faceless, anonymous Jews; Chamit's daughter recognized Ciupak and the others because "they were my close neighbors."[37]

"AN IRREPROACHABLE OPINION"

In the town of Węgrów in September 1942, around thirty men from the volunteer fire brigade, in uniform, assembled in front of the synagogue during the liquidation of the town's ghetto, which the Germans had surrounded during the night. Aside from the German and Polish police, they were the only group allowed to enter its confines. Although the five firemen who were put on trial, among them chief Wincenty Ajchel, claimed that they were only there on the orders of the Germans to fight fires and to guard the Jewish goods that were being heaped up in the ghetto square, the town's wartime mayor, Władysław Okulus, and fellow fireman Ignacy Flaga, who did not take part in the day's events, were adamant that those firemen "'did it voluntarily and in the hope of profit.'" The firemen had gone house to house on their own, dragging Jews from their hiding places and leading them to the main square, or to the cemetery, where executions were taking place. One Polish witness described seeing Ajchel's cousin throw Jews from a rooftop to Germans in the street, who then finished them off with gunshots. Okulus estimated that 4,000 Jews were sent to Treblinka that day, and another 1,000 were killed on the spot. In exchange, the firemen allegedly received a discount on purchases of "post-Jewish" goods from the Germans.

In the course of the trial, a survivor, Moszek Góra, came forward with details of the liquidation. Collecting food for his family outside of Węgrów on the fateful day, Góra went to his family's prearranged hiding place upon his return, only to be told by other Jews there that his wife and children were already dead. After a few days, the hiding place was uncovered by two Polish policemen and Wincenty Ajchel, who dragged them out, cursing them as "commies" and barking commands in German: "Los . . . raus" (Let's go . . . get out). Ajchel took a bribe offered to him but did nothing. After being held prisoner in a granary with thirty other Jews for a day, Góra and his fellow captives were given food and water by six firemen led by Ajchel and told that they were going to be put to work. The Jews were ordered to carry boxes of ammunition to the cemetery, where two German policemen, two Polish policemen, and two firemen, including Ajchel, loaded their rifles and opened fire. Góra played dead until he was struck with the flat of a shovel by the gravedigger, who shouted, "If you're alive, run for it."[38]

Although Okulus, himself a former fireman, claimed that "public opinion condemned" the fire brigade's actions, he admitted that given the "mass of incidents" the Underground "had not taken any position" regarding the crimes. Furthermore, Flaga stated that the collaboration had done little, if any, harm to their standing in the community: all the defendants "enjoyed and continue to enjoy an irreproachable opinion; all are employed, none harmed or are harming Polish society." They were working variously as concrete pourers, telephone repairmen, surveyors, farmers, butchers, and bakers. All had been members of the fire brigade since before the war, some for over twenty years at the time of the crimes, Ajchel included. A respected activist for the Polish Socialist Party, Ajchel had been a teenage volunteer in the Polish-Soviet War. He had saved the town's church bells from being scrapped by the Germans, and had allegedly been relieved of his position after absenting himself in the fire brigade car to avoid responding to fires on German-owned property. Okulus, despite being one of the lead prosecution witnesses, praised him as a "brave man."[39] Completing the picture of hostility to the occupiers, Ajchel's brother had died at the hands of the Germans in 1944.

Here, as elsewhere, the presence of a crowd suggested that not only had many people witnessed the crimes, they were voting with their proverbial feet in endorsement of them. Okulus said that aside from the fire brigade, "many people went to the ghetto to plunder," and that toward the end of the liquidation, so many firemen from the surrounding villages "invaded" Węgrów, dressed in their uniforms and looking for a share of the spoils, that he had to drive them away.[40]

Firemen did not function solely as auxiliaries; they were more than capable of autonomous action. Many perpetrators appeared to have no difficulty reconciling their patriotic duties with the persecution of Jews, and indeed seemed to revel in both. Apolinary Sokołowski, for example, was a well-known figure in the town of Burzec, where he ran a grocery store and worked as the regional fire brigade chief. A founder of the local parish, he had fought in the Polish-Soviet War of 1920 in the Eighth Infantry Division, the same unit in which a chaplain was famously killed delivering the last rites on the battlefield, and again in September 1939. In the spring of 1942, he and three other firemen had transported "with great pomp" the town's Jewish families on their carts to the designated collection point in the county seat of Wojcieszków, after which they got drunk with their German counterparts. Even before then, in 1941, he had flagged down a German patrol on a local road to arrest a man he had detained, shouting, "You mangy Jew, you won't wander about here." Later in 1942, he was seen by several residents leading a teenage Jewish boy through Burzec on a rope to the headman for transport to the Germans. A fellow fireman who later reproached Sokołowski and was relieved of duty in retaliation, recalled that Sokołowski, dressed ceremonially "as if going to a ball," had pulled the Jew along "with great pride." Another neighbor described the boy's appearance as so haggard that "it was simply horrible to look at him." But Sokołowski, who was said to have received a post-Jewish house, had not confined himself to seizing individual stragglers. He had also organized an alarm system in the surrounding villages, providing them with noisemakers of sheet metal to sound in the event of the appearance of Jews. He himself frequently set off the alarms and was seen amidst the assembled villagers, armed with an iron bar and a flashlight. His initial accuser alleged that Sokołowski had taken part in the brutal killings of two Jewish families in hiding, although the prosecutor does not appear to have investigated those charges. Nevertheless, the village headman and his neighbor, even as they delivered damning testimony about Sokołowski, insisted simultaneously that he was a "good Pole" and had interceded to prevent the arrest of others by the Germans, who had frequently lunched at his store and were on good terms with him.[41]

Firemen and others who found themselves in the dock could always point in their defense to the standing orders of the Germans for all Jews to be arrested. But the high degree of initiative required to ferret out Jews in hiding, especially when no Germans were present, the robbery that invariably preceded death, and the implacability of the perpetrators all suggest that the exterminationist rationale of the occupiers had been internalized.

Near the village of Godziszów, twenty-two Jews, some of them barefoot, were taken prisoner in a forest—the court noted that their hiding place had posed no danger to anyone—on a bitterly cold winter's night in late 1942 by three firemen whose leader also happened to be a Home Army member. Villager Józef Powrózek, along with a number of other townspeople, went to gawk at the captives, who were held for several hours before being transported to the German police at the county offices (*zarząd gminy*). He remembered how one Jewess, a former resident of Godziszów, pleaded with his cousin to release her and her family, saying that she had already given "two thousand in gold" in bribes. Finding no response, she changed tack, offering that she was "already old" but begging him to "look at my children, who want to live, like flowers." "Seeing this tragedy," Powrózek left. The next day, on the way to a neighboring town, he saw their bodies by the road: "In particular I recognized that Jewess . . . who was lying there dead, holding two children, one under the right arm, the other under the left, also dead."[42]

WATCHMEN

When it came to the persecution of Jews, the village watch differed little from the volunteer fire brigades. Either they took the initiative, launching raids on Jews on their own, or they responded to complaints from residents or other members of the village administration, resolving specific "problems" and distributing the "rewards" among themselves and the community.

While it was the German-appointed county administrator who mandated the creation of a "village police" in Majdan Leśniowski, its composition reflected popular choice; members were elected by their neighbors, as was their superior, headman Aleksander Jagnicki, who had been serving in that position since 1929. Although their main role was to collect agricultural contingents, oversee the corvée laborers and village watch, and generally aid the headman, they understood their mission broadly.

Thus it was in December 1942 that Jan Głaz and Franciszek Oszust were out gathering firewood in the forest a kilometer outside of town when they noticed footprints in the snow and followed them to an abandoned quarry, where they confronted several Jews living in a cave—later identified as the three Lejb brothers, one of whom was a small child, their sister Chana, and a certain "Judka," all known to them from Sielec, a town six kilometers to the north. When their request for a bribe of leather goods was rebuffed, they reported the Jews to Jagnicki, who ordered the two men and their colleagues Stanisław Taras and Feliks Hałaj to seize the Jews and deliver them to the police in the neighboring town of Leśniowice. When they arrived, the four older Jews broke into a run; the little boy was grabbed by Głaz, who listened to his sobs as the screams of his siblings and Judka intermingled with the shouts of the men giving chase. Taras managed to catch up with the oldest brother, striking him dead with his axe, whereupon he wheeled and ran down Judka and the other brother, killing the latter and leaving Judka bleeding from a wound to the head. In the chaos, Chana managed to escape. The bodies were stripped and a passing cart was flagged down.

One wonders what the cart driver thought or said as he trundled along with a wounded Jew, a small boy, the corpses of the boy's siblings, and their killers, but no record of that remains. Instead, we have to reconstruct the social atmosphere in large part from actions rather than words. In Leśniowice, the Germans took charge of the two living Jews—they would be shot the next day—and ordered the burial of the dead. Apparently, no item was too gruesome

Stanisław Taras, shown here on a German-issued ID card, killed two brothers with an axe during a raid on a group of Jews hiding in a quarry. When criticized for "doing what the Germans do," he responded, "What do you care about the Jews?" (Photo: AIPN)

to scavenge; one of the burial party admitted to taking home the victims' blood-spattered bedding. Another villager, appalled by the sight of the victims' bare feet dangling from the cart, approached Taras, who was washing the blood off his hands at a well, and upbraided him for "doing what the Germans do," to which Taras responded, "What do you care about the Jews?" After the liberation of eastern Poland in 1944, Taras joined and fought valiantly in the First Armored Corps of the Polish Army in the East. After the war, he, Głaz, and Oszust were accepted into the local circle of the Polish Workers' Party, of which Taras was the secretary at the time of his arrest. Questioned as to how it was that he was accepted into the party, Taras replied that although "everyone knew" about the killings, they "chose to forget about it."[43]

Taras was far from the only perpetrator to eventually bear arms for People's Poland. After Ajzyk Wasung was ambushed outside of his native village by watchmen whom he thought were bringing him bread, one of his captors, Michał Gołębiowski, derided another watchman who took the time to bandage Wasung's bloodied face and hands. The next day, Gołębiowski, leading Wasung on an impromptu leash he had fashioned from a cable, boarded a train headed to the regional center of Lubartów to deliver his victim to the Germans. It seems safe to say that Gołębiowski was no friend of the Jews, but neither was he a friend of the Germans; in 1943 he joined the partisans, serving in the communist-led People's Army. After the liberation, he joined the police and the party until 1948, when he was fired and expelled for drunkenness.

In the village of Trzciniec, in the fall of 1942 or the spring of 1943—witnesses were often unclear as to the exact dates of crimes—the two teenage daughters of a Jewish saddle maker came to collect money they were owed for their sale of their linens by the headman and others. Instead, they were seized by four watchmen and carted off to the German police post four kilometers away. Stanisław Kurek, the watchman who was seen forcing the reluctant girls onto the cart, was hardly a sympathizer with the prewar order. Sentenced to prison for subversive activity at age eighteen in 1935, he joined the communist-led People's Army in 1943 and distinguished himself in battle with the Germans and right-wing Polish partisans, earning the Partisan Cross, the Grunwald Cross, and the Cross of Valor. In late 1944 he joined the embryonic secret police, where he served as the chief of a county office in western Poland, earning the Cross of Service in silver and bronze grades. Also a member of the Polish Workers' Party, Poland's reconstituted communist party, the local party secretary praised him as one of its "most active members" and "without fault."[44]

Police interrogators and prosecutors were interested in the merits of each individual case, not with establishing a comprehensive picture of wartime anti-Jewish persecution. Still, witnesses occasionally hinted at how commonplace and banal the crimes had become. Asked if he could recall the murder of Chaim Ajzenberg by the residents of the village of Wólka Serokomlska, eight kilometers to the south of where fire chief Apolinary Sokołowski had erected his alarm system, the former Serokomla County secretary said that he might have heard something, but couldn't be sure, because murders of Jews happened "quite often" in the county. Indeed, the details of the murder recapitulated the classic pattern: initiative, material motives, group action, acquaintance between killers and victims, and homicidal intent, tinged with sadism.

Ajzenberg was twenty-five at the time of his death on November 10, 1942; allegedly, he had gone to retrieve five meters of rye that he had bought from his prewar friend and business associate, Zdzisław Kędzierski, who also happened to be on duty as a member of the village watch that day. The next time anyone saw him, he was fleeing ahead of a mob led by Kędzierski that grew in size as onlookers joined the chase. At some point Ajzenberg flagged near the blacksmith's forge, and the mob, closing the distance, pelted him with stones until he collapsed. Kędzierski ran forward and struck him twice in the head with the back of an axe, then turned out Ajzenberg's pockets, retrieving an empty pistol, which he delivered to the Germans at the county seat in Serokomla, and some money. Kędzierski tried to convince the headman Kożuch to have someone else bury Ajzenberg, who was semiconscious and vomiting, but Kożuch, who had meanwhile pulled off Ajzenberg's shoes and later donated them to a poor family, would only agree to call for a cart, telling Kędzierski, "You bit it, you chew it." Kędzierski drove with several other men "to the pines" and dumped the still-living Ajzenberg into a hole, in the words of one eyewitness, "like a dog." The earth was supposedly still moving after they filled in the grave.[45]

In some villages, the occupier designated a *dziesiętnik* (literally, tenth man) as a sort of senior watchman, obliged to inform, like the headman, and entitled to "modest compensation."[46] In the mountainous south of Poland in August 1943, *dziesiętnik* Stanisław Kwaśniowski, a veteran of the Polish Army from 1918 to 1921, was accused of helping to capture a Jewish family in the forests after a female member came to beg for bread in his town. Disturbingly, Kwaśniowski did not lack for company in the execution of this onerous duty. Witnesses recalled that "several children," referred to elsewhere as a "band of adolescents," helped guard the Jews as they were marched over six kilometers to the nearest German police post, suggesting that the prospect of sending several Jews to their deaths did not in itself awaken fear or revulsion among the children. Although the investigation did not attempt to identify Kwaśniowski's accomplices, the witnesses interviewed by the police included two children who would have been fourteen at the time of the crime and one who would have been twelve.[47]

HEADMEN

The village headman, or *sołtys* in Polish, was an institution with roots in medieval German systems of administration imported to Poland. Its ubiquity is reflected in the fact that the common last name "Schulz" is itself a derivative of the German original, *Schultheiß*. Responsible for the lowest level of government, usually a village or several small settlements known as a *gromada*, he was an eminently visible fixture of Polish rural life before, during, and after the occupation.

Headmen and their deputies are among the most common figures to appear in some capacity in the murders of Jews in the countryside, and yet not a single one of the cases in my sample involves a headman who killed with his own hands, indicating their importance as coordinators who were capable of either setting an example and leading the way or delegating responsibility in the transfer of captive Jews to the German and Polish police.

Stanisław Kwiatkowski, headman of the *gromada* of Osiemborów, was arguably acting in both the private and the public "good" when he showed up with five other men to search Marianna Chojecka's home. According to several witnesses, Kwiatkowski had relayed a message from the Germans that betrayals of Jews would be rewarded with seventy kilograms of sugar, a valuable windfall in the wartime countryside, and he himself planned to claim a reward. But he was also performing a service. As Szymon Szwarcberg related in a refugee camp in Germany after the war, in January 1943 his sister Riwka and their cousin Chaim had gone to Osiemborów to recover some linens that Chaim's father had entrusted to a man named Jędrzej Sliz in order to pay for their own upkeep in hiding with another farmer. Sliz instead had set his dogs on them, causing Riwka to flee to Chojecka's house. Sliz, naturally, turned to the proper authorities for help; having found Riwka in Chojecka's attic, one of the search party punched her in the face, and Kwiatkowski punched and

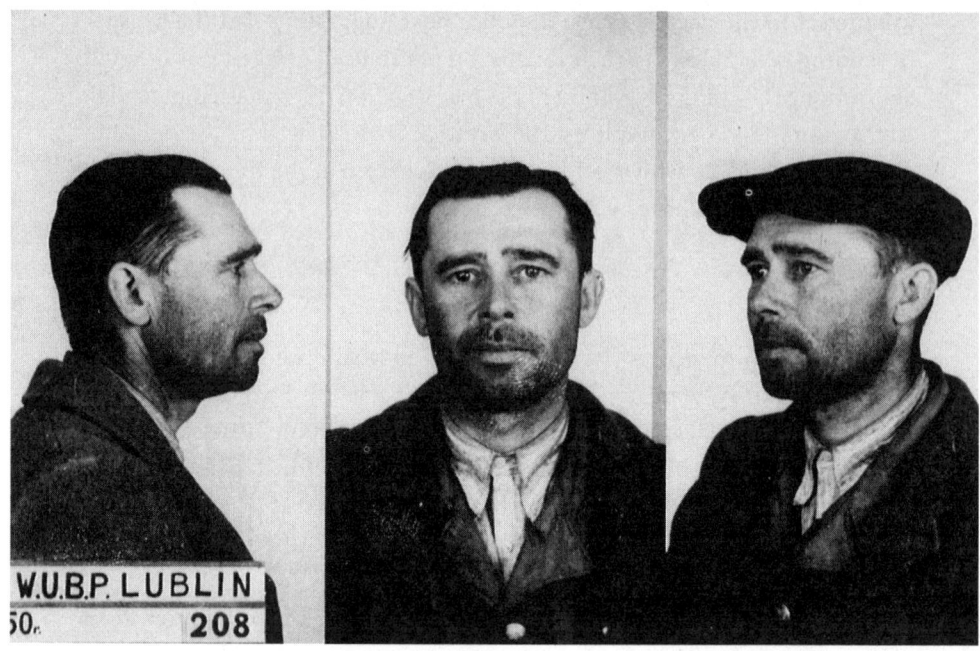

Acting on the orders of the village headman, Bolesław Gabriel and three other watchmen seized a Jew and his daughter and transported them to the ghetto at Łęczna, which was shortly thereafter destroyed. Gabriel was sentenced to five and a half years in 1951 and was likely paroled in 1953. (Photo: AIPN)

kicked her in the street before sending her away to the Germans. Szwarcberg also testified that Kwiatkowski had arrested three escapees from the Warsaw Ghetto who were trying to make their way to the partisans and had the misfortune of stopping at Kwiatkowski's house to ask for directions. As for Kwiatkowski's sugar, Szwarcberg reported that the Germans had said that Kwiatkowski would only get it upon Szymon's capture. The farmer hiding him reported that Kwiatkowski was still coming around in the summer of 1943 to ask if anyone had seen Szwarcberg.

Aleksander Abramowski, a seventy-five-year-old farmer, agreed in June 1943 to take in a Jewish tailor who had approached his son in the fields, looking for work. A few days later, he was speaking with the Jew in his barn when he saw headman Bolesław Abramowski (no relation), peering through a crack in the wall. Before he could react, the headman burst in. The terrified Jew tried to climb a barn pole, but Bolesław grabbed him and led him out by the collar, shouting that he had caught a Jew, whereupon the locals "flew out" of their houses. Aleksander Abramowski was punished with a night in jail by the Polish police—the Jew, of course, was taken away by the same police to the Germans to be shot—and had to pay a bribe to the headman to obtain his release. The former commander of the Polish police station in the town of Kałuszyn couldn't quite remember whether the headman Abramowski had come in with a Jew, saying that there had been "a lot of such incidents."

In the town of Niemójki in the fall of 1942, "after the closing of the ghettos," sixteen-year-old Krzysztof Tomaszewski, son of the elected headman, Hieronim, was accompanying a Polish police patrol in his father's absence, implying that he understood what the headman's role was. A Jewish boy, only slightly older than Krzysztof, managed to escape undetected from the two policemen as they searched a barn, but he was cut off by a crowd of townspeople as he ran through the settlement and then was grabbed by Krzysztof. Was Krzysztof's father in any way an unusual role model? Witnesses stood up for him, arguing that whatever toes he stepped on during the war, he "did what he had to do and no one else would have been better in his position."[48] The local communist party circle, of which Hieronim was a member, and the communist youth organization submitted a testimonial praising Krzysztof's "loyalty" during the war.

CIVILIANS

Civilian perpetrators, unlike watchmen or headmen, had no designated role, but they were not, of course, lacking in the material motives or sense of communal responsibility that helped spur village functionaries to crime. Where a motive can be discerned, the transfer of goods—whether through expropriation, robbery, or reward—and the necessity that Jewish victims should die were common threads.

Rather than let it fall into the hands of the Germans just before the expulsion of the Jews from Annopol in 1942, Chil Brenner had entrusted his property to a "good acquaintance," Antoni Chruściel, who removed it in several cartloads in 1942. Chruściel, an illiterate farmer, must have become accustomed to the idea of the Brenner family belongings remaining his in permanence. When Brenner, freed from a labor camp during a communist partisan raid, returned with his son in February 1944, Chruściel and his daughter imprisoned them in a pigsty before beating and stabbing them to death with pitchforks and a wooden stake; witnesses reported that the body of Brenner's daughter also washed up on the banks of the Vistula River a few days later.

Homes changed hands in this way. A Jewish tanner and his family perished after the two Polish families now occupying their former home agreed on the necessity of betraying their presence in the outbuildings. But while the instantaneous acquisition of property that had accumulated over a lifetime, or a house, or even a few bolts of fabric might have been a tempting prospect, many people were moved to murder Jews for significantly less. Jan Welo's wife and son had previously helped capture a teenage Jew whose family had entrusted the Welos with their valuables; a witness testified that when Jan spotted smoke from a Jewish encampment on Christmas Day 1943, he reported it to the Germans and received a pair of the victim's shoes in return, which he gave as a present to his wife. Elsewhere, capturers of Jews received 100 złotys, a bowl of soup, or a pack of cigarettes for their pains.[49]

The speed with which ordinary men and women could transform into killers within moments of chance encounters was remarkable. Nineteen-year-old Marceli Miszczuk and a colleague were unwinding after a day of road work when they spotted a local cobbler crossing some fields in 1943, whereupon they promptly ran him through with a pitchfork. When another villager, shocked by the sight of the Jew in his death agonies, demanded an explanation, Miszczuk, who went on to become a decorated soldier in the Polish Army, shrugged him off—"so what if I did do it"—and told him to go home if he couldn't handle the spectacle.

Farmer Władysław Chaciński was said to have boasted of slashing the throat of a Jew who had come begging for work, taking his money and jewelry, while Bronisław Król, who happened by pure coincidence to come across the tailor Icek as he was having his shoes repaired, beat him to death with three others and took his clothes.[50]

If a crowd of civilians often appeared in the ambiguous role of spectators at an execution, alluded to only obliquely in the condensed format of the interrogation protocol—"there were many people present"—there were those cases where the crowd acted as a collective.

Villagers were whipped into a frenzy at a Sunday fair by a man whose large cache of "post-Jewish" goods was rumored to be the reason behind his recent robbery, allegedly by a group of Jews. Shouting "Let's go to the Jews!," he led the crowd, described as the "entire settlement," in besieging a barn where, by various accounts, from eight to eighteen Jews were hiding.

Some cases had a stronger whiff of ethnic cleansing than others. In Przybysławice, a group of "several dozen" villagers—including two who were later communist partisans—surrounded an empty house, tearing the planks off the boarded-up windows to expose the dozen Jews inside. The house was pelted with stones to keep the Jews from attempting to escape, and the one man who did manage to make it out the window was immediately set upon by three villagers and beaten to death. The participants would later testify that the Jews had been stealing, a statement corroborated by the former county commander of the communist People's Army partisan group and a representative of the Sejm, the Polish parliament, whose father was among the suspects. However, other evidence cast doubt on the claims, given that nine of the Jews were women and children and none were armed.

In the largest incident of its kind in my sample, the headman mobilized all 250 residents of Wola Przybysławska, where earlier in the year a group of men had beaten to death a Jewish tailor. While reburying the bodies of several hundred Jews slaughtered by the Germans in a nearby forest, the villagers uncovered a bunker with about thirty Jewish men, women, and children in it. Some said that a villager had been stabbed and wounded when he tried to enter; regardless, the bunker was surrounded and the prisoners were marched back to town, surrounded by over 100 people, some of whom beat them along the way. When one man's wife, watching the procession, recognized her friend among the captives and began to cry, the deputy headman reportedly confronted her and said, "What do you care about these Jews, if you don't like it you can go with them." In town, the women, children, and infirm were loaded into carts, while the men were made to walk the nine kilometers to the German police station.[51]

Another common motive for anti-Jewish action that frequently intersected with others was the elimination of "liabilities," whether that meant Jews who had exhausted their funds and could no longer pay for their upkeep, Jews whose presence was regarded as dangerous or inconvenient, or Jews who were regarded as pests. Where the antagonists did not try to resolve their "problems" themselves, they resorted to the trusted conveyor belt of the village machinery to do it for them. As the father of one headman said of a woman who denounced her Jewish charge to the village watch, "That's people for you, as long as [the Jewish woman] had goods it was fine, but now she comes to report her."[52]

The commingling of material and hedging motives, as well as sadism, were in evidence in the case of Henryk Janczuk, who was only twenty years old when he chased down and struck Hersz Flechtman, who had been hiding with Henryk's uncle, killing him instantly. In his first and most open interrogation, Janczuk said that his uncle had urged him to kill Flechtman, who was "known to all" in the village, to prevent him from revealing with whom he had been staying. In his defense, he claimed that the headman had condoned the act, commenting after the fact, "Don't worry, you did good, it would have been worse otherwise." The headman's wife, for her part, put a slightly different spin on the killing; when she asked Henryk why he had done it, he had replied, "No one will keep the motherfucker for free, who is going to feed him for free?" She also heard from a neighbor that the Janczuk family had appropriated Flechtman's five suitcases. Interestingly, the Janczuks happened to be long-standing friends of the "new reality." In a deposition on his son's behalf, Henryk's father, the present headman, stated that "in 1939, after the entry of the Soviets to Chełm, I realized in deed the rules of the democratization of my surroundings by taking the position of deputy chairman of the Social Democratic committee. Among the members, my son Henryk took active part in this organization."

A witness also recalled seeing Henryk walking around with a "red armband" during the Soviet occupation in 1939. Immediately after the liberation in July 1944, father and son had joined the Polish Workers' Party and Henryk also joined the police, where he was wounded and from where he was eventually called up to officer school. The wartime headman's wife recalled him boasting of being in the security services, known colloquially as the "*Resort.*"[53]

Similarly, Andrzej Wąsala agreed to take in Hela, the teenaged sister-in-law of an acquaintance, in exchange for a cartload of goods. But when Hela's sister was captured and killed by the Gendarmerie, Wąsala took fright and hatched a plan to silence her. Using a letter, ostensibly from her sister, to lure her off the farm—it read, in part, "We should chat, and I don't think that we would lack for topics"—Wąsala's eighteen-year-old apprentice and a friend bludgeoned her with a hammer. When Wąsala checked and found her still breathing, he suffocated her by kneeling on her chest. He instructed the apprentice to

"No one will keep the motherfucker for free" was twenty-year-old Henryk Janczuk's stated reason for killing a Jew who had hid with Janczuk's uncle. He received a reduced sentence on the grounds of "intellectual immaturity." (Photo: AIPN)

tell people that partisans had killed her, but the boy went around bragging anyway.

Smaller transgressions, like stealing milk from cows, were also more than enough to get people killed. Two Jewish girls said to have been stealing carrots from the garden of Paweł Maksym were brought to the Gendarmerie and shot. Despite the fact that Maksym was a local figure of considerable prestige—he had been the "political commander" of the local Peasant Battalions partisan unit during the war and afterward served as the president of the peasant self-help and social welfare organizations, as well as the vice chairman of the local branch of the Peasant Party—he claimed he had no idea that the girls were Jewish.[54]

THE BLUE POLICE

If the occupation made every Gentile a potential policeman, there still remained the actual policemen. And for many Jews, delivery into the hands of the Blue Police marked the end of the conveyor belt that had begun with capture by villagers, firemen, or watchmen, and continued with transfer to the headman. Although the Blue Police had the option of calling the Germans to come do the dirty work of killing the captives, they themselves executed Jews, operating with little oversight or instruction from the Germans, which is all the more remarkable when one considers how little the Germans trusted this otherwise severely compromised force. Nevertheless, the fact remains that the Blue Police were an institution whose purpose was, among other things, to arrest and destroy the remnants of Polish Jewry. That having been said, the cases under review also reveal a police force that was capable of discretion when it came to Jews, helping some and massacring others. Even more so, the Blue Police were capable of shielding the populace from the Germans, whose reaction was unpredictable when it came to people accused of hiding Jews.

Few Blue Police documents survive—most were destroyed, deliberately and otherwise, at the war's end—but the case records left behind by Warsaw's Nazi courts from the years 1940 to mid-1942, before the mass deportations to the death camps began, depict a police force active in sequestering and repressing urban Jewish life. Jews, who had little choice but to flee to or trade on the Aryan side if they were to survive, were constantly being arrested by Polish policemen for leaving the Ghetto without permission, for not wearing their armbands, for riding the trams and trains. When asked about a detail of an arrest he had made two months prior, policeman Franciszek Ilczuk responded that "he could not recall with certainty, because in the meantime he had arrested too many Jews."[55]

Although the punishments were not draconian by the standards of early 1943—when the Warsaw Blue Police received permission to kill any Jews found on the street without warning—the consequences of a fine of several hundred złotys or a prison sentence of several months, meted out by the German courts, could be devastating for people clinging to the margins of existence.

Chena Kac was arrested by a Polish policeman while trying to re-enter the ghetto with ten kilograms of horsemeat in October 1941. Although she pleaded that her husband was in a camp and she had two small children to support, she was sentenced to ten months in jail, which would turn out to be only a death sentence, since in August 1942 all Jewish prisoners became subject to "resettlement in the East" as well. The court files reveal similar tales of woe: a widow with six children trying to resell twenty-five packets of coffee, two adolescent brothers supporting a sick father who "took off [their Star of David] armbands because nobody would want to sell a Jew anything," and a woman desperately trying to reach a gynecologist for treatment.[56] Many died before trial or before fines could be collected.

In more complex cases involving Jews, such as prostitution, counterfeiting, and smuggling, the investigations could be transferred to the Polish Kriminalpolizei, or Kripo, the former detective arm of the Polish police that had been merged with its German civilian criminal counterpart, where Polish detectives doggedly solved cases entirely by themselves. For example, Artur Jeruchem, posing as an "Aryan," was arrested in January 1942 in a café by an SS officer following a denunciation. The actual investigation, however, was conducted by Sylwester Rusiniak, a junior Kripo detective. Rusiniak carried out the search of Jeruchem's person and hotel room, interrogated his employer about his false travel passes, called doctors to check whether Jeruchem was circumcised, tracked down his mother in the Ghetto to identify his photograph, and then confronted him with her testimony, after which Jeruchem confessed. The investigation file included Rusiniak's sarcastic notes on the interrogation:

> [Jeruchem] concocted a story that he had lost his parents as a child and that a Jew ... had adopted him ... [regarding his request to be examined for circumcision]. He was probably counting that the doctors wouldn't be called or that they wouldn't know their stuff. In the meantime the examination didn't turn out well for him.

The Polish detectives possessed the kind of intimate knowledge of Polish Gentile-Jewish distinctions that the Germans did not. In one of the multiple interrogations of a suspected Jewish prostitute, she was grilled by Polish Kripo officers about "the circumstances of Catholic belief ... knowledge of the Old and New Testament ... the Ten Commandments, Church commandments, prayers, the Holy Family ... who baptized the Apostles and how many were there ... when is Easter."

Another suspected prostitute was placed under surveillance by a female detective, Alina Fabian, after being accused of sleeping with with German soldiers. Over the course of three months Fabian and two other Polish detectives established that the woman's identity documents had been obtained under false pretenses. Numerous witnesses were interviewed, who reported various rumors or confirmed that she was Jewish, positive identification was obtained through correspondence with German policemen in her hometown who showed her photo to the local inhabitants, and in January 1942 she was sentenced to three years in prison, which, of course, was effectively a death sentence.[57]

By the end of 1942, with the bulk of the deportations concluded and the survivors sequestered in much-reduced ghettos, the Germans issued orders that any Jews found outside these special areas without permission were to be shot on sight. Confusingly, the Germans also issued an instruction that all captured Jews in Warsaw should be delivered to the Kripo for "further administration," and that a report should be drawn up every month listing the Jews caught. Only a handful of such reports survive, all from the Blue Police command for the suburb of Praga, on the eastern bank of the Vistula. From May 23 to July 21, 1943, thirty-three Jews were apprehended by Polish policemen and sent to the notorious headquarters of the Nazi Security Service (Sicherheitsdienst, SD) on Aleja Szucha in Warsaw. In late June 1944, just one month before the Warsaw Uprising began and the entire city police force was interned and deported to Germany, Polish policemen were still arresting Jews.[58]

Anecdotal evidence suggests that in the countryside, orders permitting the local Blue Police to kill Jews without German involvement were issued orally or informally. Wacław Skwara, a policeman who had served since 1925 and had rejoined voluntarily in 1939 for the pension benefits, reported that the "first time Jews were caught we sent them to [the neighboring town] of Siedlce, later they called the chief from [the town of] Siedlce and told him not to send any Jews, but to deal with them in his own area." Skwara was estimated to have executed about twenty Jews from March to May 1944 alone.

Commenting on the execution of two siblings denounced by their hider, a local Blue Police commander and member of the Union of Armed Struggle—the precursor to the Home Army—mentioned that although the Germans had given standing orders to the Blue Police to hand over all Jews, they did not look into shootings of Jews but in fact "silently approved" of such conduct.

A veteran detective, who had fought the Germans and Ukrainians in the First World War, admitted to being present at the shootings of a Jewish boy and woman by other Polish Kripo members. Their German superior had instructed them that if they were "to meet a Jew in hiding, or a prisoner of war, there was no need to arrest him, but to shoot him on the spot." Likewise, a policeman from Radomsko testified that the Kripo there "liquidated Jews itself when the need arose, without consulting with the Gestapo."

The free rein of the Blue Police to kill Jews was common knowledge. In a ruling from April 1948 the District Court in Siedlce wrote that it was a "notoriously known" fact that Blue Police chiefs had "given subordinate police officers orders to take active part with arms in the liquidation in 1942 and 1943" of Jews in hiding.[59]

But precisely because they were not the Germans and were fixtures in the localities where they lived, the Blue Police could act with considerable discretion. The home of Bronisława Witosińska was searched several times by Blue Police looking for a group of Jews who had escaped an ambush by a unit of the socialist-aligned Polish People's Army (not to be confused with the communist People's Army). On one occasion, one of the policemen struck her and her children, screaming, "We're fighting with Jews to wipe them out and you're sheltering them!" Finally, in February 1944, the Blue Police caught up with the family that hadn't yet abandoned Witosińska's property: Abram Gutman and his wife, father-in-law, and parents. Allegedly, policeman Jan Faliszewski responded apologetically to their pleas, saying that "if it were up to me, I'd let you go, but there are a lot of you here and people are coming to the station and denouncing you, so we had to come out here." While the Jews were led out one by one and shot to death by other officers, Faliszewski and his superior agreed to doctor the incident report so that it would appear that the Jews had been captured in the forest and Witosińska would not be put in any danger.

The court trying Walenty Chojnacki, a policeman who had been serving since 1921, found that the Blue Police in Okuniew, where his station was located, had "very wide freedom of action and were only sporadically inspected by the Germans." Thus it was that Chojnacki's family could adopt an eleven-year-old Jewish girl in 1943 after her original hider kicked her out. The girl testified that she had been treated very well and had even converted to Catholicism. Other Jews who crossed paths with Chojnacki fared much worse, however. After a Jewish woman and child appeared at the police station for unknown reasons, witnesses had seen him take the two to the Jewish cemetery, where he shot them both in the head.[60]

A few Blue Policemen helped individual Jews, even if they still continued to implement the overall policy of extermination. One policeman stood trial for killing two brothers but had turned a blind eye to escapees while standing watch in his town's ghetto. Another spared the young son of an acquaintance even as he was said to have arrested or shot at the family members of other Jews. Speaking highly of the veteran policeman who had smuggled him to Warsaw in a covered wagon and brought Jewish children from the Lublin area at great personal risk and without any reward, a Jewish doctor commented that the man "couldn't have been a 'saint' working in the Blue Police."

On the other end of the spectrum were policemen who made a sport out of killing Jews. Czesław Smietanko was a rookie who was accused of a string of murders, rapes, and extortions of Jews in the area around the town of Adamów. In the words of a colleague who broke down as he recalled Smietanko's cruelties, "killing for him was a pleasure." Adam Grzechowiak, a policeman from western Poland forcibly resettled by the Germans, was accused of taking part, jointly with the Germans and by himself, in the killing of over fifty Jews from 1941 to 1944, shooting children in their genitals to increase their suffering.[61] In Ruda Opalin in 1941, Jan Wielebski, the chief of police and a heavy drinker, allegedly offered his son the opportunity to shoot an injured Jewess who had apparently jumped from a passing train. The son recalled,

> She was destined to be sentenced to death, that is as a Jewess—[so my father] asked me if I wouldn't take the opportunity to kill her with a firearm. At that time I, as a young boy [aged sixteen], seizing the gun, agreed to do it. The Jewess was brought out and I carried out the execution. I didn't see if I killed her or only wounded her.[62]

More numerous were the cases of policemen who seemed to take a workaday approach to the business of genocide, for whom the killing of Jews, far from the supervisory eyes of the occupiers, was a service they rendered to their communities, diligently and dispassionately disposing of the "problems"

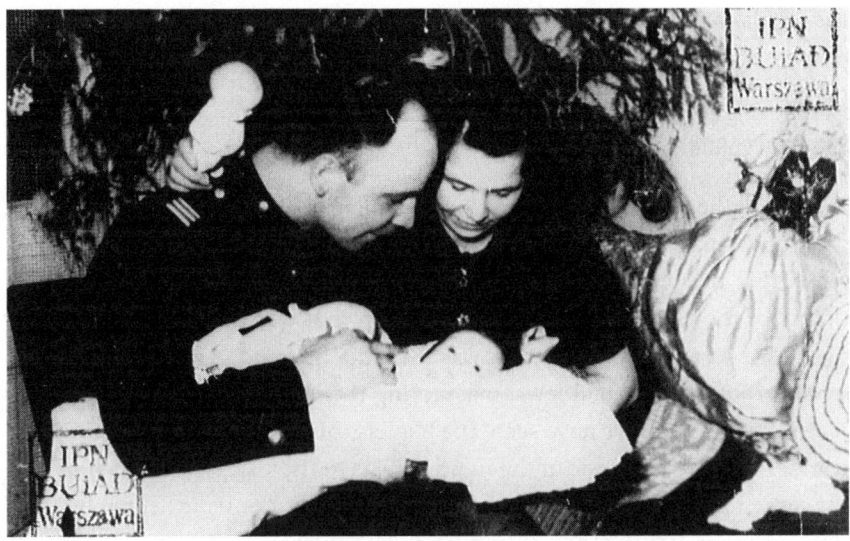

The wartime uniformed Polish police were considered totally untrustworthy by the Germans, except when it came to participation in the Holocaust. Policeman Adam Grzechowiak received seven death sentences in 1950 for murdering dozens of Jews, but was released in 1961. (Photo: AIPN)

that were passed along to them by concerned citizens and other village functionaries.

When the Jewess Schmidt, her adolescent son, and her sister sought shelter at the home of Aniela Strojna, with whom they had previously stayed, Strojna sent her son to alert the headman, who phoned the police and roused the two villagers on duty that night for burial detail. Officers Ludwik Słomiński, a twenty-year veteran, and Mieczysław Krawczyk, a twenty-three-year-old rookie, arrived well after dark and arrested the Jews. When the prisoners asked where they were going, one of the policemen responded, "To heaven." About a kilometer outside of town, Słomiński and Krawczyk, both members of the socialist Underground, trained their flashlights on the captives and shot them down. Likewise, Franciszek Kuś shot two Jewish children, an "emaciated" brother and sister hiding in a haystack in the town of Charlejów, in front of a crowd of onlookers. His superior in the police said of him apologetically that "as a policeman at that time [he] had to fulfill his obligations." Ironically, Kuś, who had allegedly been in the Home Army during the war and in the regular and secret police afterward, had himself almost become the victim of the occupier's mass reprisals in 1940 after being mistaken for a civilian.[63]

THE UNDERGROUND

If all the other segments of society—the villagers, the townspeople, the village functionaries, and the Blue Police—could claim, as their last line of defense, that they committed crimes against Jews only because such were the orders of the Germans, then the one group that was immune to the occupiers' threats and blandishments was the Underground. And yet units of the Underground also killed Jews, massacring them in groups or picking them off individually. As we have seen, the Underground considered and depicted wandering Jews to be one of the main threats to the villages, so much so that the supreme commander of the Home Army issued an order in September 1943 implicitly sanctioning their suppression, although the order was but the culmination and official confirmation of attitudes that had already coalesced at the ground level. In the Białystok area, for example, the local Home Army commander had already issued orders in July 1943 to "liquidate without mercy... communists and Jewish-communist bands." Judging by the dates of similar killings documented in the postwar trials, the anti-banditry order clearly coincided with an intensification of anti-Jewish operations by the Underground in the war's final two years. One senior officer of the Peasant Battalions recalled a "printed order... coming from Warsaw about fighting banditry... in 1943 and at that time our actions on the terrain against various traveling robbers were intensified."[64]

However, the organization of the Underground in the countryside and the lines of command were not always clearly defined. For example, in 1943 about one-third of the populist Peasant Battalions amalgamated with the Home Army, while the rest were spun off into independent organizations with similar names—the People's Security Guard, the Security Corps, the Autonomous Guard—that still answered to the Delegatura, the underground state. Defendants were often not entirely clear themselves whether they had technically been in the Home Army or Peasant Battalions at a given moment, and sometimes used the terms interchangeably. Complicating the picture, also operating in the rural areas of the Generalgouvernement were smaller but significant partisan units from the far-right National Armed Forces, a splinter group from the National Military Organization that had refused to accept amalgamation in the Home Army, and the pro-communist People's Guard.[65]

Much of the evidence in both this study and others suggests that, in this confused situation, the actual decisions to kill Jews were dependent on the initiative and discretion of local Underground commanders, rather than originating in explicit orders from the national command. The crimes of the Underground were not only programmatic, but sympathetic—imitating the behavior of the wider society—and opportunistic: "Certainly among the most important reasons for which Polish partisans killed Jews was the desire to remove them from 'their' territory, reinforced by the prospect of 'war booty' from the victims."[66]

Despite the official pretext of combating Jewish "banditry," postwar investigations reveal that these killings differed little in modus operandi or targets from those carried out by villagers. Defenseless individuals or isolated groups of Jews, irrespective of sex or age, were put to death to clear the terrain of ethnically impure elements and to expropriate their valuables.

Polish scholars have already uncovered several shocking examples that no doubt reflect established practice around the Generalgouvernement. For example, the famed Wybranieccy (Chosen) partisan unit of the Home Army and its charismatic leader, Marian "Barabasz" Sołtysiak, were revealed to have regularly robbed and murdered Jewish men, women, and children hiding in the Kielce area, including one of their own soldiers, who was discovered to be Jewish.

Near Kraków, the commander of a unit of the 106th Home Army Division had to write an after-action report to his superiors in the district command justifying his conduct during his unit's massacre of six Jews who had been hiding with a local farmer. It was not, however, the massacre that the superior officers objected to—it had been carried out on their orders with the aim of "removing armed Jews terrorizing the population," though no weapons were recovered—but the meticulous robbery of the victims, down to their clothes.

Large-scale massacres occurred as well. En route to bolster the Polish forces during the Warsaw Uprising in August 1944, the partisan unit Barwy Białe (White Colors), as part of the Second Infantry Division of the Home Army and apparently acting on the orders of the district commander, slaughtered thirty unarmed Jews bivouacked in a forest, all escapees from the HASAG factory labor camp near Kielce. The unit's leader, Lieutenant Kazimierz "Zawiszy" Olchownik, also ordered that the unit's doctor be executed after becoming convinced that the man was a Jew.

Near Kraśnik outside of Lublin in late 1943, the county command of the National Military Organization, soon to join the far-right National Armed Forces, ordered the execution of forty Jewish prisoners of war who had escaped from a camp in Lublin after first defrauding them of their money on the pretense that they would be given weapons. To the southwest of Warsaw, another unit of the National Armed Forces requested that the Gestapo release three of its members in recognition of their services rendered in the "'liquidation of Jewish-communist bands.'" The Gestapo officer confirmed in his internal correspondence that these "'nationalist bandits had decisively declared war on the communist bandits and liquidated a substantial number of Jews.'"

Nor were these killings confined to explicitly nationalistic partisan formations. Tadeusz Maj, the commander of the Świt (Dawn) partisan unit, integrated his forces in the communist People's Army as its second brigade in the spring of 1944, after which they committed a variety of atrocities against Jews in hiding, many of them escapees from the notorious Starachowice labor camp.[67]

The crimes committed by partisan units in my sample likewise demonstrate that these were hardly the acts of renegade soldiers, but instead were the products of careful deliberation and contact with superiors, aimed against victims who were known to pose no threat. Discussion of banditry or thievery was only a pretext to plunder and exterminate under official auspices.

Residents of the area around the town of Łopiennik Górny reported that there was indeed a crime wave, though the perpetrators were variously described as Poles, Soviets, or Jews, and none of the witnesses positively identified them. A local farmer who reported being robbed eighteen times during the war said that he was once robbed by a group of mixed ethnicity, but that otherwise the Jews who turned up "didn't steal, but only asked always for newspapers, to get world news, salt, matches, and to eat. I didn't give them anything, but my wife did."

Just why the shadow of suspicion should have fallen on the fourteen-strong group of Jews, all natives of Łopiennik Górny, living in a nearby forest clearing near their hometown was never explained. They certainly did not present a picture of battle-readiness: among them was Berek Lustman, his wife Liba, the three Kestelman brothers and their aged mother, as well as a fourteen-year-old and his father. Kazimierz Mielniczuk, who later took part in their killing, testified that there were no actual robberies in Łopiennik, and that in fact it was their former neighbors who were refusing to return the goods they had deposited with them.

At any rate, Jan Pawelec, the commander of the local unit of the Security Corps, received an order in the winter of 1943 from his county-level superior to kill the Jews in the forest. According to Pawelec, the local five-man communal council also knew of the impending "liquidation action." To supplement his forces, the seven local platoons of the Home Army, numbering about 100 men, received orders to link up with Pawelec. At the meeting he informed the assembled platoon leaders and enlisted men of their orders and asked whether they accepted them, which they indicated by acclamation. The encampment was surrounded and the Jews flushed from their bunkers; a few managed to escape the initial cordon, but they were apprehended, brought back on carts, and executed. At the time of his arrest, Pawelec held the rank of captain and was a company commander in the postwar Polish Army. For his service during the war he had received the Cross of Valor, the Partisan Cross, the Silver Cross of Service, and the Victory Medal.[68]

Less deliberation seems to have gone into the extermination of eight Jews hiding in a field near their hometowns of Bogucice and Marzęcin. There too, an order had allegedly been issued at some time in 1943 by the county commander Jan "Wojnar" Pszczoła to his subordinate, Bronisław Chojnowski, to eliminate bandits "regardless of ethnicity." But how and whether that factored into this massacre was never made clear. Indeed, the Jews were killed the same day they were discovered, and the decision to do so was made on the spur of the moment. It began when a rank-and-file member of the Peasant Battalions was checking on the grain in June 1943. Having spotted the Jews sitting in a field, he reported them to his superior, who gave orders to retrieve firearms and bayonets hidden in a local cemetery. From there, four or five partisans made their way to the bivouac site and surrounded it. The testimonies about what happened next are vague and conflicting, but one of the villagers who came upon the bodies described finding the corpses of three men, four women, and an infant of twelve to fifteen months, all of whom had been shot, except for two women, who had been stabbed to death. The villager was puzzled by the killings: "They were poor Jews, they hid where they could, and what the reason for their murder was I don't know." The local headman echoed him: "I personally knew several of these Jews, they weren't rich, they were artisans, they made a living from their hands, sewed shoes and clothing and helped people, for which they received food. . . . I never heard that they stole or robbed anything, as far as I know they lived peacefully and the local people helped them."[69]

The approach of the war's end seems to have increased the urgency of "clearing the forests." In September 1944, just a few months before the area's liberation by the Red Army, a patrol from a 400-strong Home Army guerilla unit encountered thirteen escapees from the Starachowice ghetto, to whom the patrol leader falsely promised work as artisans, tailors, and cobblers attached to the partisans. After the discovery was reported, the unit's commander, Wincenty Tomasik, a former noncommissioned officer and member of the Home Army from the earliest days of the war, ordered his deputy to recruit twelve volunteers to execute the Jews. A similar fate befell another five Jews who had the misfortune of encountering a patrol from the same unit later that month; they were initially left in peace after an ID check, but orders were eventually issued to kill them as well. While claiming that he had spared "fifty Russians" under his command, Tomasik insisted that his superior officer had "continually ordered me to liquidate persons of Jewish ethnicity and to not accept them in the unit."[70]

In other cases, the profit motive was clearer, as in the extermination of three families hiding in the towns of Chruszczyna and Bełzów. Local units of the Peasant Battalions and a special sabotage brigade of the Home Army carefully coordinated their efforts, prepared intelligence, and attacked with overwhelming force, dividing up the money, gold, and clothes they took from the victims.[71]

Even members of the Socialist Party–aligned Polish People's Army were not above preying on Jews; three partisans and their commander, Mieczysław Błędowski, who later distinguished himself in the Warsaw Uprising, ferreted out a group of twelve Jews hiding in a barn in the village of Szczerbówka. Although most of their party would eventually die at the hands of the Blue Police, the victims narrowly escaped execution when one of their number tackled one of the partisans, creating a distraction that allowed them to escape ahead of a mob of angry villagers.[72]

The fact that the war was almost over offered Jews no respite from these attacks. In November 1944, only two months before the arrival of the Red Army, Tadeusz Chojnacki, a battle-hardened eighteen-year-old partisan and member of the Home Army military police, was reportedly still laying ambushes for Jews on the site of an abandoned gunpowder factory on the terrain of the former ghetto in the town of Pionki.[73]

A POISONED CHALICE

The war was leaving millions of Polish victims in its wake, and the postwar government would have to find legal remedies to assuage their anger. But the most unwelcome part of the equation was that the war had also created a class of Polish perpetrators. The damning implications of their enthusiastic involvement in the signature Nazi project—the extermination of the Jews—could not be shrugged off like the run-of-the-mill requisitioning and domestic disputes that made up the bulk of Polish-on-Polish crimes. The crimes that had been committed by Poles against their Jewish neighbors bore the hallmarks of ideological ethnic cleansing—the systematic, overt killing of non-Poles, motivated by a mixture of racial hatred and greed, dependent for success on collective, often community-based action independent of the Germans. As a dictatorial entity that nonetheless demanded a level of institutional competency, the postwar government could not ignore these crimes. But if it was to have any peace, it would have to reach a legal and narrative consensus with its ethnic Polish constituents about what had happened.

3   HEARTS GROWN BRUTAL

THERE WAS NO QUESTION that Polish society would be out for vengeance at the war's end. Even before the Soviets arrived in the summer of 1944 and began pushing the German armies out of Poland, exacting revenge had been at the forefront of public consciousness. Several thousand collaborators were "liquidated" in targeted assassinations carried out by various underground groups, and thousands of German police and soldiers were killed maintaining the occupation. But five years of terror, violence, deprivation, and lawlessness had resulted in an extraordinary accumulation of psychological pressure, the explosive power of which was frightening to contemplate, even for other Poles. Writing as early as 1942, the Catholic intellectual and Underground activist Zofia Kossak-Szczucka vividly described how the countryside fervently awaited

> the defeat of the Germans and the corresponding day of reckoning, the payback to enemies, the revenge for injustices inflicted. For the moment of release. Just what that release will consist of, the village still doesn't know. Depending on local circumstances, a sudden depressurization could unleash itself on Germans, on Volksdeutsche, on deportees, on Jews, on the manor house, on the owner of the mill, the sawmill, the tavern, the store. The dream of this day is always linked with the concept of someone's liquidation.[1]

Popular rage didn't aspire to overturn all the changes wrought by the occupation. Some of it was directed toward the maintenance of a new status quo. In August 1943 the head of the foreign bureau of the Delegatura, the underground government, warned that

> the return of the Jews to their jobs and workshops is completely out of the question. . . . The non-Jewish population has filled the places of the

Jews ... this is a fundamental change, final in character. The return of masses of Jews would be seen ... as an invasion against which [the population] would defend themselves, even with physical means.²

Seven months later, the Bureau of Information and Press of the Delegatura reported that the peasantry viewed Jews, Germans, and Ukrainians as equally "unwanted peoples": "In general the prevalent mood of the peasant population is that a postwar Poland has to be purely ethnically Polish.... All the government's promises concerning minorities published in the [Underground] press have been received with shock and mistrust."³

The Polish historian Marcin Zaremba has likened the upheaval of the immediate postwar period to the "Great Fear" that spread across revolutionary France in 1789 as the old order collapsed, with no clear way forward:

> The war left behind a cauldron of national phobias and neuroses, hatreds and desires for vengeance. At the bottom of this cauldron was a thick layer of prewar anti-Semitism. The emotional climate of the postwar period—political fear, acute feelings of defeat and multifaceted impermanence, the huge problems in everyday life—did not permit a return to psychological stability, while the growing interethnic distance fed the fire under the cauldron.⁴

The result was an "explosion of nationalism" at war's end, abetted by "the idea of a monoethnic state, realized by the communists, and their policy of ethnic cleansing of Germans and Ukrainians, for which they had a mandate from the Allies ... and the support of a decisive majority of the population."⁵

When Polish wrath finally fell on the heads of the Germans, it was brutal, but not without a certain logic. Many of the punishments and indignities inflicted on them were those that Poles had been subject to during the occupation—expropriations, detention, restrictions on freedom of movement, forced labor, identifying markers, and expulsion. In the "Recovered Territories," the formerly eastern German lands transferred to Poland in 1945, the agitation to "cleanse" the areas of Germans was especially intense; a letter sent to the central government in October 1945 from the city of Koszalin, formerly Köslin, demanded

1) that no ethnic German man or woman, even if they did not act to the detriment of Poland and Poles during the occupation, be a citizen of Polish society

2) that Germans of all categories be immediately confined in detention camps [*w obozach odosobnienia*] and made to perform forced labor, and that all the rest be immediately deported . . .

. . .

4) that all Germans be fully deprived of civil rights and wear markers [*odznaki*] distinguishing them from Polish society

. . .

6) that those Poles holding German citizenship—so-called "*Reichsdeutsche*"—who stubbornly insisted before the war and during the occupation on their Polishness, be immediately returned to the homeland in line with the principle that:

> "No German can be part of the Polish Nation, but likewise no Pole should be left to Germandom!"

The resolution was signed by the local representatives of almost the entire Polish political spectrum, including the Polish Workers' Party, the Polish Socialist Party, the Peasant Party, the Democratic Party, the Federation of Unions, and the communist, socialist, and peasantist youth movements.[6]

Trying to make his way from Kraków to Katowice after being liberated from Auschwitz, the Italian writer Primo Levi was warned not to speak German by a policeman who "replied with an eloquent gesture, passing his index and middle fingers, like a knife, between his chin and larynx, and adding very cheerfully: 'Tonight all Germans kaputt.'" But that same day he was warned by a French-speaking Polish lawyer not to identify himself as a Jew either: "*C'est mieux pour vous. La guerre n'est pas finie.* [It's better for you. The war is not over]."[7] The zero-sum attitude toward ethnicity was not confined to the former occupiers. Boding ill for the eventual airing of crimes against those minorities, the desire for vengeance was engulfing all "unwanted peoples" still tarnishing the near-homogeneity of postwar Poland.

Around 20 percent of the small Belarusian minority that had remained in Poland after the annexation of western Belarus to the Soviet Union in 1939 fled across the border in the immediate postwar years. They were driven in part by "pacifications" carried out by nationalist Polish partisan units, the most notorious of which was the execution of thirty cart drivers in the village of Puchały Stare in January 1946.[8] In the southeast of the country, the genocidal campaign of the Ukrainian Insurgent Army against ethnic Poles provoked reprisals and an anti-partisan campaign that culminated in the forced resettlement of the remaining Ukrainians in 1947.[9]

Nor were picayune groups spared. In a 150-year-old settlement near Łódź, ethnic Czechs were robbed and beaten in broad daylight by neighbors who resented the formerly privileged status of Czechs under the occupation. The Poles delivered threats such as "We'll make butter out of you" and "Go back to the Czech lands, but wearing only your pants." The police refused them protection, instead taking part in their humiliation and seizing the goods of those leaving via the town's train station. Several Czech teachers were suspended for asking that some subjects be taught in their native language, and Czech children were barred from school for several weeks. The local administrator publicly stated that "Poland is only for Poles" and drew up an illegal decree ordering Czech property to be confiscated. Young and old alike were said to be fleeing.[10]

Christian minorities too were in the crosshairs. A memorandum from the Jehovah's Witnesses listed more than 400 violent attacks, including several murders, of believers in eastern Poland from 1944 to 1948. The attackers, frequently armed and uniformed, "almost always" demanded that victims renounce their faith, hang icons in their home, and take the Catholic sacraments. Local Catholic priests were accused of instigating violence by denouncing the Witnesses to their parishioners as communists, a charge that the Church had officially propagated even before 1939. According to a letter describing several incidents, the perpetrators were quoted as declaring, "'We'll get rid of all the communists and Witnesses, and then all will be well in Poland'" and "'Communism is spreading but Poland must remain Catholic!'"

Administrative chicanery was another type of harassment. Members of the Old Catholic Church sect who leased a formerly Lutheran church building in the town of Konstantynów were pelted with rocks by schoolchildren, allegedly egged on by a nun and a priest who disrupted their service. Shortly thereafter, the town's Catholic priest broke into the building with the help of a policeman, threw out the sect's religious paraphernalia, and changed the locks. Asked for help, the local police chief said that if the church wasn't going to be Catholic, he would rather turn it into a movie theater. A letter from the town council put it bluntly: "Our society, raised in a purely Catholic spirit, doesn't want any other religious sect."

After returning from six years in a concentration camp, the rector of the Evangelical-Augsburg Parish of Bytom wrote to complain in January 1946 that his community's church buildings had been almost entirely occupied by Catholics in what he described as "religious looting." He added bitterly, "As the irony of fate would have it, in this church where [parishioners] prayed in Polish on [territory annexed to the Reich], they are not free to pray in Polish in Poland."[11]

THE WAR AFTER THE WAR

Particularly ominous for the course of postwar justice was the intensity of anti-Jewish feeling. If rural Ukrainians and some minor religious groups might be written off, the reappearance of Jews—associated in the popular mind with Christ-killing and communism, and now coupled with claims to lost property—was bound to arouse special ire.

The occupation of Poland by the Red Army did not put an end to the depredations against Jews. On the contrary, anywhere from 600 to 3,000 Jewish returnees and survivors perished in a wave of anti-Semitic attacks across Poland from 1944 to 1946. Reports of the embryonic Soviet-backed Polish government, the Polish Committee for National Liberation (Polski Komitet Wyzwolenia Narodowego, PKWN), from the fall and winter of 1944 describe a climate of "continuous fear" for Jews in the recently liberated territories. Killings and assassinations occurred regularly, and some Jews were so frightened that they continued to live under their assumed "Aryan" names or stayed in hiding. The head of the Education Section of the PKWN reported that anti-Semitic feelings were such that Jewish children could not even attend class in the same buildings as Polish children, let alone sit in the same schoolroom with them.[12]

American diplomatic correspondence from the immediate postwar period depicted a vengeful mood. A US Army officer visiting Kraków some weeks after the pogrom of August 1945 described the "feeling against Jews" as "violent" and "very vindictive" among "all people with whom I spoke."[13] A February 1946 cable prepared for the US secretary of state noted:

> A casual question as to the number of Jews in Poland typically evokes from the "average" non-Jew the remark: "Too many," without hesitation

and before any numerical reply is attempted. Jews are frequently used as scapegoats for many problems of Poland; they are blamed for communism, for land reform, for nationalization of industry, for strong-arm methods of the present regime, for disloyalty to the Polish nation and so forth. Biting comments are heard about their alleged preponderance in the Government, in the Security Police or in the "NKVD" under assumed names etc.

Contradictorily, the cable continued, Jews, otherwise suspected as communists, were also feared for very capitalist reasons: "Evidence of a latent antisemitism ... seems to be most prevalent in the smaller communities and among the 'new group of small businessmen or shopkeepers.' Non-Jews who have taken over stores or other establishments formerly operated by Jews live in the constant fear that the owner or some legitimate heir may appear on the scene and under the 'recovery law,' will take away the enterprise."[14]

Dr. Samuel Margoshes, a Polish-born, Yiddish-American journalist touring the country, found that "there isn't one Jewish store under a Jewish name" in Warsaw, owing to a "general boycott" and a campaign of death threats. According to him, the society was "so virulently anti-Semitic as to make a self-respecting life on Polish soil almost impossible." And people were acting on their hatreds—hundreds of Jews were being slain in killings across the territory of the former Generalgouvernement. There was no clear accounting of these murders. During Margoshes's stay in Tarnów, a Jewish refugee named Glick who had recently returned from the Soviet Union and demanded that his house be vacated was shot dead along with his wife by several masked attackers, leaving behind two orphans, but the town's Central Jewish Committee was "too afraid to give [Margoshes] anything in writing" and the incident had gone unreported in the press. In Kielce, Dr. Kahane, the chairman of the Jewish Committee, told Margoshes that 220 Jews had been murdered in one county alone since June 1945. Margoshes couldn't know it, but Kahane too would be dead within six months, a victim of the Kielce Pogrom.

Those Gentiles who had helped Jews were fair game as well. Another of Margoshes's Jewish interlocutors, Gustawa Wiesenfeld of Kraków, told him that she was trying to scrape together a thousand dollars to secure the release of her dead sibling's children, who had been concealed during the war by a Polish family in the town of Mielec. She did not begrudge the family's request, because they "have done a noble deed and they are entitled to every possible consideration. . . . But the important point is that until this very day those children are kept in the garret of the house, hidden away from the neighbors for fear that the neighbors discover that the Christian family saved the Jewish children and vent their vengeance on the whole family and this one year after the liberation."[15]

American military intelligence in Germany, trying to get the bottom of the influx of Jewish refugees to the American sector of Berlin, uncovered a wide divergence in motives among refugees from different Eastern European countries. Of 230 Jews from Poland interviewed, all but six "gave virulent anti-Semitism in all walks of Polish life as the primary cause of their leaving the country. More than 100 had received threatening and vilifying letters from such illegal resistance groups as the Armja Krajowa [Home Army, sic] and the Nardone Sily Zbronje [National Armed Forces, sic]. . . . Instance after instance of personal violence and oppression was recounted." By contrast, of 110 Hungarian Jews interviewed, "none . . . expressed any fear of personal violence."[16]

The violence was but the most outward sign of a general demoralization and brutalization that had overtaken society. Wincenty Rzymowski, minister of culture and later foreign minister, related an anecdote of seeing several children building something out of sticks and pieces of coal. When they were asked what they were doing, they responded, "'We're playing at burning Jews.'" Said Rzymowski, "It's truly hard not to weep at the spectacle of the dehumanization of little, unformed souls. Themselves at death's door, they were playing 'as if' at killing, at the burning of victims of the Hitlerite regime equal to them in misfortune."[17]

Two years after the war ended, a newspaper could still run an article bemoaning the denunciatory "mentality," inspired by a letter to the editor describing a scene in which a woman who refused to pay her tram fare threatened the ticket collector with the words, "'I'll put you where you haven't been before.'" Commenting that "unfortunately these kinds of expressions are heard quite often," the editor concluded that "it is necessary to battle with the atmosphere of personal grudges, denunciations, and anonymous letters, which is felt by the authorities, institutions, and editorial boards alike." As a solution he suggested reporting casual denouncers to an already established venue for liquidating the remnants, spiritual and physical, of the occupation: "the courts which are today punishing renegades and 'Gestapo' informers."[18]

FEAR OF BOOMERANGS

Unlike the authorities in neighboring Czechoslovakia, who let vigilantes and mob justice run rampant for two months after the liberation before finally issuing their "Great Decree" on the punishment of war criminals, the PKWN hastened to publish their decree when most of Poland was still under German occupation. If they wasted no time in setting about reconstructing the architecture of the Polish state, it was in part because, unlike the Czechoslovak government, they were painfully aware of their illegitimacy.

Dr. Margoshes, who was otherwise gushing in his enthusiasm for the new Polish government, praising it as the "best hope . . . in the realm of a new venture in the domain of freedom" and earnest in its "desire to cure the evil of anti-Semitism," did not mince words when it came to its popularity. "Tied to the Soviet chariot," it had "practically no roots at all in the Polish people":

> Throughout my trip, I have encountered . . . thousands of people . . . I have yet to meet a Pole who is not a Communist who has a good word to say about this Government. Beginning with the trolley conductors with whom I conversed and ending with the chauffeurs who have escorted me on my journey, no one thinks this Government can possibly last.

In particular, the government suffered because of its association with Jews in the popular mind:

> The general charge against the Government is that it does not know how to keep order; that it is sold to Moscow; that it is corrupt and principally that it is sold to the Jews. . . .
>
> It made no difference to most of my Polish friends that I explained to them that Jews would really be accepting the [Nazi] Nuremberg laws if they were to accept . . . that Jews have no right to . . . high positions. . . . The emotional reaction was that there were too many Jews in the Government. . . . At any rate, it is my profound conviction that the present Polish Government would have been in dire straits any way even if

it had not employed a single Jew but that the presence of a number of Jews in high positions was just so much water on the Government mills.[19]

The result was, from the earliest days of the government's existence, a hypersensitivity to accusations of favoritism, as well as a simultaneous reluctance to acknowledge the especially precarious position of Jews in postwar Poland.

The initial cabinet of the PKWN included Dr. Emil Sommerstein, a distinguished lawyer, Zionist activist, and interwar member of the Sejm who had been arrested by the Soviets in 1939 as a "lifelong anti-communist."[20] The fragmentary record of the meetings of the PKWN contains a clash from September 1944 in which the other members leaned on Sommerstein, then serving as the head of the War Reparations Section, to write an apology for a speech he had published in *Pravda* condemning the perpetuation of "hidden Hitlerite practices" in the organs of Polish local self-government. Despite being criticized as "incorrect," "damaging," and unfair, Sommerstein steadfastly refused to write a retraction. Two months later, during a discussion of whether to extend a large credit to the Central Committee of Polish Jewry, General Zygmunt Berling fretted that "we have to contend with the existence of anti-Semitism in Polish society. I'm afraid that if we approach the issue in this way, instead of combating anti-Semitism, we'll add oil to the fire. A society in which anti-Semitism is deeply rooted—because it was educated that way for twenty years—will be unusually sensitive to actions like furnishing aid to the Jews." Although the credit was finally approved, others agreed with Berling that the credit risked inspiring Jewish "separatism" and reactionary elements.[21]

Speaking of the successor to the PKWN, the Provisional Government of National Unity (Tymczasowy Rząd Jedności Narodowej, TRJN), Margoshes wrote, "[It] seems to be aware of its difficult position vis-à-vis the Polish population in the matter of the Jewish question . . . it feels that it has gone out as far as it would dare, and perhaps a little farther than it is healthy for it, in the matter of accommodating the Jews."

Edward Osóbka-Morawski, the titular premier of both the PKWN and the TRJN who had pressured Sommerstein in 1944, rebuffed Margoshes's suggestion that the government launch an educational campaign against anti-Semitism, for fear that it "might be a boomerang." Margoshes reported that the authorities, conscious of their "impotence" and offended by the international "outcry" over anti-Jewish violence, were instead choosing to "minimize Jewish suffering": "With regard to those excesses, the official Polish reaction is first, they did not occur; second, they are exaggerated; third, they are part of the anti-government campaign conducted by the Fascists or the bands led and financed by the rival Polish Government in London." Their sensitivity, he wrote, was "really a self-defense measure in a way."[22]

A confidential note from Ambassador Arthur Bliss Lane to Washington that same year confirmed that "despite the Jewish background of many influential members of the Government . . . [it] has taken no action publicly which could be construed as pro-Jewish." That did not necessarily mean that the government was perceived as dismissive of the suffering of Jews. In the same memo the ambassador relayed that Sommerstein was "entirely satisfied with the attitude" of the TRJN to the Jewish question, while military intelligence reports from Germany indicated that refugees considered the government "well-intentioned but too feeble under the present circumstances to cope with the problem" of anti-Semitism and that it was not a "lack of interest . . . but rather a lack of public support" which hobbled them.[23]

But the line between caution and calculated indifference could be hard to discern. A dispatch produced by a Captain L. Gran, an interpreter of "Russian Jewish extraction" attached to an American military mission to Poland in January 1946, described the "Communists" as "none too perturbed" about the rapid diminution of the Polish Jewish community. One interlocutor, a "prominent Communist," put it in conversation:

> "Look, we are trying very hard to achieve some sort of a working arrangement with the other political parties, and we aren't going to quarrel with them just because of the Jews. Anyway, there won't be any Jews in Poland in six months or so."
> "Do you think they will be all polished off by then?"
> "Not at this rate," he laughed. "No, they will all be gone by then."[24]

Indeed, Jews were a receding demographic and political quantity whose significance was fast being crowded out by more pressing priorities. At a 1946 meeting to discuss a draft of a law on combating anti-Semitism, which would have increased penalties for anti-Jewish agitation and violence, the lack of enthusiasm was palpable. Attended by representatives of all the political parties, the Central Jewish Committee, the Presidium, and the relevant ministries, the session was characterized by the back-and-forth between the Jewish Committee representative, who pleaded the necessity of a new law, and the representative of the Polish Peasant Party (Polskie Stronnictwo Ludowe, PSL), the country's largest party and also the main opposition party, who claimed that there was no anti-Semitism in the country and that such a law would besmirch Poland's honor. Tellingly, the representative from Poland's de facto Communist Party, the Polish Workers' Party (Polska Partia Robotnicza, PPR), said that although the PPR agreed on the need for such a law "in principle," the fact that the Sejm elections of January 1947—widely seen as a test of the PPR's ability to Sovietize the country—were rapidly approaching "raise[d] certain doubts," and he asked for more time to consider it. Likewise, the representative of the much-feared Ministry of Public Security cautioned cryptically that the proposed decree would "bring into relief both the political and the legal-material sides," and that because the existing laws were sufficient for the punishment of anti-Semitic crimes, the "political aspect" was "so important" that it required serious thought before making a decision. A judge chimed in that it was necessary to rethink the sensibility of the decree at a time when "the most bitter political battles" were raging.[25]

FIRST STEPS

The PKWN desperately needed to create a basis of popular support, or at least grudging acceptance, where none existed. In a country emerging from five years of Nazi terror and where, at most, only 70,000 people were educated beyond a high-school level out of a surviving population of 24 million, the quickest route was to respond to the demands of the peasants and the hatred of the occupier.[26] In the short manifesto proclaiming the creation of the PKWN on July 22, 1944, the only domestic policy proposals that did not involve simply overturning the impositions of the Germans or restoring sovereign institutions were for free education at all levels, redistribution of all farms over 20 acres in size, and a guarantee that "no German war criminal, no traitor to the nation" would escape the justice of independent courts.[27] Tellingly, the official decree on land reform was the first law to be passed following the promulgation of the August Decree six days prior.[28]

The breaking up of large agricultural estates, many of them belonging to the most famous and politically influential families of the Polish aristocracy, was further evidence that the war had brought Poland to a revolutionary "zero hour" in which the centuries-old structuring of society along feudal lines had been irrevocably and radically abolished.²⁹ The poet Czesław Miłosz described the interwar Polish republic as being a "bureaucrat-peasant country" in which the feudal dichotomy between the nobility and peasantry endured in the form of the divide between officeholder and citizen.³⁰ The war had destroyed this hybrid aristocracy-bureaucracy, and now the PKWN was uprooting its economic basis; eventually, 2.47 million acres of land would be divided among 1.1 million peasant families.³¹

The blank slate that the war provided was also a chance for the Soviet-backed government to reestablish a degree of continuity with Polish sovereignty by reviving institutions that might then enlist some of the surviving university-educated in the work of the new state, especially that which might be construed as apolitical. In this respect, the judiciary was an excellent choice, because not only would it satisfy long-standing popular expectations of governance and professionalism that were much higher than in other, less developed countries in Eastern Europe, but because it would be in a position to literally litigate a new common narrative to cover the caesura of the war years.

But whether the government wanted to be saddled with an independently minded judiciary that would have its own say in the writing of the past was another question. Leszek Kubicki, who would become a minister of justice in postcommunist Poland and who served during the war as a teenage member of the Underground, commented that the new government was simply obliged to abide by a "certain tradition of a certain level of state life." As much as the Polish Stalinist leadership wanted to "politicize, 'democratize,' [and] 'renew' everything, it saw that it had to do so in a limited fashion." The "deprofessionalization" of the state apparatus, which an ideological clean sweep would have entailed, was "forbidden" in Poland. Poland remained "not just the happiest barracks [of the communist bloc, a well-known epithet of the Cold War period], but [the one] which to the strongest degree preserved that feeling of the meaning and weight of the state . . . and a certain indispensable professionalism."

Naturally, "it was understood that justice was an important instrument."³² Thus, the PKWN set about reassembling the judicial system only days after the announcement of the establishment of the PKWN in late July 1944 and just before the conquest of Lublin, the first major Polish city west of the Curzon Line to fall to the Red Army and therefore acceptable to Stalin as the launching point for a Soviet-aligned Polish government.

Leon Chajn, a prewar communist activist and lawyer of Jewish origin, had spent most of the war deep inside the Soviet Union on an oilfield in Bashkiria. He was plucked from exile by his old acquaintance Jakub Berman, one of the éminences grises of the PPR, and sent to work for the Soviet-backed Polish Army newspaper. From there he was summoned by the PKWN premier, Edward Osóbka-Morawski, and appointed deputy director of the Justice Section, making him the acting head in the absence of its titular director, Jan Czechowski, a peasant activist with no legal experience.

Among Chajn's most pressing duties was the drafting of a law to deal with the numerous accused collaborators who had already been arrested but for whom no statute existed.[33] Although the law his office eventually produced would remain on the books, with various revisions, for the duration of the People's Poland, its genesis was already in motion before he took office.

THE AUGUST DECREE

The need to prepare the legal ground for a systematic accounting had not been lost on any of the factions competing to determine the character of postwar Poland. In March 1943 the Polish Government-in-Exile in London published a largely notional decree, "On Responsibility for War Crimes," which provided for unspecified jail terms and the death penalty for persons who, "in contravention of international law," committed acts helpful to Germany and its allies and harmful to the Polish state or its citizens. Not to be outdone, the so-called State National Council (Krajowa Rada Narodowa, KRN), the communist Underground's rival to the London-affiliated Delegatura, issued its own decree in February 1944 on "criminal responsibility for participation in fratricidal murders, denunciations, and collaboration with the occupier."

But neither project would come to fruition. With the Red Army set to occupy Poland and the KRN being an unauthorized creation of Polish communists living under the German occupation, as opposed to the embryonic pro-Soviet government that Stalin had been cultivating inside the USSR since early 1943, both proposals would inevitably be superseded.

Instead, the ordinance that would eventually launch more than 30,000 trials was a laconic document that made up little more than one printed page, entitled "On the Punishment of Fascist-Hitlerite Criminals Guilty of Killings and Mistreatment of Civilians and Prisoners as well as of Traitors to the Polish

Nation." The Decree was promulgated by the PKWN on August 31, 1944, and thus popularly known as the "August Decree." Despite its dogmatic-sounding name and Soviet genesis, the August Decree has been described by a chief of postcommunist Poland's Constitutional Court as "not a communist law in content." Indeed, it remains in force to the present day.[34]

The Decree had nine articles, only two of which actually addressed specific crimes, and those in very broad terms:

> Art. 1. Whoever, acting in the interests of the German occupation authorities:
>
> > a) took or is taking part in the commission of murders of persons from among the civilian population or prisoners of war, in the mistreatment of them or in their persecution
> > b) acted or is acting to the detriment of persons on the terrain of the Polish State, in particular through the capture or transport of persons sought or persecuted by the occupation authorities for whatever reasons (excluding pursuit for the commission of common crimes) is subject to the death penalty.
>
> Art. 2. Whoever extorted or is extorting such persons or their close ones under the threat of capture of those persons and handing-over into the hands of the occupation authorities is subject to a prison term of 15 years to life.

Article 3 excluded the consideration of the most likely mitigating factors:

> Criminal responsibility for the commission of crimes described in art. 1 and 2 is not excused by service to or orders or force from the enemy occupation authorities.

Article 4 declared that in addition to the crimes above, attempted crimes, incitement, and abetting were also subject to punishment. Continuing the spirit of severity, Article 5 provided:

> In the event of sentencing for a crime foreseen by art. 1, 2, and 4 . . . the court additionally pronounces:
>
> > a) the loss of public and honorary civil rights
> > b) the confiscation of all property of the guilty party, and moreover [the court] may pronounce the confiscation of the property of the spouse and children of the accused.

The final articles specified that the Decree was applicable to crimes committed since August 31, 1939, and that they belonged to the jurisdiction of Special Criminal Courts.[35] The decree establishing those courts followed twelve days later. There would be one for each appellate area in Poland, the prosecutors and judges attached to the courts would be equivalent in status to those of the Appellate Courts, and trials, except where decreed otherwise, would follow the rules of the prewar codex on criminal proceedings, including the requirement for a defense lawyer to be present. Where the Special Courts diverged from their civilian equivalents was in their summary character. Suspects were to be arrested immediately, the formal pretrial inquiries usually conducted by an investigating magistrate were to be dispensed with in favor of a shorter investigation conducted by the police or prosecutor, indictments were to be issued no later than fourteen days after an arrest and trial dates set within forty-eight hours of the indictment, and all sentences were final, subject only to commutation by the chairman of the KRN.[36] Finally, the Special Courts were to hear cases in an entirely new composition, consisting of one professional judge and two lay judges nominated by the local national councils.

For reasons that will be made clear below, both the initial iteration of the August Decree and the Special Courts themselves would prove controversial and short-lived. Although no one could have known it at the time, the August Decree was the legal descendant of a secret decree of the Presidium of the Supreme Soviet of the Soviet Union of April 19, 1943: "On punishment for German-fascist evildoers, guilty of killings and mistreatment of the Soviet civilian population and captured Red Army soldiers, for spies, traitors to the fatherland from among Soviet citizens and for their helpers."[37] The tone of the first two articles of the Soviet decree, vague, broad, and categorical as they were, found their echo in the first two articles of the first August Decree:

1. To establish that German, Italian, Romanian, Hungarian, and Finnish fascist criminals, involved in the commission of killings and mistreatment of the civilian population and captured Red Army soldiers, and also spies and traitors to the fatherland from among Soviet citizens are to be punished with death by hanging.
2. Helpers from among the local population, implicated in the rendering of assistance to criminals in the commission of massacres

and violence on the civilian population and captured Red Army soldiers, are to be punished by deportation to penal labor from 15 to 20 years.

The remaining three articles specified that cases were to be heard by divisional military courts whose verdicts were to be confirmed by the division commander and carried out immediately, with executions to be public and the bodies of those hanged to be left on the gallows for several days as an object lesson.

In April 1944 the invasion of Poland by the Red Army appeared imminent. Among the units of the invasion force was the First Polish Army, trained and equipped by the Soviets, and whose recently appointed commander was General Zygmunt Berling, a career officer suspected of Bonapartism by the civilian Polish communist leadership grouped in the Union of Polish Patriots (Związek Patriotów Polskich, ZPP), the forerunner to the PKWN. After Berling established an unauthorized army codification commission to prepare a new Code of Military Justice, the ZPP, not to be outdone, quickly responded by organizing its own commission under Dr. Emil Sommerstein to issue directives for the codification.[38]

The ZPP commission's makeup hinted at the dualism that would characterize the future Polish government's commitment to legality. On the one hand, Sommerstein was a nonparty technocrat and an experienced jurist. Suffering from chronic illness after his release from Soviet captivity in 1942 and surviving on subsidies from the Polish Government-in-Exile, Sommerstein was left with little choice but to affiliate himself with the ZPP after Stalin cut off relations with the Government-in-Exile in 1943.[39] Counterbalancing him were at least three prewar communists who went on to senior positions in the party and secret police hierarchy, in addition to a legal analyst from the ZPP and the head of the Army's military court.

The directives set by the ZPP commission reflected this tension. On the one hand, they called on the army commission to make use of existing Polish codices and laws, to link itself as broadly as possible with Polish legal tradition, concepts, and institutions, to use Polish legal terminology, and to build on the "advanced accomplishments of Polish legal thought." In particular, the future Code of Military Justice was to take as its foundation the "principle of subjectivism," which characterized the most recent Polish Criminal Code, issued in 1932. On the other hand, the Sovietizing influence made itself felt in instructions to take into account the "legal protection of the interests of democratic forces from attacks by external and internal reaction" as well as the "ideology of the states fighting against Hitlerite aggression." Apart from their instructions regarding the military code of justice, Sommerstein's commission also recommended that the Army Commission draft a decree on war criminals and collaborators, to be adopted at a later date by a future Polish government.[40]

At least as far as the decree on war crimes was concerned, the Army Commission does not seem to have taken the ZPP Commission's directives to heart, for the document it produced, the decree of the Polish Armed Forces (Polskie Siły Zbrojne, PSZ) of May 30, 1944—"On punishment for German-fascist evildoers [złoczyńców], guilty of killings and mistreatment of Polish civilians and POWs, for spies and traitors to the Polish Nation among Polish citizens and their henchmen"—was virtually a word-for-word translation of the Soviet decree of 1943, right down to the use of "złoczyńców," corresponding to the Russian "zlodeyev." In addition to the single-instance courts and absence of appeals, which foreshadowed the procedure of the Special Courts, it likewise included the instructions that all cases should be heard within forty-eight hours of an indictment reaching the court.[41] Despite its date, the PSZ decree was only promulgated on July 31, 1944, and thus was in effect only for a month before it was superseded by the August Decree. Military investigators were collecting evidence and carrying out arrests during that time, but their actual prosecution would be turned over to the Special Courts.

Although the PSZ decree was, in turn, used as a template for the August Decree, it would be wrong to assume that the August Decree was nothing more than a slavish imitation of its Soviet predecessor. While the minutes of several of the sittings of the PKWN leading up to the August Decree's publication are missing, those that do survive, coupled with a number of early drafts, reveal a clear evolution away from the use of the Decree a political weapon.

That the PKWN considered repurposing the military's decree is clear from a draft, under PKWN letterhead and dated "Lublin, __ August 1944." which was almost an exact copy of the PSZ decree, including its title, with only a few emendations. There was also a draft of the decree on Special Courts that hewed closely to the final version, except that in this version they were referred to as "National Criminal Courts" and cases were to be heard by two professional judges and only one lay judge.

To judge by radically different drafts of the August Decree that made mention of a law of August 15, 1944, the final version was hammered out in a little over two weeks. One version, which changed the mention of "German-fascist evildoers" to "fascist-Hitlerite criminals" but otherwise kept the reference to "spies" and "henchmen" in the title, appears to have tried to encompass those crimes as well with additional articles. The three core crimes of the August Decree—killing, capture, and blackmail—were all subject to a mandatory death sentence in the first article. The incitement of crimes by a hostile occupying government also had a mandatory death penalty, whereas "praising" the crimes of the occupier was punishable by a minimum of ten years imprisonment, up to death. Seemingly out of place, a fourth article made the sabotage of industry—through damage of goods, interference in the "pace of work," or substandard production—punishable by a ten-year minimum sentence, life imprisonment, or even death. A fifth article made the taking of enemy citizenship punishable by a minimum of five years, with a death sentence possible. The "National Criminal Courts" were to hear these cases. A page of handwritten notes that accompanies the draft seems to indicate misgivings about its grab-bag character: "The title has the word 'spy' but the activity described . . . cannot be considered espionage."

Yet another draft did away with the articles about incitement, praise, and enemy citizenship, keeping only the first article and the article on sabotage, and an even more stripped-down draft got rid of the latter, completing the exclusion of crimes unconnected to the occupation. "On Punishment for the Commission of Killings and Acting to the Detriment of the Polish State, Its Citizens and Persons Located on Its Territory" appears to have been the second-to-last draft, reducing the penalty for capture, transport, or blackmail of persecuted persons from death to fifteen years to life and referring to the Special Courts.

While it has not been possible to reconstruct the role of the senior members of the PKWN in the drafting of the Decree, there was clearly a part of the leadership that wished to "instrumentalize" the courts. Jakub Berman, the leading Stalinist, who would be expelled from the party in 1957, stated at a meeting of the Presidium the day the Special Courts were announced that the "breadth and severity" of the courts regarding the death penalty "should be feared." A few weeks later in October, his future deputy and head of the secret police, Stanisław Radkiewicz, fretted that the "issue of courts for [arrested] members of the Home Army still has not been addressed" and that prosecutors could not be trusted with their cases. He therefore proposed filling this "gap" by "extend[ing] the Decree on [Special Courts] to also cover this category of criminals."[42]

Nothing came of Radkiewicz's suggestion, but that did not mean the budding communist regime was letting crimes against the state go unpunished. The articles on sabotage, praise of fascism, and enemy citizenship that had been in the early drafts of the August Decree found their way into an eighteen-article section on "Crimes of State" in the Code of Military Justice, published eight days before the August Decree on August 23, 1944. On October 30, 1944, the PKWN promulgated a decree "On the Defense of the State" that restated many of the articles from the military codex and made clear the government's choice to separate the prosecutions of the anticommunist resistance from the civilian and special court system. Instead, the military courts would have jurisdiction over those offenses.[43] As Aleksander Tarnowski, the head of the legal department in the Ministry of Defense and a career Soviet Red Army officer, wrote in late 1945, these courts bore the "'whole weight of the struggle with subversive elements, with secret anti-state military organizations, with diversion, sabotage [and] with traitors from the ranks of the NSZ.'"[44]

Indeed, for the duration of its existence the Stalinist government appears to have maintained a division between the courts handling legitimate accusations of collaboration and those handling strictly political crimes. Even when the government did eventually use the August Decree, beginning in 1950, to prosecute high-profile members of the wartime Underground on fabricated charges, these political trials took place in specially created "secret sections" of the Warsaw City Court and corresponding courts of appeal whose existence was a carefully guarded secret from other judicial and ministerial workers.[45]

STRANGE BEDFELLOWS

Whatever the PKWN's pretensions to be instituting a "new system," they would need the help of prewar experts if they were to rebuild the shattered country. From its inception, the ZPP had endeavored to present the Moscow-aligned government as the rightful heir to Polish sovereignty. The Polish

Army nominally under its control, for example, fought under the traditional national symbol of the white eagle, albeit missing its crown, and soldiers were issued the *rogatywka,* the emblematic four-pointed Polish military cap. Continuing in that vein, the inaugural manifesto of the PKWN, issued on July 22, 1944, declared the reactivation of practically the entire court and legal structure as it had existed prior to the German invasion in September 1939.

But like every other structure of Polish statehood, the court system had been devastated by the occupation. Along with the rest of the city, the Ministry of Justice in Warsaw had been burned to the ground and the national criminal registry had been shipped off to Germany. The whole area covered by the District Court of Białystok was said to possess only a single copy of the Bulletin of Laws, from 1923. Libraries were so denuded that the Justice Section of the PKWN had to launch an appeal for the collection of all surviving legal literature not essential for the functioning of what local government existed. In the Kraków area, prosecutors were still complaining in 1946 about the lack of accommodations, heating fuel, and even window panes; the majority lacked even a copy of the prewar legal bulletin.[46] And the material damage paled, of course, next to the human toll.

As representatives of the intelligentsia and prominent citizens, court officials had been among the first to fall victim to Nazi terror. In Lublin, the presiding judges of the Appellate and District Courts, along with two representatives each from the bar, the professoriate, the high school teaching staff, and the prefecture, were taken hostage in November 1939 and executed on Christmas Eve. A numbingly long report from Warsaw detailed losses there:

> The following personnel died in camps: presiding judge Łuński, deputy presiding judge Sochaczewski, and judges Dulęba, Wysocki, Kozłowski; notaries Wilczyński, Sima; . . . notary Zieliński was shot; secretaries Jagodziński and Szymański died in camps.
>
> The young assessor Jerzy Szper was killed in defense of Warsaw, and along with him the talented, promising jurist Jerzy Zalewski. That wise educator of legal interns, Tadeusz Semadeni, was killed during the uprising. Stefan Grzebalski was felled by almost the last bullet; in the ruins of the Appellate Court bailiff Eugeniusz Borzęcki died. . . . In the ruins of the Ghetto they shot the beloved learned bibliophile, prosecutor Jan Różycki and Judge Kazimierz Komorowski.

In Białystok it was reported that "at the moment of the liberation . . . from the Germans there was only one judge left from the entire roster of the district and municipal courts. All other judges, prosecutors, and administrators had either been deported to Germany or fled."[47]

The losses were such that, combined with the interruption of the years-long legal apprenticeship process by the occupation, as late as April 1946 there were still only 1,920 judges employed in all of Poland, compared to 3,500 before the war.[48] Consequently, for the sake of "securing . . . public order," the new government was faced with the "necessity of the appropriate use of surviving legalists for the rebuilding and functioning of the justice system." The decision predated Chajn. At his first meeting with Osóbka-Morawski, he was told that the PKWN would be rehiring former judges and prosecutors. In fact, as Chajn later admitted, the Ministry of Justice would be the "only ministry in reborn Poland" to rely "exclusively on the old cadre." Given the "enormous difficulties" he was anticipating, Chajn requested in August 1944 that all persons with legal experience be exempted from conscription and that Poles with similar qualifications residing in territories annexed to the Soviet Union—western Belarus and Ukraine—be resettled in Poland.[49]

A greater remnant of the judiciary had survived in the area of the former Generalgouvernement than in those Polish territories annexed directly to the Reich, where all traces of Polishness had been suppressed. In the Generalgouvernement, Polish law had remained in force insofar as it was not superseded by German decree, which indeed it was to a considerable degree. Although the infamous German Courts (Deutsche Gerichte) and Nazi Special Courts (Sondergerichte) had jurisdiction over political and most criminal offenses, reduced Polish courts continued to hear contractual and inheritance disputes, as well as misdemeanors, providing much-needed employment for a small number of jurists during the occupation.[50]

The readiness of the new authorities to make use of the surviving judicial cadre would have been unremarkable had the judiciary in interwar Poland not been involved in anticommunist repression. Activists of the Communist Party, banned in Poland since 1919 for its support of Soviet Russia, had been regularly tried and sentenced to prison terms that, while mild by the standards of the neighboring USSR or Nazi Germany, nonetheless instilled a lasting bitterness toward the old apparatus of state.

The mistrust, wrote Chajn in 1945, was mutual. The judiciary was loyal in the main to the London Government-in-Exile, whereas the PKWN had come to power "at the head of people whom the courts had punished for their struggle with prewar Poland."[51] In his memoirs Chajn recalled that Zenon Kliszko, head of personnel for the PPR and himself a defendant in an interwar case, upbraided him for not having "categorically opposed the rebuilding of the judiciary on the old principles." Władysław Gomułka, the future premier of Poland and a veteran of the penal system, demanded the recruitment of "new, young people" and the "systematic cleansing" of all those who had been overzealous in their persecutions of leftists. And Mieczysław Güntner, the chief prosecutor of the new Appellate Court in Kraków, lamented in a 1946 speech that an attitude of "party chauvinism" was driving a wedge between the executive and the judiciary: "Many democratic activists can't forgive their prewar accusers for their role at that time. For example, one of them presently in a high official position . . . publicly states that all prosecutors should now be in jail."[52]

Sixty years later, Leszek Kubicki, a minister of justice in postcommunist Poland who began his acquaintance with the legal milieu as a law student interning at the ministry in 1952, explained the compromise as growing out of the tension between those communists who favored a more moderate, so-called Polish road to socialism and the "dogmatics" who preferred close imitation of Moscow.

Chajn, who enjoyed the confidence of the country's de facto Stalinist leaders, Bolesław Bierut and Jakub Berman, nevertheless adopted a conciliatory tone from the beginning. In 1945 he openly praised the judiciary for its "moral purity, patriotic attitude, and struggle for legality." Jurists had remained a "powerful bulwark against the depraved and demoralizing influences of the occupation." If they had heeded the appeal of the new government to return to work, it was not from a "conviction about their obligation to work and the need for the building of a new Poland, but for fear of the disappearance of legality in Poland and the triumph of lawlessness."[53]

KEEPERS OF THE FLAME

The seriousness with which the judiciary took their role as upholders of national life was apparent from the speed with which they returned to work, often even before the guns had fallen entirely silent. Tales of heroism and examples of selflessness abounded. In the relatively small section of eastern Poland under the control of the Red Army and administered by the PKWN between July 1944 and January 1945, when the Red Army relaunched its westward offensive, there were already three Special Courts, three Appellate Courts, eight District Courts, and ninety-two municipal courts that had either been newly formed or returned to service. Many began functioning within just a few weeks of the PKWN's creation. Judicial personnel simply walked back onto the job. The director of the Appellate Court in Lublin reported that a majority of prewar judges from the area had returned to work and that with the addition of several others, the personnel complement was full. Władysław Grzymała, who had been a young judge in the village of Adamów when the war broke out, made his way to the larger town of Siedlce, where all the judges and prosecutors had returned to work, save for one who declined. Through an old contact in the Home Army, he obtained a job as a deputy prosecutor.[54]

Others sometimes ran through hails of bullets. In Otwock, a suburb of Warsaw on the right bank of the Vistula, the municipal court there opened in late August 1944, when the area was still within artillery range of the Germans. On January 12, 1945, the day the Soviet offensive began, the newly christened Ministry of Justice held a meeting at which sixteen functionaries were divided into three operational groups corresponding to the major axes of the offensive—Kielce and Radom, Warsaw, and Kraków and Silesia—whose responsibility would be to follow behind the front, securing court buildings and property and restarting the justice system. In the reconquered territories, the courts sprang back to life. The presiding judge of the District Court in Poznań recalled how an appellate judge, prosecutorial secretary, and bailiff made their way under German fire to extinguish the flames in the burning court building and save its contents. Around the country, court workers, judges, and prosecutors dug out files, seals, crests, and legal books that had been hidden in mineshafts and under haystacks at considerable personal danger. One judge borrowed a horse cart to gather up surviving functionaries, rescued the civil register from a roadside ditch along the way, and typed out the new laws to display in the town square. Three days after the liberation of Kraków, the operational group had registered 550 court workers, and within five days of the liberation, the first verdicts were being issued by the city's Appellate Court.[55]

As Chajn correctly observed, Poland's judiciary was conscious of being the custodians of a young, fragile national sovereignty, which, having been resurrected in 1918 after 123 years of foreign occupation, had lasted only twenty-one years before being overthrown again. Like a medieval guild, their education and training set them apart from ordinary people. They had passed through one of the country's small number of university law departments, completed an arduous apprenticeship at court, and passed several exams. Theirs was a "somewhat hermetic milieu." When at trial, judges wore a gorget bearing the national eagle, and lawyers wore a purple sash with the same emblem above the script "Law—Fatherland—Honor."[56] Many had a history of self-sacrifice, service, and patriotism. Bolesław Sekutowicz and Stanisław Bryła, the two Lublin judges executed by the Germans in 1939, had both been lawyers during the First World War, when they had served in various organs of local self-government and "salvation committees" created to deal with the chaos of that conflict. Aleksander Chrościcki, a deputy prosecutor in the town of Siedlce who came out of retirement at the age of sixty-seven, had been held as a hostage in Russia for two years after the outbreak of the Polish-Soviet War in 1919 and returned to Poland ill and destitute.[57] His younger colleague, Judge Józef Karwowski, a graduate of the Law Department of the University of Warsaw, had served as an officer cadet in the Polish-Ukrainian and Polish-Soviet Wars.

Patriotic feelings were imbibed from a young age. Prosecutor Władysław Grzymała recalled that during the First World War, when he was only a child, he had thrilled to tales of Piłsudski's Legions and that his sister had collected donations for the Macierz Szkolna, the Polish cultural-educational organization, which had operated illegally before the war. As he put it, he had been "inculcated with the spirit of freedom." Poland's new Soviet neighbor to the east inspired no sympathy in him. The Red Army soldiers who occupied his village in 1920 were undisciplined and ragged, some barefoot or wearing women's hats. His brother, along with other locals, was dragooned to serve as a cart driver, and the family's cart and horse were stolen. Back at school after the war, he looked with "pride and envy" at the older students who had returned from the front decorated. Less than a year into the German occupation in 1940, he joined the Polish Underground along with a fellow judge at the invitation of a lawyer acquaintance.[58]

Despite their devotion to the state, court officers of the interwar period, especially judges, were expected to be independent and above politics. Judges were forbidden to belong to political parties, and, so claimed Grzymała, there were no "behind-the-scenes influences" on the courts. The reality was more complicated, especially after Piłsudski's 1926 coup d'état, which inaugurated the reign of his autocratic, semi-dictatorial Sanacja clique until the German invasion in 1939. When, in 1931, eleven former Sejm deputies who belonged to the united center-left opposition were arrested on the express orders of Piłsudski and put on trial on trumped-up charges of planning to overthrow the government, the manipulation of the legal system was plain for all to see. But even Wacław Barcikowski, a lawyer with communist sympathies who defended one of the accused at the ensuing "Brześć Trial" and went on to become the Chief Judge of the reconstituted Supreme Court in 1945, conceded that the vote for acquittal by one of the three judges hearing the case was proof of the judiciary's determination to remain independent, even if it was "rather a heroic exception" among judges "trembling for their careers." A year later, representing leftist activists who were accused of starting a riot in which two policemen were seriously injured, Barcikowski credited the three presiding judges with "not only carefully investigating the nature of the event, the intentions of each of the defendants and the quality of the evidence, but also showing real independence." After allegations of the mistreatment of the defendants in custody surfaced, the prosecutor indicted several policemen.[59]

Nor was the judiciary an ideological or ethnic monolith. One of independent Poland's first Supreme Court judges in 1919, who would reprise his role in People's Poland, was Emil Stanisław Rappaport, a lawyer of Jewish origin who held a doctorate from the University of Neuchâtel in Switzerland and had been active in the defense of Polish revolutionaries before the First World War. An expert in international criminal law, he also helped prepare Poland's criminal code and lectured at the private Polish Open University, whose humanistic atmosphere was a haven for Jewish students and others fleeing persecution at the public universities in the 1930s. There he was a close colleague and mentor of Rafał Lemkin, who later wrote the UN Genocide Convention.[60]

But overall, the prewar legal milieu in Poland was, according to Leszek Kubicki, "very right-wing," and as such was hardly immune to the xenophobic discourse that had overtaken public life. The situation was perhaps even more acute among jurists, because Jews, who made up 10 percent of the interwar population, were traditionally overrepresented in "free professions" such as law and medicine; in 1928–1929, Jews made up more than a quarter of legal students. Ultranationalist student movements dominated student organizations at virtually all Polish universities during the interwar period, and anti-Semitic agitation was said to be strongest in the medical and law schools.[61]

At the law school of the University of Warsaw, said to be a "bastion" of the All-Polish Youth Academic Union, the student organization affiliated with the main far-right grouping in Poland known as National Democracy (Narodowa Demokracja, or Endecja), physical violence had become a regular occurrence by the early 1930s. In Kraków, the "majority" of law students were said to be active in the "radical-nationalist camp."[62] A newspaper account from November 1932 described first-year law students in Warsaw streaming from their off-campus classes onto the university campus, "raising anti-Semitic cries. In front of the gates they came upon a group of Jews, whom they beat severely with sticks. Next they cleansed the remaining classrooms where Jews were hiding."[63] Incidentally, one of the nationalist demands was that Jews should be allowed to attend only one university, and that it be the Open University, where Lemkin and Rappaport taught.

Among practicing lawyers, the economic crisis of the Depression sharpened existing antipathies. The High Polish Bar Council had tried to block Jews from its ranks in 1921 but was countered by the Warsaw Bar. Stanisław Gross, a prewar lawyer who refounded the Bar Council in 1945, criticized "older lawyers of nationalist temperament" for being unwilling and unable to oppose the younger radicals,

> overcome as they were by the selfish intention to limit the number of people practicing law, the income from which had fallen due to the economic crisis and the growth in the number of lawyers. On the outside things were prettied up with claims about caring for the moral level of the legal profession, which was allegedly threatened by pauperization.

Separate offices for "full-blooded" Polish lawyers, chicaneries against Jewish lawyers, and "barroom" diatribes at professional meetings were a "daily occurrence," culminating in the closing of admissions to the Bar by the Ministry of Justice in 1938.[64]

Given that the judiciary and civilian lawyers sprang from the same source, it may be surmised to what extent a worldview was shared by segments of both. Grzymała, the prosecutor, stated plainly that "before the war the majority of us sympathized with National Democracy."[65] That sympathy may have influenced verdicts. According to one analysis, during the waves of anti-Jewish violence that swept Poland from 1935 to 1939, the courts had been "very forgiving" of those accused of carrying out the pogroms, whereas cases against Jews and other ethnic minorities for supposed "disparagement of the Polish state" had been zealously pursued. While only 500 guilty sentences, many of them for less than a year, were handed to pogromists from 1935 to 1937, 1,500 minority members were sentenced for "defamation of the Polish Nation" in 1936 alone.[66]

How would the "rather strong anti-Semitic current" in the prewar legal community be expressed in "reborn" Poland? In the words of Leszek Kubicki, the "experiences of the war hadn't always broken these people." Early signs were worrying. At the PKWN's meeting of November 20, 1944, Stanisław Skrzeszewski, the head of the Education Section, announced gravely that "reports are reaching us from the Special Courts that prosecutors, court interns, and so on are succumbing to anti-Semitism."[67]

Regardless of how the government approached the issue of anti-Semitism and the war, the state's weakness, lack of popularity, and dependence on prewar technocrats meant that it could not unilaterally impose an interpretation of the occupation—whatever narrative of the past it decided on would have to pass muster with a vengeful populace and a wary judiciary. Although its manifesto had promised to "secure" the rebuilding of Jewish "existence, as well as legal and actual equality," it was and remained a Stalinist entity for whom the greatest good was the maintenance of the power, a goal that would be put at risk by the investigations into the wartime ethnic cleansing of Jews by their Polish neighbors.

4   THE SPECIAL COURTS

FOUR DAYS AFTER Christmas 1944, 500 ticketholders crowded into the national theater in the war-ravaged, provincial town of Rzeszów, which was serving as the temporary seat of the Special Court for the historic city of Kraków, still under German occupation 160 kilometers away. Lit by only candles and lamps—electricity in Rzeszów had been cut off the night before—the court's first trial, of a Ukrainian railway policeman named Aleksandr Miśkiwa, was followed with "tremendous interest" by the spectators. The verdict—death by hanging—was greeted with "general acclaim."[1] Miśkiwa's trial was part of a trickle of a little more than sixty cases that reached the nascent Special Courts in 1944, only to turn into a flood in 1945, when prosecutors forwarded almost 10,000 cases to the courts.

These trials were the beginning of an unprecedented legal experiment that was simultaneously intended to serve as an equally unprecedented ritual of national catharsis. As such, they raised, from the outset, a host of legal, procedural, and logistical questions that lacked easy or satisfactory answers. The venues they were held in, the penalties prescribed, and their legal bases would all be the subject of scrutiny and revision that would influence successive August trials. Cases of crimes against Jews would face an additional hurdle, one common to all such postwar reckonings around Europe—namely, that the centrality of the Holocaust to the German war effort was neither understood nor acknowledged. The trials were meant neither to examine the Holocaust in depth nor to shed light on popular involvement in it. Instead, the trials were meant to document and avenge ethnic Polish martyrdom at the hands of the Germans, of which the Holocaust was a corollary.

Early trials and punishments were marked by violent, cathartic outpourings of anger reminiscent of the "wild purifications" in places like France and the Czech lands, only this time channeled into a legal framework. Leon Chajn admitted that he had made a mistake in letting six German guards from the extermination camp at Majdanek be marched on foot through downtown Lublin to the first trial of its kind in Poland in late November 1944. A crowd of 15,000 people thronged the police escort, screaming at and spitting on the prisoners. Warning shots had no effect on the crowd, and only the timely appearance of tanks prevented a lynching.[2]

While public executions were rare—most death sentences issued by the Special Courts took place *in camera*—they consistently drew masses of people, testifying to the depth of feeling. At the hangings of eleven staff members of the Stutthof concentration camp and the former Nazi governor (Gauleiter) of western Poland, Arthur Greiser, days apart in July 1946, tens of thousands swarmed the execution grounds. Once the condemned were pronounced dead, the crowds were allowed to rush the gallows, where they tore at and beat the corpses. Some took away patches of their clothing as souvenirs, while others took fragments of the nooses, believed to have magical properties. The spontaneity of the crowds as well as the unseemly "picnic atmosphere" in which beer and ice cream were sold unnerved the authorities and intellectuals alike. The Catholic weekly *Tygodnik Powszechny* referred to public executions as a "great moral and social danger" and pleaded with readers to think of "punishment, not vengeance," while the communist essayist Jan Kott argued that "most [spectators] came to satisfy their desire for cruelty, which we should condemn, and not their feeling of vengeance, which we can respect."[3]

With the support of Osóbka-Morawski, who expressed his "doubts" about public executions "to which even tickets are being sold," Minister of Justice Henryk Świątkowski, citing the "unhealthily incensed masses of people hungry for sensation," put forward a resolution to discontinue the practice, which was adopted in August 1946 by the State National Council.

The concern of the government was disingenuous, because they both encouraged and benefited from the popular rage. In February 1945 the leadership of the PPR acknowledged that the hatred for the Germans had "'create[d] a great opportunity to unite this society in a single uniform national front.'"[4] As Leszek Kubicki, who skipped high school classes to watch the trial of Ludwig Fischer, the Nazi governor of Warsaw, remembered, the trials of major war criminals had the "full approbation of society" and were a "legitimizing factor" for an otherwise unloved government that "formed the basis for the conviction that [we were] in a Polish state, delivering justice to those who wanted to annihilate that state."[5]

For example, the proceedings that Kubicki witnessed, as well as those against Greiser mentioned above, were part of a group of seven heavily publicized trials held between 1946 and 1948 of high-ranking Nazi officials and Auschwitz guards—all Germans—that were meant to illustrate the breadth of Nazi crimes in Poland, including the ghettoization, deportation, and extermination of the Jews. These cases were heard separately by the Supreme National Tribunal (Najwyższy Trybunał Narodowy, NTN), a temporary body made up of personnel from the Polish Supreme Court and meant to serve as a "Polish Nuremberg" that would educate domestic and foreign audiences alike.[6] However, both the NTN and lower courts that tried German war criminals "maintained that the Holocaust had been but the beginning of a large-scale genocidal campaign against Slavs."[7]

Official pronouncements about Germans were full of venom, urging citizens to maintain their righteous indignation and be on the lookout for the "fifth column" of *Volksdeutsche,* those Poles of partial German ethnicity who had accepted German nationality during the war. Articles with titles such as "On the Scales of Justice" and "Their Traces Must Be Burned Away with Fire" were prepared by the press office of the Ministry of Justice in 1944 and 1945, and the two press conferences held by May 1945 were on Volksdeutsche and Auschwitz.

A 1944 article, "What Must Not Be Forgotten," reminded readers:

There are no decent Volksdeutsche, there are only traitors to the nation. This must not be forgotten. They must be punished in proportion to their guilt—with a camp, prison, and if need be, with the gallows.

Besides those who rejected their nationality, by directly crossing to the enemy camp—all those must be punished who soiled the good name of Poland and those Polish women, who not for bread, but for white rolls and five years of comfort, didn't hesitate to give up their honor for the rest of their lives.

There are renegades among us, there are enemies. . . . We must find them, even if they try to hide themselves in the heart of Germany. This is the duty of our Polish justice. . . . So many years have we waited for vengeance.[8]

Fragmentary statistics about the workload of the Special Courts gives some idea of the extent to which cases involving Germans or the taking of German nationality dominated the docket initially. In Warsaw, a copy of the docket from October 1945 reveals that of 61 defendants awaiting trial under the August Decree, 32 were described specifically as Volksdeutsche, while another 5 or so had German names, in addition to two Ukrainians.[9] The issue of the Volksdeutsche was particularly time-consuming. Three million Polish citizens were estimated to have signed the so-called *Volksliste,* accepting one of four categories of Germanness and renouncing their Polish nationality, under conditions ranging from whole-hearted consent to outright threats of arrest or worse. According to a decree of November 4, 1944, those Poles who had taken German nationality on the territory of the Generalgouvernement, where inscription had not been mandatory, were to have their cases reviewed by the Special Courts and, if sufficient guilt was found, were to be remanded to a detention camp to await trial. Thus, although the crime of taking German nationality did not fall under the August Decree, it swamped the prosecutors and courts responsible for trying collaborators.

PUBLIC TRUST AND PROFESSIONAL DOUBTS

Of course, the dissemination of anti-German propaganda by the government did not mean that there was anything inauthentic about the public's reaction. At a time of considerable instability and anxiety over the future of the country, the Special Courts stood, at least for some, as islands of reliability in a sea of uncertainty. They were a vent for popular rage, a site of expertise in a decimated society, and a symbol of sovereignty amidst a foreign occupation. But professional judges and prosecutors who staffed the courts would have to struggle with a crushing workload, the ambiguity of their role in a Soviet-backed administration, and mounting evidence that the public was selective in its memory of the war and ambivalent about the punishment of collaborators. In particular, the voice of the public, exercised through testimony, reactions to verdicts, and the institution of lay judges, would shape the evolution of postwar retribution.

Surviving evidence regarding public opinion is scant, but the mass of cases certainly suggests that people did trust the courts in the matter of retribution. At the Special Court in Kraków, one of the few districts for which statistics are available, the prosecutor's office reviewed a stunning 16,774 cases in 1945, of which 5,486 were for August crimes, and 11,288 were for signing the *Volksliste*. Prosecutors had forwarded 787 indictments to the court, and 5,687 suspected Volksdeutsche had been remanded to custody. It was said that the court had heard 2,000 cases pertaining to the decree of November 4 in just 114 days of sittings. Of the 129 guilty verdicts handed down by the court, 45 were death sentences.[10]

In the end-of-year report of for 1945, the presiding judge at the Kraków Special Court reported that the court

> enjoyed truly wide trust in society, which is confirmed by the diverse requests and letters addressed to the court on issues which have no connection to the court's activities.
>
> These requests touch on the border disputes and other similar issues and not uncommonly questions of a personal nature.
>
> That people would . . . entrust the court with the resolution of these problems testifies undoubtedly to the trust placed in it.[11]

The voice of the people was arguably being heard not just through witness testimony, but though the involvement of lay judges in all August trials. The inclusion of the lay judges has been maligned by modern commentators as a barely disguised attempt to stack the courts with pro-regime sympathizers, but internal documents from the Special Courts and successive instances paint a much more complex picture. Both the judges and prosecutors of the Special Court in Kraków attributed the trust it enjoyed among the local population to the "civic factor" of the lay judges, who had "turned out to be a very valuable co-actor in the administration of justice." The court praised the "conscientiousness" and "attention to detail" of their lay judges, most of whom

> come from the political groupings of the PPS [Polish Socialist Party] and PPR, they are mainly former political prisoners and therefore extremely sensitive to the fate of every defendant.
>
> This accounts as well for the rather significant number of postponed cases, since even the smallest evidence submitted by the accused is the subject of research before a verdict will be issued.[12]

Lay judges were not unknown in prewar Poland, where they had been incorporated into the adjudication of labor and commercial disputes, but the decision to have August crimes heard by one professional and two lay judges marked a considerable widening of the institution's reach. For the new government, the fact that citizens could now outvote the professionals was a populist move to suggest that justice had been "democratized," as well as providing a surrogate to the feelings of righteous anger which had been denied an outlet in the form of French or Czech-style "wild retribution." Contrary to the suggestion that lay judges were a barefaced attempt to subvert the judicial process, their presence was praised by people who were otherwise unstinting in their criticism of the "new judicial forms." Władysław Chojnowski, a judge of the Warsaw District Court and a prewar investigating judge who was unsparing in his disdain for the entire institution of the Special Courts, nevertheless commended the summoning of lay judges as "sensible and useful" and expressed confidence that, under the tutelage of the professional judge, the lay element would always vote correctly.[13]

The initial criteria for selecting the lay judges, who were to be chosen by the local national councils, approved by the State National Council, and forwarded to the courts, were broad: "They must be persons over the age of 21 who have taken or are taking part in active armed struggle with the occupier, or in civil actions of self-defense or resistance, including propaganda, or in the rebuilding of Polish statehood in the political, social, economic, or cultural sphere."

For a society that had been united in resistance to the occupier, many people fit this bill. Only suspected collaborators and those accused of "fratricidal conflict" with the "democratic" (that is, communist) Underground were excluded.[14] The lay judge was meant to be a rotating responsibility; candidates had to take time off from their day job and travel to the court, and the government took the principle of rotation seriously. A circular from 1946 chastised the courts for not having a large enough roster of candidates and changing lay judges infrequently or not at all:

> It must be kept in mind that given the small number of lay judges taking part in certain courts . . . there arises the danger of the degeneration of the institution; the too frequent use of these same persons in hearings misses the basic goal of introducing into the judicial system constantly new, vigorous factors representing public opinion.

It cannot be ignored that the too often summoning of those same persons, working in their own professions, causes the overburdening of them with work to a degree often exceeding their capabilities.[15]

Contrary to the idea of the lay judges as communist plants, they often either submitted to the will of the professional judges or behaved idiosyncratically, exercising a braking effect on the punitive intention of the laws and contributing to a high rate of acquittals that frustrated the government. At the Special Court in Toruń, the lay judges were appreciated by their professional colleagues for their "valuable familiarity with local relations during the occupation and . . . reflect[ing] the actual opinions of society." The court fretted, however, that "many . . . approach cases subjectively and not like a judge. For example, a lay judge who is a tailor will try his hardest to avoid sitting in judgment on another local tailor, while another lay judge who lost a leg while in the Reich is extremely harsh and that affects the sentencing and evaluation of evidence." That having been said, "in general the professional judge's vote has the deciding significance and outvoting by the lay judges is the exception." Their comportment suggested that they were anything but iron instruments of Sovietization. Lay judges, in a scenario familiar to anyone who has had to perform jury duty, were often late and sometimes failed to show up at all.[16]

Meanwhile, the career judicial personnel were wrestling with the ambiguity of their own position, caught between meting out justice and potentially legitimating a regime that many of them considered illegitimate. Each judge or prosecutor presumably had his or her private reasons for continuing on the job, whether it was the necessity of earning a living, a commitment to the profession and a determination not to abandon it to the "enemy," ideological sympathy, or some combination thereof. As Leszek Kubicki pointed out, the prewar judiciary "was not ideologically monolithic."[17]

Several days before the actual liberation of the capital city in January 1945, Witold Mniszewski, the presiding judge of the Special Criminal Court in Warsaw, delivered a speech that explained, in surprisingly frank terms, what he saw as the courts' mission and his decision to support it. The Special Courts were an institution "conceived for the merciless suppression in Polish lands of Germandom in all its forms and manifestations." He went on to discourse on the monstrous manifest destiny of the German people, the "eternal enemy of all Slavic tribes" and the "most adept at racism, chauvinism, brute force, and the illusion of superiority." Actions that "would be inconceivable to a member of any other nation [are] perfectly comprehensible to a German."

Outnumbered ten to one by the combined populations of Germany and the Soviet Union, Poland was "doomed in advance to massacre and terrible defeat" in an armed conflict with either. The only solution was to make an alliance with one, which of course had to be the USSR, Poland's savior from certain destruction. He challenged those in the audience who disagreed to imagine the slaughter that would ensue if the German Army returned tomorrow. Finally, Mniszewski warned against a strange complacency about the war that had begun to descend the moment the "sounds of the cannons died away and the salvos of machine guns fell silent behind the last German." Only a few months ago, people had "greedily seized" upon even the Nazi-approved "gutter press" to wring the smallest details of the Red Army's advance. Now, "sate[d] with the luxury of freedom," voices had begun to mutter that "under the Germans it was better, since butter cost such-and-such an amount, but now it costs more, and before we waited only an hour in line for rations, but now it's an hour-and-a-half."[18]

The prosecutor of the Appellate Court in Kraków and one of the presiding judges at the NTN, Mieczysław Güntner, recorded a similarly pragmatic exchange on the eve of the Soviet offensive:

> "What are you planning to do when 'they' [the communists] arrive?"
> "Nothing, I'll still be sitting at this desk."
> "So what then when the London government[-in-exile] comes back?"
> "That's not important right now. What's important is that the Germans get out of here as soon as possible. As for the government, it can be anything they like, as long as it's ours. We'll worry about its form later."[19]

In the memoirs of prosecutor Władysław Grzymała, an anticommunist who observed that the new government would have been dispatched "with ease" if it had not been for the presence of the Red Army and NKVD, little is said about the initial trials of war criminals and collaborators. Instead, Grzymała remembers the years 1945 to 1946 as a time when he and other members of the prewar judiciary were a bulwark of legality in lawless, dangerous eastern Poland. He learned with horror of the activities of the "hooded courts," summary courts that were attached to the civilian courts on paper and often staffed with absentee personnel from the state security apparatus who produced death sentences ex post facto for anticommunist partisans who had been shot out of hand after capture.[20] Much of his activity was directed toward negotiating with and mitigating the damage caused by the poorly disciplined political police, officially known as the Office of Public Security (Urząd Bezpieczeństwa Publicznego, UB), who behaved as a law unto themselves. Among other things, he agreed to knowingly keep an innocent landowner under arrest to prevent the man from being sent back to the UB prison, and he also investigated a drunken shooting committed by a small-town mayor under the protection of the UB.

Grzymała's is not the only testimony to the view that a court presence was a hedge against official impunity. The national council of the town of Garwolin, southeast of Warsaw, claimed to be speaking on behalf of the public when it pleaded for the creation of a Special Court there, hoping to "put an end to any possible kinds of abuse" by the local office of the UB, who were arbitrarily arresting and then releasing residents without trial or explanation.[21]

AN "AVALANCHE OF DENUNCIATIONS"

Between January 26, when it opened its doors, and June 30, 1945, the prosecutorial office attached to the Special Court for Kraków was besieged with 1,983 complaints made under the August Decree and almost 4,000 cases of suspected Volksdeutsche. In that same time, with a staff that grew from five to nine prosecutors and around two dozen office workers, it managed to generate only 119 indictments, while 1,054 persons, presumably all Volksdeutsche, were sent to "separation camps" to await further processing. This "insane overburdening" had already caused several court workers, whose low salaries forced them to take second jobs to support their families, to fall ill. To make matters worse, wrote the chief prosecutor, the "persistent pestering" of families of detainees to have loved ones' cases expedited ended up consuming an "unbelievably large amount of time" in of itself.[22]

Władysław Chojnowski, the Warsaw judge, went so far as to claim that Special Court prosecutors were "helpless" when confronted with the crushing "mass of work" and the difficulties of mastering their "too large" jurisdictions. Whereas the "prosecutorial districts and internal borders" of the districts, Poland's basic units of judicial administration, had been "established on the basis of many years' experience, such that the prosecutor easily masters the flow of cases . . . and knows his region," the Special Courts had been created to correspond to each of Poland's eight appellate areas.[23]

Prosecutors were transferred around the country as needed, and some were entirely new to the job. To patch the holes in the judicial quilt, prewar assessors and interns—court officers who had recently finished their legal studies and were effectively apprentices—were rapidly promoted, and lawyers too were inducted with little ado. At the Special Court of Warsaw, for example, of the nine prosecutors in January 1946, there were three former lawyers, one assessor, and two interns. Of the eight judges in April 1946, one had been a lawyer, one a mortgage clerk (a type of court official in the Polish legal system), and the presiding judge, Henryk Cieśluk, was a prewar communist activist with no prior legal experience.[24] "Not every lawyer is fit to be a prosecutor or judge," warned Chojnowski.

Although skilled investigative judges—who were responsible for pretrial investigations under the prewar legal system—knew how to examine a crime scene and secure evidence, "many legal personnel . . . don't have the necessary experience . . . and don't realize the great importance . . . of this activity":

> Please just compare the requests for court assistance . . . by regular and Special Court prosecutors . . .
>
> They often demand . . . the interrogation of witnesses who, based on the case files, are obviously dead or living elsewhere. These requests contain fundamental material faults. They often don't request the most important basic judicial operations, like exhumations and autopsies, although they do send the case back to the court several times for the interrogation of additional witnesses before criminal charges are formulated, which can alert the accused and cause his escape, etc. etc.

The problem with delegating municipal courts to interview witnesses whom the prosecutors didn't have time to reach themselves was that the case was then reliant on the individual judge's determination to get to the bottom of the matter. If he was uninterested, the court would have to file new requests for re-interrogations, and the cycle would be prolonged.

Ultimately, the creation of the Special Courts put attached prosecutors in the "impossible" position of trying to get a grip on the case influx of their "gigantic" jurisdictional area, while prosecutors from the regular courts were left with nothing to do. "Nothing surprising then, that with this distribution of work, only a tiny fraction of the Hitlerite-fascist criminals end up in the dock, while the best-concealed criminals escape justice even if an investigation is opened against them."[25]

Anecdotes from the field suggest that Chojnowski was not wide of the mark. Although matters were said to be improving thanks to the heroic exertions of the prosecutorial team, which "in almost all important cases [did] not rest on the results" of investigations conducted by the police, the review of 1945 from the office of the prosecutor of the Special Court in Kraków admitted that "the slender personnel of the prosecutor's office does not permit the quick examination of the avalanche of denunciations and mass of prisoners. Investigations drag on for months. Huge numbers of suspended cases."[26]

Suspended cases were so numerous that they outnumbered indictments.[27] The decision to proceed with or suspend a case was entirely at the prosecutor's discretion. According to Alina Skibińska, a leading scholar of August crimes who has worked with a vast quantity of prosecutorial files, many cases were suspended "exclusively due to the will and decision of the prosecutor, and not for lack of guilt."[28] My own research fully corroborates this assertion, but in fairness to the judiciary, there was also a tremendous amount of "noise" that had to be tuned out, especially in this early period. The aforementioned "avalanche of denunciations" included many "false, rash accusations" by people trying to "settle personal, political, and financial accounts," causing "huge difficulties" for prosecutors sifting the real from the false. The Special Court prosecutor in Kraków attributed the "large percentage of suspensions" to the "great dishonesty of certain segments of society wishing to settle their personal accounts with enemies by means of false accusations, based on the exploitation of all possible appearances against [the accused]." This was coupled with the "lack of expertise" of the UB and MO, who "botch[ed] difficult and incriminating cases."[29]

Even so, cases at the Special Court in Lublin which the judges felt would have been better off suspended by prosecutors due to the "poor quality" of the investigations were forwarded to the courts anyway, pushing up the number of acquittals. Although much of the correspondence from the early years of the Ministry of Justice has been lost, evidence suggests that ministerial authorities were partly to blame. The prosecutor in Lublin defended his record by referring to instructions from the Office for Oversight of the Special Courts, which had ordered prosecutors to send "doubtful cases" to the courts to decide, rather than suspending them.[30] At the court in Lublin, 17 out of 41 verdicts in February 1946, the month before the report was produced, had been acquittals. Since the court had begun operation in November 1944, there had been 95 defendants sentenced to death, 87 to prison terms, and 102 (just over one-third) acquitted. In 1945 at the Special Court of Kraków, there were 76 convictions—24 of them death sentences—and 82 acquittals along with 6 suspensions.[31]

Public reaction could be fickle:

> The press, after finding out that an indictment has reached court . . . and without analyzing the evidence, announces [the case] with great fanfare, often exaggerating the crime and in advance condemning the accused, often in a very blatant way. When an acquittal results, the reaction of society is very vigorous and . . . surprised. With it come unjustified attacks on the court.[32]

Judicial difficulties were compounded by false accusations, witness-tampering, and, perhaps most unexpectedly, an ambivalence about the accused. In private correspondence, judges and prosecutors raised questions about the reliability of witnesses. Under the prewar procedural code that remained in effect, defense lawyers had a right to be present at the preliminary interviews of witnesses carried out by prosecutors and investigative judges. But witnesses who otherwise spoke freely clammed up when the counsel for the accused was present. Due to the "general decline of security, the prosecutor and judge cannot at present guarantee the witnesses' security for them to speak the truth. Oftentimes witnesses—who do not want at any price to appear in the files, correctly fearing for their life, freedom, or property—will contact the judge and offer confidential and very valuable information in solving a crime."

The suspect, for his part, using the ill-gotten gains from his collaboration, "can find a smaller or larger number of witnesses who will whitewash him for money and sing hymns of praise." The Special Court prosecutor, who delegated the interrogations to other judges or law enforcement due to the workload and size of his jurisdiction and sometimes did not speak with the witnesses until trial, was at a disadvantage: "In general in cases of this type a disproportion is observed between the forces leading the investigation and the defense of the accused. The investigation is conducted by unprofessional and unschooled personnel—the security authorities—[whereas] the defense are experienced lawyers, who due to their occupation and education have a big advantage over the former."[33] Moreover, judges who interviewed witnesses at the prosecutor's behest could not officially opine as to the truthfulness of the statements, something which prewar investigative judges usually did in their summations.

Score-settling was clogging the system. In Kraków, "in the first months after the liberation, many citizens came forward with denunciations" to the Special Court, which they were unable to substantiate at trial. Instead, they "often exposed the background" to their complaints, which turned out to be the "malicious satisfaction of private vengeance" and the settlement of "personal accounts." The prosecutor's office echoed the judges, writing that "society's attitude" to the trials "cannot be praised": "On the one hand they exploit the decrees against criminals and traitors for personal accounts, knowing full well that pretrial arrest is mandatory, wherefore the huge quantity of false accusations."

But at the very same time a strange permissiveness toward the accused was becoming apparent, suggesting that society's theoretical vengeance was faltering when confronted with the reality of punishment:

On the other hand, however, the prosecutor encounters excessive leniency, understanding, false mercy toward collaborators, and in particular Volksdeutsche—a false shame about denunciation, especially Volksdeutsche.

In almost every serious case one comes across a group of witnesses, who struggle to whitewash the criminal or traitor. It's hard to determine whether the actual motive in such cases is mercy or certain material influences.

Where there's no body or no serious abuse, in general persons involved in the case will want to forgive the defendant. It's typical Polish softness of heart, a defect, which may permit the remains of a fifth column to stay in the country.[34]

Leon Chajn commented on the same phenomenon: "In almost every trial against Hitlerite thugs responsible for the deaths of hundreds, thousands, and even tens of thousands of people, witnesses came to testify in their favor.... They came from different backgrounds: Poles and Jews, priests and partisans. Almost every criminal, big or small, had his moments of 'weakness'—mercy."[35]

Moreover, it was not just professional judges, but lay judges who protested against what they considered the overly harsh penalties mandated in the August Decree and who preferred to acquit defendants threatened with death or a long prison term. Lay judges in Kraków also favored a relaxing of the regulations about obligatory pretrial arrest and felt that the November 1944 decree on Volksdeutsche was too severe. The prosecutor of the Special Court in Kraków went so far as to complain of an "unhealthy leniency" among the lay judges. The "struggle of the prosecutor with this attitude" was all the more difficult because the verdicts of the Special Court were final and there was "no possibility of correcting them to the detriment of the accused."[36]

Twenty-five years after the end of the war, an in-depth study of lay judges by Leszek Kubicki, the author of the first legal monograph on the August Decree, found that citizens who tended to be harsh in abstraction, when considering the matter from the perspective of a potential victim, suddenly changed when sitting in judgment, instead looking at the crime through the prism of the perpetrator.[37] As lay and professional judges in the August trials alike had discovered, it was hard to remain objective when there was precious little to distinguish patriots from perpetrators.

THE THIN GREEN LINE

As we have seen, the law enforcement organizations on whom the Special Courts relied were themselves an obstacle to functioning effectively. The Soviet-backed PKWN had established two police organizations. The regular criminal police force was replaced by a new Citizens' Militia (Milicja Obywatelska, MO), whose name, in conscious imitation of the eponymous Soviet police force, was meant to evoke its supposedly democratic character, unlike the prewar State Police. The functions of the political police, on the other hand, were assumed by the UB, whose main task was quelling armed opposition to the State and public dissent. In theory, both institutions were meant to be stocked with ideologically reliable cadres drawn from the ranks of PPR members and former communist-aligned partisans arranged around a nucleus of hand-picked personnel trained in the Soviet Union. In reality, the unpopularity of the government and the chaos of the early postwar years were such that the doors were open to almost anyone with the right class background who was willing to risk his life wearing an official uniform in a climate that has been described as one of "civil war."

According to one estimate, the "most numerous group" in the MO were "young men 20–25 years in age, not uncommonly 'infected' by a wartime mindset, and demoralized." Although the UB, by contrast, was supposed to be the Praetorian Guard of the regime, they were hardly more élite. From 1945 to 1956, only 24 percent of UB members had attended high school, and only 2 percent had any kind of university education. The result was an epidemic of the problems one would have expected: drunkenness on the job, misuse of firearms, theft, and abuse of office. Illustrative of the turmoil in the security services is the fact that by 1949, 90,000 workers had been fired or resigned from the UB, an organization which at its peak strength in 1953 counted just over 33,000 members.[38]

Unfortunately for the prosecution of collaboration, this disruption was occurring at precisely the time when law enforcement was being entrusted with more responsibility than ever before. Poland, like much of continental Europe, had had an inquisitorial system of justice during the interwar period, in which an investigating judge would build a criminal case, interviewing witnesses and securing evidence before forwarding it to the prosecutor, who would then issue an indictment. In the interest of expediency and given the greatly diminished number of judges, the PKWN had decreed that the traditional inquiry of the investigating judge would be replaced by an abbreviated investigation conducted by the local UB or MO office.

Naturally, some members of the judiciary were aghast at this state of affairs. At a 1946 conference, Władysław Chojnowski, the prewar investigating judge, concluded that the new laws issued since 1944, including the decree on the Special Courts, had "failed the exam." Policemen, who were now subject to military justice, "were not afraid" of the regular courts and only carried out the orders of prosecutors "when they felt like it." He took particular issue with the transfer of the highly experienced investigative judge's responsibilities to law enforcement:

> How on earth can one imagine that an untrained security functionary or militiaman can uncover a well-concealed Gestapo informer and establish the extent of his activity.... The aim of such an inquiry is not only the establishment of one such incident of harming an individual, but ... the entire activity of the informer, the exposure of his accomplices and helpers. It requires such subtlety that it can't be entrusted to an unintelligent and unexperienced person.

In fact, the "whole weight" of the investigation instead ended up "resting on the municipal courts and investigative judges" anyway whom the Special Courts were empowered to ask for assistance, "because the material collected in these cases by law enforcement is unfortunately insufficient for prosecutors to issue an indictment. These cases demand the interrogation of sometimes more than a dozen witnesses, and the security organs don't know how to do this and don't have the patience. Their interviews are most often modeled with stereotypical questions, whose reworking and answers are so demanding of an investigator not possessing enough skill in writing that interviewing 100 witnesses takes him several months, whereas it would take an investigative judge several days."[39]

Chief Judge Barcikowski shared these concerns:

> A policeman cannot be a judge. The combination in one person of the executive organ and those duties which decide the fate of the defendant is neither correct nor sensible. The usual attitudes of the policeman, the desire to show off his "abilities" to his superiors, an unsophisticated treatment of evidence and so on reduce the investigation to a mechanical action without use for the purposes of justice. The value of even a scrupulous inquiry is often cast into doubt when the court touches it with its scalpel, all the more so for a police investigation, being the work of an official assigned to the observance of public order.

The new system had "demoralized" the courts, who, despairing of the competency of the police, were now returning far fewer cases for further investigation.[40]

Tensions were no doubt exacerbated by the consciousness of the new police organizations of being the offspring of political upheaval, unbound by the traditions of their prewar forebears, the intoxication of being given guns and power with little commensurate vetting, and their social and educational gulf from the well-educated judiciary. As one prosecutor put it, "It's necessary to start almost from ABCs, because the hand of the policeman, who until a few days prior was a partisan, is quicker with a gun than a pen."[41] In the words of the prosecutor of the Special Court for Kraków,

> despite numerous courses and training sessions, investigations are still being carried out poorly . . . the organs of the MO and public security are still unschooled. They are recruited in large part from ideological considerations and inspired by the best intentions, but without respect for professional considerations, often almost from the ranks of illiterates. The effect is the transfer of a huge amount of investigative work to the regional prosecutors and an extreme slowing of the work tempo.[42]

A year later, problems persisted. Working with the UB and MO was still an "uphill battle"; both regulations and training were lacking, "not to speak of the fact that, unfortunately as everywhere here too criminal elements have crept in." Recruited primarily from "boys from the forest," or former partisans, they were "amateurs" who had not acquired a respect for legality in the "partisan atmosphere." Often they defied or ignored the courts. A prosecutor had ordered the MO to arrest several criminals "belonging coincidentally to a certain political party, only to have the UB release them." Functionaries of the UB, as they were called, ignored subpoenas and defied court orders to vacate properties occupied illegally.[43]

In December 1944 the prosecutor of the Warsaw Special Court, temporarily seated in the town of Siedlce, informed the Justice Section of the PKWN that the UB was refusing to forward him the cases of hundreds of accused collaborators being held in local camps: "The UB in my jurisdiction acts completely independently, there is no connection between their activity and my intentions, and as a rule I'm not informed about their investigations. . . . Suspects often spend weeks in UB jails without me being informed. This situation is creating distrust in society of judicial institutions and an atmosphere of panic." To top it off, there was evidence of "massive theft" of the property of suspects, otherwise subject to confiscation by the state.[44]

The UB, in turn, interpreted signs of disregard of their work by the Special Courts as a snub. In a memo from the local UB office in Rzeszów to the Ministry of Public Security, they claimed that the prosecutors and judges of the Special Courts too often refused to bring cases investigated by the UB to trial and instead released the defendants, who often went into hiding: "No matter that every case possessed the strongest and most concrete compromising materials. Even the prosecutor said that the confession of the accused has no value. I wish to communicate that the prosecutor of the Special Court made us to understand that he doesn't want to cooperate with the UB."[45]

The new crypto-communist government and its security services, above all the UB, were and are identified by many Poles with the alleged establishment of "Jewish" control over Poland. Given the disproportionately large numbers of ethnic Jews in the prewar Polish communist movement, the fact that some Polish Jews fled (or were deported) to the Soviet Union ahead of the Nazi invasion in 1941, and the hostility that many survivors encountered during and after the war from mainstream Polish society, it was unsurprising that some of those who chose to stay in Poland after the war, unlike the majority who emigrated rapidly to north America and Israel, embraced a utopian ideology that espoused colorblindness and promised a clean break, however improbable, with the openly racist society of the 1930s.

Of roughly 400 "leading" positions in the Ministry of Public Security between 1944 and 1954, it has been calculated that 37 percent were occupied by ethnic Jews. But away from Warsaw and in the countryside, Jews were few and far between in the ranks of the UB. In early 1946 in Lublin province, heart of both the anticommunist insurgency and a former center of Jewish life in eastern Poland, less than 2 percent of the UB personnel were Jews. Although the concentration of Jews was highest in Silesia and the "recovered territories" of western Poland after the war, in the former province only 10 percent of the leadership positions were occupied by Jews while in the province of Greater Poland, home to the city of Poznań, 95 percent of the "Ubeks" were Poles.[46]

If anything, the men of the UB and MO were representatives of the local societies in which they operated, both mentally and demographically, and consequently they too were susceptible to anti-Semitism. UB and MO personnel were implicated in the two most notorious outbreaks of mass postwar violence, the Kraków and Kielce pogroms, and incidents of hostile comportment by both the MO and UB were recorded nationwide. As we shall see, it was not at all uncommon for accused wartime persecutors of Jews to turn up in the ranks of the local MO and UB. After all, who better to police the community than its own members? Even former members of the wartime Blue Police were initially permitted to join the MO, where their experience as law enforcement veterans was in demand. One Jewish woman, seeking the return of belongings left behind when a Polish Kripo had arrested her and her young daughter, who later died in Auschwitz, came face to face with the same Blue policeman, now in the MO, who had been on duty the day she was brought in in August 1943.

The creation of these new, "democratic" security services offered Jews no guarantee of security and instead raised serious questions about whether the MO and UB would investigate crimes against Jews with impartiality. Based on interviews conducted with Jewish refugees from Poland in 1945, American military intelligence reported the troubling information that "many minor officials, particularly in police agencies, are people who collaborated with the Nazis."[47]

PROBLEMS WITH THE AUGUST DECREE EMERGE

Looking back on the Special Courts and the various laws on collaboration in an article published in 1946, Antoni Landau, a veteran left-leaning lawyer appointed to Poland's Supreme Court by the new government, sarcastically quoted the nineteenth-century French statesman Louis-Napoléon Bonaparte. Bonaparte had famously justified his 1851 coup d'état that overthrew the French Second Republic by insisting that it had been necessary to "depart from legality in order to return to justice." The play on words explicitly contrasted the legality of the dissolved National Assembly, which had refused to alter the constitution to allow him to run for a second term as president, with the broader right (*droit*), or justice of the soon-to-be emperor's popular mandate, which had just been confirmed ten-to-one in a plebiscite based on universal suffrage.

Landau was upset because he felt that the ends did not justify the means—namely, circumventing certain legal protections and creating special venues, however temporary, for these cases. But his indignation laid bare the dilemma facing the adjudication and administration of war crimes and collaboration in not just Poland, but all over Europe; law and "justice" did not always overlap, nor could they always be reconciled. As Lawrence Douglas has written of the trials of German perpetrators elsewhere in Europe, this was the classic contest between "two warring impulses ... the desire to submit extreme outrages to the rule of law, and the refusal to permit the law to be misshapen."[48]

In the course of their roughly two years of operation, Poland's Special Courts would issue 721 death sentences for August crimes. By contrast, France, a country with an actual collaborationist government, carried out fewer than 800 death sentences from 1944 to 1951.[49] Objections to such severity were bound to be raised, and they were almost as soon as the August Decree itself was issued.

Behind the unanimous desire for revenge against the Germans and the harsh rhetoric about local collaborators, there was disagreement not only about the letter of the law but also about its implementation. Inveighing against war criminals, opportunists, and profiteers was one thing, but ordinary citizens, professional judges, and the head of state himself wavered when it came to the actual application of mandatory sentences—the death penalty not just for murder on behalf of the occupiers, but also for the broadly defined "capture or deportation" of "wanted or persecuted" persons—in the August Decree. Criticisms from unlikely quarters also extended to the institutions set up to enforce the Decree. Perhaps the fundamental quandary was that the Decree, like its cousins around Europe, was an attempt to address by legislative means the desire for retribution, which by its nature is outside the purview of the law.

These difficulties were foreseen even before the first cases started rolling in. In a memo from early October 1944, the chief prosecutor and presiding judge of the newly formed Special Criminal Court in Lublin wrote to the Justice Section of the PKWN to air their concerns. The August Decree did not permit what was known as the "extraordinary mitigation of punishment" in cases of "little import"; that is, it did not allow courts to issue sentences below the mandated minimums in light of mitigating factors. The judge admitted that "for political reasons it would not be advisable either to so empower the Special Court[s] by means of an amendment [to the Decree] at the present time. The Special Court will therefore stand before the dilemma of either letting the accused off scot-free or applying a disproportionately heavy sanction."[50] In fact, the memo was a treatise in favor of bypassing the August Decree. It proposed that courts should make use of Articles 100–104 of the prewar Criminal Code—still in force where not specifically superseded by postwar decrees—which covered in even broader terms crimes against the state in time of war.[51]

Others went after the Special Courts themselves. Looking back in 1946 on a year's worth of Special Court activity, no less authorities than the Chief Judge of the Supreme Court, Wacław Barcikowski, and one of his colleagues, Antoni Landau, questioned the rationale behind the courts. The fact that both men were prewar lawyers—Barcikowski had also spent time as a prosecutor—who had been involved in the defense of left-wing political prisoners at the Brześć Trial and who owed their elevation to the advent of Soviet-aligned "People's Poland" testifies to the fidelity to legal principle that persisted among some even in the pro-regime camp.

Barcikowski stated flatly that the introduction of the Special Courts was "misguided" and was "undermining the authority of the regular courts":

> The regular courts are no less capable of adjudicating cases under the jurisdiction of the Special Courts. This state of affairs . . . has unnecessarily distanced the regular courts from contact with the security authorities and the administration, making them second-class courts and depopularizing them.
>
> The Special Courts have no political responsibilities which would demand their exclusion from the competence of the regular courts. We should join, not separate the judiciary.

In spite of its revolutionary pretensions, the government was strangely emulating the tendency of the prewar administrations to split up the court system among various ministries—treasury courts, rail courts, insurance courts, and so on—creating "unheard-of chaos."[52]

Landau agreed in a separate article that "every Special Court is a dangerous strike at the concept of the courts, all the more painful because it was not necessary: by no means are the Appellate Courts overburdened, and with the added help of lay judges they would have dealt with the new issues."[53]

Much of the carping about the August Decree and the Special Courts could be traced back to their provisional, stopgap character. Their procedural irregularities—the lack of appeals, permission of indirect evidence, hurried tempo, and lay judges—were to be attributed to the desire for swift and summary justice to satisfy society and head off vigilantism at a time when the front was still moving. The mission of the Special Courts, in the words of their defenders, "could not be achieved in the framework of existing legal norms, containing many abstract rules which must be applied in a normally functioning society and state, but could not be allowed to interfere in the application of repression in the face of the national catastrophe provoked by the methods of the occupier."[54]

As Jerzy Sawicki, lead prosecutor at the 1944 Majdanek trials and later a principal member of the Polish delegation to the International Military Tribunal at Nuremberg, put it: "No one denies that the first sprouts of the law about the Special Courts arose in an atmosphere of especial emotional tension. The entire accumulated hatred . . . for the occupier and his collaborators in the country was looking for an outlet to the fastest and most severe repression. Obviously, such a climate didn't aid subtle legislative work."[55]

These special laws responded to the "emotional needs of the moment," specifically the "need for reprisal," because "only repression in the form of pure vengeance can appease an enraged society." Antoni Landau also observed that the "somewhat too violently born" August Decree betrayed "traces of haste." Its authors had "given up on correction and education" as the end of punishment, and were instead resurrecting practices "long ago consigned to the dustbin of history"—namely, the principle of "retribution as well as . . . exclusion from society." Barcikowski in his memoirs grumbled vaguely about the "feverish work to create new laws, derived from ready-made models, not always suited to our [Polish] reality, which brought to life heretofore unknown institutions."[56]

DEATH PENALTY DEBATES

The designation of the death sentence as the only possible punishment under Article 1 of the August Decree was particularly controversial. The mandatory death penalty was not part of Polish legal tradition, and such a provision was unique in twentieth-century Polish law. A part of the judiciary had also opposed the death penalty out of principle. During the writing of the Criminal Code of 1932, designed to replace the welter of laws that had existed in the different partitions of Poland before the First World War, much debate had gone on between members of the codification commission as to whether to keep the death penalty. Emil Rappaport, who served on the Supreme Court both before and after the war, had been opposed, although public opinion was in favor. Barcikowski, the postwar Chief Judge of the Supreme Court until 1956, had also been opposed to the death penalty since before the war as a member of the left-wing League for the Defense of the Rights of Man and Citizen. Leon Chajn, the acting chief of the Justice Section of the PKWN and therefore responsible for issuing opinions on clemency to Bolesław Bierut, the chairman of the State National Council and true authority in the government, remembered being surprised by the complexity of the cases that went before the Special Courts, describing the many "sleepless nights" that resulted and Bierut's grilling him about the merits of individual cases.[57]

Vengeance in theory and vengeance in practice turned out to be two different things. The violation of traditional judicial prerogatives and the potentially broad application of the death penalty led to pushback whose extent is hard to gauge, but was significant enough to warrant notice by leading government figures.

While insisting that the desire for revenge "corresponded to ... the opinions of the majority of society," Chajn conceded that "there were, however, numerous voices who claimed that the wave of cases was an impediment to the process of unification of hearts and minds, so necessary to a shattered and damaged society."[58] At a meeting of the judiciary for the appellate area of Toruń in western Poland in November 1945, the new minister of justice, Henryk Świątkowski, noted, "In society two conflicting views are clashing, one aiming at the most severe sanctions on the rules of revenge, the other, which demands greater leniency from the judiciary, believing that the republic can afford it."[59]

Although Świątkowski was speaking about the rehabilitation of Poles who had taken German nationality during the war, the same phenomenon was observed in the Special Court in Kraków in 1945. The lay judges of the court explained that the high number of acquittals was due to the "too great severity of punishments provided by the August Decree." In a typical case, some "mild infraction" would be demonstrated whose "basis was rather a shortcoming of national education," and as a result of the "disproportion" between the crime and the prescribed punishment, they preferred to vote for acquittal, feeling that time served was more than enough.⁶⁰

Indeed, the mandatory punishments were viewed by professional judges as an attack on their prerogatives. Czesława Żuławska, a Supreme Court judge in postcommunist Poland whose father had been the presiding judge at one of the Special Courts, describes a "protest movement" that sprang up around the issue. Her father submitted a memorandum with the grievances of his colleagues to the Judicial Section of the PKWN along with his resignation. Interestingly, without mentioning Jews, her father justified his stand by citing a scenario that was employed regularly in cases of crimes against Jews: "It was impossible to demand from an individual the kind of heroism under threat of death—in the realities of the occupation—that was involved in a refusal, for example, to betray people in hiding, thereby exposing oneself, one's family, and often the entire village to certain death."⁶¹

Revealing its sensitivity to social and professional pressures, the government yielded. As of February 16, 1945, the August Decree was amended. The decision to do so specifically mentioned the experiences of the Special Courts, which often found that individuals guilty under Article 1b—capture or deportation—did not merit death and, without the option of extraordinary mitigation, acquitted them.⁶² The revision changed Articles 1a and 1b of the original August Decree to Articles 1.1a and 1.1b, added the crime of "pointing out" wanted persons—that is, denunciation—to 1.1b, and retained the death penalty for both. Article 1.1b also did away with the condition that offenders had to have committed crimes "on the territory of the Polish state," allowing for the pursuit of *Kapos* in concentration camps located in Germany, for example. The real innovation of the revision, however, was to introduce an entirely new article, 1.2, which in essence functioned as an escape hatch from the still severe Article 1.1 and was sufficiently nondescript as to allow virtually any crime to be so classified: "Whoever, playing into the hands of the German occupation authorities, acted or acts in a way other than foreseen in [Article 1.1] to the detriment of the Polish state, the civilian population, or prisoners of war is subject to a prison term of between 3 to 15 years, or life imprisonment, or death." Finally, Article 2, which had originally covered only blackmail, was expanded to include all persons "exploiting a situation created by the occupation" for material benefit, and the minimum sentence was reduced from fifteen to three years.⁶³

Despite these concessions, the dilemma posed by the death penalty persisted. A little more than a year after the revision, a prosecutor from the Special Court of Lublin found that lay judges were still struggling with cases that qualified unquestionably under Article 1.1: "In cases where the intensity of malice of the offender isn't excessive and the harm rendered by him is not large, the lay judges, without the intermediate option of a prison sentence, are mostly inclined to acquit, rather than condemn [the accused] to death."[64] As it turned out, the standards by which "intensity of malice" and "harm" were judged would be far from universally agreed upon.

NO CRIME WITHOUT LAW OR NO CRIME WITHOUT PUNISHMENT?

The death penalty was not the only issue that was attracting the criticism of jurists, regardless of their affiliation with the new government; another heated legal debate was taking place across postwar Europe regarding several key legal principles descended from Roman law that were invariably contravened by the special legislation instituted to deal with the legacy of the occupation. The intertwined principles were two of the most cherished in Western legal thought: *lex retro non agit,* which holds that new laws may not obtain retroactively; and *nullum crimen sine lege,* which holds that there can be no crime without a corresponding law. The August Decree had infringed upon the former by applying itself to all acts committed since August 31, 1939, and upon the latter by creating new categories of criminal acts connected to the occupation, rather than relying on the existing penal code.

Strikingly, even in Poland, where a third of the legal profession had perished in the war, Leon Chajn claimed that the retroactive nature of the Decree initially aroused "much controversy and resistance" in the legal milieu, requiring him to mount a press and radio campaign in its favor. The thrust of the argument in favor of the Decree was that unprecedented crimes required unprecedented solutions. An article approved by the PKWN, entitled "In the Struggle with Legal Illiteracy," lambasted critics as "blinded by their narrow little world of stiff norms and regulations." There were no "legal clairvoyants who could have foreseen the whole range of Hitlerite crimes," but that was "no reason to let crimes escape punishment."[65]

Jerzy Sawicki, who also served as the head of oversight for the Special Courts, wrote that the compromise of some principles "considered untouchable by a liberal conception" was inevitable, given the need to come up with a legal formula in the absence of any "exhaustive" definition in international law which could encompass all violations and all war criminals. He pointed with pride to the catchall Article 1.2 of the revised August Decree, whose "broadly conceived factual state" (or, some might say, lack thereof) permitted the prosecution of all acts not covered in Article 1.1 but which "according to the customs of international law and the postulates of conscience" had to be penalized.

A municipal judge commenting in the country's major legal periodical defended the trade-off inherent in the violation of "no crime without law": the need to "protect society against the criminal" had superseded the need to safeguard the "subjective rights" of individuals against the state. Instead, *nullum crimen sine poena*—no crime without punishment—was the order of the day. Like Sawicki, he vaunted the success of the special laws, including the August Decree and the decrees directed against Volksdeutsche, in differentiating between "passive" and "active" traitors and establishing separate procedures of trial and sequestration.[66]

Antoni Landau, the Supreme Court judge, took a darker view of the process. The special laws represented not rationalization but "chaos," raising as many questions as they answered. If the judicial code was founded on the assumption of a confrontation between accuser and accused, just where did a former Volksdeutsche submitting a rehabilitation request fall? Was he or she a "self-accuser"? How was one to know when to try a Volksdeutsche under the regular criminal code and when to apply the "mere" terms of detention? Why were there three different laws mandating total seizure of property of suspected collaborators, a punishment theretofore unknown in Polish law? All these questions, as well as the breaking with the traditions of Roman law and the "doctrine of liberalism," were, in his opinion, being glibly shrugged off.[67]

STRUGGLING WITH LEGALISM

These debates were a textbook case of an intellectual approach that the American scholar Judith Shklar would criticize twenty years later as "legalism." In her view, legalism was the political philosophy prevalent among legal professionals which held that justice was simply a "matter of the equal application of rules" and that this "mode of social action" was "superior to mere politics," which "looks only to expediency."[68] This dogma concealed the sordid reality that law is just one "form of political action, among others," is only "occasionally . . . applicable," and that "policies of justice must constantly compromise with other social demands."[69] The process of postwar retribution exposed the "rigidities and unrealities" of the legalistic approach, attempting as it did to shoehorn perpetrators of genocide and exponents of ideologies of violence into the framework of a "model criminal trial within a municipal system." The International Military Court at Nuremberg, in particular, had missed "enormous potentialities" to delve deeper into the root causes of crimes against humanity, treating them as "aberrations" from, rather than disturbingly regular byproducts of, the "civilized order."[70] But Shklar conceded that "it is indeed doubtful that legal provisions *can* be devised for events of this sort."[71] "Crimes against humanity were an organized corporate enterprise expressing a policy deeply rooted in a national ideology. . . . One is not dealing here with a handful of deviants, but with a social movement, and this makes the relationship between the causes of and responsibility for these acts exceptionally problematic."[72]

The August trials were confronting state, judiciary, and the public with incontrovertible evidence of that "social movement." To avoid the "exceptionally problematic" implications, an alternative history would have to be synthesized.

5   REWRITING THE NARRATIVE OF THE PAST

UP TO THE PRESENT DAY, the misconception prevails that the Special Courts were an instrument of Soviet-style Stalinist justice—that is, a venue for preordained show trials intended to smear and suppress the opposition. As one Polish legal scholar recently described them, the Special Courts tried "German criminals, as well as persons who acted against the new order." Supposedly, the communists "controlled" the courts by installing "their people," the lay judges, for the purpose of ensuring "severe sanctions against political opponents."[1]

Much of the internal documentation, if it ever existed, that might have shed light on the inner workings of the Special Courts, which functioned from October 1944 to October 1946, appears to have been discarded during an archival purge in the 1950s and 1960s. The only way, then, to reconstruct judicial thinking is to analyze the case rulings themselves. Although my access was limited to only two of the four Special Courts covering the area of the former Generalgouvernement—Lublin and Kraków—I found no evidence of politically motivated prosecutions in the two appellate areas with the highest concentration of anticommunist partisan activity, nor am I aware of any such documented case from any other Special Court.[2] As we have seen, the government made a conscious decision in October 1944, the month when the first Special Court began its work, to try persons accused of organized resistance to the state in military courts, which were entirely under the control of the Soviet-backed security services. Likewise, when armed resistance was equated with "banditry," defendants could be sent before the "summary" courts, which in practice were essentially adjuncts to the military courts. It was not until 1950 that high-profile members of the Underground began to be tried under the August Decree outside of the military court system, and then only in the explicitly political "secret section" of the Warsaw City Court.[3]

If the trials at the Special Courts were not scripted and their outcomes not predetermined, they were still arguably being steered in a particular direction, just not by any single, deliberate force. This process was not a top-down effort but instead represented separate segments of society feeling their way to a usable past in the aftermath of the war. Each party to the trial—the state, the judiciary, and the population at large—influenced the verdicts in different ways and at different times to deflect attention from popular involvement in ethnic cleansing. In doing so, they gradually worked toward the common goal of codifying a legally binding memory of the war from which the most compromising parts had been excised. As Donald Bloxham has written of the Nuremberg Trials, which ran concurrently with the Special Court trials, in them "lay the seeds of the misrepresentations that were to characterize portrayals of Nazi criminality in the postwar era and in some cases up to the present day."[4]

The tools available varied. At this early stage during the two-year tenure of the Special Courts, the government appears to have limited itself to tinkering with the August Decree and adjudicating clemency requests; only later, as will be discussed in Chapter 6, did it feel confident enough to begin asserting itself more directly through avenues such as the Supreme Court and the national prosecutorial office. Instead, the terrain was largely ceded to the professional judiciary, which exercised control through its members and influence on lay judges, and to the public, which interceded through the changing testimony of witnesses and the testimonials—signed attestations to the character of the accused—of dozens and even hundreds of acquaintances of the defendants. As for the charge that lay judges were an instrument of the state, they arguably took the side of the public; the only instances found by this author in which they diverged from the presiding judge were those in which they voted for a lesser penalty or acquittal.

The outcomes were not uniform. Sometimes the groups involved wholly or partially exonerated the accused, and sometimes not; periodically they worked at cross-purposes. Many cases before the Special Courts ran aground for the reasons they do everywhere: lack of proof and witnesses. But where the evidence was stronger and the case clearer, courts were often still either reluctant to convict or mitigated punishment. A review of the records of the Lublin and Kraków Special Courts shows that, in at least a third of the cases heard by them, dubious interpretations of the evidence and laws—sometimes at striking variance with the facts—by professional and lay judges, courts of appeal, and even the government itself materially affected sentencing or contributed to acquittal. Although these observations are based only on the work of two Special Courts, the strategies employed would become so routine in later years that it is fair to speak of a pattern, and one Supreme Court judge would even give the phenomenon a name: the "stretching" of verdicts.

This rewriting of the narrative of the past scrambled the chain of responsibility and eliminated the agency of local people. Broadly speaking, it consisted of either faulting Jewish victims for what had befallen them or exonerating Polish perpetrators, or both. Individual Jews were depicted as having brought misfortune on their own heads by some indiscretion or lack of common sense. Polish defendants were made out to be victims of circumstance—they mechanically submitted to external pressures, or their well-meaning actions were tragically misconstrued. To be certain, this was not an all-out whitewashing of guilt—some of the accused were still sentenced to comparatively long prison terms—but the intention was clear: the cutting edge of the August Decree should be blunted and the rough edges of the wartime narrative should be smoothed over.

The evidentiary standard stacked the odds against obtaining a conviction for anti-Jewish crimes. Virtually no forensic evidence of any kind was collected, and exhumations were rare, even when the location of bodies was known. Witness testimony was the only means of assessing the merits of a case. But Jewish victims, as targets of Nazi exterminationist policy, had rarely survived, and on many occasions the only advocate for the victims in the courtroom was the prosecutor. The hurdles to be cleared were numerous. Even when a Jewish witness had survived, it was his or her word against that of the defendant and as many friends, neighbors, and family members as the defendant could muster. Even if community members were willing to incriminate one of their own, the courts had to be willing to accept their accounts. Finally, if the case was appealed, the arguments had to pass muster also with the Supreme Court.

EARLY SEVERITY

The one characteristic of the Special Court trials that did not hold true for later trials was their relative severity. From their creation in September 1944 to their abolition in November 1946, death sentences accounted for almost one-fifth of all the guilty verdicts they issued; a year later, death sentences made up a little more than 5 percent of all guilty verdicts.[5] There are no statistics about how many of those sentences were carried out, although the commutation of the death penalty would become the rule rather than the exception by the late 1940s—more about that later. But by way of illustration, of 45 people condemned to death by the Special Court in Kraków from November 1944 to January 1946, 24 were executed, 11 had had their sentences commuted by Bolesław Bierut, and another 10 were awaiting execution as of February 1946.[6]

Indictments for crimes against Jews also made up a small proportion of the Special Court caseload at this early stage. At the Special Courts in Warsaw and Kraków, only 5 percent and 13 percent, respectively, of indictments made reference to Jews. By contrast, at the Regional Courts—which had jurisdiction for August crimes after 1951—of the city of Warsaw and the Warsaw region, 22 percent and 39 percent, respectively, of cases involved anti-Jewish offenses.[7] Compared to the thousands of defendants who would stand trial later on, the number of people being tried for crimes against Jews was also numerically small. Sixteen Poles were tried by the Special Court in Lublin for crimes against Jews, as opposed to twenty-four Volksdeutsche, Germans, and Ukrainians, while the court in Kraków heard the cases of seventy-three Poles, and only ten Ukrainians or Germans. With only five acquittals and eleven guilty verdicts, the Special Court in Lublin managed to convict 69 percent of the accused, and seven of those found guilty, or 63 percent, were sentenced to death. As we shall see, the early Lublin court was something of an outlier; more common would be the experience of the Kraków Special Court, where the numbers were reversed. Fifty-eight defendants, or 79 percent of the accused were acquitted, and five death sentences were passed, representing one-third of the guilty verdicts.[8]

Just why the Lublin Special Court should have been so severe is unclear, but it may have had something to do with the fact that it was the first such court operating in the country and therefore determined to be exemplary in its harshness. In any event, the Special Courts declared themselves willing, at least in theory, to be true to the spirit and letter of the August Decree and to punish complicity as firmly as criminal authorship, reflecting the uncompromising rhetoric of the immediate postwar period.

Jan Kamiński was an ethnic Slovak who had assimilated into Polish society after being sent in 1943 as a seventeen-year-old SS volunteer to Poland, where he took part in anti-partisan operations and mass killings of Jews as a concentration camp guard.[9] In his case, which would eventually attract attention at the highest levels of government, the court found that the "fact alone" of his SS service was "sufficient basis" for finding him guilty under Article 1 of the August Decree, with its mandatory death sentence, "since as is commonly known and requires no special proof," the SS, like the Gestapo and the SD, took regular part in the mass murder of civilians.

The Special Court of Kraków, handing down a death sentence to former Blue Policeman Władysław Rzepa for his role in anti-partisan sweeps, applied the August Decree's broad definition of a capital crime:

> The accused has admitted that in 1943 he took part with different German police and Gendarmerie formations in the raids on partisans hiding in the Dulecki, Jastrząbski, and Zawadzki forests. . . .
>
> It is a matter of indifference what role he played: whether he stood on the road, by a house, in the house, in the forest, outside the forest; what is essential, rather, is that he took active part in the execution of the plan of the occupier, our enemy.

Neither Kamiński nor Rzepa was convicted on the basis of mere guilt by association or for persecuting Jews alone.[10] Both had been accused by multiple eyewitnesses of serious crimes against Poles, and Rzepa also received a separate death sentence for brutally beating numerous Polish and Jewish civilians. But the important thing to note is that in certain instances, the Special Courts were prepared to apply the principle of collective guilt and issue the correspondingly harsh judgments set forth in the August Decree in a way that would become ever more uncommon as time progressed.

Courts would become particularly loath to condemn perpetrators whose crimes against Jews lacked "especial" brutality, who could produce commonly accepted pretexts for their actions, or who had witnesses who changed their testimony in the defendants' favor, which is why the case of Stanisław Sot is instructive. Sot was a small-time farmer who, like many others, during the war had made extra money bootlegging and smuggling. How his case came to the attention of the UB is unknown, but he appears to have been unpopular with some in his village, possibly, in his telling, for his refusal to let the locals pillage bunkers for timber. Sot admitted to having detained four Jews on two separate occasions and, with the help of the headmen and neighbors, having transported them to the Gendarmerie. Sot's explanations for his actions changed repeatedly. Initially he claimed that two of the men he had captured had ignored warnings that they were entering a military zone and that they had gone to the Gendarmerie willingly. Later, after other witnesses testified that two of Sot's victims were a father and son living with a local man who had been deported to Germany as punishment, Sot would allege that he had caught them stealing. Likewise, Sot insisted that he had only arrested the other two men on the suggestion of the local cobbler's mother-in-law, who spotted two Jews hanging around her house during a wave of robberies that had affected Sot too. Sot admitted to acting on his own initiative and receiving only the coat of one Jew for his services.

At trial, the testimony of witnesses was hardly unequivocal. Two of the chief prosecution witnesses retracted their claims to have seen Sot arrest the Jews, saying that they had only heard about it. The cobbler said that while the captured Jews had been unarmed, Sot did claim to have been robbed, and the headman recalled that although there were no robberies he knew of, Sot had become preoccupied with the threat of German reprisals and that otherwise Sot had never harmed any Poles. Even one of Sot's accomplices, who claimed he helped arrest the Jews only because Sot had threatened him, admitted that opinions in the village about Sot were varied and that he had never denounced anyone. One of Sot's fellow cattle traders testified that together they had witnessed farmsteads being burned by the Germans, and that shortly afterward Sot had become obsessed with capturing Jews who he said had robbed him, before finally witnessing him capture two in the presence of "many" villagers, assisted by the headman and others. Still others stated that although they too had been robbed, they had no idea whether Jews were responsible.

The court, under Judge Henryk Jasionowski, found that Sot's actions "fully met" the criteria of Article 1 of the August Decree and sentenced him to death. Its "opinion" of his clemency request, which the court was required to send to the head of state to aid in the decision making, was also negative. By acting on his own initiative not once but twice, Sot had shown a "high degree of malice." He had threatened others, and his fellow villagers thought ill of him.

Even in the harshness of the verdict, however, we see the outlines of an exculpatory impulse. Sot was singled out for the ultimate punishment, leaving unaddressed the material roles of individuals like his accomplice, the headman, the cobbler's mother-in-law, and others. In its verdict the court asserted that the "residents of the village of Maciejowice feared Sot and avoided him so as not to be denounced" to the Gendarmerie. But not only did Sot not stand accused of denouncing any ethnic Poles, he had acted at the behest, with the assistance, and in the presence of numerous other villagers when arresting the Jews outside the house of the cobbler's mother-in-law.[11]

GOVERNMENT RESTRAINT

Indicative of the emerging trend are cases in which one or more parties to the trial intervened to mitigate the responsibility of the defendants or those who had assisted them. In the absence of more detailed documentation, it is impossible to know to what extent and in exactly what ways the Soviet-backed government may have attempted to tip the scales, but the surviving evidence suggests that they allowed the courts to issue their own judgments, and only later became involved when necessary through the appeals process.

That the government carefully weighed the political implications of sentencing from its earliest days and was prepared to intervene within the limited permissible legal framework of clemency is apparent from the epilogue to the case of Jan Kamiński, the teenage Polish-Slovak SS volunteer condemned to death in Lublin. Kamiński had not ended the war in the ranks of the SS—in May 1944 he had deserted to the communist-led People's Army partisan group, where his bravery was confirmed by numerous veterans, including no less a figure than Mieczysław Moczar, who would later go on to notoriety as minister of the interior and organizer of the anti-Semitic campaign of 1968. After the withdrawal of the Germans, Kamiński joined the MO, where he was serving when he was denounced to the Soviet security services by an ex-girlfriend.

Deputy Minister of Justice Leon Chajn laid out the case for clemency in a memo to President Bierut. The purpose of the punishments prescribed in the August Decree was either the "elimination forever of individuals who have no value for society" or the "correction" of those for whom there was still hope. Because Kamiński had already given proof of his "segregation from a criminal group [by] fighting for ideals which were the opposite of his there-

Jan Kamiński deserted from the SS to the Polish communist partisans, becoming a policeman after the war. His death sentence was discussed at the highest levels of government. (Photo: AIPN)

tofore worldview," he was neither without value, nor did he require correction; he had already "recouped" his guilt by risking his life. According to Chajn, Kamiński could serve as a model for others:

> Society sees in him not only a criminal but also a hero. His execution could lead others to think that active remorse has no purpose. At a time of a growth in criminality, the rewarding of an autonomous correction has socio-educational significance, just as intimidation does. Society—and masses of former partisans are interested in this case—will receive a visible example, that social integration [*uspołecznienie*] can erase the results of the greatest crimes.

Indeed, according to the "latest criminological trends," courts in the future would be able to find defendants in similar cases guilty, but without imposing punishment. Clemency in this instance would be a "proper correction to the principles of the Criminal Code of 1932, which were based on other assumptions about social-penal policy."[12] Subsequently, Bierut reduced the penalty to ten years.

With the eventual introduction of an appeals process, the government would gain another potential avenue for influencing the August trials, but they do not appear to have made use of it during the tenure of the Special Courts. Initially the courts' verdicts had not been subject to appeal; when it was created in January 1946, the Supreme National Tribunal was officially given oversight responsibility for the Special Courts, and the prosecutors of the Tribunal were empowered to appeal their verdicts. Beginning in the fall of 1946, shortly before the Special Courts were themselves abolished, Tribunal prosecutors began issuing appeals of lenient verdicts to the Supreme Court.[13] The Supreme Court, in turn, began issuing decisions in the spring of 1947 that would provoke controversy and contribute to greater government involvement in the composition of the Supreme Court. Kazimierz Bzowski, head of the court's Criminal Section until 1951 and a close collaborator with the government, would be a constant during these changes, but at least during this early phase the Supreme Court took a mitigating approach that sided with defendants and put it at odds with state prosecutors.

"MAYBE IF IT DID HAPPEN"

For the presiding judges of the Special Courts, their lay colleagues, and the public who appeared before them as witnesses, the challenge was to account for the involvement of a whole swath of village society in the routine work of genocide and the actions of defendants whose prominence or banality defied the popular image of a "fascist-Hitlerite criminal." The accused and witnesses did so by advancing versions of the past that the professional and lay judges could reject, accept, or embellish as they saw fit. These novel interpretations of what had happened recast evidence of criminal intent as the unfortunate misperception of harmless or incidental conduct, glossing over the incriminating statements of defendants and witnesses, while blaming victims for carelessness or passivity. At worst, defendants were said to have been acting under duress, performing the bare minimum required of them by the occupier.

That the minimizing of responsibility for collaboration in the ethnic cleansing of the Jews was on the mind of the judiciary and the public from the very beginning is apparent from the trial of Aleksander Obarzanek, who may have been the first Pole—not a Ukrainian, German, or Volksdeutsche—to stand trial under the August Decree for participation in the Holocaust.[14] Obarzanek was a dairy farmer who had worked on an SS-administered agricultural estate near Lublin, to which a camp of 150 Jewish forced laborers was attached. His trial took place on November 18, 1944, less than three weeks after the Special Court had heard its very first case. Obarzanek, who had labored in Germany as a young man during the First World War and spoke fluent German, functioned as the interpreter and "enforcer" on the estate, in addition to his official role as the head milker, with a staff of two Polish and two Jewish assistants.

In September 1944 several Polish workers had come forward to the military police to report that they had seen Obarzanek going out on raids with SS men, dressed in a German uniform and carrying a rifle, to search for Jewish fugitives, and that he had beaten Jews. One Polish woman also blamed him for denouncing her theft of a bag of grain to the Germans, for which she spent eight months in prison. No one claimed to have seen him kill anyone, although the estate's coachman reported that in 1943 Obarzanek had taken the reins from him and, without having to ask directions, driven a group of SS men to the site of a previous day's massacre of runaway Jews.

Interrogated by the military police and the UB, Obarzanek denied denouncing the woman, hunting for Jews, or driving the coach, conceding only that he had beaten workers out of frustration and that he had "carried" a gun as an interpreter for the Germans. By the time of his trial, however, Obarzanek had refined his story considerably. He had never beaten anyone, only struck employees for insubordination. Nor had he hunted Jews with the Germans; he had only traveled around in 1942 with "Jewish commandants" from the Judenrat, the Nazi-mandated Jewish council, trying to persuade Jewish shirkers to return. It was true that he had held a rifle during the visit to the site of the massacre, but that was only because the four SS men happened to have brought five rifles and needed someone to hold one for them. A witness, Stanisław Kotarski, insisted that the defendant had beaten one of his Jewish subordinates in the courtyard of the estate, to which Obarzanek replied, "The beating of the Jew in the courtyard didn't happen—I didn't beat

Jews. The witness obviously has a grudge against me, but maybe if it did happen, it was a joke." Kotarski said he didn't know whether it was a joke, since all he heard were the screams, and that other Jewish workers complained about Obarzanek, though no Poles did.

In a pattern that would become commonplace, key witnesses would walk back parts of their testimony later in the investigation or at trial. That this was not simply the retraction of untrue statements is clear from the selectivity, partiality, and inconsistency of the withdrawals. Just why they did was rarely fully explained, but it often indicated a desire to downplay the witnesses' own implication in crimes, as well as an awareness of the gravity of the charges that a former friend, neighbor, or colleague was facing. Kotarski, who had at first admitted to serving as an overseer of the Jewish slave laborers, suddenly denied it, and qualified his earlier statements by saying that he had only "heard from others" that Obarzanek had searched for Jews. On the stand, Obarzanek's subordinate in the cowshed altered his earlier statements that his boss had ridden on missions with the Germans, instead stating that Obarzanek, unarmed, had accompanied the Germans on trips to "recruit" local Jews to the estate. He confirmed, however, that Obarzanek beat and kicked Jews for "not paying attention to work" and "whenever he felt like it," including the man Kotarski had seen in the courtyard. The beatings were "heavy . . . more than once a Jew was knocked down from the blow."

Only the coachman stuck to his story from the investigation, although he suddenly volunteered on the stand that Obarzanek had denounced the female grain thief, before just as suddenly withdrawing his statement. The other seven witnesses called to trial had nothing of substance to add. The prosecutor, in his closing statement, halfheartedly asked that "in the event" that the court was unable to convict Obarzanek under Article 1 of the Decree, that it find him guilty under Article 2, regarding blackmail. Evidently, in this period before the addition of the "everything else" clause in the February 1945 revision of the Decree, the prosecutor was already anticipating the court's reluctance to apply the mandatory death sentence of Article 1.

The court accepted this awkward compromise. Although Obarzanek had beaten Jews "two to three times a week," in the court's opinion it did not rise to the level of "mistreatment" outlined in Article 1. Instead it was "violence, behind which undoubtedly always hid the threat of handing the workers over to the occupier." He was sentenced to two years under Article 2. Furthermore, the court accepted the argument that the defendant was a "recruiter of Jewish workers," a claim that Obarzanek himself had never made, insisting that he had merely "persuaded" Jewish runaways to return to work.

Almost two years later, the chief prosecutor of the Supreme National Tribunal, Tadeusz Cyprian, who had been a member of the Polish delegation to Nuremberg, filed an appeal, arguing that the Special Court had failed to address key evidence in its judgment, that the classification of the crime as Article 2 was faulty, and that even if the beating of Jews did not qualify as mistreatment, "in any case it is action to the detriment of persons pursued or persecuted" as laid out in Article 1. In its brief dismissal, the Supreme Court under Judge Kazimierz Bzowski maintained that the qualification of the crime had been correct and ruled that the charges of taking part in the capture of Jews and in the massacre were not covered by the indictment and so could not be considered, although, bizarrely, the indictment was for capturing Jews.[15]

THE DISSENT OF THE LAY JUDGES

At the Special Court of Lublin, otherwise notable for its severity, lay judges were the driving force behind two highly questionable verdicts, declining to punish to the full extent of the law two defendants whose actions had led directly to the deaths of several Jews, even though the actual business of killing was left to the Germans.

Wacław Kania was a twenty-five-year-old farmer who was picked up, while drunk, by the military police for bootlegging in October 1944. In custody he confessed spontaneously to having captured a Jew fleeing across a field from Polish and German police "after the harvest" in 1943. The pursuers had shouted at him to stop the man, whom Kania later identified as a local, Pejsach, which he did "gladly, because I don't like Jews." Kania had had time to reflect on his actions, because Pejsach offered him 500 złotys for his freedom, which Kania refused. At his second, pretrial interview before an investigating judge, Kania denied ever having said that he disliked Jews, and that he didn't know why he was so recorded. Rather, he said he had been afraid of the pursuing policemen. At trial, the metamorphosis in his testimony was complete. There had been several people fleeing, he did not know they were Jews, shots were being fired, and somehow a pursuing German, far enough away so that the accused was still able to chat with Pejsach yet close enough to make himself heard despite running with a rifle, had shouted, "'Catch him, or I'll shoot you!'" and aimed his gun at Kania to drive the point home. Also, Kania was especially afraid because, as he said, his wife's first husband had been killed for hiding Jews.

Shortly before trial, the defense called six witnesses, four from Kania's home village of Piotrawin, including his brother-in-law, and two from the neighboring settlement of Natalin. By a quirk of the Polish judicial system, none of these witnesses was interviewed by the prosecution or law enforcement before trial, meaning that there was no way to check the consistency of their statements over time, unlike prosecution witnesses and defendants, who were generally interviewed at least three times: once by law enforcement, once by an officer of the court in the pretrial phase, and again at trial. All six of them testified that Kania had "known" about other Jews hiding in the village, yet had taken no action against them. There were no specifics about who these Jews were, when exactly they had been in hiding, or where, or indeed if they had ever actually existed.

Perhaps indicating the thin line separating the police from the policed, Władysław Jezierski, the military policeman who had arrested Kania and recorded his comments about not liking Jews, appeared at trial and, recounting the defendant's initial confession, confirmed that the Germans had ordered Kania to capture the Jew at gunpoint, a critical detail that Jezierski had somehow inexplicably omitted in the record of the interrogation.

Lay judges Dymowski and Rymski reasoned in their verdict that Kania was acting under higher necessity when he caught and held Pejsach, but because the German would likely "have limited himself to beating" Kania as punishment for allowing the Jew to escape, he still bore some criminal responsibility. The August Decree still lacked a mechanism for considering mitigating factors at the time of sentencing, so they applied Article 22.1 of the Criminal Code of 1932, which stated that a person "is not subject to punishment who acts with the aim of avoiding direct danger threatening his welfare or another's, if the danger cannot be otherwise avoided," as well as Article 59.1, which permitted the substitution of a death or life sentence with a minimum of five years imprisonment in the event of "extraordinary mitigation of punishment." Given his "very low level of intellectual development, culture, and civic refinement as well as weak legal sense," Kania was sentenced under Article 1 to eight years in prison.

In his dissenting opinion, Judge Antoni Furgała found no grounds for applying Article 22. The danger "must be real, not imagined." Furthermore, higher necessity required that the preserved good be greater than the sacrificed good: "the life of a person, hunted by the Hitlerite perpetrators, is obviously of a greater value, than the moment of pain, occasioned by a beating."

Once again, Tadeusz Cyprian filed an impassioned appeal, arguing that Kania had to have known whom he was capturing, since he described Pejsach as "bearing down" on him. More importantly, Article 22 of the Criminal Code could not apply to the crimes of the August Decree, which explicitly forbade force or orders as an excuse, all the more so because Kania had still enjoyed "free will" at the moment of the crime. Weighing the preserved and sacrificed good, Cyprian reasoned that

> there are no values, the preservation of which can justify collaboration, or even the execution of orders of the occupation government.
>
> ... In an instance where someone acts "to the benefit of the German occupation authorities" ... there can be no measure of the proportionality of the goods, since the sacrificed good is not life, health, or property of the persecuted, but the good of the Nation and Polish State as a whole, being in a state of war with the Germans.

Likewise, the finding of the court that the accused was of limited intellect could only be the basis for clemency, not a mitigating circumstance in itself. The Supreme Court curtly dismissed Cyprian's appeal, ruling that Kania's "justified fear of repression," as established by the lower court, met the criteria for extraordinary mitigation of punishment according to the December 1946 revision of the August Decree.[16]

Defendants like Obarzanek and Kania had operated in the shadow of the Germans, but perhaps the most commonly tried anti-Jewish crime—and the one that would be the subject of debate in the Supreme Court into the 1950s—was an act that took place in the absence of the occupier: the capture and transport of Jews by villagers.

Asked by the MO why he had waited until June 1945 to report Aleksandra Mrozowska, who in January 1943 had brought the Ukrainian "village police" to the quarry on her property where he, his children, in-laws, and two Jewish women were hiding, Szloma Ziserman was recorded as saying that his "conscience didn't permit" it. At trial, he explained further that he hadn't alerted the authorities sooner "because I was occupied with my farm, which is located in the same settlement as the defendant. I intended to stay on that farm and live among the people. . . . Finally, when I gave up on the farm I took up this case."

Mrozowska never denied contacting headman Michał Gregoruk about the Jews hiding on her land in the small settlement of Bezek-Kolonia. Instead, she claimed in the run-up to trial that she had tolerated their presence for weeks after spotting their tracks in the snow, and only asked Gregoruk to remove them when complaints and threats from local Ukrainians to denounce her became intolerable. Gregoruk, she alleged, had released the Jews outside of the village after receiving a bribe. Although the Ukrainians, including Gregoruk, would be cast as a sinister presence at trial, none of the witnesses suggested that there was anything unusual about their conduct, nor had any known there were Jews hiding in the settlement until that day.

Mrozowska, in a carefully worded, typewritten request from prison to have the charges against her dropped, emphasized the legality and propriety of her action in alerting the "local headman, elected by a normal vote." Indeed, the captives had been held overnight at the house of a Pole, and guarded by "two Poles and two Ukrainians." Eighty-one villagers signed a testimonial in support of Mrozowska, who had relied on the kindness of neighbors while her husband, a reservist, was a German prisoner of war.

During trial, a substantially more colorful and outlandish narrative emerged. Mrozowska now testified that an imminent "rabbit hunt" by the Germans had been the immediate impetus for removing the Jews from her property. She had warned the Jews, but they were resigned to their fate: "They responded that it was all the same to them whether they died here or somewhere else." In any event, the Ukrainians, she had been told, had released the captives after Ziserman agreed to pay for a party (*bal*) for them. Naturally, none of these details had been in the lengthy, self-justifying memorandum that she had filed before trial. Likewise, witnesses suddenly recalled the details of a rabbit hunt that none had mentioned in previous testimony.

No one disputed that of the eight Jews, six had disappeared, never to be seen again. Ziserman recounted how he "threw" his son from the cart transporting them to Chełm and then took off running with him, while the others who tried to escape, including his daughter, were recaptured and presumably sent to their deaths. But the two lay judges unquestioningly accepted the story of the "rabbit hunt" and the "release" of the captives. Indeed, they found it difficult to discern malice in the actions of any of the participants:

> Had the intention of the headman and his helpers been the desire to give over the captives to the Germans, they undoubtedly would not have carted away the detainees, but rather awaited the arrival of the Germans, who in fact conducted a hunt [for rabbits] that same day. Moreover, it seems doubtful that [Ziserman and son] could have escaped in broad daylight without the agreement of the rather large escort.

Still, for depriving the Jews of their hideout and exposing them to danger, Mrozowska was sentenced to the minimum punishment, three years, under Article 1.2, the catchall article of the revised decree.

In his dissent, Judge Łanowski vigorously protested:

> All the residents of the village knew well what is commonly known, that headmen were obliged to capture hiding Jews and deliver them to the Germans. On the basis of the very admission of the accused it was necessary to recognize that she committed the crime laid out in Art 1.1b and sentence her to death. The fact that the trial did not clearly establish where the persons taken captive by the headman were sent and what fate they met is completely immaterial for the qualification of the act. . . .
>
> In these circumstances the qualification of the act by the lay judges . . . and the assigning of the lowest punishment appears to be in blatant contradiction with the conclusions of the trial.

Shockingly, the Supreme Court responded to Tadeusz Cyprian's appeal of the case by acquitting Mrozowska entirely. The Special Court's findings were accepted in their entirety:

> Although the appeal is predicated on widespread knowledge of the fact that headmen were organs used by the occupying authorities for the capture of hiding Jews . . . in light of the determinations in the present case regarding the headman's actions, there is no basis for accepting that the captured Jews were given to the Germans, and as for the [Mrozowska], that she intended and agreed to that and with that aim exposed them to the headman.

Given that the lower court did not find any intention to act for the benefit of the Germans, but only a refusal of shelter, which was not a crime, the court had no grounds for sentencing her, and she was therefore acquitted. Here again, Kazimierz Bzowski was the presiding member of the troika that heard the appeal.[17]

Likewise, the lay judges at the Kraków Special Court defied their reputation as simple ideological tools. In the case of Adam Juny, a young Polish Kripo member who had arrested a Jewish woman and her daughter who lived in his boardinghouse and brought them to his commanding officer, Lindert, the two lay judges drew a distinction between his "bringing" of the women, allegedly on orders, and Lindert's "arresting" of them. This, despite the eyewitness testimony of the surviving woman—her daughter had been "incinerated" in Auschwitz—and the boardinghouse owners. Not only was Juny said to have stolen the bribe that the survivor had offered him, the UB had recovered archival evidence from a wartime Underground court that Juny had been awarded 2,500 złotys for "special distinction in the capture of Jews." Judge Mieczysław Kądziela, in his dissent, argued that it was immaterial whether Juny had been acting on orders, per Article 3 of the August Decree, which excluded acting under command as an excuse, and that the crime met all the criteria for capture under Article 1.1b. Tadeusz Cyprian's appeal to the Supreme Court restated Kądziela's objections, but the high court under Judge Bzowski merely extended the sentence by six months.[18]

IT TAKES A VILLAGE

Cases of the arrest and handover of Jews were challenging precisely because of the way they could enmesh whole communities in the business of ethnic cleansing; one way to get around this was to inflate the responsibility of some lesser member of village society. Even Judge Jasionowski, who accounted for four of the six death sentences passed on Poles by the Lublin Special Court, yielded to a separate logic in the case of Józef Pudzianowski and Wojciech Molęda.

The basic facts of the case were not in dispute. Then seventeen years old, Pudzianowski had encountered three Jewish escapees from a deportation train on his family's farm in Gołębiów near Radom on the morning of January 11, 1943, most likely when they approached him to ask for something to eat. With the assistance of his father and several villagers, he had brought them to headman Molęda. A discussion among a large group of villagers ensued, which concluded with the decision to send the Jews to the Blue Police station in Firlej, five kilometers away, rather than a nearby German forestry outpost. The Jews' requests to be released were rebuffed. Several men from the village convoyed the Jews, who would have been—and this simple truth was never acknowledged at trial—either executed by the Blue Police or transferred to the Germans for the same outcome.

The case hinged on the headman's claim to have been intimidated by the teenaged Pudzianowski. Molęda, a respected veteran of the Polish-Soviet War, was supported by his successor, a wartime member of the Military Organization resistance group, and produced a testimonial signed by over eighty villagers. In their telling, the Pudzianowski family was feared—the young man for his friendship with the German forest guard, and his sister for her fraternization with Germans. Molęda insisted that he had the Jews' best interests in mind. He had sent the Jews to the Polish police because he "thought that they, as Poles, would release them." A supporter painted a more dramatic picture: "All of us [villagers] present" opposed Pudzianowski's wish to send the Jews to the Germans, and "thanks to the opposition of the assembled villagers," it was decided to send them to the Blue Police. The testimony of three other villagers at trial belied the assertion that the young Pudzianowski had intimidated anyone, let alone the village chief. Two eyewitnesses present during the discussion over the fate of the Jews heard no threats, nor did they think that Pudzianowski had a bad reputation. One described a "disagreement of opinion" among the group over whether to deliver the Jews to the Polish or German authorities, with several people on each side. There was no hint that humanitarian motives had anything to do with it. In all probability, the villagers simply considered it safer to dispose of Jews with fellow Poles.

The normalization of genocide that the occupation had instituted was evident in the nonchalance with which witnesses admitted to participating in the detention and transport of the Jews, offenses that were clearly punishable under the August Decree and were frequently pursued in later years but provoked no response from law enforcement or the judges when revealed at this trial, held in August 1945. One man freely admitted that his son had helped transport the Jews to Firlej, while another, the watchman on duty that day, admitted it as well.

Perhaps their comfort level before the court helps explain why Jasionowski and the lay judges were so forgiving of the headman; he was just doing his job. The court, citing the high regard for Molęda and his testimonial, found him to be acting under higher necessity according to Article 22, at the same time crediting him for "still giving the captured Jews the chance to save themselves." None of the case's illogicalities or inconsistencies were mentioned in the verdict, beginning with the fact that the Jews were consigned to almost certain death. It was not explained why a supposedly implacable, teenaged Pudzianowski would have agreed to sending the Jews to the Blue Police unless he felt they would meet the same fate as with the Germans, and why, if everyone else had been against the detention of the Jews, they didn't simply release them. Pudzianowski fared worse than Molęda; he was sentenced to death, but his sentence was commuted on the recommendation of the court, because he had been a minor at the time.[19]

THE THREATENING VICTIM

A strategy that would become commonplace was to argue that Jewish victims had forced their killers to act by threatening them or their communities. Henryk Janczuk, who had killed the man being hidden by his uncle, mixed elements of that argument with the supposed resignation of the victim. Ordered to leave, Hersz Flechtman, Henryk claimed, had said "it was all the same" to him whether he died there or elsewhere, then set off, saying he would report the Janczuks to the Germans for sheltering him. In his first interrogation, Henryk said his uncle told him to retrieve Flechtman. In his second, he said he flew into a rage upon being threatened. In any event, he bashed Flechtman's head in with a cudgel. Before trial, the prosecutor suspended the investigation of the uncle, deciding that there was no "causal link" with the murder despite evidence to the contrary.

At trial, Henryk produced a fantastic story about Flechtman's inadvertent discovery of the hiding place of a Soviet partisan, "Koczumów." Acting on Koczumów's orders, Henryk had killed Flechtman and taken the blame on himself to avoid exposing the partisan. When asked why he hadn't come clean earlier, Henryk alleged that he had been threatened at gunpoint by the military prosecutor who had interrogated him. The court would have none of it, judging the tale "clearly deceptive and contradictory." But the court did accept the premise that Flechtman's threats had precipitated the murder, leaving aside testimony that Henryk had killed him because he didn't want to "feed him for free," that Flechtman had "bothered the neighbors enough," and that the Janczuk family had stolen the dead man's five suitcases. In the meantime, the defense had changed tack completely, arguing that Henryk was mentally unfit. His elementary school teacher said that he had a short memory and trouble concentrating, and was supposedly "dropped on his head" as an infant.

While the court declined to acquit him, it did give credence to the testimony of two psychiatrists called by the defense who, though excluding any mental illness, diagnosed "intellectual immaturity of an unknown level, which in certain instances, in particular moments of panic, can cause a reduction of competency to a significant degree." He was sentenced to ten years imprisonment on the basis of Article 18 of the Criminal Code, which provided for extraordinary mitigation of punishment in cases of reduced competency. Presumably, it didn't hurt that Henryk was a member of the PPR and in MO officer school at the time of his arrest, and had been a member, with his father, of the local "Social-Democratic Committee" during the Soviet occupation in 1939–1941. If the villagers resented his family's earlier collaboration with the Soviets, there were still forty of them willing to sign the testimonial in his favor.[20]

"THEY THEMSELVES DECIDED ON THIS" AND THE PHANTOM BLACKMAILER

The case of Stanisław Kwaśniowski was a good example of how witness testimony could evolve to minimize the guilt of defendants with each new telling, transforming captured Jews into willing captives and inserting hobgoblin-like figures to diminish the agency of other perpetrators. Although each of the various witnesses interviewed appears to have told a mixture of truth and fiction, all essentially confirmed the story that Kwaśniowski had told in his first interrogation—namely, that in the summer of 1943 he had been approached, as the watchman on duty, by fellow villager Józef Handzel and asked to help capture a Jewess who had come begging. Together with Handzel and his fourteen-year-old son, as well as several other local residents and teenagers, Kwaśniowski had captured a five-member Jewish family from the nearby village of Zabornia and marched them over seven kilometers to the nearest Gendarmerie post, where he waited for several hours until the Germans returned.

Successive witnesses confirmed the story, while adding or subtracting elements to mitigate their involvement or that of other participants. A local woman was the first to mention the supposed presence of a Volksdeutsche, Szymalik, among the perpetrators. She claimed to have seen Kwaśniowski and Szymalik leading the captured Jews while Józef Handzel supposedly followed at an oddly distant remove of 100 meters. She had also seen Kwaśniowski strike a woman with his truncheon when she dropped her wool scarf.

Handzel, despite his evident interest in deflecting blame, did not mention Szymalik in his first statement to police, although he otherwise carefully described the course of events. Nor did Wiktor Nieć, the man in whose house the Gendarmerie unit was quartered. Nieć stated that Kwaśniowski had been accompanied by a "couple of teenagers." He also said that Kwaśniowski had claimed at the time to have merely shown the Jews the way to the German police at their request.

Perhaps Szymalik had indeed taken part in the capture, but even if he had, neither Kwaśniowski nor Handzel considered his presence significant enough to warrant mention in an action that had involved at least half a dozen residents. Only two weeks later, at his second interrogation, did Kwaśniowski suddenly claim to have been "blindly" following the orders of the dreaded Szymalik, who had commanded him to join him in the hunt for Jews.

By the time the court under Judge Sawrycz issued its verdict nine months later, the version of events laid out in it was almost unrecognizable from the testimonies that had begun the investigation. Almost every hint of Kwaśniowski's guilt had been carefully scrubbed from the narrative. In this retelling, Szymalik, now a "German policeman," had ordered Kwaśniowski to help him escort the "already captured" Jews, with which Kwaśniowski had reluctantly complied, following the group "at a distance of several dozen paces." In the court's opinion, this hesitation showed that "in no way did Kwaśniowski follow behind the Jews to guard them, nor did he in the least involve himself their capture, but fearing Szymalik, went in the same direction, thereby hoping to appear to be fulfilling the orders of Szymalik."

Whereas a witness had earlier claimed to have witnessed Kwaśniowski beat one of the Jewish women, the court uncritically accepted her new trial testimony that the defendant had "only nudged" the Jewess with his stick in order to draw her attention to a scarf she had dropped. And although the Handzels still maintained that Kwaśniowski and Szymalik had headed to the forest together, the court discounted their testimony because they were the "indirect cause" of the Jews' capture and because due to the "large number" of people present, they could have been mistaken about the defendant's presence.

Instead, blame was transferred to the victims. On the stand, Wiktor Nieć altered his original statements. Gone was any mention of the teenagers who had escorted the Jews with Kwaśniowski, and in their place, Szymalik appeared. Minimizing his own guilt as their jailer, Nieć testified that he "only" kept the Jews under "lock and key" overnight. They could have "left unobserved if only they had wanted to through the windows of the hut . . . which had no bars." In his words, the Jews "preferred to be presented to the [Gendarmerie] commander, since they had no means of survival and for that same reason had no intention to escape whatsoever." The court embraced the notion that the Jews had desired this fate for themselves:

> In light of these testimonies and the fact that the Jewess who ran from the Handzel house had time to inform [her companions] about the possibility of a chase, as well as the ease with which the Jews were seized, it is clear that their capture occurred only because they themselves decided on this, having no possibility of survival. This decision could also have arisen from the conviction that, as the Germans were claiming, they would be brought to the ghetto and that their lives were not threatened by any direct danger.

The court did not dwell on what the appropriate level of difficulty for capturing an old man, two women, and two children should have been, or whether anyone in Poland could still have been under any illusions about the fate awaiting captured Jews in the summer of 1943. Naturally, the court took at face value the testimony of Kwaśniowski's sister and a neighbor that the defendant had in fact risked his life to help Jews, and that of five other witnesses testifying to other good works the defendant, a veteran of the Polish-Soviet War, had performed in the village. Finding that "the entirety of his presence consisted only of pretending that he was not refusing the orders of

Szymalik, and that in any case the capture of the Jews came about only because they themselves aimed for it and agreed to it," the court acquitted him. No charges were brought against the Handzels, the other teenagers, or Wiktor Nieć.[21]

AIDING THE VICTIMS

When evidence of action or agency were incontrovertible, it was still possible for defendants to argue that actions intended to kill or capture Jews were gestures meant to help or save them. Given the low evidentiary bar involved in the trials, even highly implausible scenarios could pass muster with courts. In the case of Franciszek Barglik, accused of denouncing several Jews hiding in a forest near the town of Skawa in July 1943, the judges accepted Barglik's assurances that he had "consciously chased [one of the victims] in such a way as to allow her to escape."[22]

With no witnesses to the killing of a Jewish family in a forest near the village of Wadowice Górne, Blue Policeman Mieczysław Głogowski could have denied it, but instead he claimed that he had actually helped a woman to escape moments before his colleagues reached the encampment and killed her companions. Although he initially said that the woman was unknown to him, he changed his mind twice, eventually settling on the version that it was a neighbor of his whom he ended up sheltering and had recently emigrated to Italy. The court chose not to contest any part of his story.[23]

Judge Sawrycz of the Kraków Special Court strove to explain away every incriminating moment in the case of two volunteer firemen (and later MO and PPR members) who had scoured an estate for hidden Jews. But the one moment that could not be explained away was when they took part in the beating of a Polish farmer as one shouted, "I'll teach you sons of bitches to keep Jews!" As Sawrycz reasoned,

> That this is the only area where the explanations of the defendants have turned out not to be true cannot affect the question of the defendant's guilt, since it is necessary to accept, in light of the entire comportment of [the defendant] who in any case was drunk as is clear from the statements of [the beating victim], that his exclamation was rather just a sort of kidding around.[24]

SERVANTS OF THE PEOPLE'S STATE

As mentioned earlier, members of the postwar security services, drawn as they were from among local people, regularly cropped up as suspects in wartime crimes against Jews. The fact that their fellow officers were sometimes responsible for investigating them raises obvious questions about conflict of interest, as well as whether their true allegiance did not in fact remain to the communities of which they formed a part, contrary to their image as steadfast supporters of the Soviet-imposed "people's state" and its agenda.

When Franciszek Czaja, a member of the Polish communist party since 1928, was arrested in 1945 for having played a leading role with other firemen in the wartime capture of two Jews, he was working at the UB county office in Dębica, which was charged with handling his case. But his eventual conviction did not shake the confidence of the apparatus in Czaja. His commanding officer in the UB still sent an affidavit to the court praising Czaja's record and asking that his minimum sentence of five years be reduced or overturned completely.[25]

For reasons that were never fully explained but most likely involved fear of his discovery by the Germans, Wohlfeiler, a Jew hiding in the town of Kaszów, was detained and handed over to the Blue Police, who executed him. Of the estimated 200 villagers who corralled the victim, only headman Franciszek Gałecki stood trial, and the only two witnesses who confirmed his claim that Wohlfeiler had "threatened" the village were both serving in the UB in Kraków. But doubt was thrown on Gałecki's defense by Józef Paszkot, a Jewish MO officer also in Kraków who had changed his name from Henryk Kenner. Paszkot stated that he had fled the "unpleasant atmosphere" that appeared in Kaszów shortly before the incident, and that he had heard from others that "concerned villagers" had decided to have Wohlfeiler killed by the Blue Police "in order to avoid the betrayal of anyone who had sheltered [him]."[26] We are left to speculate why Paszkot suddenly and completely reversed his earlier statements at trial, but the role of the UB officers and Paszkot's subordinate status as a regular policeman hardly seem coincidental. Interestingly, the court, either assenting or bowing to the community's decision, decided in effect that since everyone was guilty, no one was guilty; the killing was chalked up to a "collective psychosis of fear" and "unfortunate coincidence."[27]

The only outright acknowledgment of police interference in this author's sample comes from the trial of Jan Wojciechowski, a young worker on an agricultural estate who, an anonymous denunciation reported, had arrested two Jewish women to whom his mother owed a small amount of money. The original case was dismissed by the prosecutor for lack of evidence after Wojciechowski recanted his confession, claiming that he had been pistol-whipped on the soles of his feet during his initial interrogation by the UB. Three years later, the UB, in a rare move, reopened the case. Multiple witnesses from the first investigation now incriminated Wojciechowski, but only one offered an explanation for his reversal:

> My interview of March 28, 1946 was written up when I was serving in the MO and [my superiors] told me to sign the transcript as it was written and at the time I signed the transcript in which it was said that as a night watchman, policemen came to me and I took them to the cowshed [where the Jews were hiding].... I signed because they told me, "Sign, what's it to you," even if it didn't happen that way.

Was this true, or was this just part of the smoke and mirrors that a Stalinist political police force was supposed to practice? There is no way to know for certain, but the fact that it was the only explanation offered suggests it was not part of a structured plan by the UB. Nor, if this was a frame-up, did Wojciechowski, who was ultimately sentenced to three years, play along. He continued to deny the most serious charges, although he now said that some Blue Policemen had forced him to take part.[28]

JUDICIARY AND SOCIETY SET THE PACE

While my sample of Special Court cases is small, they indicate that a degree of unspoken consensus had formed in the way different interest groups in society approached the involvement of ethnic Poles in the wartime ethnic cleansing of Jews. No one force—not the government, not the judiciary, nor society—could be said to control the process in its entirety, as a result of which the outcomes of the trials were not predetermined, contrary to the blanket condemnations of postcommunist scholars of postwar justice in Poland. On the contrary, the government had arguably ceded the terrain to the professional judiciary and public.

Three cases presided over by Judge Dr. Stanisław Król illustrate this consensus and passivity of the state. Król, as the holder of a doctorate, would have been one of the most educated people in a country where perhaps one-third of 1 percent of the surviving population had an education beyond high school. Serving as a judge since 1929, Król was also swept up in the mass arrests of Polish jurists by the Soviet NKVD in January 1945 on suspicion of collaboration before being released.[29] Although it is impossible to know for certain, Król's social status and life experience meant that he was almost certainly not a communist sympathizer.

But in his verdict on UB officer Franciszek Czaja for participating in the capture and handover of two Jews who were executed by the Blue Police in late 1943, Król indicated that he was no less concerned with the disrepute that might redound to the nation:

> The enabling of this action of the occupier ... was in line with [the occupier's] interests—all the more so, since the capture and murder of Jews was conducted by Poles—because those facts could be used abroad by the perfidious German propaganda [to claim] that the Polish nation not only supports [*solidaryzuje się*] the liquidation of the Jews, but also actively aids this action.
>
> Taking part in such an action damaged not only the Jewish population, but also the Polish state, which must be free before history of the shadow of the accusation of taking any part in the massive and unheard-of persecution of a whole people.[30]

The alleged mastermind of the raid, Wincenty Omelański, was sentenced to death in a separate trial, also presided over by Król, for that crime and for denouncing the husband of a woman he was having an affair with to the Germans. But in both the cases of Czaja and Omelański, the state took a moderating position. President Bierut commuted Omelański's sentence to fifteen years after Omelański filed a clemency request claiming one of the Jews he captured had supposedly killed his entire family—parents, brother, sister, and three small children. Somehow, Bierut overlooked the fact that Omelański's justification had changed radically from the one he gave at trial, when he said he was simply motivated by a general hatred of Jews stemming from a letter he received in 1942 stating that a Jew had killed his parents, a claim that Judge Król had deemed "empty."[31] In the case of Czaja, the Supreme Court under

Judge Bzowski rejected the majority of the prosecutorial appeal and added one additional month to Czaja's sentence.[32]

The public also made its voice heard in the Omelański and Czaja cases, successfully obfuscating the role and thereby limiting the legal exposure of up to seventeen men from the village watch of Wola Wielka who may have taken part in the raid. Omelański was depicted as a dreaded denouncer and collaborator, although at both trials headman Andrzej Żuziak stated that he simply refused Omelański's requests to organize a raid without any consequences.[33]

The thesis that the government did not have a clearly conceived plan for the immediate future of postwar retribution but instead deferred to the public and the judiciary is supported by the addition of the catchall clause to the August Decree in 1945 and the schizophrenic situation that had arisen in which the country's chief prosecutor was regularly butting heads with the Supreme Court. Their contrasting positions and the lack of guidance in war crimes policy were illustrated by the trial of a Blue Policeman, Stanisław Kuczyński, who had participated in blockading the ghetto of Tarnów during its final liquidation in 1943.

As has been established, the only aspect of their political program that the Nazis trusted the Blue Police enough to carry out independently was the capture, sequestration, and execution of Jews. But Judge Król found Kuczyński's involvement too "loose" to constitute participation in murder or action to the detriment of persecuted persons, instead giving him a minimal sentence of three years under the catchall Article 1.2. The voice of the people also made itself heard clearly in the case. No less than 200 townspeople signed a testimonial on Kuczyński's behalf requesting clemency, which was followed by a letter of support from the chairman of the communal national council, who praised Kuczyński for his selfless aid to fellow Poles throughout the war, as well as his unblemished record as an adolescent volunteer in the Polish-Soviet War, again in the defense of Warsaw in 1939, and in the Underground during the occupation.

Jerzy Sawicki, a member of the Polish delegation to Nuremberg, wrote in his appeal as Prosecutor of the Supreme National Tribunal that the Kraków Special Court

> did not take into account that the act of the accused cannot be considered in isolation from the entirety of the interconnecting events at that time. . . .

The Germans, in organizing the liquidation of the ghetto followed a plan, surrounding the area with Blue Police posts, while bringing in units for direct action. Their mutually complementing activities made up the whole of the *Aktion*. In this state of affairs, the behavior of the accused, who was on duty, preventing escape, is directly linked with the entirety of the event and fulfills the concept of taking part in the [crime of murder] covered by Article 1.1a [of the August Decree]. For the legal qualification of the conduct of the accused it is irrelevant whether he directly committed the acts specified in the Decree or, by preventing the persecuted persons from escaping, contributed to their capture and murder by other participants of the *Aktion*.

The lower court itself, Sawicki pointed out, had decided that Kuczyński had accepted the consequences of his actions. The Decree was not concerned with whether he had intended to kill Jews directly by his actions or merely accepted that he was contributing to their deaths, albeit at the hands of others. But the ruling of the Supreme Court under Judge Bzowski was completely at odds with Sawicki's interpretation of the August Decree. While Kuczyński had been present at the ghetto liquidation, there was "no basis for considering him guilty of involvement in the killings, committed on this occasion by the German criminals, which did not form part of his intent, but rather were an excess on the part of the Germans." The defendant, in the court's opinion, was guilty only "within the limits of *his own* intention." The court cited Article 28 of the 1932 Criminal Code, which stated, "The instigator or accomplice carries responsibility in the limits of his intention, independently of the responsibility of the person, who committed the intended act."[34]

The finding exposed yet another contradiction in the August Decree. On the one hand, the Decree had been designed specifically to override the limiting provisions and narrow definitions of the prewar, peacetime laws; on the other hand, the Decree stated that all the regulations of the prewar Criminal Code applied to its crimes unless explicitly excluded, including Article 28. It was clear that, sooner or later, the government would have to interject itself more forcefully into these debates. But whether the government could afford or sustain a unilateral approach, without taking into account the desires of the judiciary and the people, was another question.

6   BETWEEN POLITICS AND RETRIBUTION

THE GOVERNMENT WAS dissatisfied with the outcomes being achieved by the courts in the immediate aftermath of the war, but not because it disagreed with the vision of the past that was being enacted. Although individual critics would point out the disturbing willingness of professional, lay, and Supreme Court judges to minimize crimes of collaboration, the government made it clear that its problem was with the insubordination to the "new order" that excessive leniency implied. The administration expressed its anger through public and private attacks launched by officials within the Ministry of Justice, but at the same it clearly tried to meet the judiciary and the public halfway by responding to some of their biggest complaints about postwar retribution, dismantling the legally irregular Special Courts, and introducing provisions for mitigating circumstances.

As was to be expected from a communist government, official criticisms pushed the idea of a simplistic, Manichaean confrontation between the new "people's power" and "reactionary holdovers" from the prewar period, shifting all blame onto the alleged ideological shortcomings of the latter. But the bombast concealed a more complex reality. Divisions were not simply between Left and Right, they were also within Left and Right, between socialists and Stalinists, between veterans and *arrivistes,* between those wary and those favoring accommodation. Participants were divided by ideology, judicial philosophy, life experience, and a law that was vague enough to allow everyone to make of it what they would.

The reasons for the resistance of the judiciary were several. Memoirs indicate that at the ground level of the Special and District Courts, some judges and prosecutors were indeed motivated by opposition to the communist government or by anti-Semitism that prejudiced them in favor of defendants. But on both the lower and the upper rungs of the judiciary, the adherence to the rules-based philosophy of legalism was also in play. There was a deep-seated antipathy to any attempt to place "'expediency or the public interest or the social good'" above traditional legal rights. Legalism's equation of rule-following with justice also meant that exasperating technicalities and narrow interpretations were embraced as part of the spectrum of justice.[1] In the encounter between a cynical communist leadership and a deeply legalistic judiciary, the imperative for revenge inherent in war crimes trials therefore inevitably led to conflict. As Judith Shklar wrote of Nuremberg, a war crimes trial is where the "policy of justice . . . is most starkly confronted by political aims different from, and often opposed to, its own."[2]

RATES OF CONVICTION

Between October 1946, when the Special Courts were abolished, and July 1949, Poland's District Courts would hear more than half of all the cases of collaboration tried in the country. A quirk of record-keeping prevents us, unfortunately, from knowing exactly what the rate of conviction for August crimes was at not just the Special Courts, but also all subsequent judicial instances.[3] Although the Polish authorities made a precise record of the number of individual convictions handed down during each phase of the postwar retribution, they kept a tally only of the number of cases heard by the courts, and because many cases featured multiple defendants, it is impossible to calculate what proportion of defendants were convicted, or even how many defendants there were.

All that can be said with certainty about the rate of conviction for August trials is that it was definitely and possibly significantly below 56 percent from 1944 to 1949. If we assume that the average number of defendants in each August case remained stable over the years, then it appears that the overall conviction rate, whatever it was, remained relatively stable as well during this period.[4]

The conviction rates in the available sample for wartime crimes against Jews showed great variation. Rates ranged from just under 40 percent in Warsaw to a mere 15 percent in Kielce. Only one Polish defendant out of more than 100 was sentenced to death solely for having killed Jews by the District Court of Warsaw, and his sentence was commuted. In Siedlce, where at least a dozen defendants were accused of taking direct part in the murder of Jews, the harshest sentence pronounced by the court was eight years, not including a life sentence passed in absentia. Only in Lublin did the conviction rate meet or substantially exceed the 50 percent mark.[5]

ACCUSATIONS OF "PASSIVE RESISTANCE"

In the December 1945 issue of the new *Democratic Legal Review*, Deputy Minister of Justice Leon Chajn firmly but diplomatically voiced his dissatisfaction with the speed and sentencing of the courts. They were "not mastering the influx of cases and the process [was] extending to infinity." According to Chajn, the sluggish pace of justice was "emboldening criminals" and depressing the public. Worse yet, the courts were treating suspects with kid gloves at a time when "severe penal repression" was necessary to offset the "depravation and demoralization of certain segments of society by the occupier." Searching for the origins of this situation, Chajn observed that the "sore point of our courts in the prewar period" had been the light sentences, with most prison terms lasting less than a year and suspended sentences commonplace. Ironically,

> this state of affairs only deepened during the Hitlerite occupation . . . it's commonly known that Polish courts gave the lowest sentences during the occupation. Such a position . . . was the expression of a hostile attitude to the occupier . . . it was a position of passive resistance. In particular since general crime in this period was often on the edge of political crime, aimed at the occupier.[6]

One of the "fronts of battle" was the "slowing of cases" and issuance of "low sentences" by the Polish courts on occupied territory. However, Chajn noted that "observing the activity of the courts in liberated Poland, it's clear that this justified attitude in the conditions of slavery has become habit and continues up to the present. . . . The courts must do away with this leniency toward criminals, a leniency which makes justice totally illusory."[7]

Within a few months, the government's criticism was much less restrained. Early in 1946 Zygmunt Kapitaniak, the chief of the Judicial Oversight section, a new and controversial office within the Ministry of Justice, published a stinging article in which he likened the judiciary to a medieval "guild" trying to remain "on the margins" of the "economic, social, cultural, and political upheaval" taking place in Poland. Kapitaniak accused judges, clothed in archaic "togas and berets," of maintaining a feudal mentality and venerating "overgrowths of legal formalism, a fetishistic approach to the writ of the law, detailed, elaborate legal language ... all this testifies obviously enough to the 'isolationist' tendencies of the courts, to the desire for artificial elevation above other fields, to the tendency to the creation of a professional ghetto."

Although Kapitaniak was responding mainly to the judiciary's resistance to his office and their unwillingness to have their work supervised by anything other than a higher judicial instance, he sarcastically took them to task for their verdicts as well:

> No matter that the Ministry of Justice, not to mention society, comes across incidents where one court sentences, and another acquits for the same act. No matter that sentencing gravitated and gravitates to the legal minimum, contrary to the intentions of the codex and the express judgments of the Supreme Court. No matter that the suspension of sentences is commonplace and leads to the belief of criminals that their first crime will go unpunished.

Behind the scenes as well, Kapitaniak complained at interdepartmental meetings that judges were "in a position of internal emigration (passive, waiting), absolutely not aiding a positive attitude to work." Internal assessments of prosecutors in April 1946 similarly found a "lack of interest in work, failure to conduct investigations, [and] partiality in proceedings," in addition to a "lack of a trained investigative service" and "continuing difficulties in cooperation with the police."[8]

The new authorities continued to hammer away rhetorically at the judiciary in 1946. The *Legal Review* carried an article by Stefan Bancerz, director of the Legislative Department of the Ministry of Justice, on the occasion of the first nationwide convention of PPR-affiliated jurists. The "deficiencies" of the court system had "two main sources: the first in human materiel, the second in organizational structure":

> The Ministry of Justice is the one which rests almost entirely on prewar cadre. Before the war these cadre, though supposedly apolitical, were a useful instrument in the hands of the governments of the era. In spite

of that, the democratic camp has rebuilt the courts on the old cadre so as not to lower its quality, having assumed that the war and its consequences wrought radical changes among them too. Has a spiritual metamorphosis indeed occurred? Unfortunately, not in all [judges and prosecutors] and not to the necessary degree.

Among court workers, those individuals "hostile to the governing camp" were influencing "that passive mass of the undeclared—that is, those without a party affiliation." These internal enemies, Bancerz proposed, should be removed and replaced with people of "sincere democratic convictions."[9]

By July 1946, on the second anniversary of the founding of the PKWN, Chajn had harsh words for those in the judiciary whom he felt were stalling progress. Admitting that only a "small group of Polish legalists" had responded to the new government's initial call, he wrote that the "rest of the legal world, with a few exceptions, hostile to the camp of democracy and cherishing their promotions from the so-called government-in-exile in London, adopted a wait-and-see attitude, engaging ever more intensively in their work only as the specter of 'London' faded from view."

While he praised the judiciary overall for its "unusually positive role" in the "great historical examination" facing Poland after the war, one had to be conscious that a "part of our judges and prosecutors" had "failed" the test, "closing themselves in articles and paragraphs without a clear view of real life" and taking a "negative attitude to the basic structural changes" in society. They were incapable of adapting themselves to the "needs of a state in complicated circumstances which demanded to a great degree Platonic 'freedom of action.'" What those members of the judiciary called jurisprudence, "we call legal ossification." As a result of their incompetence, there were already "thousands" of incorrect verdicts and rulings. Due to the untrustworthiness and hostility of these judges and prosecutors, the government had transferred the "most important part of criminal sentencing"—"crimes against the state," meaning the cases of anticommunist partisans—to the "military courts, which ensure fast and efficient justice." Accusing intransigent members of the judiciary of wanting to subvert the new order, Chajn assured readers that they were "being replaced by the new, young cadre, which is graduating from the reformed universities and legal schools."[10]

The threat, however, was more empty than not. Jerzy Jodłowski, director of the Department for Legal Education in the Ministry of Justice, stated in his address at the opening in April 1946 of the legal school in Łódź that an additional 1,000 judges and prosecutors alone were needed in the Recovered Territories in western Poland. Whereas 2,000 university students had graduated every year with a law degree in prewar Poland, in 1946 there were only several dozen. The Łódź school was the first of six intended to circumvent the traditional five- to six-year university education with an abbreviated curriculum of only half a year to quickly produce ideologically reliable judges and prosecutors. But with few prerequisites for students other than a correct class background, it was conceded a year later at interdepartmental meetings of the Ministry of Justice that the legal schools had "ever worse material," and that it was necessary to return to intensive recruitment from the law departments of the universities.[11] For the time being, the judiciary and the ministry would have to continue to abide by one another.

THE END OF THE SPECIAL COURTS

The end of 1946 saw important changes in the pursuit of August crimes. On October 17, 1946, the Special Courts were abolished, and responsibility for trying wartime crimes was devolved to Poland's numerous regular District Courts (*sądy okręgowe*), of which there were several for each of the appellate areas that the Special Courts had formerly covered. As we have seen, the institution of the Special Courts had never been popular among even the left-wing members of the judiciary, and, almost a year and a half since the German capitulation, the extraordinary practices associated with them, like the absence of the right to appeal and their compressed procedural deadlines, were considered extreme. In the District Courts, the August trials would continue to be heard by one professional and two lay judges, but with defendants now enjoying the right of appeal to the Supreme Court.

The August Decree, too, underwent its penultimate revision. The revised version, published on December 11, 1946, was the fruit of several months of meetings between the legal experts of virtually all the relevant ministries—Justice, Defense, Public Security—the offices of the President and Council of Ministers, and representatives of the Supreme Court and the Prosecutor's Office, including familiar faces like Antoni Landau, Jerzy Sawicki, and Tadeusz Cyprian. The *in camera* discussions also included legal authorities from outside the apparatus of government, like Stanisław Śliwiński, the deacon of the Law Department at the University of Warsaw who had co-authored the

Underground state's 1943 decree on war crimes, and Julian Makowski, the former rector of the country's oldest economics school and an expert on international law.[12]

The ostensible reasoning behind the revision was to incorporate jurisprudence from the International Military Tribunal at Nuremberg, but naturally the two most substantive additions reflected the pressing needs of the Polish judicial system. The August Decree had lacked a clear means of punishing people for whom no specific criminal actions could be proven, but whose activity, like administrators in a concentration camp, fell within the concept of "conspiracy." On the other hand, as we have seen, there was widespread demand for a mechanism that would allow persons convicted under Article 1 to avoid the mandatory death penalty.

The solutions were Article 4 and Article 5.2, hereafter referred to as Article 5. Article 4, which provided anywhere from three years' imprisonment to death as punishment for belonging to a "criminal organization" whose aims were "crimes against peace, war crimes, or crimes against humanity," also criminalized membership in the Nazi Party, the SS, the Gestapo, and the SD. Article 5.1 recapitulated Article 3 of the original Decree, which had specified that force or orders did not excuse a defendant from punishment. However, a second clause was added, stating that "in this event the court may apply extraordinary mitigation of punishment depending on the character of the perpetrator or the circumstances of the act," which mirrored Article 8 of the International Military Tribunal Charter.

It should also be noted that clauses "A" and "B" of Article 1.1—the sections of the Decree concerning participation in murder, capture, and denunciation—were renumbered as Article 1.1 and Article 1.2 in the new revision. For the purposes of clarity, they will hereafter be referred to collectively as "Article 1." The previous catchall Article 1.2 was renumbered as Article 2 and will be referred to as such.

The transfer of jurisdiction for August crimes to the District Courts and the dismantling of the Special Courts, whatever the latter's merits and demerits, meant that the trials would now be in the hands of a much larger number of prosecutors and judges who were unversed in dealing with issues of collaboration. Because the personnel of the Special Courts were merely being returned to the regular court system, it was true that some judges and prosecutors continued to handle the August docket, but in the main, the transfer represented a broader test of the restored judicial system's abilities. Indeed, 77 percent of all August cases would be heard by the normal criminal courts.

In its supervisory capacity, the Ministry of Justice mandated regular on-site inspections of all the District Courts in the country, though only a few of the written reports produced have survived. One set, regarding the District Court and prosecutor's office in Zamość, near the postwar border with Ukraine, described the situation that had resulted from the new burden of the August cases. As before, poor security and partisan attacks hampered the investigative work of the MO, who in any case were overworked, under-trained, and constantly behind schedule. While the reports generally commended the diligence and work ethic of the prosecutors, despite their low pay and difficult material circumstances, the transfer of cases had resulted in their "overburdening." In one section of the office, only half as many personnel were dealing with regular crimes as before, due to the reallocation of personnel to work on crimes of collaboration; the idea was mooted of reinforcing the prosecutors with graduates of the Łódź legal school.[13]

NATIONALISM AND ANTI-SEMITISM IN THE JUDICIARY

That there was ferment within the ranks of the judiciary even before the transfer of the August trials is clear enough from the above-cited polemics that ran in the pages of the *Legal Review* in 1946. But unlike those of the ministerial officials, the grievances of the judiciary, which had the potential to impinge on their adjudication of cases of collaboration, could not be aired in a public forum.

Naturally, the most germane for the purposes of this study is the issue of anti-Semitism. Without directly addressing its prevalence, Wacław Barcikowski, the communist fellow traveler and Chief Judge of the Supreme Court, nonetheless claimed in his memoirs that the "label of anti-Semites," as well as that of "retrogrades," was applied indiscriminately by the ministry in an attempt to disqualify candidates for the Supreme Court who had been prewar judges.[14] If the ministry ever attempted to quantify or study the existence of anti-Semitism in the country's legal system, no record survives, but the fact that the topic was omitted from the otherwise biting published criticisms of the judiciary suggests that the government preferred not to know.

Fortunately, the unpublished memoirs of Władysław Grzymała, the District Court prosecutor in Siedlce and later Białystok, provide anecdotal insights into the opinions of at least part of the judiciary in the early years of People's Poland. For Grzymała, the Jews were ethnic and racial adversaries of the Polish nation who ungratefully turned on their Gentile compatriots after the liberation, provoking the civil war of the immediate postwar years:

> Following the arrival of the Red Army in all the larger cities, Jews emerged from the ground like mushrooms after a rainfall. Perhaps it speaks well of Poles . . . that a significant part [of Jewry] survived. Only a few exceptions [among Poles] handed them over to the Gendarmerie, and that was most often for fear of their own lives.
>
> Therefore it was not without surprise that we observed the massive enrollment of the surviving Jews into the UB and MO. Their activity in these organizations commenced with acts of vengeance on Poles suspected of any kind of antipathy to their fellow tribesmen. Torture and arrests multiplied. This action brought forth in turn a counter-reaction from Poles.

Grzymała goes on to describe several notorious Jewish UB and MO members who were assassinated. Pondering the villainy of these individuals, he offered an explanation allegedly given to him by a Jewish classmate of his from boyhood, a Dr. Samuel Jedwab:

> He and his wife hid with a peasant family near Siemiatycze. He was preparing to leave for France when I met him in Siedlce in 1945. When I asked him why, he responded that, after how [his] fellow tribesmen had behaved toward Poles, nothing good can meet the Jews. He added that the more honest Jews, being less resourceful, had died out. The scum remained—various porters, butchers, rope-makers etc. Speaking about this with sadness, he encouraged me to leave with him.

Although, as we shall see, Grzymała was the prosecutor in several highly contentious cases of wartime anti-Jewish violence in both Siedlce and Białystok, he says little about his work on August crimes in the former venue. But that he and perhaps other members of the judiciary were prepared to undermine cases which he felt were foisted on them is evidenced by his handling of the case of several rank-and-file Home Army partisans who were on trial for raiding a collective farm and whose leaders had already been murdered by the UB. It was the first "political trial" at the Siedlce court, and Grzymała carefully rehearsed his arguments, which consisted of casting the defendants as misguided youths who had been following orders from abroad. In a break between sessions, he and the presiding judge agreed on minimal sentences in advance. As Grzymała put it, the experience was a "guide for me on how in the future to prosecute those whom it was necessary to defend."

In Grzymała's telling, the political orientation of his colleagues helped determine the strategies they adopted to resist or mitigate the unwanted responsibilities imposed on them by the new system. As a member of the "younger" generation of the prewar judiciary whom the new regime hoped to win over, Grzymała was selected in 1948 to attend a special six-week course on "Marxism-Leninism-Stalinism" at a resort south of Warsaw with fifty other junior prosecutors from all around Poland. Aged between thirty-five and forty-five, they were, ironically, all "of the generation that had finished its legal studies before the war, and therefore of a political orientation, in the majority, represented by Roman Dmowski, Rybarski, Stroński"—leading figures of the prewar far-right nationalist movement. In this atmosphere of mutual confidence, they debated during long walks along the banks of the Vistula about how best to survive in the new and enduring reality Yalta and Potsdam had created:

> How to save what could be saved. To join the party or not. Jurek Wiśniewski, who was already a member, was of the opinion that a party member could do more good for the country than a nonmember. It wasn't without a certain logic. They would pay attention to the voice of such a prosecutor in the party committees, whereas a nonmember would be taken for a reactionary.
>
> On the other hand, the fact that the role of the individual didn't count for much after all militated against such a course of action. The prosecutor, as a member of the party, had to dutifully fulfill all the orders of the executive, and if he didn't, he would be treated worse than a nonmember.
>
> That's why to the end of my time in the prosecutor's office I stayed without a party affiliation. Some sought shelter in the Peasant Party or

the Democratic Party [two other noncommunist parties allowed to exist in order to give People's Poland a semblance of multiparty democracy]. But none of that accomplished anything. The only people who mattered there were those who had been delegated from the PPR [as infiltrators], and all the others were considered to be shielding themselves from being forced to join the PPR.

Instead of a final exam, their instructors tried to start a discussion "in order to figure out what we were now thinking," but the class avoided being drawn in.[15]

Inspection reports from 1948 corroborate Grzymała's depiction of a wary and skeptical judiciary. In Kraków, only seven of the nineteen prosecutors, delegated judges, and assessors at the District Court had a party affiliation, and only two of those belonged to the PPR. Their involvement in extramural party life was "relatively insignificant" and the prosecutor's office as a whole was judged to be "pleasantly indifferent" to the political situation. Of twelve prosecutors in Radom, seven had party affiliations, and only two were PPR members, one a rookie recently graduated from one of the fast-track legal schools. UB Major Józef Światło, later to become one of the most famous defectors of the Cold War, complained that there was "not one single person in a leadership position" in the civilian court system in the Kraków region "with whom it would be possible to cooperate with complete certainty as to [that individual's] loyalty to the present political reality."[16]

Grzymała's memoirs make reference to another important bone of contention between the judiciary and the new government—namely, the new political appointees in the Ministry of Justice and, to a lesser extent, in the field. Having written off the Jewish "riffraff," Grzymała also took the "Jewish intelligentsia" to task. Yes, he wrote, many had emigrated, but "many" others had "entered immediately into high positions in all the ministries, and a significant part into the Ministry of Security and the Ministry of Justice."[17]

POLITICS AND ETHNICITY IN THE MINISTRY OF JUSTICE

Chief Judge Barcikowski of the Supreme Court, though no right-winger, mentioned the same situation in his memoirs. Knowing well the suspicion with which it was viewed by the traditional intelligentsia, the new government surrounded itself, especially in the beginning, with above all those people who in the prewar period had stood on the Left. Among them were many intellectuals of Jewish origin. In large part mistreated before the war, they saw in the Left the basis of their dignity. Many of them had ended up on the territory of the Soviet Union and served in the army. Those who had survived the conflagration of the war, hiding in various corners of the country, also reported for work. Acquaintances recruited other acquaintances, because at that time you could only count on people you trusted.

But Barcikowski soon detected a power play by the Ministry of Justice, under the de facto control of Leon Chajn, to stock the administration with unqualified parvenus, beginning with Chajn himself: "The actual chief of the Ministry of Justice [Chajn] was a former intern of the lawyer Kulczycki . . . and the leading positions were occupied by interns as well. That made a bad impression on me. I knew many judges and lawyers, and among them many progressive, deserving, and experienced people, who better merited being entrusted with those positions."

Barcikowski's relations with Chajn were "as bad as could be" from the very beginning. He viewed the deputy minister as a talented and politically well-connected figure from the Kościuszko Division, the embryonic formation of the Polish Army in the Soviet Union, but fundamentally dishonest and arrogant. Chajn was a careerist who energetically fulfilled party orders, brooked no criticism or advice, and selected subordinates who "didn't interfere with his independence." For his part, Chajn, along with his appointees, was incensed that Barcikowski's nomination had taken place without their input, creating an impediment to the full subordination of the Supreme Court to the ministry.

The man who hired Barcikowski, Adam Wendel, was also a former legal intern from Warsaw who had been selected by Chajn to be the head of the Organizational Department. When Wendel ran into Barcikowski on the street in Lublin in 1945, he offered him the post of Chief Judge and forwarded his name to Bierut and Gomułka, who confirmed Barcikowski's appointment the next day. Bierut had been acquainted with Barcikowski from his work on behalf of left-wing causes both before and during the Second World War. Perhaps he accepted his appointment as a counterbalance to Chajn, or perhaps, as Barcikowski claims, "questions relating to justice were not at that time the most important point of the political program. Nor were they later."[18] Whatever the reason, this division of influence was yet another sign that justice would remain an arena of competing interests, rather than the forcibly fused-together product of top-down decision making.

From the scant surviving documentation it is impossible to fully corroborate Barcikowski's depiction of himself as a well-meaning but increasingly hapless idealist whose insistence on legality was shunted aside in the name of "revolutionary necessity." But in addition to his early published criticisms of the Special Courts and aspects of the August Decree as having a demoralizing effect on the court system, he also spoke out against the Offices of Judicial and Prosecutorial Oversight, arguing in the February 1946 issue of the *Democratic Law Review* that it violated the separation of powers for the executive to be overseeing the work of the judiciary. If supervisory responsibility was not returned to the Supreme Court, it risked becoming an "isolated island of priests of the law," divorced from the life of the lower courts, while prosecutors would be more inclined to "routinize" their work, subordinating themselves to the oversight office. All this in the same issue in which Kapitaniak lambasted the judiciary for allegedly sneering at the new oversight office from the "height of the judge's bench" in the belief that the "only permissible form of criticism of verdicts and control of justice is by means of judicial instances."[19]

Barcikowski did succeed in nominating Henryk Świątkowski, a prewar lawyer and Sejm deputy of the Polish Socialist Party, to become minister of justice in May 1945—he reported that Leon Chajn appeared to have been forced to accept his suggestion—but Świątkowski remained, as his predecessors before him, a figurehead. Meanwhile his frustration with cronyism in the ministry grew. He resisted attempts to place unqualified candidates, "mostly former legal interns" recruited "on the buddy system," on the Supreme Court. To Barcikowski, the haughty "new dignitaries" of the ministry were "youth with little experience" in the court system whose "knowledge of the law came from private law offices and whose conceptions of justice had been formed entirely by the customs of their parents and bosses."[20]

Whether guided by ideological considerations or not, Chajn had little choice but to accept the help of those few junior jurists who were prepared to affiliate themselves with the new authorities, so widespread was the initial opprobrium against collaboration with the PKWN in legal circles. Stefan Bancerz was the first lawyer to volunteer in August 1944; he was able to recruit two other locals, but that was as far as recruiting from among the Lublin legal community went. As Chajn found out, "from the moment when they began to work in the PKWN, everyone turned away from them, no one wanted to talk to them, no one greeted them, colleagues and acquaintances boycotted them. One even told me that his wife cried incessantly because all her friends ignored her, and her family wouldn't let her into their home."[21]

It was no doubt jarring for any Jews at all to be seen in positions that would have been closed to them before the war, and indeed, the government was inclined to recruit heavily from among Jewish intellectuals because they either had been left-wing before the war or had taken their chances as refugees in the Soviet Union and then, like Chajn, been hoovered into the Polish Army in the East. Ethnic Jews had also been disproportionately represented before the war in free professions like law and medicine.

During his time as a law student interning in the Legislative Department of the Ministry of Justice in 1952, Leszek Kubicki, the future minister of justice in postcommunist Poland, came to know many of the ethnic Jewish personnel who were involved in some way in the August trials, and he recalls them as being no less diverse than the old cadre who regarded them with suspicion. It is thus perhaps worth considering some of their biographies in greater detail. They were not all wet-behind-the-ears youngsters, as Barcikowski implied, nor were they all automatons mechanically fulfilling party orders. They ranged from figures like Jerzy Sawicki, whom Kubicki described as a "Renaissance man," to Henryk Podlaski, a "primitive" Stalinist who was "exceptionally efficient" at doing evil.[22]

Sawicki in particular had begun making a name for himself even before the Second World War. Born Izydor Reisler in 1910, after finishing his five-year legal internship in 1936 and entering private practice as a defender for left-wing clients, he published numerous pseudonymous articles in the major liberal publications of the day, including *Wiadomości Literackie* (Literary News) and *Bunt Młodych* (Revolt of the Youth), edited by Jerzy Giedroyc, later renowned as the editor of the Polish exile journal *Kultura*. During the war Sawicki had escaped from the Lwów ghetto with the help of his father-in-law, the noted lawyer and Jewish activist Leib Landau, and survived in the countryside under an assumed identity. His stirring, theatrical delivery at the first

Majdanek trial in November 1944, filmed and replayed as part of the news chronicle, helped propel him to public prominence, from vice prosecutor of the Lublin Special Court, to the Office of Oversight for Special Courts, and then to member of Poland's Nuremberg delegation, head of the Office for International Cooperation in the Ministry of Justice and chief prosecutor of the Supreme National Tribunal.

Sawicki was a Marxist, but hardly a conventional apparatchik. Although he joined the PPR in August 1946, lectured Grzymała in 1948 on Marxism-Leninism, and co-wrote the main Marxist textbook on criminal law in 1950, he was expelled from the party in 1951 on the grounds of leading a "bourgeois lifestyle." Having published in all the major postwar intellectual journals—*Kuźnica, Odra, Przekrój*—he also wrote under a pseudonym for the Catholic humanist journal *Tygodnik Powszechny* from 1952 to 1955. Readmitted to the party in 1956, he graduated twenty doctoral students as a professor at the University of Warsaw until his sudden death in 1967. His entry in the encyclopedia of the Polish Academy of Sciences from the 1970s noted that he had been moderate in his criticism of classical criminal law even during the domination of Soviet thought, and though his post-Stalinist public writings still included the standard vitriol against Western imperialism, Leszek Kubicki, his former student, cautioned that such "primitive, transparent" journalism was the "price" he had to pay to continue writing and publishing.[23]

On the other end of the spectrum were ruthless men like Henryk, formerly Hersz, Podlaski, who was a key figure in the arrangement of secret and show trials in the military prosecutor's office before being transferred in 1948 to head the Office of Prosecutorial Oversight and, after its transformation into the Soviet-style General Procuracy in 1950, to serve as number two and de facto head. A "dreadful character"—Barcikowski cited Podlaski and Chajn as the two most harmful presences in the Ministry of Justice—Podlaski was officially blamed for having orchestrated many judicial abuses, including the arrest of Gomułka; he was fired in 1955 and is believed to have committed suicide, although his body was never recovered.

But most of the other Jewish figures in the Ministry of Justice who worked on the August trials were more unassuming, less polarizing figures. Leszek Lernell, who, like so many of his contemporaries, changed his name to try to better assimilate and was the butt of jokes for it even among friends, came from a poor Jewish family but passed his school-leaving exams in 1930 at age twenty-four without having attended high school. He completed his legal studies and training in 1938 and spent the war years in exile in Uzbekistan, whence he returned as part of the Union of Polish Patriots, joining the Ministry of Justice in 1946 and working his way through a series of journeyman legislative analyst jobs to become the head of the Legislative Department in 1950. He also served as the editor of the *Democratic Legal Review* from 1947 to 1954. Lernell had been a member of the Polish communist party since 1936 and co-authored the same Marxist legal textbook as Sawicki, but he was sensitive to his status as a parvenu. Kubicki recalled that Lernell would take a suitcase full of Polish poetry with him when he went on a vacation, in a genuine attempt to assume the role of a member of the intelligentsia fitting to his station, since he was aware how quickly he had risen in the world.[24]

Closer in age to the "legal youth" that Barcikowski complained about was Arnold Gubiński, born in 1916 into a wealthy, religious Jewish family that was, according to Kubicki, "expressly inclined to assimilation." After fleeing to Lwów in 1939, he finished his legal studies there, only to flee again into the interior of the Soviet Union, where, along with other Polish male refugees whom Stalin mistrusted, he was attached to an unarmed construction battalion in which he befriended Leon Chajn. Discharged and with no means of survival, Gubiński was caught in a snowstorm and near death when a collective farm director driving a sleigh chanced upon him and saved his life, taking him in and giving him a job as an accountant. Eventually he ended up on an oilfield in Bashkiria, married a Bashkir woman, and made his way to the Polish embassy in Moscow in 1945. Although Gubiński owed his job to Chajn as a prosecutor, working variously in Judicial and then Prosecutorial Oversight as a "Special Plenipotentiary" for collaboration, he quit in 1951 at the height of Stalinism in Poland to write his doctorate and teach at the University of Warsaw, where both he and Kubicki studied under Jerzy Sawicki. In Kubicki's words, Gubiński had left the ministry to be "rid of any kind of administrative affiliations and dependencies." Never a member of the PPR or its successors, he had joined the Democratic Party (Stronnictwo Demokratyczne) on the recommendation of Chajn, who had been delegated there by the PPR as a plant but, unlike his mentor, remained in it until the fall of Communism.[25]

Unlike Chajn, Sawicki, Gubiński, and Lernell, Adolf Dąb spent the war not in hiding or in the Soviet Union, but in the paradoxically privileged position of a junior officer taken prisoner by the Germans in 1939. Though of Jewish ethnicity, Dąb, like other officer POWs, enjoyed protected status in the relatively humane conditions of Oflag II-C near Woldenberg, where he arranged law courses for fellow inmates. Like Barcikowski, he had been a member of the League for the Defense of the Rights of Man and Citizen before the war and, as a Socialist Party activist, represented left-wing defendants, including, by coincidence, Leszek Kubicki's uncle. While he served simultaneously as a Supreme Court prosecutor and head of Prosecutorial Oversight for a time and later sat on the Supreme Court in the early 1950s, he was eventually forced out because of his resistance to the PPR's absorption of the Polish Socialist Party, which he represented in the Sejm, as well as his "revisionist" views. He subsequently went into private practice and eventually became a professor at the University of Warsaw.[26]

By way of comparison, it is worth noting that the pasts and interests of some of the non-Jewish ministerial personnel who appear in the course of our story were just as variegated. Tadeusz Cyprian, the prosecutor at the Supreme National Tribunal whom we have already encountered filing one fruitless appeal of Special Court verdicts after another, had a particularly colorful biography. As a teenage conscript in the Austro-Hungarian Army, he was taken prisoner by the Italians in 1917 and from there volunteered for the French-equipped Polish Army of General Haller, where he became a lieutenant in the new Polish Air Force and was wounded during the Polish-Soviet War of 1918–1921. Between the world wars, he authored Poland's leading textbook on amateur photography and rose to become a Supreme Court prosecutor, before joining the Government-in-Exile in 1939. In 1945 he joined Jerzy Sawicki as one of four members of the Polish delegation to the Nuremberg trials, finally quitting government in 1950 to spend the rest of his days as a university professor.[27]

The man who penned the angry screed against the "professional ghetto" of the prewar judiciary, Zygmunt Kapitaniak, was no parvenu, but himself a prewar judge. A decorated veteran of the Home Army and the Warsaw Uprising, he had been active in the underground Democratic Party during the war and remained a leading member for the rest of his life. After the war he headed the Office of Judicial Oversight from 1946 to 1949, then worked as a

Supreme Court judge from 1952. Dismissed in 1954, he was reinstated in 1956 and served until 1971, suggesting that he was not someone whose record was considered irreparably compromised by his service during the Stalinist period.

PENAL POPULISM

Yet another potential threat to the thoroughness and integrity of the August trials was the communist government's inclination toward what Leszek Kubicki called "penal populism," the treatment of justice as a series of "campaigns" in which select crimes would be prosecuted vigorously and with great public fanfare. First was the pursuit of "anti-state" crimes; then, once armed resistance had been suppressed, came the campaign for labor discipline, then for the defense of social property, then the campaign against hooliganism, and so on. The problem was not only that it gave the impression that criminal policy was fickle, but that, once again, it encroached on the prerogatives of the judiciary. Despite its reputation for conservatism, the judiciary was "consistently excessively liberal" in their sentencing, unwilling to let it be swayed by trends of the moment or by guidelines from the executive branch and choosing instead to "resis[t] every appearance" of penal populism.

Ironically, the campaign-oriented policies of the new Ministry of Justice were in large part a "continuation" of those of its "reactionary" predecessor, the Ministry of Justice of the Second Republic. Likewise, the confrontation that resulted was similar to one that had arisen before the war between the ministry and the judiciary. Then, too, the authoritarian Sanacja government, which assumed power after Józef Piłsudski's death in 1926, had attempted to curtail the independence of the judiciary. When in 1945 Leon Chajn blamed the "light sentences" of the prewar period for the "constant" rise in crime during the Second Republic, it no doubt caused many of the judges and prosecutors who had returned to work after the war to make unfavorable comparisons.

Indeed, the contemporary objections to rapid proceedings and harsh mandatory penalties were reminiscent of those published in 1937 by one of the grand old men of Polish jurisprudence, Juliusz Makarewicz, as a rebuttal to demands for the same at the third Congress of Polish Legalists in Katowice.[28] Makarewicz, who was the principal author of the first unified Polish criminal code of 1932, rebuffed calls for more severe penalties in response to growing crime. A focus on the act rather than the perpetrator and the corresponding focus on "rendering the perpetrator harmless" was tantamount to a return to the "views of the 17th century," including collective revenge and draconian punishments like branding and amputations. In any case, longer prison terms—instead of treatment facilities for alcoholics and other substance abusers, which the Ministry of Justice was unwilling to pay for—would do little to deter recidivists whose crimes were driven by addiction. Finally, "even Nazi law" placed the emphasis on the individual rather than his crime:

> The 20th century is and will be the century of the deepening of the problem of individual and subjective guilt, in particular in the public interest. It is not about depriving someone of life at all costs (just because we need to frighten others or because we need a body to hang publicly on the gallows), rather it's about the state being able to best manage all the data regarding the individuality of a given criminal in order to correctly treat him in the area of punishment as well as in the area of supplemental restrictions [środków zabezpieczających]. Evolution is driven in this direction not by the influence of some doctrine, but by the social interests of the masses.

The overhasty sentencing of minor or incidental criminals to prison would only damage them psychologically and transform them into career criminals. There was no doubt, in Makarewicz's mind, that a *"cheap* (i.e., *fast) justice system"* would be *"very expensive."*[29]

SENTENCING UNDER SCRUTINY

As we have seen, however, in practice it was difficult to know which lenient sentences were the result of "liberalism," which were the result of real "passive resistance," and which were due to the complex nature of the cases themselves. Certainly, some combination of the three was contributing to a situation that the Ministry of Justice found galling. A September 1947 memorandum, signed by Adolf Dąb in his capacity as director of Prosecutorial Oversight and distributed to all Appellate Court prosecutors, who in turn oversaw all District Court prosecutors, tore into the leniency of the courts and the inactivity of prosecutors. The "state of justice in criminal cases" was, in his words, nothing less than "catastrophic":

> Reports are arriving from many District Courts about the poor state of sentencing. Sentences are too low, do not correspond to the guilt of the accused, and the courts make generous use of . . . suspended sentences. In some District Courts the number of conditional suspensions leads sometimes to incredible numbers, up to 80% of all sentences for general crimes. . . .
>
> The situation is all the more threatening, since this leniency of the courts is commonly known and makes criminals bolder. The conviction has even arisen, that the first crime can be committed without consequence, since the court will suspend the punishment.

The report alleged that prosecutors in large measure bore responsibility for this state of affairs:

> Prosecutors do not use in the correct way their legal powers and do not contribute to the improvement of verdicts by their appeal. Even if they take legal means in some cases, they quickly become discouraged as soon as the Appellate Courts refuse to hear a few appeals.
>
> Attention to the correct application of penal repression is however a basic obligation of every prosecutor. The inactivity of prosecutors in this area is drawing the attention of even the Appellate Courts, which often express the opinion that they find sentences inappropriate, but are helpless due to the unwillingness of prosecutors to appeal.[30]

Although Dąb did not specifically mention the August trials, an article by Chajn four months later in the *Legal Review* mentioned, among others, the example of a questionable verdict in the case of a murder of several Jewish children during the war, demonstrating that while perhaps August crimes were not at the forefront of the ministry's attention, they were part of the panoply of cases whose outcomes were less than satisfactory:

> Does a prosecutor who does not appeal the acquittal of three persons accused under [Article 1] of the [August Decree] of organizing and taking active part in a raid on three Jewish children in hiding—seizing them and handing them over to the German police who shot them, as

well as taking part and organizing raids on persons selected for forced labor in Germany—understand the importance of his functions? ... This despite the fact that the trial fully confirmed the guilt [of the accused] in the capture and handover of the hiding children.

Troublingly, even the Supreme Court was seen to be falling short in its rulings. In the same article, Chajn reproached the Supreme Court for precisely those things that Makarewicz had upheld as virtues—the unwillingness to treat justice as a prophylactic, placing the act ahead of the perpetrator, and not sentencing harshly just because the crime in question was spreading. He even cited "similar" faulty reasoning in verdicts from "1934, 1935, 1938," and sarcastically wondered whether the Supreme Court had "noticed" that a "revolution" had taken place in Poland in 1944. But most disturbingly, a recent article by Jerzy Sawicki and Arnold Gubiński had exposed the highly questionable "value of some rulings of this court in cases of war criminals and collaborators." The Supreme Court, he charged, was "clinging compulsively to the easiest, and at the same time most unreliable grammatical interpretation" of the laws. Its judges were failing to "provide an example to the lower courts through their rulings of ... an interpretation of the prewar laws which would make of the courts a co-creator of the new democratic legality."[31]

Chajn's speech may have been cluttered with communist jargon, but he was touching on another issue regarding the August crimes that had emerged in the wake of the dismantling of the Special Courts: there was precious little guidance or consensus on how to interpret the August Decree, of which the Supreme Court's rulings had become the most glaring proof.

The August Decree was a law that had been pasted together in haste, and its seams began to show once they were put under scrutiny. Writing in the December 1946 *Legal Review,* a municipal judge commented that if the Special Courts had only succeeded in hearing 58 percent of their caseload, it was not just because of the quantity or quality of the cases, but because judges were operating in the "absence of whatsoever ready examples and rulings against the backdrop of a totally new body of law without precedent in history." The "broadly stitched framing" of the Decree "placed the courts ... in front of a difficult task demanding an enormous effort."[32]

Given the impossibility of conducting a sweeping, fundamental analysis of what constituted "Hitlerite crimes" beforehand, the Decree had been left deliberately vague, foregoing an explicit catalog of war crimes and limiting itself to a blanket description of offenses designed to cast as wide a net as possible. The responsibility for interpreting the Decree was thus left up to "court practice and the doctrine of the law." Poland's legal system was one of civil law, predicated on codification. But with a law as threadbare as the August Decree, precedent-setting court rulings would necessarily have an "incomparably higher degree" of influence in guiding subsequent decisions, similar to the Anglo-American precedential common law system. In particular, the Supreme Court, as the sole instance of appeal, would have the power to "directly shape the interpretation of all the most doubtful problems."[33] With three-quarters of its judges having served on the bench before the Second World War, the Supreme Court was also vulnerable to criticism over legalistic thinking.[34]

ON MURDER

The Supreme Court appears to have begun hearing appeals in August cases from both the defunct Special Courts and the District Courts in early 1947, and controversial interpretations of the August Decree resulted almost immediately. This was, of course, in part the fault of the wording of the Decree. The first point of Article 1 had abandoned the individualized "traditional construction" of the legal description of murder in the 1932 Criminal Code—"whoever kills a person"—in favor of one encompassing all participants in the act—"whoever takes part in killing."

Such a construction was indeed necessary to address the phenomenon of mass killing, where the commander was often many, many steps removed from the executioners, and the executioners were only able to carry out their work because a whole array of personnel streamlined and organized the process. Nor was the concept of collective responsibility for crime unknown in Polish jurisprudence. Article 240 of the 1932 Criminal Code, which otherwise addressed only crimes by individuals, provided for the punishment of persons taking part in a brawl or beating resulting in death or injury.

But Article 1 of the August Decree not only broadly described the categories of victims—"persons from among the civilian population or military persons or prisoners of war"—it also made no attempt to define or delimit what constituted "taking part" in murder. Lawmakers obviously wanted to "embrac[e] the whole range of possible actions," but it was precisely the span of this range that ended up becoming the subject of controversy. The high Nazi officials of the Generalgouvernement were clearly guilty, but what about the Polish peasant who had driven a captured Jew on his cart to the police for execution?

The judgments of the Supreme Court would seesaw between two positions: one held that a defendant was guilty if it could be proven either that he acted with direct intent to harm the victim (direct responsibility [*dolus directus*]) or that he foresaw the potentially harmful consequences of his action and nonetheless accepted that possibility (indirect responsibility [*dolus eventualis*]). The opposing position excluded indirect responsibility, holding that only direct intent "colored" by a high level of malice (*dolus coloratus*) could justify a conviction.

In the opinion of Kubicki, who was inclined to consider the prosecution of the aforementioned cart drivers as an example of the overzealous reading of Article 1, the Special Courts had initially indulged in an "excessively wide interpretation" of the article. As time passed however, their practice became "more cautious, and even in the immediate aftermath of [the Special Courts'] abolition—too cautious."[35]

This caution was plainly stated in the Supreme Court's rejection in March 1947 of an appeal of a verdict in the case of Edward S. from the Special Court in Kraków. Explaining that because Article 1 of the Decree carried a mandatory death penalty, "from this consideration alone it should be especially narrowly interpreted." Given that Edward S. was accused only of "providing information to the German authorities" in the case of two Polish men arrested for hiding weapons and "taking part in the search" for Jews hiding in a forest who were then murdered, the Supreme Court determined that his crimes did not meet the strict reading of Article 1. Specifically, because S. had not "denounced or captured" the Poles, but merely "provided information" about them, and because he had been seen going to the forest armed with only a stick as part of a German search party that later killed the Jews, the court decided that he had taken part only in the search, not the murder. Because Article 1 made no provision for taking part in a *search*, he was rightfully sentenced, in the court's opinion, under Article 2, for crimes "other than foreseen" in the first. As the court concluded, "not *ratio legis ampla* [a broad understanding of the law], but on the contrary *ratio legis stricta* [a restricted understanding of the law] should be applied here."³⁶

ON CAPTURE AND DENUNCIATION

The interpretation of the second clause of Article 1 regarding capture and denunciation was even thornier and its import even greater because its language was more confused and the number of offenses to which it applied was potentially more numerous, since collaborators had often identified or transferred victims to third parties like the Germans and the Blue Police for execution.

The clause had gone through three iterations: Article 1b of the original August Decree had stated:

> Whoever, acting to the benefit of the German occupation authorities:
> ... acted or acts to the detriment of persons residing on the territory of the Polish State, in particular through capture or deportation of persons sought or persecuted by the occupation authorities for whatever reasons (excluding pursuit for the commission of general crimes) is subject to the death penalty.

Article 1.1b of the revision to the decree of February 16, 1945, had slightly expanded to include explicit mention of denunciation. In its final version, issued on December 11, 1946, the second clause of Article 1 was thus phrased: "Whoever, acting to the benefit of the authorities of the German state or an ally, ... by denunciation or capture acted to the detriment of persons sought or persecuted by the authorities for political, national, religious, or racial reasons is subject to the death penalty."

The offense of "denunciation or capture" was something altogether new in the grim "catalogue" of war crimes. Whereas the law of war in the prewar period had been principally concerned with crimes that occurred on the battlefield, the Second World War had shown that an occupation itself could bring out the worst in human nature. The problem, however, was that the second clause of Article 1 did not precisely define who constituted "persecuted persons," nor did it define what constituted denunciation and capture. The construction "sought or persecuted" was particularly infelicitous, because it was redundant. That was not the only part of the wording that caused confusion; unlike the first clause of Article 1, which described participation in killing, the legislators had not written "who takes part in capture" but simply "capture." Much hinged on the interpretation of this difference. There was no agreement over whether the crime of "capture" meant only the "direct physical capture" of individuals, or other subsequent functions like the guarding of captives. The upshot was increasingly convoluted judgments which had the effect of greatly narrowing the scope of the law, bringing forth "not only contrary doctrinal views, but even contrary verdicts."[37]

A variety of linguistic contortions were indeed used to deflect the appeals of prosecutors dissatisfied with lower-court convictions under the lesser, catchall Article 2 of the August Decree. In the case of Roman Sz., the Supreme Court emphasized that whereas the first clause of Article 1 might permit a collective interpretation, the second clause was about an "individual act" of denunciation, capture, or deportation, "not about taking part in those acts." This, despite the fact that Roman Sz., a Polish Kripo officer, had ordered three different men to accompany him to Gestapo headquarters, where they were arrested, with one dying in a concentration camp. Accepting the questionable reasoning of the Special Court of Lublin that, because in other cases the defendant had warned people of impending arrests, he must have sincerely believed that he was only "bringing" the victims to a "meeting" with the Gestapo, the Supreme Court concurred that he had not "captured" the men but was at most guilty of "not permitting their escape." Likewise, a ruling issued at the same sitting of the Supreme Court declared that in contrast to the crime of homicide, the August Decree made no provision for punishing participation in the crime of capture, as a result of which "'only the perpetrator can be punished, not the accomplice or inciter.'"[38]

An even more peculiar construction was to be found in a ruling from March 1947 that, like the one cited above dealing with the first clause, stated Article 1 had to be "interpreted as narrowly as possible." Ordering a retrial on the basis of what it considered questionable evidence, the Supreme Court also dismissed the prosecutor's appeal of the qualification of the crime, deciding that the defendant's key action—the alleged reporting of a man for owning a radio, resulting in his death—did *not* constitute denunciation, but was instead the "occasioning of persecution" and therefore fell under the lesser article.[39]

The semantics of who exactly constituted a "sought or persecuted" person were no less tortured. A slew of rulings from early 1947 advanced the notion that the "'denunciation of persons not yet pursued cannot fall under Article 1 of the Decree.'" This meant, for example, that a person suddenly denounced for violating German prohibitions—possessing arms, radios, or forbidden literature—could not be considered "sought or persecuted" unless the Germans had *already* been searching for the person at the time of their denunciation. The high court based its reasoning on the vagueness of the second clause: "If the legislator uses the expression 'persons sought or persecuted' it is necessary to assume that he wanted to limit the circle of persons to whom it applied—namely, those persons already actually being sought after."[40]

Whatever the merits of this claim, it was leading the court to some startling conclusions. In March 1947 the Supreme Court rejected an appeal by the prosecution in the case of Józef R., who, as a Gestapo informer, passed along information on the resistance activities of two women and a man who had been arrested. The judges concurred with the lower court that the Germans "already possessed sufficient incriminating material" regarding the victims and that Józef R.'s "providing of information" did not amount to "denunciation or capture."[41]

While there was never any dispute that Jews had been a persecuted group during the war, it is worth noting that confusion reigned over which categories of Poles to include. After all, Poles were one of the underclasses in the Nazi worldview. Was it necessary to "consider only certain groups of Poles, or all Poles"? Among the persecuted groups at first excluded were conscripts in the Baudienst, the mandatory German labor service for young Poles and even deportees designated for forced labor in the Reich.[42]

CONTRARY TO THE LAW

The ministerial response arrived in the form of a June 1947 article in the *Democratic Legal Review*, "The Logic of Intention or the Logic of Verbalism?," penned by Jerzy Sawicki and Adolf Gubiński. The article, which consisted of a detailed analysis of the Supreme Court's rulings regarding August crimes up to that time, was, in effect, a broadside against the Court's opinions, hammering home the message that their highly restrictive interpretation of the August Decree was contrary to the law, or *contra legem*.

While Gubiński and Sawicki took care not to impugn the judges or their motives, they implied that there was no other explanation for the convoluted readings of the Decree. The article began with a quote from a 1922 issue of the *Illinois Law Review*: "Whether certain laws will be enforced depends in no small degree on the personal, legal, economic, and social views of those people who are currently sitting on our tribunals. A different . . . view is based in large part on fiction, which is not substantiated in a detailed analysis of court rulings."

The consistently "narrow" positions taken by the Supreme Court had "overruled in large part" the body of precedent created by the Special Courts, and were "also contrary to the rulings of the International Military Tribunal in Nuremberg." Such an interpretation was only permissible when the meaning of the words could be variously understood, such as when the court has a choice of "two conceptual types of expressions used by the lawmaker," but given that the "legal concepts" of the Decree awakened "no or almost no doubts as to their conceptual range," an observer would naturally deduce that the real purpose was to interpret the law *contra legem*—"overriding the law's purpose."

Moreover, the "verbalistic" approach heretofore taken by the Court did not hold water. Citing the case, mentioned above, of Edward S. and his role in the "hunt" for Jews, the authors compared the contemporary Supreme Court's extremely limited reading of "taking part in murder" with the rulings of the prewar Supreme Court regarding what constituted "taking part" in a fatal or serious beating according to Article 240 of the Criminal Code. In various rulings from the 1930s the Supreme Court had gone so far as to state that actually striking a blow was unnecessary to find someone guilty of "taking part" in the crime, and that a brawl was to be considered a single, unified offense, even if it contained pauses, changed locations, or involved different people. Not only was the construction of Article 1 of the August Decree similar to Article 240, the concept of "perpetratorship and co-perpetratorship" was so broad in Article 1 that lesser categories of criminal responsibility were clearly meant to be limited to "exceptional instances." Inciters and accomplices were clearly understood by the authors of the Decree to be included among those "taking part" in murder.

In defense of the public order, the Supreme Court before the war had not hesitated to go further in its rulings than the authors of the Criminal Code, accepting participation in Article 240 in its widest range, and limiting [forms of lesser guilt] in this construction to a minimum.

Should not the Supreme Court set the same goal in defense of the Polish legal order destroyed by the occupier, in defense of the violated norms of the Hague Convention, [and] in defense of... the "rights of man"?

The first clause of Article 1 had been explicitly constructed with the co-perpetration aspect of mass murder in mind:

Crimes of this kind cannot be as a rule committed by individuals, a whole group of persons is required whose activity is often in competition, but most often is complementary.

The killing, for example, of children in the villages of the Zamość region or Jews in the ghettos would have been impossible or significantly harder were it not for the deliberate surrounding, besieging, and searching of the terrain, transporting to the collection point, etc. etc. Of those who took part only a tiny number participated in the "technical putting to death" [*techniczne uśmiercanie*]. "Techniczne uśmiercanie" would, however, have been impossible had not all the links in the chain used by the occupation authorities taken part.

The jurisprudence of both Nuremberg and Poland's own Supreme National Tribunal also militated against the narrow interpretation of the Decree. The International Military Tribunal had traced responsibility for murder all the way back to the planning stage, and the Supreme National Tribunal had found both Arthur Greiser and Ludwig Fischer, the Nazi governors of western Poland and Warsaw, guilty of murder, although in the "vast majority of cases the 'techniczne uśmiercanie' had taken place sporadically at a much later date and was carried out entirely by other people." The most likely purpose of the Supreme Court's verbalism, then, was the "reduction of punishment, contrary to the aim of the law."

The second clause of Article 1 did not include the words "taking part" when referring to denunciation and capture, but Article 28 of the prewar Criminal Code, which still applied to the August Decree, provided for collective guilt by holding each accomplice responsible "within the limits of his intent," irrespective of the responsibility of the chief perpetrator. The Supreme Court, however, appeared to be selectively ignoring that provision by sentencing accomplices in capture and denunciation under lesser articles of the Decree. Gubiński and Sawicki referred to two different Supreme Court rulings, one in which a man took part in rounding up deportees for forced labor, and the other in which a man helped the Germans arrest three people, one of whom later died in a camp. The high court refused to requalify either of those crimes under the second clause of Article 1 on the grounds that there was no provision for "taking part" or "co-perpetration." Exasperated, the two authors asked, "Why is it that an accomplice in a misdemeanor is culpable within the limits of his intent . . . but in a case [of collaboration] is charged not according to the [corresponding] article [i.e., capture and denunciation], but under . . . a lighter section of the law . . . covering . . . crimes of another kind[?]" Once again, the only explanation they could find for the "totally incomprehensible" refusal of the Supreme Court to properly qualify these crimes was that it "would then be forced . . . to pronounce the death penalty."

The hairsplitting over who counted as "pursued or persecuted" also came under attack. The Supreme Court had refused to qualify the denunciation of two Poles to the Ukrainian police, one for being a communist and the other for having stolen a list of persons to be arrested, as such because it "'had not been established that [the victims] were being sought by the occupation authorities.'" It had refused to requalify one case in which a man had denounced three others for membership in the Underground, since it had not been proven that the victims were being pursued on "political, national, religious, or racial" grounds. It had refused yet another in which the victim of a denunciation died in a camp because the lower court had not proven that the decedent was "sought or persecuted by the German police." And it had steadfastly refused to extend the label of "pursued and persecuted" to the general population of the Generalgouvernement, such as when it refused to requalify a case in which a man had been denounced for sabotaging telephone wires: "By no means can the view of the appeal be agreed with that every resident of the so-called Generalgouvernement, besides privileged minorities, should be considered pursued or persecuted. Article 1 of the [August Decree] is an exceptional law, and therefore is not subject to an expanded interpretation. It should be interpreted as narrowly as possible."

Likewise, the Court declined to requalify the case of a man denounced to the Kripo for possessing a radio and receiving large quantities of underground press—presumably for further distribution—at his apartment twice a week. He did not meet the Court's definition of a "persecuted" individual because he did not belong to an "especially harshly treated" group such as "communists, members of the Polish Resistance, the Polish Home Army, the People's Army, representatives of the Polish Underground authorities, members of the Catholic and Evangelical clergy in some parts of the country, Jews, etc."

Nor did he meet their stringent criteria of a "pursued" individual, because *before* the search was initiated he had not been among persons known to the Germans for "specific acts," such as "perpetrators of military sabotage, members of an exposed underground organization who had escaped arrest, or persons about whom the occupation authorities had established that they possessed radios, weapons, or illegal writings, etc."

Even were one to accept the second set of criteria, Gubiński and Sawicki expressed their bafflement that the Court failed to acknowledge what was "obvious to everyone"—namely, that persons who "possessed weapons, radios, or belonged to Polish political organizations ... were pursued ... for political or national reasons." Indeed, both the International Military Tribunal in Nuremberg and the Supreme National Tribunal in Warsaw had concurred that the Germans had conducted a "policy of extermination of the Polish population regardless of its activities":

> What is the point of the interpretation of these kinds of legal rules, which contrary to the Supreme National Tribunal, contrary to Nuremberg, contrary to the obvious indication of the facts and documents confirming that the Germans aimed to destroy the whole Polish nation, takes the position of *"rationis legis strictae"* and confirms that the Polish Nation as a whole was not persecuted.
>
> Does the [verbalistic] interpretation not conceal here the reality of the occupation?

Paradoxically, the Supreme Court's judgments had created a situation in which the most important element for the qualification of a crime was not the intent or actions of the perpetrator, but the identity of the victim. According to this logic, the most despicable collaborator, one combining denunciation with lies, would receive a lesser sentence for accusing *completely innocent* people of resistance activity, than if he had denounced actual Underground members. This was the "dead-end [*manowce*] to which we have been led by an interpretation which puts verbalistic logic as the highest value."

To show that the Supreme Court's understanding of what constituted "denunciation or capture" offered no surer footing, Sawicki and Gubiński singled out a number of a controversial decisions, several of which have already been cited: the assessment that "bringing in" a subject for questioning by the Gestapo was not analogous to capture, that the "causing of persecution," the supplying of redundant information to the German police, and fruitless surveillance by registered Gestapo informants were all lesser crimes. Turning to the case of Edward S., who participated in the hunt for the Jews, Gubiński and Sawicki asked how it was that he had been sentenced under the lesser article even though he had personally revealed the hiding place of weapons hidden by two men after the Germans at first failed to find them, "as if pointing out the location of hidden weapons during a search is not equivalent to a denunciation." Exasperated, the authors summed up everything that was *not* denunciation or capture according to the Supreme Court's standards, demonstrating clearly the intent of the court to restrict the crime of denunciation and capture to "improbable limits in a manner which misses the point of the law":

   a) it is not a denunciation if the German authorities (specifically the Gestapo) do not yet possess incriminating materials . . .
   b) it is not a denunciation if the German authorities (specifically the Gestapo) possess [such] materials, but from another source . . .
   c) it is not the providing of information to the German authorities (specifically the Gestapo) if the perpetrator did not 'point out' or did not apprehend the complainant . . .
   d) it is not independently bringing in [a victim to the police] . . .
   e) it is not a capture [in coordination] with other persons . . .
   f) it is not the revelation to the German authorities of the fact of possessing a radio, weapons, etc. . . .

> . . . It seems that only with difficulty can an instance be imagined in which the perpetrator would be guilty of denunciation or capture according to the rules established by the Supreme Court, such as if Person A captures (albeit independently) or denounces (albeit not in the form of the provision of information, but rather directly

e.g. with a hand gesture(!)) Person B, who was pursued by the Germans on the basis of materials already in their position, or belongs to the number of persons [defined by the Supreme Court] as persecuted.[43]

Even as the Court had hemmed in the use of Article 1, restricting which categories of victims and actions qualified, it also imposed other tests of its own invention. Gubiński and Sawicki picked apart the case of Dr. Józef Syga, a retired railway official and veteran officer of the Austro-Hungarian Army and the Polish wars of independence, who had been sentenced under the catchall Article 2 by the Special Court in Kraków to three years for denouncing two people, one falsely, as Jews. In June 1941 Syga had spotted Adolf Liebeskind, a Jewish lawyer with whom he had clashed over late fees at a legal library where Liebeskind had worked before the war, stopping him in the gardens surrounding the Old Town of Kraków and summoning a German policeman, to whom he vehemently insisted that Liebeskind be arrested for not wearing his Jewish armband. Luckily for Liebeskind, the policeman released him with a summons that led to a small fine. If he had been arrested and ended up in the prison at Montelupich, he would have been "beaten to a pulp." According to Liebeskind, Syga had cursed him in Polish, swearing that "'whether Poland survives or not, there won't be a single Jew left; this mangy Jew has to croak.'" Two years later, Syga falsely accused a Polish woman, with whom he had professional contacts in his function as a minor municipal court administrator, of being a Jew. After she was arrested, he even appeared at her interrogation at Gestapo headquarters, continuing to insist that she was a Jew, although the Germans released her shortly thereafter.

In its dismissal of the prosecutor's appeal, the Supreme Court argued that for the crime to fulfill Article 2, the defendant's intent had to be the aiding of the occupation authorities, not the settling of personal accounts. Syga's actions also did not "betray a high degree of malice," since, in the court's opinion, crimes of the second clause had to threaten the life of the victim or bring about his mistreatment, while Liebeskind had only suffered a fine. Likewise, the woman he denounced experienced "no negative consequences" as a result, according to the Court.[44]

As Gubiński and Sawicki pointed out, none of the Supreme Court's stated reasons had any actual basis in the law. Article 14 of the Criminal Code, which applied to the August Decree, declared that indirect responsibility—when a perpetrator "foresees the possibility of a criminal result or the criminality of his activity and accepts it"—sufficed for a finding of criminal intent. Instead, the Supreme Court was imposing additional criteria, demanding that a "high level of malice" be present as well. Moreover, the enabling of the destruction of a person, even if the primary motive was personal, in line with the occupier's exterminationist policies was clearly indirect responsibility. The Court's casual shrugging off of the harm done to the victims—one's near arrest and the other's actual arrest—was misguided because the crimes of the August Decree were "formal crimes," in which criminal responsibility was incurred at the moment of commission, irrespective of the consequences. Gubiński and Sawicki accused the Court of seeking to "edit" the law by transforming "formal crimes" into "material crimes."

Gubiński and Sawicki selected two other rulings on verdicts for crimes against Jews to drive home their point about the Supreme Court's logically untenable interpretations of the August Decree. In July 1943, panicked by the threat of German "pacification" campaigns in their area, the people of the village of Cholerzyn had demanded that the headman and the chief of the village police remove the Jew H. who had been hiding in their midst. When his captors refused to release him, H. then asked to be given to the Blue Police rather than the Germans, apparently in the faint hope that they would spare him. It did him no good; after beating him bloody, the village police commander took H. to the Blue Police in Liszki, who executed him.

The Special Court of Kraków had sentenced the village policeman to three years for beating the Jew, but acquitted him on all other charges on the grounds that he had acted not to the benefit of the Germans but to protect the village, and that he had acceded to the Jew's request to be turned over to the Blue Police. The Supreme Court concurred with these opinions, deciding that the defendant "shared" the Jew's hope that the Blue Police would be merciful and was not responsible for their killing of the Jew. Bizarrely, the Court explained away the sadistic beating inflicted on H., which clearly contradicted the notion advanced in the verdict that the defendant had the victim's best interests at heart, as an "exploitation of [H.'s] position." Sarcastically commenting on the alleged sympathy of the defendant for the victim, Gubiński and Sawicki made a suggestion of their own as to why H. was beaten: "because [the defendant] wished him well, obviously."

They went on: "Without analyzing at greater length the verdict of the court . . . it is worth posing the question of whether the capture and handing over of a persecuted individual (which *nota bene* led to 'further consequences') is not in itself an act forbidden by law under threat of punishment."

In particular, they took exception to the key element of the argument advanced by the Special Court and endorsed by the Supreme Court that the victim himself had "requested" to be handed over to the Blue Police and so, by implication, had determined his own fate. Aside from the fact that the only reason H. had to make such a choice was because his original captors refused to release him, the "agreement of the complainant" in his own demise was not a "circumstance excluding punishment." In fact, the prewar Supreme Court had set clear boundaries on the related topics of mercy killing and assisted suicide:

> If the perpetrator by his own actions has brought the victim to such a state, in which he requests death, then obviously there is no question of "privileging" murder, which depends on the objective meaning of the free disposition of one's own life.
>
> Moreover a condition for privileging of murder is that the "motive for the actions of the perpetrator was sympathy for the victim."

Finally, Gubiński and Sawicki used the case of Polish Kripo Adam Juny, whom we met in Chapter 5, to question the Supreme Court's sentencing practices. The December 1946 revision of the August Decree had added a second clause to Article 5, permitting the "extraordinary mitigation of punishment" at judges' discretion in cases where the defendant had been acting "under the influence of threats or orders." According to the October 1946 Decree abolishing the Special Courts, the same special procedural rules applying to appeals of "especially dangerous crimes during the rebuilding of the state" as laid out in the so-called Small Criminal Code of June 1946 would hold for the August crimes. These rules allowed the Supreme Court, as the court of appeal, to pronounce its own sentence in the event of "incorrect use of the law in the qualification or sentencing of a crime," and empowered the Court to overturn a verdict and order a retrial if it had "serious doubts as to the correctness of the facts established as the basis of the appealed verdict."

Thus the Supreme Court could and did on occasion grant prosecutorial appeals to requalify crimes under the more severe Article 1. But Gubiński and

Sawicki found that in the "majority" of such cases they also applied extraordinary mitigation under Article 5, usually doling out sentences of five years and a few months, "oscillating close to the minimum foreseen in Article 59" of the Criminal Code, which permitted a minimum prison sentence of five years in lieu of a death or life sentence. Juny, who had arrested and sent Rozalia Lieberfreund and her nine-year-old daughter to a concentration camp, where the child perished, had his sentence requalified under Article 1 but, with extraordinary mitigation of punishment, received only six more months on top of his earlier five-year sentence. Sawicki and Gubiński noted that the "apportionment of the punishment near the permitted minimum . . . seems disproportionately low and incomprehensible," as it did in most of these cases. If a willing, armed, and official collaborator with the Germans whose actions had resulted in the death of a young Jewish girl could not be punished to the full extent of the law, then who could be?

> Did the accused, voluntarily accepting the responsibilities of an informer, not in advance agree to follow orders? The Supreme National Tribunal took a similar position in the cases of Greiser and Fischer. The International Military Tribunal [in Nuremberg] adopted the construction of responsibility for participation in criminal organizations proceeding from such assumptions.
>
> How then can a person, who alone voluntarily took upon himself the obligation of obedience to the commission of crimes in the German apparatus, claim when he is brought to justice that he had no alternative and had to carry out the order[?]
>
> That was not the aim of the statute of [Article 5] on extraordinary mitigation of punishment.[45]

PAPER APPEALS

We cannot know whether feelings about Jews played a role in the rulings of the Supreme Court, because sources are lacking; but the presence of several jurists of Jewish descent—Maurycy Herling-Grudziński, Antoni Landau, Emil Rappaport, and Mieczysław Szerer—among the nineteen judges employed in the Criminal Section of the Supreme Court as of early 1947, as well as the fact that the Court was restricting the use of Article 1 across the board, suggests that other factors were at work. In this same period, around 75 percent of Supreme Court judges had served in that role before the Second World War—a lower proportion than the 90 percent rate of prewar service for all judges throughout Poland, but still considerable.[46] Some, like Emil Rappaport, were opposed on principle to the death penalty, but a still greater number presumably had no desire to have to compensate for the reluctance of the lower courts to impose the mandatory death sentences required by Article 1, all the more so when the appeals were only "paper"—that is, when the Supreme Court itself did not call witnesses or even meet the defendant during its deliberations.

In a handwritten letter to Minister of Justice Świątkowski from February 1947, Mieczysław Szerer warned that the lower courts needed more sentencing options for Article 1 than just the death penalty. As matters stood, the lower courts were "stretching" their verdicts to qualify them as crimes under Article 2 and thereby permit a minimum sentence of three years, putting the Supreme Court in a very awkward position: "When the prosecutor appeals a verdict stretched in this way, the Supreme Court, should it accept the appeal, is faced with the prospect of sentencing to death a person whom they haven't seen and whom the judges hearing the original case did not want to so punish."[47]

Rappaport himself laid out the case for the Supreme Court's restraint in a gloss on a ruling in which he had overturned a verdict in an August trial, cautioning against the excessive use of the substantial expansion of the Court's power—traditionally the Court had only been able to overturn verdicts for errors of procedure or law, not on the basis of a qualitative assessment of the case itself. Not only did he state that the "paper" appeal was the "worst form" of judging the merits of the case, he emphasized that preeminence had to be accorded to the "free opinion" of the lower courts, the only evidentiary standard stipulated in the Polish legal code:

> The court of [trial], taking into account the public nature, oral testimony, and immediacy of the actual trial, disposes, at the moment of creation in the judge's psyche of an opinion on the question of guilt or innocence of the accused, of an arsenal of not only logically correct premises and conclusions, based on the explanations of the accused, arguments of the accuser and statements of witnesses, not only a base of conclusions,

resulting from the evaluation of material evidence or expert opinions, but furthermore an inestimable investigative capital of its own impressions and emotions, which no regulations can reproduce, but which in an oral and live criminal proceeding possess a premier, often decisive importance in the necessary judgment. The sentencing court does not judge "from paper," it creates the actual trial records during the questioning of witnesses, formulation of the verdict and its justification.

If the Supreme Court found some glaring illogicality, contradiction, or omission, then it was bound to take up the case, but it was not its place to exceed its role by poking around the merits "of every detail left out by the appeal." In other words, it was not the role of the Supreme Court to "compete" with the trial court.[48]

The situation was serious because the role of the Supreme Court in the August trials was only growing. As of November 1947, appeals of cases of collaborators and Volksdeutsche made up three-quarters of the Court's caseload, with the share of August cases "constantly growing." In a letter from that same month from Kazimierz Bzowski, the deputy chief judge and chairman of the Criminal Section of the Supreme Court to his superior, Wacław Barcikowski, Bzowski referred to the article by Gubiński and Sawicki, whose conclusions he judged "harsh, but correct." He added that Stanisław Śliwiński, the chair of the Law Department at the University of Warsaw and a prewar Supreme Court judge who had sat on the Codification Commission behind the 1932 Criminal Code, had reviewed the rulings of the current Supreme Court and concluded that they did not "stand on a high level."[49] The response of the government seems to have been to try to wait out the Supreme Court by either retiring older judges or, if Barcikowski resisted an appointment, simply leaving the position unfilled or delegating temporary judges. Thus, although there were nineteen judges in the Criminal Section of the Supreme Court at the beginning of 1947, there were only fifteen two years later. Of the nine judges from the Criminal Section whose involvement in controversial interpretations of the August Decree could be established, four were forcibly retired in August 1947 and one in 1948. Antoni Landau, the outspoken judge who had criticized the utility of the Special Courts and August Decree, was also fired.[50]

LAST REVISIONS

Even as the government shrank from revising the most controversial sections of the August Decree, it responded to the demands of the professional judiciary and the public in other ways. As we have seen, Article 5 of the December 1946 revision to the August Decree permitted the courts to apply "extraordinary mitigation of punishment" in the event that the perpetrator was acting under threats or orders. However, the last revision of the August Decree, issued on April 3, 1948, made a few small changes, with one critical addition. Where the second clause of Article 5 stated that the courts "may apply" extraordinary mitigation of punishment, a new third clause of Article 5 stated that extraordinary mitigation "is to be applied accordingly, if in cases of [denunciation or capture] there are specific mitigating circumstances." In other words, the courts were being given leeway to apply mitigating circumstances in every case—for, indeed, mitigating factors could always be invented—short of outright murder. Coming a year after Judge Szerer warned about the "stretching" of verdicts by lower courts, the amendment of the August Decree suggests that, behind the severe facade, the government sought to maintain a *modus vivendi* with the rank-and-file judiciary and the population.

The Sovietizing state certainly seemed resigned to its reliance on the prewar judiciary. Unable to do without the services of the vast mass of prewar judges and prosecutors and also cognizant of the lack of political profit in pushing the collaboration issue any further, the government was content to wait for a new generation to issue from the universities and abridged legal schools. But the quality of the graduates of the latter was low—the majority were sent to reinforce prosecutors' offices where they could perform "less complicated" tasks like preparing indictments or investigative formalities.

Even worse, from the government's point of view, those university graduates who did choose a career in criminal justice despite the low pay and difficult conditions often still deferred to and were shaped by the seniority and experience of the prewar cadre. According to Leszek Kubicki, a "huge role" in the maintenance of an independent-minded judiciary "was played by the preserved continuity of the academic tradition [in the] universities . . . the overwhelming majority [of schools of higher education], despite huge losses, kept their prewar form and tradition. This had a colossal influence on the formation of consciousness."

Even among the more poorly trained legal school graduates, Władysław Grzymała, the prosecutor in Siedlce, found allies. One of the graduates assigned to be his assistant, Błaszyk, was a "worker and a communist," but also

> a very moderate person, who understood that he had a lot to learn in order to be a good prosecutor.
> ... I soon befriended [him]. Getting to know our work, he became convinced that we old cadre were not the dark reactionaries that we had been made out to be at the school.... Soon I figured out that he was a true Pole first, and only then a communist.

As for the other graduate assigned to them, he had been a former prosecutorial administrator (*sekretarz*) and so was devoted "heart and body" to the old cadre.

Perhaps the paradoxical nature of the government's efforts to cultivate a new cadre unsullied by the old is best indicated by the irony that the thirty-nine-year-old Grzymała, an avowed anticommunist who believed that Jews were out to destroy Poland and who worked to undermine cases he thought unjust, was, after completing his six-week course on "Marxism-Leninism-Stalinism" for junior prosecutors, assigned the responsibility of educating his fellow court personnel, including actual party members, about Marxism. Grzymała wasn't bothered in the least: "In order to defeat the enemy, you have to know his fighting methods and goals."[51]

7 THE DISTRICT COURTS

THE PROCEDURE FOR THE reconstruction of the past that the Special Courts had established was carried over to the District Courts with the transfer of jurisdiction for August crimes in October 1946. The set of exculpatory narratives for anti-Jewish crimes remained similar to those first mooted under the Special Courts, but with the expansion of the concept of mitigating factors under Article 5 and the signal that the period of exemplary repression had ended, the District Courts had more flexibility to craft verdicts as they saw fit.

The weight of the evidence was such that only very rarely did the courts decide that the events in question had *not* taken place and that the defendants had *not* been present. Instead, they propagated three interpretations that dovetailed with popular sentiment: that perpetrators had been "blind tools" devoid of agency, that their "crimes" were merely a matter of misperception, or that Jewish victims themselves had been criminals. In cases where there was no basis for even those justifications, courts could look to the social, professional, or political backgrounds of defendants for mitigating circumstances. Contrary to the stereotype of August trials being a cover for persecution of anticommunists, the District Courts continued to put on trial—and excuse—both members of the security services and the anticommunist resistance.

Neither the result of authoritarian stage management nor covert rebellion, the forging of a postwar consensus about the past continued to rely on input from across the political and social spectrum. The population demonstrated its support for the accused by corroborating, inventing, or reshaping the oral history of the occupation, no matter how incredible. The government could complain, but their regular revisions of the August Decree, sparse enforcement of oversight of the District Courts, and willingness to commute sentences showed their responsiveness to public and judicial pressure. And, the judiciary, for its part, preserved lives and reputations in a devastated nation by finding guilt yet diminishing culpability. In this respect, postwar retribution was the rare state-sponsored activity in Stalinist Poland to have some democratic quality about it.

The upshot was that the punishment of Polish collaborators in the Holocaust operated within a set of understood parameters and followed a predictable pattern, resulting most commonly in acquittal or a mild sentence, rarely and only in the most extreme cases in a death sentence with a high likelihood of commutation. The suspects could pretend to have been misguided, the government could pretend to be implacable, and the judiciary could pretend to be giving each case equal weight under the law. Each side would be able to claim victory and an interpretation of the past amenable to all involved would be entered into the historical and legal record. The only party to the process who would be consistently disappointed were the rare Jewish survivors, who were confronted with the reality that redress and retribution were not the chief purpose of the trials.

ACTORS WITHOUT AGENCY

Most of these crimes involved the denunciation or capture of Jews, rather than their "technical putting to death," so there was room to maneuver and assert that perpetrators had been bystanders, stripped of psychological and physical agency, all the more so since the essential functions of guarding, transporting, and even searching for victims did not always furnish glaring examples of a "high level of malice." Culpability was also easier to minimize when offenders had acted in concert, as was typically the case in the raiding and capture of Jews which relied on group action to be effective.

Judge Czesław Kosiński, a colleague of prosecutor Władysław Grzymała at the District Court in Siedlce, presided over several trials of this type. His verdicts illustrate well the judge's role in synthesizing an exculpatory narrative that could reconcile competing claims. Detractors might argue, for example, that Wincenty Ajchel's minimum sentence amounted to a slap on the wrist of a collaborator in mass murder, but supporters could claim that it was fair punishment for a man whom even an accuser had praised for "bravely" risking his life, albeit for other Poles. The court appeared committed to having a full hearing of all the evidence, suspending the trial for three months to call new prosecution witnesses. By the same token, the short sentence it ultimately issued betrayed a strong impulse to conclude the trial as bloodlessly and painlessly as possible.

Like five of his co-defendants, Ajchel had been a member of the fire brigade charged with assisting the Germans in destroying the ghetto of the town of Węgrów. But the case against his five subordinates gradually fell apart; Stanisław Zbrozek, an officer in the postwar auxiliary police who had filed the original denunciation, suddenly declared two months later before the investigative judge that he couldn't identify any of the guilty parties. Ignacy Flaga, another fireman who had not taken part but vehemently insisted that those who did, did so voluntarily, became more reticent at trial, saying that he wasn't sure if the firemen in the ghetto had been rounding up Jews after all and, when eventually pressed by the prosecutor about his earlier identifications of the accused, suggested that his prior testimony at the Municipal Court had been "incorrectly written down."

The trial was unusual for the relatively large number of Jewish witnesses who survived to take the stand. One, Moszek-Mendel Góra, had been captured, held, and convoyed by Wincenty Ajchel to the Jewish cemetery where he and a group of prisoners were shot and left for dead. Following his testimony, the court postponed the trial for three months to summon two additional Jewish witnesses from Wrocław, almost 500 kilometers away, despite the protests of defense lawyers who objected that the investigation had already lasted a year. But on the stand, both of the new Jewish witnesses who did appear stumbled. Chana Żelizer, who as a fourteen-year-old had watched from her hiding place as uniformed firemen dragged Jews from neighboring houses, mistook Wincenty Ajchel for one of his co-defendants. Nor could Chil Szejnberg identify on a hand-drawn map from which house's attic he had watched the ghetto liquidation.

In its verdict, the court acquitted all the defendants save Wincenty Ajchel, discounting prosecution witness testimony as unreliable, inconsistent, or motivated by family feuds. The only defendant who had admitted to a criminal act, Blue Policeman Kazimierz Ajchel, a distant relative of Wincenty's who had taken a Jew to the Germans in September 1943, was acquitted because the court found plausible his explanation that the Jew he had convoyed had blithely refused an offer of escape, because "he [the Jew] knew all the gendarmes and nothing would happen to him." Szejnberg and Żelizer's statements were thrown out:

> Insofar as these witnesses might objectively testify truthfully, nevertheless their testimony stands under a question mark and cannot correspond to reality. First of all, witness Chaim [sic] Żelizer at the moment of the event . . . was very young . . . and found herself in a state of great emotional tension, caused by events threatening her with constant danger, which . . . include[d] certain death; and in these circumstances could not make normal and objective observations . . . and therefore could in good faith be mistaken as to the nature and course of these events as well as the persons taking part in them.

As for Szejnberg:

> Keeping in mind the circumstances which he was in, his mental state induced by the threat of exposure at any moment by the Germans searching for Jews, as well as the distance from which he made his observations, the court has found [his] testimony . . . true subjectively, but it may not be true objectively nor may it correspond to reality.

Góra, on the other hand, had impressed the court as "fully believable and deserving of complete credence" and as a result the judges had formed the "unbreakable conviction" that Wincenty Ajchel had led a team of Blue Policemen and firemen in the liquidation of the ghetto. However, given Ajchel's "level of malice," intellectual and cultural development, his "aid to Polish society/people," to which numerous character witnesses had testified, and his supposed help to Jews—including to the Grynbergs, whose bakery he now owned and which Szejnberg said Ajchel had seized during the war with the help of a German policeman—the court decided that "in general he protected Jews from persecution" and committed his crime "under threats and orders from the German Gendarmerie," a claim that Ajchel himself had never advanced at any point in the trial. He was sentenced to five and a half years—six months above the minimum—as well as two years' loss of civil rights and the loss of his property.[1]

Despite the damning and mutually corroborating testimony of the prosecution witnesses, prosecutor Grzymała called on the court to apply extraordinary leniency in the case of Apolinary Sokołowski, the grocery store owner and fire chief who had been seen dragging a teenage Jew by a rope around his neck. Judge Kosiński, who had been a municipal court judge in nearby Międzyrzec when the war broke out, went one better. He downgraded the charge from Article 1 to the catchall Article 2, reasoning that because no one had actually seen Sokołowski physically apprehend the Jewish boy, nor had he given him over to the Germans—headman Edward Sady and cart driver Stanisław Kopyść had transported the victim to the Blue Police—his crime did not fulfill Article 1. The whole conveyor-belt mechanism of rural denunciation and capture of Jews—the negotiation between the original captor and the headman, the designation of guards to transport the prisoner, and the handover to the Germans or Blue Police with death as virtually the only possible outcome—was completely ignored. Regarding Sokołowski's punishment, the court kept in mind that the defendant was "acting under the . . . orders of the German authorities to arrest 'wandering' Jews on pain of death," although no Germans had been involved at any time in the incident with the boy on the rope.[2] In an oft-repeated formula, the court wrote that given his "heretofore impeccable behavior, level of intellectual and moral development, as well as help rendered during the occupation to members of the Underground and Soviet POWs," Sokołowski was to be sentenced to two years in prison with time served, as well as the loss of his civil rights for two years and the loss of all his property. The verdict passed over in silence the fact that one of the witnesses called by the defense on short notice, Zygmunt Makuła, whose story about Sokołowski feeding a Soviet escapee was credited by the court, was also said by several prosecution witnesses to be the original denouncer of the Jewish boy.[3]

Chaim Ajzenberg had been stoned, bludgeoned, and buried alive by a mob led by Zdzisław Kędzierski, his former trading partner. The investigation and trial, in which both Grzymała and Kosiński took part, were a textbook case of the pressures outside and inside the courtroom that militated in favor of defendants. While witnesses agreed on the key details of the incident, many still maneuvered to minimize their own involvement, with some even attempting to throw off the investigation entirely. After testifying before the UB and then the investigative judge, still more grew reticent at trial, presumably by then aware of the danger facing their neighbor, Kędzierski.

There was no shortage of witnesses to the chase, which had been an attention-grabbing spectacle in broad daylight in the small village of Wólka.

Even so, one of them was careful to preface his account to the UB by saying that he had only joined in the pursuit because as Kędzierski passed, he had shouted that "bandits don't let us sleep" and that he would "denounce to the Gendarmerie" anyone who didn't take part. Not only did it seem like an implausibly audible and coherent thing for a sprinting man to say, no other witness alleged that Kędzierski, a respected local farmer, had threatened anyone. Deposed two months later at the municipal court in Kock, the same witness suddenly denied having seen Kędzierski strike Ajzenberg with an ax, claiming to have been threatened by the interrogating UB officer, Karol Gmur.

Coercion by the UB was a not uncommon excuse of witnesses who altered their stories in the later stages of an investigation, but it was usually belied by the fact that no one else claimed intimidation—least of all, in this case, the defendant. Interviewed by Gmur, Kędzierski was hardly the picture of a suspect browbeaten by secret policemen. Instead, he cannily insisted that he had given chase, admittedly armed with an ax, to a suspected bandit just after logging the end of his shift with the watch commander; the suspect had been brought down by stones thrown by him and others. At trial, where he now claimed to have come upon the scene when Ajzenberg was already dead, Kędzierski did not use torture or coercion to justify his reversals, but simply stated that he couldn't remember what he had said earlier and that his statement might have been transcribed incorrectly.

The strategy of depicting Ajzenberg as a criminal also appeared improvised. After at first claiming that he had only been chasing an anonymous bandit, Kędzierski then said during his depositions at the Siedlce Court that the watch commander directed him to apprehend Ajzenberg, who was making his getaway after robbing a local woman's farm. The woman, interviewed for the first time at the Kock court, declared that Ajzenberg had robbed her before. According to her, Ajzenberg had boasted that once he obtained a gun—an unloaded pistol had been recovered from him—he would have "everyone by the ears" and would leave "several dozen children," presumably a threat to commit rape. For his part, the watch commander responded that while Jews had committed robberies, he had never suspected Ajzenberg, and the woman farmer, asked why she hadn't reported the crime involving Ajzenberg, said that she had feared bringing some "misfortune" on the village.

At the actual trial, held three months after the last interviews were conducted, every single witness besides Ajzenberg's brother-in-law, Abram

Rozenman, now said that they didn't know whether Kędzierski was responsible, that they had only "heard" of his involvement, that he had been in the rear of the mob, or that they had only seen Kędzierski rifle Ajzenberg's pockets as he lay dead, and so on. Grzymała moved to requalify the crime from Article 1 to Article 2. The court recognized that while none of the witnesses at trial had admitted seeing Kędzierski strike Ajzenberg, their testimony was "not completely objective" in light of the fact that several of them had taken part in the chase themselves. Nor could Rozenman be credited, because he was not an eyewitness.

Nevertheless, the "act of the accused to a high degree went to the benefit of the German state, striving with all means for the extermination and biological destruction of the Jewish population," and therefore met the standard of Article 1. However, the fact that Kędzierski was a respected local farmer with no prior record and that he had acted "under the influence of his surroundings and the psychosis created by the German occupier," merited the application of Article 5, although the verdict had not suggested that Kędzierski had acted under threats or orders. He received five and a half years, three years' loss of civil rights, and the loss of his property.[4]

Although a compelling force could be as diffuse and generalized as unspecified "threats and orders" from the Germans, or as concrete as an actual co-defendant, more often than not it appeared in the guise of some dead, absent, or anonymous figure whose existence in the narrative of the defendants, like a sapling springing up from the forest floor, grew from practically nothing in the early testimonies to be a towering presence by trial, as in the case of the young Home Army partisan Tadeusz Chojnacki.

Chojnacki had originally been acquitted in 1945 by the Lublin Special Court for participating, along with a superior who went by the nom de guerre "Comanche," in the capture and robbery of three Jews who were later handed over to the Germans. Although he confessed to having gone on subsequent hunts for Jews with Comanche—now living in exile in Scotland, safely beyond the reach of interrogation—there was considerable official support for Chojnacki before trial. Fifty-five people signed a testimonial confirming that his whole family had been in the socialist Underground, and the local Socialist Party and PPR organizations endorsed him as well. The court's approach was to recast the crime as a repression of Jewish criminality; in the verdict, the perpetrators were said to have been sent by their commanding officer, acting on a tip about a stolen bicycle, to arrest Jewish bandits who had their "seat" in the ruins of a factory in the former ghetto. The "circumstance" that a carbine was found in the hiding place of the detained Jews "serve[d] as proof" that they were in fact bandits. Because it was still dark, rather than bring the Jews before their officer, the partisans took them to the nearest headman. As for Chojnacki's culpability, "he was only the blind executor of the orders of his leader," since after all as an expert witness testified, iron discipline held in all partisan units and the "least deviation from orders was punished with death."

Overturning the verdict in June 1947, the Supreme Court under Judge Bohdan Korsak, who had been a judge since before Polish independence, cited "serious doubts as to the rectitude" of the Special Court's findings. The Jews had had "every right to defend their lives" and their possession of the carbine proved nothing. In fact, the trial "had produced no evidence of any kind" that the victims were behind the alleged thefts or that the partisans had needed to hand them over to the headman when by the defense's own account, their orders were to bring the Jews to their commander. The Special Court had also "completely passed over" the testimony of an eyewitness who said that Comanche, contrary to his supposedly leading role, had not even accompanied Chojnacki to the headman. Nor had the Special Court addressed the discrepancies between Chojnacki's testimony at trial and during the investigation.

Three and a half years after the first trial, the District Court of Radom acquitted Chojnacki again. In this version, Comanche's role was inflated to terrifying proportions. It was Comanche who had forced a civilian at gunpoint to lead them to the Jews; it was he who ordered the Jews taken to the headman and refused Chojnacki's entreaties to release them, threatening the defendant with a "bullet in the head"; and it was he who forced the headman at gunpoint to go to the Germans with Chojnacki's note, which had also been written at gunpoint. The entire responsibility for the crime rested with Comanche, whose "utter ruthlessness" Chojnacki did not dare oppose. The court commented sympathetically that "the situation in which he found himself is one of those situations created by the war in which there is no exit. How today can we dictate a posteriori the guide for behavior to the accused when that guide could turn out to be incorrect due to our ignorance of this or that psychological or circumstantial factor within the accused speaking in his favor."

Citing "public opinion" which was "no doubt well-informed," the presiding judge concluded by opining that if the charges were true, the defendant's father "would not today be the mayor of the city of Pionki," the very town in the ruins of whose ghetto the crime had taken place.[5]

"HIS BLOWS WERE, HOWEVER, ALWAYS LIGHT AND PAINLESS"

When there was not only no denying that a crime had occurred, but evidence of particular callousness, demonstrating that the defendant had gone well beyond what might be expected of someone who took no pleasure in carrying out the policies of the Germans, a frequent tactic was to argue that all was not as it seemed, as in the case the agricultural overseer who suggested his beating of a Jewish laborer was a "joke," the villager who only "pretended" to give chase, or the labor camp guard who only "shot in the air."[6] With the help of supporting witnesses, the courts created an alternate reality of people who only pretended to beat, pretended to chase, and pretended to shoot.

At the District Court of Radom, Janusz Gombrowicz, the former owner of an estate of over 400 acres, stood trial on charges of beating and terrorizing his Jewish laborers. Three separate Polish witnesses, including a former employee who was now a UB officer, testified to his crimes, which included beatings with clubs, setting dogs on people, and locking a man in a cellar as a punishment for collecting brushwood in the forest. Like a domestic abuser, Gombrowicz took the tack that he had beaten the Jews out of compassion: "In the event that the Germans had suspected that the defendant tolerated wandering about and malingering by Jews, either a German guard would have been sent to watch them, or the Jews would have been taken [elsewhere], that is they would have met a worse fate."

To compensate for the lack of German presence while he meted out his punishments, Gombrowicz used the hobgoblin defense; not only were there denouncers "everywhere," there was an evil German administrator who was known to show up "unexpectedly." As for the Jew in the basement, the Germans supposedly wanted to execute him, so to save his life Gombrowicz had had him imprisoned. Gombrowicz's general bona fides on behalf of the Polish nation were confirmed by a raft of witnesses, including the deputy director of Polish state radio and a professor at the University of Poznań, both of whom he had sheltered during the war. However, the Radom District Court found the evidence of crime unmistakable, even as it generally credited the defendant:

> Although the witnesses to a large degree confirmed the explanations of the accused ... the difficult conditions of work and reasons for his behavior, and finally his help to deported persons ... nevertheless the court's position is that these circumstances do not stand in contradiction with the facts uncovered at trial of beatings and threats, themselves partly acknowledged by the accused but only explained idiosyncratically, and in view of the fact that the actions of the accused were undoubtedly in line with the exterminatory policy of the occupier ... in the action of the accused are all the criteria of Article 2.

But the Supreme Court came to Gombrowicz's defense, ordering a retrial on appeal. The lower court had failed to consider a defense witness who reported hearsay that Gombrowicz was trying to save the Jew in the basement; furthermore, there was no evidence that the mistreatment of the Jews was meant to aid the occupiers. "Without the establishment of external circumstances, e.g., utterances, indicating an intent to debase the national dignity of the victims, it might be necessary to qualify these acts under Articles 239 and 256," the provisions of the general Criminal Code for assault and insults. The court's decision, issued in March 1949, two years after Gubiński and Sawicki published their criticism of the Supreme Court's jurisprudence, showed that the "verbalistic logic" they had bemoaned was alive and well. By this standard, virtually no murder or abuse of a Jew during the war could be punishable under the August Decree unless the perpetrator specifically declared his desire to aid the Germans. Even though the ruling did not serve as a precedent—it does not appear in any of the published collections of Supreme Court verdicts from the period reviewed by this author and the high court continued to generally regard Jews as one of the war's especially persecuted groups—it is proof of the continued ambivalence (and independence) that reigned at the highest levels of Polish justice.

Suffice it to say that the Radom District Court under Judge Bielski now wholeheartedly accepted Gombrowicz's story. He employed Jews "exclusively to help them escape persecution," he locked the Jew in the basement out of fear that the Germans would kill the man, and he had to treat the Jews severely "for show," lest Germans or Ukrainians be sent to guard them. All the prosecution witnesses were picked apart as tendentious. The "fact" that he had been seen beating Jews was dismissed as a "superficial approach" to his actions, since the witnesses did not know "what guided the accused and assume that it was about increasing output." Most gallingly, the court made the determination, in the absence of the testimony of anyone ever beaten by Gombrowicz, that "his blows were, however, always light and painless."[7] The misunderstood Gombrowicz walked free.

That eyewitness testimony of Jewish victims, even when they made it to trial, could still be futile in the face of a court determined to construct an alternate reality is evident in the case of Piotr Siedlecki. If the civilian court system had ever had a revolutionary axe to grind, Siedlecki would have been a prime candidate; he was the son of Polish landowning gentry that had fled Ukraine after the Bolshevik Revolution. His relatively "light" offense, exploiting the labor of several dozen Jews who had paid for the privilege of leaving the Warsaw Ghetto to work as farmhands, stealing their wages, and beating some of them, probably contributed to the court's forgiving attitude. Mieczysław Górski, the surviving Jewish foreman of the work party, put it: "I wouldn't say the [beatings] were due to sadism, but rather out of frustration." Górski had been party to several beatings, including his own, after he was released by the Germans for smuggling boots. His claims were backed up by a Polish worker on the farm who saw Siedlecki and his wife beat a Jew for trying to steal a head of cabbage and "some potatoes." The Warsaw District Court seemed content to give Siedlecki a slap on the wrist, sentencing him under the catchall Article 2 to the minimum of three years in prison, but the defense successfully appealed the verdict.

Whether out of ignorance of occupation realities or in a deliberate act of "stretching," the Warsaw Appellate Court, hearing the case in the composition of three professional judges, decided that Siedlecki's behavior had, if anything, been an act of charity.[8] His employment of the Jews had been "an activity which can be considered expressly helpful for persecuted Jews and at the same time damaging to the intentions of the Germans." What evidence was there that this employment had been motivated by altruism and not naked self-interest, as was routinely the case with the exploitation of ghetto laborers? The Appellate Court cited the brief statements of two witnesses whose only contribution on the subject of the Jewish laborers consisted of hearsay from the defendant himself: "I heard that Siedlecki treated Jews well."

He told me that he took them out of mercy, that maybe his act would be counted in the heavens." The other witness had come forward to say that Siedlecki only shouted at the workers "for show" when they were shirking: "It's impossible that he mistreated them, because he is a good man . . . I heard rumors that Siedlecki was keeping Jews. He told me that he was making IDs for someone. He didn't beat workers . . . He told me that he took the Jews only from mercy, because many couldn't work. The Jews always left with full sacks."

As for the prosecution eyewitnesses, their statements "were in contradiction with the ensemble of the accused's behavior." Most disturbingly, in a somersault of logic, Górski's claims were thrown out as unreliable because he was "unfavorably disposed" to Siedlecki for beating him. That is, even as the court acknowledged that Górski had truthfully testified about being victimized by Siedlecki, his testimony was insufficient for a conviction because he as a victim could not be impartial toward his aggressor. Having invented a Catch-22, the court acquitted Siedlecki.[9]

Mitigating factors, the most common of which were patriotic service, public opinion, and family status, could technically only influence sentencing, not the finding of guilt itself; usually rattled off summarily at the end of the verdict, it is difficult to know to what extent they colored the judges' interpretation of the facts of a case, but they must have to a wide degree. It is hard to believe, for example, that the pronounced "stretching" apparent in the verdict against Franciszek Sciborowski was unconnected to the reality that his arrest, as a widower, had left his twelve-year-old as the oldest family member on their farm. The stretching was necessary because the evidence was so damning. In full view of a large crowd of neighbors who had come to gawk, Sciborowski and his brother-in-law, with the help of the headman, had handed over a French escapee from a train to Treblinka in exchange for several kilos of sugar. What was worse, he later bragged upon his return that the Jew had given him some money to buy some sausages as a last meal, but that he had cheated the man and kept the food for himself. Without missing a beat, the Warsaw District Court wrote these off as empty boasts from the illiterate Sciborowski, who "in his backwardness saw himself elevated in the eyes of the village and wanted to remain the center of attention for as long as possible."

Finally, the court credited the defendant's claim that he had offered to let the man escape once on the road to the Blue Police, but that the Jew refused. "Although the escape from the train showed will to live," the victim's reported "apathy"—just how a man on the verge of death should behave is left unsaid—in front of a crowd of onlookers after capture "indicates the truthfulness of the explanations of the accused that the prisoner consciously chose not to escape."[10] In essence, the unsubstantiated word of the two perpetrators that their victim did not object was to be believed. Sciborowski received six years, while his accomplices received the minimum of five; the Supreme Court rejected both defense and prosecutorial appeals.

JEWS AS THREATS AND NUISANCES

We have already come across several desultory attempts at painting Jewish victims as criminals—the murder of Chaim Ajzenberg by Zdzisław Kędzierski or the Jews hiding in the abandoned factory in Pionki, for example—and indeed Jews, like every other group hiding in the countryside, could engage in crime, though their small numbers, lack of arms, and alienation from much of the rural community made it an extremely risky proposition. But if actual Jewish criminals or, as it was sometimes alleged, informers were ever targeted, those cases are not in my sample. Accusations of Jewish criminality were ex post facto contrivances meant to excuse the extermination of the handful of survivors and to take advantage of the August Decree's provision excluding common criminals from victim status.

Exculpatory rationales could be mixed and matched depending on the need. The verdict in the murder of Mrs. Wolf combined compulsion, best intentions, and Jewish criminality to excuse the four defendants who had successively taken part in her killing. Józef Katra was the only apprehended member of a group of firemen who had brought in Wolf; the court exonerated him based on his claim that his presence was superfluous. According to Katra, he had been brought along because, as in the tale of Sleeping Beauty, only his voice was capable of awakening slumbering Blue Police commander Adam Bartnik. Moreover, a mysterious, unknown man approached him in the forest and warned him that if he dared to release Wolf, the spectral figure would "make use of it."

Bartnik, in turn, was initially incriminated by his subordinate Jan Kuciak, who said that he had given the order to execute Wolf. But the court accepted Bartnik's explanation that he merely wanted to transport Wolf to her "place of residence" in a local ghetto, which "can in no way be considered as acting to the benefit of the Germans." It was not his fault, therefore, that Kuciak had killed her.

As for Kuciak, he successfully adopted the tack at trial that Wolf had threatened to denounce the local people who had helped her, as a result of which he had alerted his superiors in the Underground, who conducted an apparently lightning-fast investigation and ordered her killed. If he had failed to mention any of this before trial, it was only because he had not wanted to get the Underground involved and was "afraid to tell the truth." The court did not address the consistent testimony of a witness who reported that, several weeks before the killing, Kuciak and his landlord, who was also acquitted, had come to the witness's residence to search for Wolf, who was rumored to be trying to reclaim some valuables that she had stowed with the landlord.[11] Instead, the court praised the "clarity and logic" of Kuciak's implausible narrative.

Similarly, former Blue Policeman Witold Ślezak admitted shooting Berek Szmajcer when he attempted to flee the barn where he had been hiding near the town of Opatów, but asserted that Szmajcer was wanted for banditry. None of the local residents remembered anything untoward about Szmajcer during the investigation, but by the time of trial their testimonies had changed so wildly that Szmajcer was now recalled as the "terror of Opatów," a chauffeur and informer for the German Sicherheitsdienst who had robbed and raped his way across the region.

On other occasions, the moment of truth could resemble something out of a lazily conceived stage play. Władysław Chaciński explained that he only detained the Jewish beggar who later turned up with his throat cut because a "card" suddenly "fell out" of the man's pocket, on which was written the names of five farmers who had recently been robbed.

The combination of an anti-banditry pretext with alleged ignorance of the victim's Jewish identity was a popular one. Paweł Maksym was acquitted on the grounds that he hadn't known that the two women committing "massive thefts" from his vegetable garden were Jews. It was hard to believe that a citizen of Maksym's stature—wartime political officer for the local Peasant Battalions unit, president of the Rural Self-Help Society, vice-president of the local Peasant Party organization, president of the welfare committee, and cashier at the credit union—could not have known whom he was arresting, but no doubt he was helped by the fact that the investigating MO officer could

The District Courts 213

find nothing but praise for him as a distinguished social activist and that the lone Jewish eyewitness emigrated to Germany in the three years it took to bring the case to trial.[12]

THE ACCIDENTAL CRIMINALS

The courts did not always have to rely on elaborate pretexts to justify their decisions. With the urgency of the immediate postwar period behind them and a more flexible August Decree, they could simply exercise their discretion, applying diverse penalties as they saw fit and without much explanation. The fact that most perpetrators were not habitual criminals, but opportunists who had taken advantage of the occupation to act out in ways they would never have dared to in peacetime, was significant too. These "accidental" offenders received sentences that varied greatly for similar crimes but were still well below what they theoretically risked under the law.

Zygmunt Nowak and Eugeniusz Cieślak were both credited for the "sporadic" nature of their crimes: the former for defrauding and betraying an elderly Jewish couple seeking secure housing and the latter for arresting a Jewish woman while working as a communal administrator. Left unsaid, of course, was just how many murders one had to commit to cease being sporadic. But Nowak, a one-legged man who had worked in concert with a Volksdeutsche woman, received seven years for his two victims, whereas Cieślak—a PPR member and the postwar *starosta* (administrator) of a large town in Warmia-Mazuria—was sentenced to twelve.

In two especially tragic cases, two different sets of offenders murdered the children of Hanna Margules, but received strikingly different sentences. Anna Jankowska, in whose "care" Margules's six- and nine-year-old daughters had disappeared, volunteered that she had abandoned the children in a stairwell in Warsaw. Even though the court had no trouble acknowledging that leaving them "was equivalent to their death, which was well-known to every resident of Warsaw," Jankowska was given the minimum of three years under Article 2.

To compound the horror, Margules's seven-year-old son had fallen prey to an almost identical scheme practiced by Wacław Budnicki and Lucjan Wróblewski. After being paid tens of thousands of złotys up front by desperate parents, Budnicki and Wróblewski would bring Jewish children under their "care" onto a train bound for the Reich and then jump off at the last minute, sending them to their deaths. Although "only" three such incidents were documented at trial, the court wrote that "in all likelihood the defendants practiced the described procedure for a long time with many Jewish children." Nevertheless, the court qualified their crimes under Article 2 and sentenced them to fifteen years instead of a life or death sentence, because it couldn't be said with "one hundred percent certainty that the children sent off by the defendants died," although, of course, it was not stipulated in the August Decree that a victim had to have died in order for the ultimate sanction to be applied.

In its verdict against blackmailer Kazimierz Giebułtowski, who repeatedly raped his victim, the court seemed sympathetic to the victimization "in a particularly sensitive and drastic manner for a young woman." Moreover, the defendant's "lack of remorse" and the "trifling" way he had tried to minimize his crime in his testimony by calling it an "inappropriate joke" convinced the court that "only a longer period of imprisonment would teach the defendant the proper worth of another person's life and dignity." That having been said, the punishment the Warsaw District Court under Judge Krzyżanowska—incidentally, one of the only female judges to preside over a case in my sample—found "proportional" was three years, the minimum permissible under Article 3 for blackmail.[13]

COMMUTATIONS

Even for the unfortunate few who could not elude a death sentence, there was still hope. Twelve of the twenty Polish defendants sentenced to die for crimes against Jews by the District Courts in my sample had their sentences commuted to life or a term of fifteen years by President Bierut. We cannot know the exact reasoning that went into these decisions, but judging from the materials submitted for consideration—pleas for clemency from lawyers and defendants, as well as the official recommendations, or "opinions," of the sentencing court—Bierut, no less than the courts themselves, was guided by an excess of caution.[14]

Blue Policeman Walenty Chojnacki, who had executed a Jewish woman and her small daughter on his own initiative, appears to have been saved by a long history of Polish blue-collar activism beginning in 1912 in what was then still an eastern province of Imperial Germany, as well as his family tragedy—a son had disappeared fighting the Germans in the Warsaw Uprising—and verified aid to a Jewish girl his family had adopted and converted.

Other defendants could point to more recent services rendered to "reborn Poland." Stanisław Taras, who had showed such energy chasing down and killing two Jews, invoked his wartime service to both the interwar Second Republic—falling, wounded, into first Soviet captivity in 1939 and then German captivity until 1942—and to People's Poland from 1944 to 1945. He had re-enlisted in 1944 in the Soviet-backed First Armored Corps and despite poor rations, lack of equipment and warm clothing, the extortion of his family by the anticommunist Underground, and mass desertions, stayed true to his oath, fighting through "hell on earth" in Germany until the capitulation and being decorated for bravery. After the war he had joined the PPR, earning the enmity of the "exploiter class and village fat cats."

Likewise, Władysław Zdun had been a prewar Communist Party member, a wartime member of the People's Guard, and a postwar UB officer. As his lawyer, Antoni Furgała, a former Special Court judge now in private practice, wrote:

> I bow before the justice system in reborn Poland, but I cannot not give voice to the thought that the District Court as well as the Supreme Court are cherishing the worn-out principle that Themis [the classical personification of justice] must have her eyes closed. Closing one's eyes to the very great services of Zdun in the battle for Poland and democracy ... does not correspond to a sense of justice and right.

It certainly helped if one could claim to have been a second-stringer or one perpetrator among many. Village watchmen Stanisław Betiuk and Stanisław Lewandowski had grabbed a fleeing Jewish boy and thrown him "into the mud" while their superior beat the child's father, but because they were subordinates their sentences were commuted by Bierut in spite of the court's negative opinion. Bierut also showed mercy to Józef Fijoł after the sentencing court supported clemency on the basis of his age (thirty-seven) and his having three children, and the fact that his three co-conspirators had not been brought to justice.

Events could be completely recast during the clemency phase. Andrzej Wąsala and his apprentice Lucjan Wrona had both been condemned to die for killing a young Jewish woman whom Wąsala had been hiding. The Appellate Court of Kielce, which heard their appeals, recommended clemency for both. Wrona had only been a boy and subordinate to his boss when the country was "swamped by waves of Nazi propaganda," whereas Wąsala, who had masterminded the crime and returned to the scene to finish off the wounded victim, benefited from an almost complete re-reading of his role. Although Wąsala had treated the victim as an investment, liquidating her when the risk became too high, the court turned his human trafficking into an occasion for praise:

> [His] crime is closely connected with taking in a persecuted person . . . and thus with a good act, indicating that Wąsala was not deprived of noble human feelings for another's misfortune; even if we were to accept, which was not proven with complete certainty, that he received a reward from the family of Hela, it would not stop being an act worthy of praise, an act for which the accused could have paid with his life. . . .
>
> Thus this undoubtedly good and noble act of the accused put him in a critical moment in an excessively difficult situation.

Of course, taking in a Jew for money did not necessarily communicate anything about a person's character, and many of the August cases that had been turning up in the courts since 1944 involved the murder of "guests" who were no longer profitable or convenient to their hosts. The three professional judges behind the opinion could not have been so naïve; among them was at least one, Edward Długosz, who had been hearing such cases since his time with the Lublin Special Court, where he had presided over the case of Henryk Janczuk, who had bashed in Hersz Flechtman's head after he could no longer pay Janczuk's uncle. If the judges spoke in his favor, it was more likely because they saw no point in putting him to death. Wąsala had lived an "honest and social" life before and after the crime, suggesting that it was merely the "result of disastrous coincidence" and "did not arise from [his] character and psychological traits." There was no reason to think that he posed a threat to society or the "common good," or that his "complete elimination from society was an irrefutable necessity."[15] Wąsala was another of the occupation's accidental criminals.

THE UB AND THE RESISTANCE

The image of the ruthless—and often "Jewish"—UB relentlessly hounding members of the anticommunist Underground is one of the most familiar historical tropes in modern-day Poland, and its shadow darkens every aspect of postwar justice and law enforcement, enmeshed as the secret police was in those spheres. To be sure, thousands of members of the Resistance did lose their lives in open combat with the state's security forces or were executed after cursory proceedings in the military courts, but the August trials, with some notorious and later exceptions, were not a theater of the civil war during this period. If anything, being a member of the Underground was an advantage at trial—defendants could more easily claim to have been acting under orders—whereas the new regime's security services, far from being a tool of Jewish revenge, found themselves in the awkward position of investigating their own communities and periodically their own members.

Both the MO and the UB of the town of Włoszczowa, responsible for investigating the capture of Dawid Rozenberg by a group of watchmen in the village of Ewina in 1943, pushed hard to get the case against Stanisław Spiechowicz, headman, party member, and reserve policeman, dropped before trial. Writing to his regional superiors in Kielce a month after the investigation had been initiated, the local UB chief described the crime in much the same sympathetic terms as the District Court would when it eventually sentenced Spiechowicz to five and a half years and acquitted his two accomplices. Spiechowicz, head of the village militia, had only captured the Rozenberg because he was afraid that his "evil neighbors" might denounce him otherwise. The two other men designated to escort Rozenberg to the Blue Police "encouraged the Jew to escape by leaving him several meters behind, but he didn't want to." Explaining the decision to release Spiechowicz, the UB chief concluded that "there is no guilty party in the incident . . . since it was a matter of circumstances, and what's more this Jew was already mentally ill and not in full possession of his faculties."

Władysław Zdun, a closet communist and headman who had arrested a Jew in addition to two Polish and three Russian women during the war before joining the UB afterward, was sentenced to death despite the intercession of three UB officers and the wartime county commander of the communist People's Guard partisans, who testified that Zdun had been accepted into the movement after being cleared of the same charges during an internal investigation. Zdun's boss at the county UB office in Krasnystaw defended him as a faithful member of the UB post since its very creation and suggested that the charges had been "made up by the reaction [that is, anticommunists]" for whom Zdun's diligence had been "salt in their eyes." He concluded dismissively that "had Zdun actually collaborated with the Germans, he would have given up partisans or partisan organizers rather than these two grandmas [the Polish victims] . . . and would have received much more praise for it."

In the case of Majer Rozen, who had committed suicide after being arrested by villagers, the very same MO post where several suspects worked as policemen was in charge of the investigation. Not surprisingly, the investigating officer wrote favorably of the sole indicted suspect, arguing that he hadn't understood the fate awaiting the captive, that he had been a young man at the time, and that "one might say" his role was only "passive." He was acquitted.

On the other hand, the aforementioned acquittal of Tadeusz Chojnacki, the Home Army "forest gendarme" accused of capturing three Jews in Pionki, and the minimum sentences handed out to the socialist Polish People's Army commander Mieczysław Błędowski and his subordinates for robbing Jews were indicative of the courts' light touch when it came to members of the Resistance.

In the case of the massacre of eight Jews, including four women and a child, who were shot and bayoneted by a unit of the Home Army near Marzęcin, the Kielce District Court refused to convict any of the four defendants, and the prosecutor suspended the case against a fifth suspect, Franciszek Lech, who was serving as a county UB chief on the Polish-German border. None denied their involvement, but all successfully invoked the necessity of following orders. As defendant Józef Kozioł put it, "I was a soldier and merely carried out the orders of my leaders. It is not my place to philosophize whether the order is correct or not."

The Warsaw District Court carefully avoided ascribing anything untoward to the Resistance as a whole in its verdict in the arrest of Pola Berkowicz, who had been captured by local men and then transferred to the Blue Police after being beaten bloody by members of the village Home Army cell. While it sentenced the three conspirators to eight, six, and five and a half years, respectively, it concluded that "since the [Home Army] was not an anti-Semitic organization," the incident must have been the result of the "specific conditions reigning in [the village] and the character" of their deceased commanding officer.

If there was one August trial where the new regime would have had a clear interest in obtaining a conviction, it was that of Józef Wiącek, but here too there was no evidence of bias. Wiącek, who had received one of Poland's highest awards for bravery as a leader of the famous "Jędruś" partisan detachment, had already been surveilled, harassed, wounded, and imprisoned by the UB in the months before his arrest on charges of ordering the execution of two Soviet partisans and three Jews during the war. His brother was even less fortunate; sentenced to death for desertion by a military court, he was not released until 1956. Although several civilian witnesses gave confusing and contradictory statements about what had happened, the star prosecution witness was Stanisław "Dziekan" Dorosiewicz, a member of the Jędruś group who claimed to have been privy to secret discussions in which high-ranking members of the Delegatura ordered the liquidation of Jews and Soviets. However, not only did Wiącek have a wall of witnesses speaking on his behalf, but Dorosiewicz, who was serving a fifteen-year sentence for antistate conspiracy, was discredited by reliable sources as a disgruntled expellee from the ranks of the *Jędruś* group who had worked as a German informant in Auschwitz.[16] Wiącek was acquitted.

BEHIND THE VEIL

When the courts wanted to, they could easily cut through the fog of misrepresentation. Commenting on the conflicting testimonies of one man's friends and neighbors who had helped him to capture three Jews, the Radom District Court wrote, "It's clear that these witnesses, just like the others, did not sufficiently work out the details of their made-up statements." On another occasion, a judge who was sometimes harsh and sometimes forgiving pointed out what was missing from dozens of other verdicts which exonerated village functionaries for seizing Jews in their midst. The defendants, who had taken a Jewish man his two young sons to the nearest German police post twelve kilometers away, "could and did have the possibility of resolving the whole matter in a painless manner ... the headman ... by warning the [Jewish] family to disappear from the terrain of the village ... and the other defendants by not seizing the . . . family in their hiding place and by reporting to the headman that they hadn't found them."[17]

The Ministry of Justice created Offices of Prosecutorial and Judicial Oversight, although very little archival evidence exists as to what their role was in the administration of these verdicts. In almost every August trial in my sample, the case wended its way through the regular court system with no sign of manipulation from above. In just one instance, however, a document has survived that gives us insight into the limits of ministerial intervention. It is a letter written in June 1949 by the Stalinist appointee Henryk Podlaski in his capacity as director of the Office of Prosecutorial Oversight, excoriating the handling by the court in Siedlce of the case of Apolinary Sokołowski, the fire chief who had led a Jewish child by a leash.

Although Podlaski was a notorious apparatchik, his objections were not ideological, but legal. The construction of the indictment had been "faulty," failing to address Sokołowski's larger role in the deportations or to place his crimes against that backdrop. Nor had the prosecutor indicted the headman or cartman, even though they freely admitted their involvement. The court, in its written ruling, had not given any grounds for discounting the prosecution witness in Sokołowski's roadside arrest of a Jew, and the handover of the Jewish boy to the headman obviously fell under Article 1. If the court's logic in the matter of mitigating circumstances was followed in all cases, the standing orders of the German authorities to arrest members of the Underground and hand them over to the Gestapo could be taken as the basis for extraordinary leniency, in which case "sentencing of August crimes as mandated by the law would be *a priori* impossible." Going further, Podlaski touched on the essence of what made these crimes so difficult for the court to confront: "these are not isolated cases, in which it is necessary to analyze the motivation and circumstances—rather they are two documented examples of the extermination of Jews carried out by the accused in line with Hitlerite ideology."

The court's justification for its verdict was "not thought through at all [*zgoła nieprzemyślanem*]" and "obviously incorrect." On top of that, the prosecutor had not filed an appeal. Podlaski concluded by ordering the prosecutor—Grzymała—to submit an explanation of why no appeal had been filed, and to forthwith launch new investigations of Sokołowski, the headman, and the cartman. But Podlaski's intervention imparted no renewed urgency to the case. Sokołowski was not subject to new proceedings, and two years after the letter, the headman and cartman were tried and sentenced to a year and released, having already spent eighteen months in detention.[18]

SOLE SURVIVORS

If the government, judiciary, and society all had a say in the outcome of the trials, the voice of one key party was conspicuously absent: the Jews. Even in the rare cases where a Jewish witness remained, they often could not or did not come forward. Although it had already waned significantly by mid-1948, the civil war that had raged between the government and the anticommunist resistance since 1944 made it extremely dangerous for anyone identifiably Jewish to live or travel in eastern Poland. As Grzymała mentioned in his memoirs, "Jew" was "synonymous with communist in those days." The handful of survivors usually made their way in haste to western Poland or Łódź, which served briefly as an administrative center due to Warsaw's near-obliteration. Survivors, separated from their friends and loved ones, often only learned of their demise secondhand. Fela and Guta Feldman, for instance, wrote from the safety of Łódź to the prosecutor of the Radom District Court to request an investigation of Józef Fijoł, who had allegedly lured their father and sister to his farmhouse before torturing, robbing, and denouncing them to the Gendarmerie. "We would provide witnesses," they wrote, "were it not for the fact that even now we can't travel to that village, since from the moment of our liberation, Underground groups have been marauding there and we can't risk our lives."[19]

Jewish witnesses were also constantly emigrating. One of the most common problems was that by the time a case actually came to trial, witnesses had already disappeared. The evidence against former Blue Policeman Czesław Śmietanko seemed overwhelming. He was implicated in the beating, extortion, and killing of Jews by no fewer than five Jewish witnesses, as well as a former colleague in the Blue Police, Stanisław Kania, who said that killing had been a "pleasure" for Śmietanko. According to another witness, Kania had been driven to tears by Śmietanko's cruelty. But by the time the trial rolled around in June 1946—the indictment itself wasn't issued until December 1945—almost two years had passed since the original investigation in Lublin in 1944. Not one of the defense witnesses could be located for trial. The original complainant, MO officer Ignacy Grynbaum, was dead, Stanisław

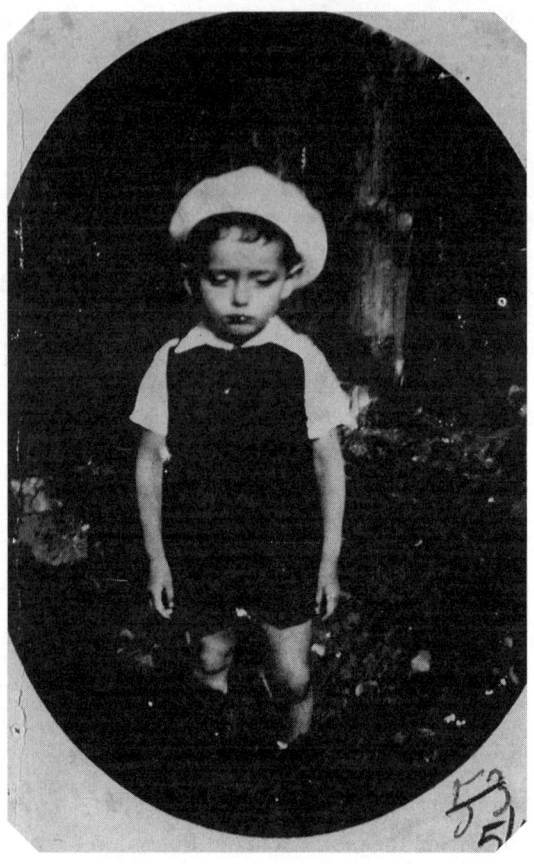

Few Jewish victims had anyone left to advocate for them; the murder of three-year-old Mojżesz Kwint came to light only because his parents had survived. Stanisława Tkacz, who had been paid to hide Kwint, confessed to having drowned him when the money ran out. Sentenced to fifteen years in 1950, she was paroled after four. (Photo: AIPN)

Kania was believed to have moved to Szczecin, and the rest of the Jewish witnesses had departed for parts unknown, most likely abroad, according to the prosecutor. After being postponed twice, the trial went ahead in their absence, but there was no chance the court would find Śmietanko guilty solely on the basis of recorded testimony, and he was acquitted.[20]

Likewise, Marian Grabuszyński was identified by two Jewish survivors as being a labor camp guard who had shot a fleeing inmate and even confessed. But both witnesses soon emigrated to the West, leaving Grabuszyński free to spin a convoluted tale about how he had only "shot in the air" on the orders of an unknown German civilian. In its verdict, the court condemned the Jewish witnesses for "not want[ing] to carry out their citizen's duty" and "intentionally" avoiding the court by emigrating. Most gallingly, it accepted at face value the preposterous claim of Grabuszyński's brother-in-law that one witness had come to him several months ago to swear that he would "retract all of his earlier statements as soon as he returned." The court applied Article 22 of the Criminal Code on higher necessity and acquitted Grabuszyński.[21]

For the same reasons it was surprising that the prosecutor at the Kielce District Court even went ahead with the trial of Natalia Kondera; a Special Court prosecutor had suspended the case eight months before. Kondera had fallen under suspicion when a Jewish refugee living in Sweden contacted the Polish Association in Stockholm to report that Kondera had recognized and denounced her during the occupation as she waited to board a train for Warsaw with her small nephew, who was later shot, while she ended up in a camp. In a notarized interview at the Polish consulate, she alleged that, after trying to hide in the bathroom, she was confronted by German policemen and Kondera. But with the witness abroad and nothing more to go on, the prosecutor had no chance of success.[22]

And, of course, if survivors were on hand, they had to be *willing* to testify. There were those who, emotionally exhausted by years of horror and suffering, simply wanted to move on with their lives. Janusz Bardach was told by his brother, "We can't find and punish everyone who hurt our family.... Let's not talk about this anymore. I made peace with what happened, and I'm going on with my life. I wish you would do the same."[23]

Others, disgusted by their experiences, had no faith in the system. Oscar Pinkus, who had survived the war in the vicinity of Siedlce, never entertained the notion of turning to the legal system:

> We were busy trying to get away with our lives—not to deal with Polish courts. We were not notified, were not asked to testify, we were ignored as much as we ignored them—expected nothing from the proceedings and received nothing. Though living in the open . . . we were in perpetual peril and even if we had been safe we would not have bothered to rely on a Polish court for justice or compensation.

In fact, Pinkus, who left eastern Poland in April 1945 in the wake of a massacre of thirteen Jewish survivors in a neighboring town and then left the country altogether six months later, assumed that the "main purpose" of the August trials was to "compromise and besmirch the Poles who leaned toward the London Government and the [Home Army]," indicating how suspect the trials could be in the wider consciousness of the remnants of Polish Jewry.[24]

Still others were deterred for various reasons. Szloma Ziserman held off on reporting the denunciation of his family because he was trying to reestablish himself as a farmer in the very same village where he had been betrayed. At the Ajchel trial, Moszek Góra is recorded as saying that he hadn't gone to the authorities when he returned to Węgrów in 1946 because he was "afraid." Revealing secrets buried with the war carried risks. Chana Żelizer had refused to name the family with which she hid, "because I could endanger [them]. . . . Poles have killed those people with whom Jews stayed."[25]

Thus, a person like Abram Rozenman, a key witness whose testimony initiated three of the cases in my sample, was a rare bird three times over: he was alive, he had stayed in eastern Poland, and he wanted to go on the record. For Rozenman, a forty-five-year-old Jew who had survived the war in the forests around Siedlce, the urge to speak on behalf of friends and family who had been annihilated, even to the extent of falsely claiming to have been an eyewitness to some events, must have been overwhelming. The war had left him with nothing to lose—his wife, child, six brothers, parents, and aunt and uncle had been killed, and Rozenman, uneducated and already middle-aged, had emerged physically disabled as well, having been shot in the right hand during a German sweep of the forests. Of the eighty-strong partisan group he had been with, only seven lived to see the end of the war, and he appeared to be the only one still living in Poland when he was interviewed by the Jewish Historical Institute in 1958. According to him, all he had left was "my little dog."

While acknowledging his contribution to the conviction of a Blue Policeman who killed two Jewish children, the court in Siedlce declared his claim to have clearly seen the events through the thatched roof of a hut located some distance away "exaggerated" and did not credit other "overwrought" details of his account. Indeed, after at first insisting that he had also seen the policeman leading a forest raid in which Rozenman's brother was killed, Rozenman admitted that he had only heard about the man's role in the hunt from others.

Interestingly, Rozenman's attitude toward Polish society was hardly one-sided. In his oral history, he described being alternately helped and hunted by local people after escaping first the extermination of the Jews in his home village of Serokomla, and then the destruction of the ghetto in Łuków. Rozenman was very much aware of what had become of both friends and enemies. He still kept in touch with a Christian neighbor's daughter who, though only a small girl during the occupation, had secured medicine for his wounds and deftly deflected suspicion about his presence. Rozenman also said that the forester who betrayed his partisan camp to the Germans still lived nearby.[26] It was precisely his familiarity with the local Poles—his role in the partisan group was that of a liaison to the Christian population—that enabled him to glean information and bring charges after the war.

But the meager results that Rozenman's testimony obtained could hardly have encouraged other survivors to risk considerable personal danger and the psychological pain of remaining in eastern Poland; of four defendants accused of committing murder tried in four separate cases based on Rozenman's denunciations, two were acquitted, one was sentenced to three years, and a fourth to eight years.[27] Jewish victims were peripheral to the proceedings of postwar retribution, whose executors saw their mission in different terms.

PATTERNS

To read the verdicts of the District Courts is to perceive the outlines of an unspoken but increasingly stable tripartite arrangement among state, society, and judiciary over the punishment of accused collaborators, one that was largely untroubled by the voices of victims and their advocates. But as 1948 drew to a close, Poland was entering an age of High Stalinism in which the government would second-guess its earlier pragmatism. The question was whether and for how long the public and the legal milieu would acquiesce to the state changing the terms of its tacit agreement, testing just how confident the "new order" was in its authoritarian rule and how willing it was to upset the consensus around the memory of the war.

8   COLD WAR CONSIDERATIONS

FOR POLAND'S Soviet-backed government, the years 1944 to 1948 were years of "struggle for political control," during which they "reined in their more radical ambitions in an attempt to win support."[1] Step by step, however, what little political opposition remained was excluded from public life. After months of harassment following the rigged elections to the Sejm in January 1947, the leader of the parliamentary opposition, Stanisław Mikołajczyk of the Polish Peasant Party, was forced to flee the country in October of that year. In August 1948, Władysław Gomułka, the secretary-general of the Polish Workers' Party who had opposed the blind implementation of Stalinism in the country, was removed from his post. With the forced fusion in December 1948 of the Polish Socialist Party and Polish Workers' Party into a new de facto Polish communist party, the Polish United Workers' Party (Polska Zjednoczona Partia Robotnicza, PZPR), Poland's Stalinists had consolidated their control over national life.

Despite totalitarianism in Poland reaching its zenith, the government remained deeply divided over how to approach August crimes and limited in its ability to influence the court system. Remarkably, in October 1950, at a time when the Soviet Union was one of only two nuclear powers in the world and its Chinese client was fighting an open war with the United States on the Korean Peninsula, the director of the Legislative Department in the Ministry of Justice, Leszek Lernell, was still fretting about "finding appropriate methods of influencing sentencing (obviously while completely preserving the independence of judges) when we see the necessity of correcting the political line of that sentencing."[2]

Although the fragmentary archival evidence does not provide a full picture of the debate, internal documents capture the struggles of competing groups of political appointees at the highest levels of Polish justice—the ministry, the Supreme Court, and the Prosecutor General's Office—over how to interpret the August Decree and what kind of sentencing policy to pursue. For a time, a harder line was ascendant, pushing an expansive interpretation of collaboration that more accurately encompassed the communal participation required for the conveyor belt of genocide to function. Suddenly, however, the effort fell apart. Partly, it was because the judiciary had successfully resisted pressure, demonstrating an unheard of degree of independence even in the darkest period of Stalinism.

But the government had also recognized that to advocate for an application of the Decree in line with the historical reality, thereby undermining the narrative of the occupation that had been carefully assembled since 1944, was to damage their own position domestically and internationally. Instead, by definitively presenting itself as an ally in burnishing the judiciary and the public's version of the past, the Sovietizing state could yet find a way to make itself indispensable to ordinary Poles. The myth of the past would become, like cradle-to-grave welfare or full employment, part of the compact between the communist state and citizens.

TIGHTENING THE SCREWS

For those in the government who favored punishment over conciliation in the matter of collaboration, 1947 and 1948 had not been successful years. The proportion of death sentences is perhaps the clearest indicator of how rigidly the August Decree was being applied. The ultimate penalty, which had been meted out in almost one-fifth of all guilty verdicts issued by the Special Courts, had fallen drastically to a little over 5 percent of all sentences issued by the District Courts in 1947 before rising to just under 8 percent in 1948. But in 1949, death sentences jumped to almost 14 percent of the total.[3]

How was this sudden change achieved? The ministerial authorities and the Supreme Court were certainly in a much better position to oversee the rapidly declining number of August cases, of which there were probably half as many in 1949 as the year before. Effective July 1, 1949, the responsibility for August trials was shifted from the dozens of District Courts all around the country to just fourteen Appellate Courts (*sądy apelacyjne*), each of which covered an entire region (*województwo*), Poland's largest administrative unit.[4] These, in turn, would be renamed "Regional" Courts (*sądy wojewódzkie*) in January 1951. In many of the Appellate Courts, August crimes made up a majority of the docket, at least initially.[5]

Presumably, the reduced number of venues also meant that the government could more easily lobby, cajole, and pressure the smaller coterie of appellate judges. The ministry boasted that the statistics spoke "irrefutably to the correction in sentencing of August cases . . . since the change in the Code of Criminal Procedure and the introduction of the Appellate Courts as the court of first instance."

To be sure, the attempts to actually replace judges were still stalled; we will return to this subject shortly, but suffice it to say that although 1949 was the first time the percentage of prewar cadre in the whole court system fell below 50 percent, the old cadre still stubbornly clung to their majority in the judiciary. In March 1950, statistics revealed that while only one-quarter of prosecutors had been serving before the war, 64 percent of judges had, and only three Appellate Courts had a chief judge who was a graduate of the new legal schools.[6]

Clearly not ready to declare victory but cautiously optimistic, Judge Kazimierz Bzowski, head of the Criminal Section of the Supreme Court, wrote in a March 1949 memo to Chief Judge Barcikowski that the sentencing of the high court was "currently, on the whole, on the appropriate level, if we consider the *entirety* of these verdicts." The "former massive suspension of death sentences for Hitlerite criminals," he wrote, "already belongs to the past. The mass of our verdicts, the vast majority, are beyond political reproof." Bzowski observed that sentencing "depends to a large degree on the personality of the judge and his political and social views. What counts is not just intellect, knowledge of the laws, often unclear and full of holes, logic, but also the legal sensibility of the judge, pushing his will in the direction of the publication of this and not that interpretation."[7]

In what was perhaps wishful thinking, Bzowski suggested at a conference of court workers in 1949 that the "judiciary of the older generation has undoubtedly undergone an important spiritual evolution" and that they were now among the "wide sections of society" to whom "healthy views of the Soviet Union have spread." He offered his own biography as an example. Although a member of the seven-judge panel of the Supreme Court that ruled in 1933 that membership in the Polish communist party should be punished under the more stringent articles on treason, rather than the lesser laws on conspiracy, he had undergone an ideological conversion during the occupation while waiting for the arrival of the Red Army, the only force capable of stopping the extermination of the Polish people. However, all was not entirely well, he acknowledged: "In the older generation of judges there exists a certain ossification, which can be ascribed to unconscious anti-Soviet and anti-Semitic instincts, which find their expression in some verdicts for whispered anti-Soviet propaganda and for betrayal of citizens of Jewish nationality."[8]

In fact, demonstrating that the August crimes were still a live issue, Minister of Justice Świątkowski had written before the conference to complain about several rulings of the Supreme Court, including one in which the high court concurred with the reasoning of a lower court that several defendants had been acting "predominantly in the private as well as the public interest" when they handed over Jews captured during a raid to the Blue Police. For the uncooperative, Bzowski warned that "no regime can tolerate a judge whose sentencing opposes the politics of the regime," and that those who continued to resist would be removed, although he preferred not to.[9]

As far as the Supreme Court is concerned, the evidence points less to an "important spiritual evolution" among the judges than to an old-fashioned administrative reshuffle. If the government had tolerated a generally apolitical stance among Supreme Court judges in the immediate postwar years, by 1947 they began to scrutinize the affiliations of the judges more closely. Of the ten Supreme Court judges most often involved in narrowing interpretations of the August Decree, Bzowski was the only one who appears to have remained in the Criminal Section of the court in 1949, the rest having been carted off by retirement (forced and otherwise) or mortality. That Bzowski, who had overseen more rulings restricting the application of the August Decree than anyone else, should have kept his job was a sign that he played an important role in transmitting or interpreting the changing wishes of the government to the rest of the court. In any event, this development did not betoken the deprofessionalization of the Supreme Court—as late as 1952, 85 percent of the positions at court were still filled by members of the prewar judiciary—but its composition was being tinkered with to achieve different results.[10]

WIDENING THE INTERPRETATION OF THE AUGUST DECREE

One of the surest and most striking signs of a renewed hard line regarding August crimes was the gradual progression toward a comprehensive redefinition of what constituted murder and capture under Article 1. Article 1 had two clauses: Article 1.1 covered "taking part in the commission of murder" of civilians, POWs, and "military persons"; Article 1.2 covered the capture and denunciation of persons "sought or persecuted" for "political, national, religious, or racial reasons." Beginning in February 1948 the legal understanding of Article 1.1 was steadily and definitively widened by decisions involving new appointees to the Supreme Court. The widening began with several rulings in the case of collaborators who performed functions other than shooting in the mass executions of Jews and Poles. As a May 1948 decision summarized it, "taking part in killing" was not necessarily to be construed as an action in "close causal relation" with the physical act of killing, but could also include indirect aid and support to the actual perpetrator, including transporting the condemned, guarding the place of execution, and all activities meant to secure the "peaceful" conduct of the execution. Most expansively, a ruling from September 1948 specified that "taking part" was "not only participation in the technical deprivation of life or attempt at the same, but all kinds of help and incitement, in a word, everything which according to the intention of the perpetrator may cause in any way the deprivation of life of the persons [mentioned in Article 1]." Of the fourteen judges I could identify who were involved in rulings to this effect, eight were recent appointees or delegates to the Court.[11]

The route to widening Article 1.2 was more circuitous. Initially the Supreme Court wavered over the issue of who exactly constituted "pursued or persecuted" persons; Jews were always understood to belong to this category, but the Court at first refused to include other groups such as Baudienst conscripts and forced labor deportees. Although the Court reversed itself on the latter group beginning in June 1947, the former group had to wait until October 1949 to receive the appropriate recognition. In September 1947, two weeks apart, the Court adopted two completely different views of whether illegal traders or smugglers could constitute a persecuted group. After at first ruling that, yes, a Pole starving during the occupation and thus forced to go against the laws erected by the Germans was "constantly in the position of a person persecuted by the occupier," the Court subsequently ruled that a smuggler could be so qualified only if his or her actions had a "political character." A rule of thumb was finally established in December 1948 that illegal traders could be considered persecuted, provided that their motives were not for profit. The overall tendency was to take a less exclusive approach, as evidenced by a December 1947 decision that the second clause of Article 1 did not apply "only to persons individually pursued . . . but also to every person in general engaged politically against Germany."[12]

The much more explosive question raised by Article 1.2 was about the criminal responsibility of those accused of denunciation and capture. From late 1947 the Supreme Court began to accept indirect responsibility (*dolus eventualis*) as sufficient proof of guilt in cases of denunciation or capture. Regardless of whether the perpetrator was acting in his own interest or directly on behalf of the Germans, it was sufficient to know that the victim belonged to the category of persons persecuted for ethnic or political reasons for a finding of guilt.

However, the court still held fast to the idea that denunciation and capture were the crimes of individuals, not groups, "limited to the person of the perpetrator." To accept otherwise would be to admit, in effect, that the capture of persecuted persons often relied on the cooperation and active participation of a large group of people—cart drivers, guards, members of raiding parties, and coordinators, whether headmen or others. An expanded interpretation of Article 1.2 would expose them to greater danger than the lesser Article 2, which provided for the punishment of offenses "other than foreseen" in Article 1. But it would also be tantamount to an assault on the memory of the occupation that the courts—including the Supreme Court—and the public had been stitching together since the beginning of the August trials, in which, at worst, a handful of "renegades" and incidental offenders had acted against their Jewish neighbors without the consent or participation of the wider community.

The Supreme Court finally took the stand that capture and denunciation could be a collective crime in June 1949, shortly before responsibility for August crimes was transferred to the Appellate Courts.[13] But the more complete ruling came several months later in the October 1949 decision of a seven-judge panel of the Supreme Court, assembled to issue authoritative legal opinions, in the case of two men convicted by the District Court in Tarnów of alerting the Blue Police to the presence of four Jewish women, who were then executed. The District Court had declined to find them guilty under Article 1.2, instead sentencing them to two years each under the catchall Article 2. The District Court verdict was in line with the restrictive, "verbalistic" approach to the August Decree, previously endorsed by the Supreme Court in a decision from February 1947, which capitalized on the fact that the second clause of Article 1 described only "individual acts" of denunciation and capture, whereas the first clause referred to "taking part" in murder. Now, however, capture was declared by the Supreme Court to be a "prolonged crime":

> Every moment of deprivation of liberty after the capture is a crime ... the state of criminality ceases from the moment of return to liberty of the captured person or from the moment of the perpetrator's loss of control over that person. ... Thus every individual, who until that moment has joined in the intent of the author or accomplices must be held responsible under Article [1], if he was aware that the captured person was sought or persecuted for [political, racial, or religious] reasons.
>
> In light of these principles and within their limits, the concept of 'capture' includes not only activities aimed at physical capture, but all those after capture which are directed toward the handing over of the captive to the apparatus of the occupier.

This was a clear triumph of the principle of indirect responsibility, intended to sweep up every auxiliary to genocide, in a word all the denouncers, headmen, watchmen, convoyers, cart drivers, and the like. The panel's position echoed the arguments of Gubiński and Sawicki: "If every murder had to be preceded usually by a string of actions leading directly to that killing, then every one of these activities ... should, as a link in this 'criminal procession' find its counterpart in the law; that is the *ratio legis* of the August Decree and should be the starting point for its interpretation."

Although the phrasing of Article 1's clause on capture was different, it was still the intention of the lawgiver to "encompass ... the full group of actions which, connected with each other and with the perspective of a conscious goal, are essential links in a genocidal action."[14] The panel cited precedents in which the Supreme Court had drawn the bounds for participation in murder "very widely" as proof of the lawgiver's intent, but it is hard to avoid the impression that this sudden turnaround was the fruit of some kind of internal administrative decision or compromise. If the Supreme Court had often been at odds with prosecutors in previous years, the panel ruling now reproduced the prosecutor's resolution almost verbatim, and in other parts engaged in logical acrobatics to avoid contradicting the Supreme Court's earlier rulings.

For example, although three judges, including Mieczysław Szerer, had ruled in 1947 that Article 1.2 applied only to "individual acts," the seven-judge panel—including Szerer—now argued that that precedent merely "excluded responsibility for 'taking part' in a crime—not responsibility for incitement, aid, or being an accomplice." The decision also moved to curtail the "stretching" of verdicts which Szerer himself had bemoaned in 1947, stating that the sentences for the crime of capture or denunciation could only be ameliorated through Article 5, which provided for the extraordinary mitigation of punishment, not by the "incorrect" legal maneuver of qualifying a crime under the catchall Article 2, which, coupled with the application of Article 5, would allow defendants to be sentenced to less than three years, as opposed to a minimum of five under a mitigated Article 1.[15]

Several factors point to the political reliability of the judges involved in the decision. Of the seven judges on the panel, three would later sit for varying periods on the rotating "secret section" of the Supreme Court, created as the appeals instance for the analogous secret section in the Ministry of Justice, which was eventually relocated to the Appellate Court of Warsaw, and from there to the Regional Court for the City of Warsaw (Sąd Wojewódzki miasta stołecznego Warszawy).[16] According to Leszek Kubicki, the secret section was initially conceived as a way of trying Communist Party members who were discovered to have been prewar moles.[17] It was soon repurposed as an instrument to ensure guilty verdicts on trumped-up charges, including August crimes, against a variety of opponents of the regime, most notoriously in the case of wartime hero General August Emil Fieldorf, who was executed after his appeal was denied by the secret section of the Supreme Court in February 1953.[18] Additionally, Rappaport, who was praised by Bzowski as "politically aware," and two other judges taught obligatory classes on Marxism to Supreme Court personnel at various times between 1949 and 1953, although as Władysław Grzymała's example teaches us, Marxism-Leninism instructors were not necessarily true believers.

LOOSENING THE SCREWS

Barely a year later, the pendulum swung back in the other direction. The occasion was the appeal of four men, including a headman and his deputy, who had been found guilty by the Lublin Appellate Court of the largely routine capture and transport of an escaped Soviet prisoner-of-war to the Blue Police. The newly formed General Prosecutor's Office requested that their appeals be dismissed, citing the now-established precedent according to which designating a cart to transport a victim met the criteria of Article 1. Instead, a panel of three judges moved in October 1950 to refer the case to the entire Criminal Section of the Supreme Court "with the question of the possibility of departing" from the previous year's ruling.[19]

As the eleven judges revealed in their decision, issued in February 1951, the 1949 ruling had failed to stop the stretching of verdicts and only caused further confusion. Since October 1949, there had been "many difficulties" in trying defendants who had "acted after the actual deprivation of liberty of the captured person as a result of pressure or suggestions" which did not however rise to the level of "threats, commands, or orders" as required for extraordinary mitigation of punishment under Article 5. In these cases, the lower courts had been "resorting" without justification to mitigating circumstances or acquitting defendants entirely. The "rule" had become "ingrained in judicial practice that those people, who only mechanically carried out their activities during the period of the delivery of the already captured persecuted person from one place to another on the order of an entity empowered to give such commands, bear no responsibility."

The Supreme Court's solution was to redefine "capture" yet again, narrowing it and shifting it more closely to the pre-1949 definition. Capture, they wrote, "ends at the moment when the [victim] is actually deprived of control over himself." True, the decision did not quite return to the definition of capture as an "individual act," since multiple perpetrators could be charged with "being an accomplice or aiding" the crime, but after the capture "all further actions intended to hand over the captured person to the German authorities *may be* [sic] punished, depending on the circumstances and motives of the perpetrator, according to Article 2."

Many of the people who had manned stations along the conveyor belt of genocide now risked much less. The example chosen by the high court to illustrate the consequences of their resolution made that clear: "Thus the... wagons, by which prisoners were transported, will be free from responsibility if the drivers only mechanically carried out the duties of a crew member of this means of locomotion, regardless of what aim they served, as long as they did not demonstrate intent to harm the captured persons."[20]

This time, the role of the government in managing the outcome was more clear. A majority of the judges behind this decision were individuals whom Poland's Stalinist leaders considered politically reliable. Of the eleven judges in the Criminal Section who signed off on the resolution, five were political appointees who had not served in the judiciary before the war, and only four did not eventually serve in the secret section.[21]

KEEPING UP APPEARANCES

Several exchanges recorded in 1951 offer insight into the aftermath of the flip-flopping over Article 1. They reveal little evidence of centralized decision-making, suggesting instead that policy decisions were being made, withdrawn, and rehashed by competing groups at the highest levels of the Polish judicial system; they also show that, having learned a lesson from the unsuccessful 1949–1950 interlude, the government would be more careful to approach the August Decree in line with its political interests—namely, the conciliation of Poland's working classes.

In April 1951, seeking to take advantage of the momentum of the February Supreme Court resolution, and reflecting the apprehension in the upper echelons of the judiciary over the mixed messages that were being broadcast to the lower courts, Judge Bzowski wrote to the Ministry of Justice, asking for their help in moderating the August Decree. While the Supreme Court's recent decision had "blunted in many cases the cutting edge of the excessively severe August Decree," Article 1, which contained the two clauses covering murder, capture, and denunciation, and prescribed death as the mandatory penalty, "had still not been revised." The minimum sentence for these crimes, even when extraordinary mitigation of punishment was exercised, was still five years and a month,

> a penalty too severe when considering that the crimes of this decree were in many cases committed as a result of the awful terror of the Hitlerite

occupier. The establishment in Article 1 of an alternative sanction consisting of a prison sentence would enable just sentencing, would reduce the number of too severe verdicts, and consequently would reduce the number of clemency requests and appeals.

The proposed revision was also intended as an olive branch to a population still suspicious of the new regime and in which the perpetrators were deeply embedded:

> Overly severe verdicts, still unfortunately pronounced in very many cases, cannot but arouse in the ranks of the sentenced, coming mainly from the class of the laboring peasantry, their families, acquaintances, and thus in the wide masses, dissatisfaction with the courts, and thus with the present government and our present order.
>
> It cannot be a good politics, which spreads resentment to the government in the widest masses of the people. And unjust, too severe verdicts, massively handed down for years, must spread that resentment.

Anticipating the ministry's response, Bzowski concluded that the "argument against the revision of the August Decree, that the Anglo-Saxon imperialists favor the Hitlerite criminals, is not a convincing argument." Justice and the "interest of our People's State demands" the revision of the decree.

Several weeks later, Leszek Lernell, in his capacity as director of the Legislative Department of the Ministry of Justice, responded that such a revision was "not politically advisable." Instead, he countered that the "negative repercussions of a rigorous application of the Decree" were already being "effectively averted" by the "correct practice of the Supreme Court" in suspending "unjust verdicts." Cold War politics, specifically the need to not appear lax at a moment when the Western powers were forgiving and re-enlisting their former enemies, dictated that the August Decree be maintained in its present form, even if, behind the scenes, the high court was doing its best to mitigate its effects:

> The present international situation, the multiplying cruelties of the imperialists, and the coddling of Hitlerite criminals does not create an auspicious climate for a legislative easing of the statutes. . . . The easing of the decree would disarm not only the apparatus of justice with regards to cases currently under review, but would undermine the basis of the

rule of law of People's Poland achieved through the issuing of just verdicts with regard to the greatest war criminals on the basis of precisely this decree.[22]

Internally, the Ministry of Justice remained conflicted. Its personnel seemed torn between the Stalinistic expectation of total control over subordinate institutions and an enduring sensitivity toward public opinion. At an intradepartmental meeting in June 1951, chaired by Minister Świątkowski and attended by representatives of the General Prosecutor's Office and the Supreme Court, fingers were pointed and criticisms were traded over the "disturbingly large" number of acquittals and the "striking liberalism" of the courts. Year-end statistics for 1951 would show, among other things, that sentences of ten years or less for August crimes increased from 79 percent of the total in 1950 to 85 percent in 1951, while the proportion of death sentences was more than halved, falling from over 10 percent in 1950 to 4 percent in 1951. More than two-thirds of all sentences for the crimes of Article 1 were being reduced by the exercise of extraordinary mitigation of punishment according to Article 5.[23]

Leon Penner, speaking for the prosecutor's office, defended his department, arguing that it was the courts that were responsible for the trend toward leniency. Although the discussion ranged over a wide variety of crimes, Judge Marian Mazur, speaking for the Supreme Court, cited the August trials as an area where the high authorities had failed to chart a clear course. Adopting a conciliatory tone, he admitted that "we have to act self-critically regarding the guidelines which we gave to the courts.... In August trials we tightened the screws sharply, but now we have changed our policy regarding these cases."

The issue was all the more delicate because the "unique attribute of the profession—the independence of judges—makes the issue of oversight often very sensitive." Even in the era of High Stalinism, this prerogative was something that had to be respected or, if not, circumvented discreetly, as with the secret sections. Mazur suggested that they should try communicating with the lower courts through "general directives, but legally sound [*merytorycznie słuszne*] ones, kept current." One of the department heads, Maurycy Herling-Grudziński, agreed that judges were being left to their own devices: "We tell them that criminal policy has to be sharpened, but we don't contribute anything beyond that." Henryk Podlaski, the Stalinist deputy general prosecutor, admitted that "on the one hand we liberalize, on the other hand give unjustifiably high sentences." He wasn't sure what to do either. Podlaski made the noncommittal statement that it was "necessary to examine specific issues and send orders to the field, for example in August cases, thefts from factories, etc."[24]

THE CHANGING "GOALS OF THE WORKING MASSES"

Handwringing notwithstanding, the Ministry of Justice and Supreme Court clearly viewed postwar retribution as a process that had run its course and continued to wind it down in tandem with the declining number of new August cases. The number of sentences being issued, and by implication the number of cases being heard, fell by more than half from 1951 to 1952. Although the total number of sentences held steady in 1953, it fell again by almost half in 1954. The Regional Court in Białystok reported with satisfaction that 1952 was the year of "breakthrough changes," when August crimes decreased from 60 percent of the caseload to 18 percent, a decline caused, they wrote, "by the ever greater passage of time since the occupation." Leszek Kubicki, the future minister of justice of democratic Poland who was interning at the ministry at just this time, agreed that collaboration as a legal issue simply "exhausted itself."[25] But, even as potential cases were being exhausted, there was also exhaustion with them in the judiciary.

As early as 1948, Emil Stanisław Rappaport, one of the most prestigious legal personalities to return to the court system after the war, had argued in a draft project on court reform that the August trials should eventually be curtailed by administrative measures if they did not end sooner:

> The cases connected with the wretched period of the Hitlerite occupation . . . are ephemeral [*okresowymi*] by their nature. They've . . . filled court dockets for three years now; in 1950, after five years of intensive effort by our courts, we have every reason to suppose that their number will be completely exhausted, and that the few remains of these cases can disappear from the docket thanks to amnesties and abolitions. After five years of pursuing these crimes. . . . People's Poland will certainly want to put an end to the further adjudication of these cases.[26]

In August 1951, six months after the decision circumscribing the crime of capture and denunciation, a Supreme Court panel of seven judges, the majority of whom were politically reliable and also sat in the secret section, officially enlarged the grounds for leniency. The specific part of the August Decree that was being addressed was the third clause of Article 5, which had been added in 1948 and called for extraordinary mitigation of punishment to be applied "accordingly," if in cases of denunciation or capture there were "particular mitigating circumstances." Exactly what constituted those circumstances had not been clarified, leading to confusion over whether, as the Supreme Court affirmed in its decision, "taking part in battle with the Hitlerite invader" or "performing a positive service for People's Poland after the liberation" should be taken into consideration.

The reasoning behind the new decision revealed the changing political calculus underlying these new legal interpretations. It was only natural, the court wrote, that new questions were arising,

> since a large amount of time separates us from the issuance of the [August] Decree, and an even larger amount of time from the crimes foreseen in the Decree. The criteria for evaluating the criminal act are changing in accordance with the goals set by the working masses in a specific given period and with the degree of danger of these acts in the same period of time.

Reminiscent of Bzowski's appeal earlier that year not to alienate the "laboring peasantry," the restrained tone of the ruling was one of understanding for defendants, hinting at the impending obsolescence of the August Decree. The courts had to ensure that "those people who, under the influence of specific circumstances of the occupation, allowed themselves to commit criminal acts" should not be confused with the more dangerous "criminal and fascistic elements." If Article 5 had been left vague, that was "no omission on the part of the legislator," but a signal that the facts of each case "must be understood and interpreted in keeping with the changing conditions of social life with an emphasis on their class content." After all, "with the passage of time the very character of the perpetrator undergoes change and transformation."

In the poor, authoritarian, and highly stratified world in which almost all Polish adults had grown up, there were few people who had not experienced at least one of the mitigating factors the Supreme Court listed that, as we have seen, were in use from the beginning of the August trials: "neglected social or civic upbringing, lack of education, the negative influences of the milieu in which the perpetrator was raised or moves, youth and lack of life accomplishments"—in a word, anything that "alone or together could have impeded the perpetrator's understanding of the entire moral-political and social consequences" of his or her act.[27]

Across the board, the state's criminal policy was entering an openly conciliatory phase. In October 1951 a new law on parole, which had been in the works for almost a year, introduced credit for good behavior and reduced the time served necessary to qualify for parole from two-thirds to one-half of the sentence. Those serving life sentences had to spend ten years in prison, rather than fifteen, before becoming eligible. Even more importantly, a year later in 1952, the first amnesty to affect August crimes was announced. It was a general amnesty meant to commemorate the passage of the first constitution of the newly rechristened Polish People's Republic (Polska Rzeczpospolita Ludowa, PRL), but it also applied to those convicted under the catchall Article 2 and Article 3 (the blackmail clause) of the August Decree. In the words of Henryk Podlaski, it was meant for those unfortunates who had "erred due to insufficient consciousness."[28] According to its terms, death and life sentences would be automatically commuted to penalties of fifteen and twelve years respectively, and all sentences above three years would be reduced by one-third.

"CONTRARY TO THE SOVIET EXPERIENCE"

Although the percentage of prewar cadre in the judiciary fell precipitously in the early 1950s, the decline belies the government's continued reliance on and nuanced handling of these veteran jurists, whose remit still included August crimes. Unlike in the Soviet Union and numerous other satellites, years of attempting to usurp the prerogatives of the judiciary had come up short. Judging from the documentary and memoir evidence, the legal and political worldviews of the prewar cadre, ranging from legal conservatism to ideological nationalism and anti-Semitism, appear to have continued to influence their decisions and those of less-experienced colleagues incapable of fully replacing them. Likewise, lay judges continued to be an ameliorating force on verdicts, as they had been since 1944.

In a retrospective study from 1954, issued on the tenth anniversary of the founding of the postwar Ministry of Justice, the authors noted, in the stilted jargon that was by then commonplace in official documents, that the replacement of the "old judicial cadre, educated in the spirit of fascism," had reached its "peak intensity in the years 1950 to 1953." The proportion of judges serving since before the war had fallen steadily from 64 percent in March 1950, to 57 percent by the end of 1950, to 45 percent in April 1951, to 26 percent by 1954. But the feelings of the ministerial authorities about these changes were hardly unambiguous, and the changes were not necessarily as earthshaking as they seemed at first glance.

For one thing, the apparatus still needed its veteran judges during those years, and not merely to occupy seats. Although plans drawn up in 1950 called for 2,000 new judges and prosecutors, the ministry's makeshift legal schools were only cranking out 300 graduates a year, most of whom went to work in prosecutor's offices, in addition to the 200 university law school graduates (out of over 1,300) who on average chose a career in public service. Moreover, the "'new cadre' was not always good cadre." Two years in the abbreviated schools were insufficient to master the required material, and the graduates' "general level of preparation" was described as "feeble." In the long term, the legal schools would need to be as long and as rigorous as their university counterparts.[29]

Behind the frustration of the ministerial officials was a continued commitment to a high professional standard for all judicial workers, and the conciliatory realization that the old cadre were an integral part of maintaining that professional standard. At a meeting at the Ministry of Justice in April 1951, Zygmunt Ratuszniak, a judge at the Warsaw Appellate Court and director of the Administrative Department, acknowledged that while it would be great if the "new cadre fit us perfectly . . . experience however teaches us, that that's not always the case." He reminded the other participants that they had kept on prewar judges precisely because of their "considerable professional qualifications" and emphasized that the "quality of the people whom we let into the judicial system" had to be raised. At a time when forced conformity and purges were the order of the day throughout much of the rest of the Soviet bloc, Ratuszniak warned against generalizations: "The mechanical division between 'old' and 'new' cadre may turn out to be erroneous, since the so-called 'new' cadre, which includes people who were formed in capitalist conditions, is by no means always suitable to our needs and a whole group of them have had to quit the apparatus."

Minister of Justice Świątkowski concurred that one had to "take an individual approach" in this "exceedingly difficult" question. Judges needed to have "not only high political, but also professional qualifications." Maurycy Herling-Grudziński, another judge and departmental director, asked whether it was really necessary to retire all 1,133 prewar judges and prosecutors. He proposed making a more careful analysis, because "if we don't have to fire them right now, then we could better educate the new cadre." The director of the Office of Judicial Oversight, Henryk Chmielewski, criticized the current practice of promoting legal school graduates directly to the status of assessor, the most junior official empowered to hear cases, without requiring the traditional internship:

> It's thought that [these] judges are politically and professionally mature, that the Office for Judicial Oversight doesn't have to hold them "by the hand." However, for every young judge running a small court who gets by, there's also a judge going straight to court after a year's schooling who runs into huge difficulties. If we fire 400 people from the "old cadre" without sufficient professional preparation of their successors, then we can expect a very serious decline in the level of rulings. The division into "old" and "new" cadre cannot go on. We need to divide cadre into "correct" and "doubtful." . . . We can't reconcile these two mutually contradictory aims—"judges of a very high quality" and "very rapid change"—without either slowing the speed of the change or giving up on the quality.

In response, Director Szyguła, who had called for the rapid firing of 400 people, insisted that he "did not at all have in mind laying off only people from the old cadre." Instead, he proposed classifying the judiciary into five different groups, with the lowest-ranking 400 being laid off over a period of eighteen months, as new workers entered the system.[30] Despite being part of the Soviet bloc, the Polish judiciary was not an instrument like a thermostat that could simply be adjusted to suit the government's needs.

It was even possible to say no—not without consequences, but without suffering the more extreme fates that befell dissident voices in the other countries behind the Iron Curtain. Edward Osmólski, a judge at the Warsaw Appellate and later Regional Court, refused to serve on the secret section and had the temerity to complain to Stalin's Polish proconsul himself, President Bolesław Bierut, about pressure being put on judges by the chair of the court. "In the USSR he would have disappeared the next day," but instead a commission composed of three politically reliable officials was assembled and Osmólski was fired after being subjected to withering criticism for various "errors" in his work.[31]

The recognition of the administration that their legal cram schools could not replace the university law schools and would have to become more like them—in fact, the new legal schools would all be closed in 1952—meant that, as before, old and new university-educated cadre alike would continue to exert both their independence and an oversized influence over their less-educated colleagues, rather than vice versa. While only 45 percent of judges serving in April 1951 were still from the old cadre, 72 percent of those in "leading positions" had begun their careers before 1944.

Noting that barely a quarter of the judges in the Gdańsk region belonged to a political party—countrywide figures from the same period showed that around 60 percent of judges and prosecutors had no party affiliation, and only 16 percent belonged to the PZPR—a report from October 1950 observed that new hires, suffering from an "inferiority complex" about their "lack of professional preparation and general education," were incapable of influencing the "political-ideological stance of their nonparty colleagues." As late as 1954, the Białystok Regional Court was reporting with consternation that

> the new people in our apparatus are not always on the offensive ... often only the resistance of the petty bourgeois milieu endures, the resistance of the old consciousness, based on the myth of a university diploma.
>
> More than once it has happened that young comrades have succumbed to the charms of professionalism of the old colleagues, that they become infected with petty-bourgeois and small liberalism.[32]

As for the lay judges, the "citizen factor" that was supposed to have revolutionized and democratized justice—and was still two-thirds of the decision behind every verdict in an August trial—the ones in Gdańsk still "show[ed] a tendency to unjustified leniency" and a "too often subjective submission to emotional factors ... in ignorance of the legal statutes." Citizens nominated by the local national council for duty "seek by all possible means to avoid their obligations and be removed from the list," and no-shows were so frequent that they were like a "bullet in the leg" of the court. In Białystok, the role of the lay judges was "not great, often none at all." A "large part" were guided by "emotional views," or "show[ed] passivity and an uncritical sharing of the opinion of the professional judge." They also demonstrated an "express tendency to liberalization . . . inclined to suspend punishment as well as apply the lowest possible sentence." According to a countrywide survey of their role, conducted in 1953:

> Their commitment . . . must be characterized as average.
> . . . The familiarization of lay judges with the case files is limited to a briefing by the [professional] judge on the day of trial . . . their activity . . . at trial is low. The majority of lay judges . . . listen passively and rarely ask questions.
> . . . A certain liberalism . . . appears in cases where the defendant is of a working-class background. . . . In general lay judges show a tendency to lighter punishments, not taking into account the necessity of general prevention. They often wait for the [professional] judge to take a position, and then line up behind his opinion. It even happens that lay judges strive to "whitewash" the accused, acting in the role of the defense counsel.[33]

The review of the last ten years drawn up by the Office of Judicial Oversight in 1954 insisted that the liberalism of the lower courts, an "expression of passive resistance to social change" with which the old cadre had attempted to "infect" the new, had by that time been "decisively broken." But all was not well. "Confusingly," it was now the Supreme Court and the General Prosecutor's Office that were mitigating the more severe verdicts, either on appeal or, in the prosecutor's case, by moving to have cases reheard under its discretionary powers of "extraordinary revision."

The fact that half of all judges had been working for only three years, and one-fifth for not even that long, was contributing to verdicts that were "perfunctory, incomplete" and which "insufficiently analyzed" the evidence, failing to convince even the "spectators in the courtroom" and leading the verdicts to be overturned on appeal. The other side of the coin was the continued "poor preparation of cases" by prosecutors, which was corroborated by other reports of passivity in the courtroom, like prosecutors whose concluding statements were sometimes only, "I support the indictment." The Office of Judicial Oversight itself had been and remained "under attack from Left and Right":

> These attacks have been expressed in accusations of the type "stop leading the courts by the hand, leave the judge to his own devices," "no one has the write to criticize rulings other than the higher court," and so on. Contrary to the Soviet experience, these sorts of voices have been heard even to the present in tendencies to liquidate the oversight office.

Without giving percentages, Judicial Oversight also pointed out that "that part of the new cadre recruited from university graduates," while possessing greater "theoretical-legal knowledge," had a much lower rate of membership in the PZPR.[34] Even at this late date, the judiciary retained a high degree of independence and never fully became a tool of the regime.

TRYING AUGUST CRIMES FROM SIEDLCE TO BIAŁYSTOK

Statistically, the composition of the judiciary might have been changing in the early 1950s, but the world of Władysław Grzymała, who was working as a deputy prosecutor and lecturer on Marxism-Leninism at the Siedlce District Court when we last saw him, stayed more or less the same. In fact, Grzymała, himself a member of the old cadre, was promoted and transferred in 1949 to become deputy prosecutor—and, incredibly, "nonparty Marxist" on the judicial education commission—at the reorganized Appellate Court in Białystok. The independently minded chief prosecutor there, a former radical nationalist who had been converted to socialism during his time in Auschwitz and whom Grzymała greatly admired, was eventually relocated to Warsaw after clashing with local officials once too often. But, as Grzymała recalled, the new chief, a graduate of the abbreviated legal schools who was assumed to be a PZPR appointee, nevertheless "treated us older legalists with respect and consulted us in the more important cases in which the investigation had been carried out by the UB." Grzymała also became fast friends with his immediate superior, a prewar graduate of Poznań University, despite initially fearing that the man might have "some Jewish blood in his veins."

In Białystok, Grzymała carried on what he seems to have considered his true calling, covertly intervening on behalf of Poles whom he believed to have been falsely accused of collaboration by Jews and, now, ethnic Belarusians. According to him, there were more August cases in the region than elsewhere because it had changed hands several times during the war, beginning with the Soviet occupation in 1939, and therefore there were more vendettas between the "activists" of the changing regimes. Because the local UB and MO were recruited "primarily" from among the ethnic Belarusian population, it fell to the judges and prosecutors to prevent unjust convictions. As Grzymała put it, "I'm not in a position to mention all the cases where I managed to save the liberty of a person, and often even his life." Among these were a female Polish medical student accused of assisting the Arbeitsamt in deporting Belarusians for forced labor—Grzymała suspended the investigation—and a barge captain implicated in wartime requisitioning—Grzymała tipped off the man's wife that the case hinged on the testimony of a single witness, who was persuaded to change her tune.

As before, Grzymała blamed Jews for making unfounded accusations:

> Indeed, few of them had survived in this area either. But those who remained alive ever more bitterly pursued revenge on those who had been involved in the deaths of their brethren.
>
> ... They were afraid to go alone to the hamlets in the areas where they had hidden during the occupation. Instead they gladly listened in the towns ... to rumors about who among the Poles had taken part in the liquidation of the Jews, then themselves appeared at trial as eyewitnesses.
>
> In this way the two Hryciów brothers ... fell victim to the [Jews'] ignoble schemes.

The family of the Jew Jankel Jęczmien, composed of several women and children, had perished during the war while hiding in a forest bunker. An enemy of the Hryciów family, who lived near the site, had allegedly told a Jewish survivor, one of "three or four" Jews who regularly petitioned the prosecutor's office, that the Hryciów were responsible. In Grzymała's telling, the survivor then went to the UB with several confederates, one of whom claimed to have been present at the murders. Grzymała had his doubts, and the situation was all the more critical because one of the lay judges for the trial was the Jewish sister-in-law of Minister of Industry and notorious Stalinist Hilary Minc. Over lunch, Grzymała and the presiding judge conspired to liberate the defendants. In a bold move, he adjourned the trial to visit the crime scene, where the eyewitness was unable to point out the correct part of the forest. Furthermore, the farmer who had been helping the Jęczmien family came forward to say that "some armed band" had killed them with firearms, which an exhumation supposedly corroborated; Grzymała then withdrew the indictment.

In the separate case of a young man who had taken part in a Jedwabne-like pogrom in the summer of 1941 in the town of Siemiatycze, when Jewish residents were forced to tear down a statue of Lenin erected during the Soviet occupation and give it a "funeral," the same Jewish witnesses from the Hryciów case accused a pharmacist of egging on the crowd. Grzymała interviewed a range of witnesses who spoke positively about the pharmacist; he managed to suspend the investigation and keep it closed, despite the complaints of the Jews to the authorities in Warsaw, who ordered it reopened but never followed up.

Tired of wrestling with the UB in various other political cases, Grzymała filed his resignation as soon as it was permitted in 1953, but was only allowed to partially resign and continued working part-time in the prosecutor's office until 1957, when he quit for good and went into private practice.[35]

A NOT-SO-IRON CURTAIN

At the apogee of Stalinism in Poland, its conservators had retreated from confrontation with the "working masses" and a still independent judiciary, instead embracing and endorsing the exculpatory version of the past that had been synthesized since 1944. Years before Nikita Khrushchev initiated the famous "Thaw" in the Soviet Union, a different thaw was already beginning in the treatment of August crimes. But rather than admit it outright, the authorities preferred to maintain the architecture and appearance of retribution while accommodating their constituents who were put on trial. As the postwar reckoning with collaboration entered its final phase, repression spiked before falling into a rapid and unbroken decline.

9   THE PRINCIPLES OF SOCIALIST HUMANISM

A FEW DAYS BEFORE New Year's 1954, Apolinary Sokołowski, the fire chief whose perfunctory sentence at the District Court of Siedlce in 1948 had earned prosecutor Władysław Grzymała a reprimand from the Ministry of Justice, mailed a letter to the Council of State (Rada Narodowa). A free man since 1950, Sokołowski wrote to request that the still-unexecuted confiscation of his property be commuted. Aside from the standard invocations of his misfortune at having "collided with criminal justice due to the express orders of the German occupier" and his otherwise blameless conduct, Sokołowski also appealed to the state's sense of fairness. Although he had served only two years in prison for dragging a half-starved Jewish youth by a rope around his neck for delivery to the Germans, he noted that "presently, verdicts for this kind of act are significantly lighter."[1]

Due to archival limitations, this chapter is confined to studying the work of one court, the Appellate Court of Lublin from 1949 to 1950 and then in 1951, after it was redesignated the Regional Court of Lublin. But the cases of anti-Jewish persecution heard by the Lublin court clearly chart the sudden spike in sentencing from 1949 to 1950, documented in the previous chapter, and the rapid deceleration afterward to the situation described by Sokołowski.

A close inspection of the verdicts suggests that the punitive interlude between 1949 and 1950 was not the inauguration of a qualitatively different phase in the history of the August trials. If previously the courts had accepted exculpatory narratives without question, they were now more willing to interrogate some of those narratives, but the increased skepticism was matched by the advent of an administrative de-escalation in punishment, whether in the form of mitigating factors, parole, or amnesty.

Although outright acquittals, especially in the face of considerable incriminating evidence, grew rare, the newfound readiness of the Appellate Courts to dissect the kinds of flimsy defenses that had been commonly accepted in the District Courts was accompanied by an almost blanket application of mitigating circumstances. The high leadership of state also carefully lessened the consequences of increased repression. Of the nineteen death sentences pronounced by the Appellate and then Regional Court of Lublin between 1949 and 1951 for crimes against Jews, only one was issued after 1950 and only one would be carried out. Four were reduced by the Supreme Court on appeal, and fourteen were commuted by President Bierut.

After 1950, the passage of time since the war, public opinion, and "socialist humanism" would be regularly invoked to justify the dwindling prison terms handed down, in many cases of a year or less. The understanding that postwar retribution was coming to an end did not mean that the judiciary had lost its capacity for independent thinking—individual cases could still take unexpected turns and, as late as 1954, the General Prosecutor's Office and the Supreme Court were still butting heads. But, in the twilight of Stalinism in Poland, there was no real impetus or reason to revise the story of the occupation cemented over the last decade; the country was on the brink of momentous changes, and the war was an increasingly distant memory.

CUSHIONING THE BLOWS

From 1949 to 1950, a new stringency was apparent in the adjudication of August crimes. What the courts had previously ignored was now acknowledged—the pressure on witnesses, the behind-the-scenes deals, the alternately threadbare and elaborate explanations for the conduct of the defendants—but the actual consequences of this newfound candor were uncertain.

The Appellate Court of Lublin dispensed with the typical flurry of last-minute defense witnesses and the backtracking of others in the case of the firemen of Chrzanów who, under their leader Władysław Ciupak, had captured or killed dozens of Jews. In its verdict, the court did not hesitate to state plainly what had been obvious in so many other similar cases: "The Polish witnesses at trial were testifying to the benefit of the accused under an undefined psychological pressure which was evident from the content of their statements. Even witnesses who hid the family of Sława Chamit [the key witness and survivor] and to whom she owes her life now deny their act as it if were something undignified."

It was unbelievable that in such a small village, residents who otherwise admitted to witnessing crimes like the capture of Chamit's son or the cutting of another man's throat could not recognize the firemen involved. The court noted that, by contrast, a Polish witness who no longer lived in the village did not relate such "unbelievably favorable moments" for the defendants, corroborating the "existence of an atmosphere" in the area which had made Chamit afraid to go to the authorities "even after the liberation." The death sentences on Ciupak and his three co-defendants were upheld by the Supreme Court, which noted additionally that a number of defense witnesses were unreliable either because they had likely denounced the Jewish victims whose capture they were testifying about or because they feared "mutual accusations from the defendants' families about still uncovered collaborators."[2]

Nor were the old excuses about phantom perpetrators and Jewish bandits as successful as they had been. In the past, the District Courts might have exonerated Antoni Paskudzki based on his claim, supported by the conflicting statements of his friends and relatives, that a mysterious gang of Polish Kripo officers had raided his farm, killed Szajndla Zysman, and forced him to bury her body. But it was not enough to offset the initial panicked confession he had made when the woman's brother-in-law, tipped off by a neighbor, came calling in 1949.[3]

Antoni Chruściel argued that he had beaten to death the Jewish man who had given him his property and stabbed the man's son because he feared they were criminals. But the court pointed out that all his excuses had been introduced at later stages of the investigation and were a transparent attempt to pretend that he was acting in a state of higher necessity. Condemning him to death, the court concluded that "such bestiality and dehumanization displayed toward unfortunate and moreover familiar acquaintances deserves the most severe repression, all the more so since it sprang from greed. His behavior, for which there are no words, in any event dictates that his name cannot be tolerated among the living."[4]

The court could be cutting when it wanted to be. The most glaring incident transpired between the father of Franciszek Kupczyński, one of nine men on trial for denouncing and murdering dozens of Jews in local forests, and Lejba Hot, a survivor of the raids. Mistaking Hot for another key witness, Kupczyński's father had offered Hot 4,000 złotys, apparently on the advice of his son's lawyer, as well as "flour, kasha, and eggs." All he asked was that Hot change his testimony to say that Franciszek was not present at the raid, adding that he had already "worked it out with the witnesses."

Mulling over the sudden recantations and reversals of defendants and witnesses alike, the court wondered "what kind of operations preceded [them]," since the excuses offered were "eye-popping" in their "illogicality." Some claimed that earlier confessions had been beaten out of them, although those confessions had been partial or were repeated in front of the investigating magistrates, while co-defendants interrogated by the same UB officers reported no compulsion and did not admit to anything. Some simply said they couldn't remember why they had so testified, while others strove to paint one defendant as a blameless "half-wit or even idiot." It was "obvious," the court wrote, that "it had been agreed upon" between the accused and the defense witnesses to "transfer the accusations against them" to the one participant who was "absent from trial and possibly deceased." The extrajudicial "stage management" of witnesses and defendants was so quick to react that a witness was even found to testify on short notice that Kupczyński's father was senile and therefore not in his right mind when he tried to bribe Hot.[5]

It would be wrong to imagine, however, that the Lublin Appellate Court was distinguished by its iron fist. In spite of the death sentences pronounced, the norm was the consistent application of mitigating factors to defendants whose crimes were hard to tell apart from those of their less fortunate peers, even as the court discounted their stock defenses. Perpetrators who had captured Jews were given lesser sentences on the grounds of "frustration and feeling[s] of injustice . . . caused" by unrelated thefts, while others, who had grown up in German-administered western Poland, were said to be involuntarily "imbued with the spirit of Prussian militarism, demanding absolute obedience to all orders from authority."[6] As before, social background, "intellectual level," and partisan service also excused those convicted from longer or more serious sentences.

And lest the Lublin Appellate Court be suspected of being a more pro-communist instance than its predecessors, it displayed no special partisanship in two cases in which former members of the anticommunist resistance figured prominently, finding grounds for leniency in both. Although both defendants likely belonged to not just right-wing, but far-right resistance groups—the National Military Organization and the National Armed Forces, it seemed to have no bearing on their verdicts. In fact, the one partisan who admitted to shooting a man in front of the victim's wife and daughter (themselves later executed) successfully argued, in contradiction to his earlier testimony, that he had not known the victim was a Jew. The court found him guilty of murder under the regular Criminal Code—since he was not "aware" that his act benefited the occupiers—and sentenced him to ten years, which according to standing amnesties from 1945 and 1947 was immediately reduced to four.[7]

Of the above defendants, only Ciupak faced the gallows. The death penalties of Paskudzki and Chruściel were commuted to terms of life imprisonment or fifteen years by President Bierut. The courts themselves had a hand in this, because the official opinions of clemency that were furnished to aid the president in his decision making were not always negative, nor did the courts of first instance and those of appeals always agree with one another. In Ciupak's case, the Appellate Court diverged from the Supreme Court in its recommendation, voting for clemency given his low level of education and the "atmosphere of anti-Jewish racial hatred" stoked by the prewar government, which left him vulnerable to the "stupefying influence" of Nazi propaganda. Moreover, he did not "belong to the class of rich farmers."[8]

But Bierut also commuted the sentences of defendants about whom the courts were unanimous in their condemnation. The Appellate Court's opinion, shared by the Supreme Court, of Adam Grzechowiak, a Blue Policeman who was sentenced to no less than seven death sentences, could hardly have been more damning:

> The direct, active participation of the accused in multiple murders of Jews, the large number of his victims, his cruelty and torture of the decedents—[shooting] them first in their genitals and then finishing off the wounded—his express service to the Gestapo, his greed for Jewish property and his vengeance when it was not rendered to him ... all of this demonstrates that the defendant is an individual deprived of any moral scruples.
>
> His repugnant character traits, his prominent antisocial and asocial instincts, along with a complete lack of any circumstances ... which could lighten his guilt, justify the necessity of the most complete elimination of Adam Grzechowiak from society.[9]

And yet ten days later, Bierut rejected that possibility. Then again, by the time the sentences pronounced in 1949 wended their way through the appeals process and landed on Bierut's desk, it was already 1950—in Grzechowiak's case, 1951—suggesting that the almost blanket commutations were a foreshadowing of impending changes in sentencing policy in 1951.

THE BEGINNING OF THE END OF POSTWAR RETRIBUTION

After the Supreme Court greatly restricted the statute on capture in February 1951, the high court began systematically curtailing harsh penalties pronounced only a few months before, while the reorganized Appellate Courts, now renamed as Regional Courts, took a decidedly more forgiving approach to those convicted, handing out negligible sentences for crimes against Jews.

The government continued in a conciliatory direction with its new law on parole, issued in October 1951. While the staunchest enemies of the regime—political opponents convicted of "espionage, terrorism, and sabotage"—were excluded from consideration, all other categories of criminals, including those sentenced under the August Decree, became eligible for release after serving half their sentences. Both of these gestures—a retreat and an olive branch—seemed to amount to an acknowledgment by the government that it had gone too far in 1949 and in 1950 in advancing a punitive agenda. The fact that the defendants were overwhelmingly peasants whose crimes had been committed in the relatively "distant" past was an added argument against a hard line.

The spirit of pragmatism was reflected in the language in some of the Supreme Court's revisions of lower court rulings after 1950. Reducing by half the sentences of six watchmen convicted in 1950, the high court took the unusual step in June 1951 of directly chastising the Lublin Appellate Court for not foreseeing the changing climate. "In the matter of prison terms," the lower court had "completely" failed to "factor in the time that has passed since the crime" and had "failed to recognize the principles of socialist humanism, by which it should be guided in sentencing."[10]

Clearly, this latest phase of socialist humanism entailed the de facto abolition of the death penalty, the source of so much controversy over the preceding seven years, even if it remained on the books. In January 1951, the Supreme Court had upheld the death sentence of Piotr Kłyza, who had hacked to death two Jews in his care while a neighbor watched out of morbid curiosity, but two months later sharply disagreed with the lower court's negative opinion in the matter of clemency. While it agreed that the murders had been "bestial," the Supreme Court still felt that the Appellate Court had "omitted" to consider

> the fundamental reservation which one must have about the expediency and necessity of the application of the death penalty in peacetime... all the more so in the present case, when eight years have passed since the commission of the crime.... This circumstance brings into question the purpose of carrying out the death penalty... as a means of general prevention.[11]

Needless to say, Bierut commuted the sentence.

Within days of its February 1951 resolution redefining capture, the Supreme Court began striking down death sentences. But it wasn't just the harshest sentences that were subject to revision. They also worked to bring less severe recent verdicts of the Appellate Court into line with the February resolution. As long as defendants could attribute the actual "moment" of capture to someone else, however tenuously, they were resentenced invariably to the minimum of three years—or less, given mitigating factors—provided for under the catchall Article 2. Interestingly, the possible penalties under Article 2 ranged from three years to death, but neither the Supreme Court nor the Regional Court would ever go above the minimum, demonstrating that Article 2 remained what it had always been—namely, an escape hatch from more severe verdicts.[12]

Part of the new reality was that a sentence of fifteen years, the longest defined prison term in prewar Poland and one rarely encountered during the tenure of the District Courts from 1946 to 1949, now became the stand-in for the death penalty or life sentence in those cases where it was otherwise impossible to ignore the malice of the accused. As before, the creative application of Article 5 permitted a downgrading of the mandatory death penalty in the spirit of "socialist humanism."

The beneficiaries included Stefan Gansiniec, a young SS volunteer from Polish Silesia who had worked as a guard at the Majdanek extermination camp. Gansiniec received only fifteen years for shooting to death a female Jewish inmate because he "undoubtedly acted in the framework of the general order to shoot in cases of contact with prisoners" and, most disturbingly, because he had allegedly executed the woman, whom he claimed had already been wounded by another guard, "out of mercy to end her suffering," a detail he himself had recanted at trial.

The situation was eerily reminiscent of one that had moved Jerzy Sawicki and Arnold Gubiński to pen their probing analysis of August trial verdicts in the country's main legal journal four years earlier. Then, in 1947, the Supreme Court had refused to add more than six months to the sentence of Adam Juny, the young Polish Kripo officer who had arrested a Jewish woman and her daughter who later died in a concentration camp. Now, in 1951, the Supreme Court reduced Gansiniec's penalty from fifteen to seven years, only eight months after his original sentence had been pronounced. The high court offered no explanation for its decision, other than that the Regional Court had failed to "take into account to a sufficient degree" the alleged mercy nature of the killing or "other established circumstances reducing the guilt of the accused, as a result of which the pronounced sentence turned out to be strikingly severe."[13] The decision was clear evidence that the courts, high and low, were returning to the sort of practices that the Ministry of Justice had once tried to blame on an insufficiently enthusiastic old cadre. Ironically, having rearranged the judicial system to be more responsive to the political leadership, the high authorities had decided to embrace a vision of wartime victimhood so broad that it encompassed even concentration camp guards.

MINIMUM SENTENCES

Like the District Courts before it, the Regional Court of Lublin settled into a pattern of giving sentences at or near the minimum—five and a half years under Article 1 with mitigating factors applied—to people who performed the most common, workaday tasks along the rural conveyor belt of genocide—namely, capturing Jews and convoying them to their destruction, with the difference that now only the initiator or leading party of each incident had to receive more than a token punishment, while all the others could be treated as accessories after the fact according to the February 1951 Supreme Court resolution, regardless of whether their actions had been coterminous or of equal import. Indications that unwilling executioners or supposedly passive accomplices had been anything but were typically glossed over.

The one-page verdict sentencing Józef Socha to the minimum for arresting a Jew he found in his cowshed was typical. In it, the court placed the blame on a dead headman and noted favorably that the defendants "did not beat or tie up the Jew, who went with them freely." This was, of course, a rather innocuous reading of Socha's own testimony, according to which he had not bothered tying the victim's hands "since we knew he wouldn't escape because he was frozen and could barely walk." Stefan Kilanowicz, who had helped Socha, was "free of criminal responsibility" because his role was limited to the "mechanical escorting" of the victim, though there was certainly something very intimate about the crime, with Socha lighting the wintry five kilometers to the nearest Blue Police station with a flashlight while Kilanowicz, armed with a club, brought up the rear.[14]

The Supreme Court's 1951 resolution also cleared the way for the "significantly lighter" penalties that ex-convict Apolinary Sokołowski mentioned in his letter to the authorities in 1954. The partitioning of the crime of capture, an act requiring the close coordination and cooperation of multiple parties, into an "original" sin followed by supposedly lesser, "mechanical" functions, meant that numerous instances of sadism and moral turpitude were now subsumed under the catchall Article 2, whose minimum penalty was three years. With mitigating factors applied, the actual sentence could be a fraction of that. One villager, who had beaten a thirteen-year-old captive with a farm hoe while the boy's father looked on, received a year in prison; two watchmen who had taken a Jew, a metal cable tied around his neck, via train to the Germans received a year and two months; a deputy headman who captured a man and then organized an overnight guard in shifts to watch the prisoner received one and a half years; and another, who arrested a whole family, received just ten months.[15]

What longer sentences were issued were liable to be revised downward by the Supreme Court: the high court reduced from five and a half years to one year the sentence of Paulina Welo, who had denounced the Jew her son had locked in their barn. Of more than a hundred villagers from Wola Przybysławska who had marched thirty Jews into German captivity, the four defendants convicted of participation in the convoy all had their minimum sentences under Article 1 cut down to between one and a half and three years. And of three cart drivers convicted of hunting down the Lejbus family, the one sentenced to the longest term had his penalty reduced from eight to six years.[16]

CONTINUING EVIDENCE OF FREE THOUGHT

If the handling of August crimes was characterized by broad trends, certain cases show that, even at this late date, the trials were not subject to a purely automated, predictable regimen. Indeed, the most surprising verdict of the Regional Court involved precisely that group which is now customarily assumed to be the principal victim of the Soviet-backed government: veterans of the London-affiliated wartime Underground. Acquitting all five defendants, veterans of the Home Army and Peasant Battalions, of the massacre of two Jewish families hiding in the forest outside their hometown, the court accepted in May 1951 that the families had been bandits and that the killings were a "justified action taken on the orders of the Polish underground government ... for the purpose of liquidating banditry." Fascinatingly, a military court, the dreaded arm of political justice in Poland, had acquitted the overall commander of the action on the same grounds in 1949, although the verdict was soon overruled by a superior military court.

Here too, the Supreme Court stepped in, overturning three of the acquittals and sentencing three former partisans to between ten and fifteen years in March 1952 in a decision that betrayed no sign of ideological animosity. As soldiers following orders, they were all subject to leniency, although there was "nothing" in the victims' dugout to suggest that they had been thieves. On the contrary, "a consistent picture [was] established from the very first interrogations [and] throughout the entire investigation that this action was about Jews." The order read aloud by the commanding officer to the hundred-odd partisans assembled was

> clear and unmistakable; it was necessary to liquidate the Jews in hiding. The number of summoned persons, the provision of battalion members with guns, the approbation of the commands, the movement in battle order through the forest, the surrounding of the forest to prevent escape—all of this indicates that by 'liquidation' the gathered Peasant Battalion members understood the killing of the Jews in hiding. That was the goal and Jan Pawelec and the defendants achieved that goal.

In this instance, the precedents set by the Supreme Court were unambiguous. Regardless of the defendants' function that day, indirect aid and support to the direct perpetrator of murder fulfilled the criteria of Article 1. The ruling's conclusion, although it was penned by three judges who later sat on the secret section of the Supreme Court, also avoided ideological condemnation of the Resistance: "Units of the Peasant Battalions and Home Army were an extra-military organization whose activity was legal and patriotic when they battled the German occupier or its agents—on the other hand when they conducted fratricidal battles with civilians, it was treasonous and cannot enjoy the protection of the law."[17]

THE CALMING OF OPINION

The sample used for this study ends in 1951, but by all appearances the trends established at the Regional Court held steady during the rapid deceleration of the August trials until their de facto cessation in 1956. By way of illustration we might consider the afterlife of the trial of Bronisław Szewczuk and Aleksander Turowski, two opportunists who had stumbled across a Jewish bunker in the forest in 1943 and reported it to the Germans in exchange for the belongings of the slaughtered inhabitants.

Per the Regional Court's operating procedure in what was a fairly open-and-shut case, Szewczuk received fifteen years and Turowski seven, a sentence upheld by three Supreme Court judges. Among the mitigating circumstances taken into account by the lower court were that the two men "did not allow themselves to commit this crime out of racial or ethnic hatred, but rather from backwardness." Turowski, in accordance with the 1951 law on parole, was released after serving half his sentence in April 1954 and a few months later the Regional Court endorsed Szewczuk's clemency request, citing the good opinion of his jailers, his family status, and the "importance of raising agricultural production at the present moment." The same three Supreme Court judges now concurred, arguing that since Szewczuk and Turowski shared responsibility, their penalties should not differ. However, the General Prosecutor's Office refused to forward their recommendations to the Council of State, leading the Supreme Court to pen an unusually long and critical clemency recommendation again in September 1956, after that year's amnesty had reduced Szewczuk's sentence to ten years. Evidently annoyed, the judges explained that they had originally upheld the verdict because 1951 had been "much closer" in time to the "tragedy of the occupation." But in 1954, they were instead motivated by the "calming of opinion after a long passage of time."[18] Szewczuk was released two months later, part of the amnesty wave sweeping the country.

10   THE MATH OF AMNESTY

THE YEAR 1956 was when Poland regained a significant degree of sovereignty within the confines of the Soviet bloc and, not coincidentally, when postwar retribution effectively ended. That year the state would merge the winding down of the unpopular August trials with the process of de-Stalinization, contributing to the lasting impression that the punishment of collaborators had been a fundamentally illegitimate undertaking. By forgiving both acts of resistance against the communist state and August crimes in its sweeping 1956 amnesty, the government further confused the necessary punishment of collaborators with the Stalinist suppression of political freedom in the eyes of the public, tacitly disavowing both postwar retribution and postwar repression. That the state should consign the August trials to the same dustbin of history as Stalinism shows how little their legacy concerned a government focused on seizing the future. Having helped shape popular memory of the occupation, the state's actions now shaped the popular memory of the trials themselves.

The euphoric year of 1956 was the climax of several earthshaking events that had come to pass over the previous few years, beginning with Stalin's sudden death in March 1953. His demise immediately precipitated a slow but steady "thaw" in Soviet politics and society that radiated out to the empire's colonial periphery. In Poland, the destabilization of the Stalinist edifice precipitated the defection in December 1953 of high-ranking secret policeman Józef Światło, who back in 1948 had complained about the political unreliability of the Kraków courts. Światło's tell-all broadcasts from the West about the scandalous inner workings of the Polish communist leadership rocked the establishment and forced them to fire the dreaded Minister of Security Stanisław Radkiewicz in December 1954. That same month, Władysław Gomułka, in detention since 1950 for his dissenting opinions, was released.

In 1956 the dam broke. Only two weeks after Nikita Khrushchev delivered his damning indictment of Stalinism in February 1956 at the Twentieth Communist Party Congress in Moscow, Bolesław Bierut, Stalin's Polish epigone who had been in attendance, died of heart failure; he never returned to Poland, but the text of Khrushchev's speech did, circulating widely. In June, protests over living standards in Poznań devolved into anti-party rioting and borderline insurrection. Though suppressed, the demonstrations sparked countrywide mass unrest, frightening the PZPR into appointing Gomułka as party secretary to general acclaim, despite the misgivings of the Soviet leadership, which was only dissuaded from mounting an invasion of Poland after face-to-face meetings in October between Gomułka and Khrushchev. In the world of limited options that was Soviet bloc politics, it was an unmistakable and remarkable victory for the Poles and their ruling party alike, so impressive that it helped set off the tragically unsuccessful Hungarian Uprising that same year.

THE LEGAL THAW

The legal component of the Polish Thaw was the amnesty of April 27, 1956, which essentially released everyone serving five years or less for a broad range of offenses, anti-state crimes pointedly included, and slashed all sentences longer than that. Terms between five and ten years would be cut by half, terms above ten years by one-third, and life imprisonment and death sentences would be reduced to terms of twelve and fifteen years, respectively. Almost all offenses committed by Poles in exile would be forgiven, provided they returned to Poland by July 1957.

In the recollection of Leszek Kubicki, the former Justice Ministry intern who was by then working in the Organization of Polish Jurists, the 1956 amnesty had "colossal meaning" not only for persecuted dissenters and anticommunists but for society in general, allowing the "whole political opposition to return" and "preparing" the way for the events of October. Indeed, close to 450,000 persons were affected by the amnesty, including 35,300 who were released from prison immediately and almost 300,000 who had proceedings against them halted. Nor was it just the former political prisoners and their families who had reason to celebrate. The same conditions were applied to all prisoners sentenced for August crimes, with the exception of those convicted of murder under the first clause of Article 1. Furthermore, all current investigations into August crimes were to be suspended immediately, and no new ones were to be opened, once again with the exception of direct participation in murder.

The stated reasons for including crimes of collaboration in the amnesty were familiar from the verdicts of the Appellate and Regional Court period:

> This is justified above all by the passage of a very long period of time from their commission. It should also be taken into account that these are crimes which cannot be repeated, that the perpetrators generally did not benefit from ... previous amnesties, that these crimes had no statute of limitations, and moreover, that the verdicts in these cases especially in the first years after the liberation were very severe.

But expediency aside, what was implied in their coupling with anti-state crimes in the 1956 amnesty was that the August trials, having taken place for the most part during a period of violent Sovietization, were effectively associated with that process and had now therefore become a casualty of de-Stalinization.[1]

Copies of amnesties from the "people's republics" in Romania, Czechoslovakia, and Hungary collected by the Ministry of Justice through 1955 indicate that the authorities were studying the various possibilities before 1956, but the specific impetus was the desire of the legal milieu to help the reformist "Puławska" faction of the PZPR strike a blow against the hardline "Natolin" wing in 1956. According to Kubicki, the chief lobbyist behind the amnesty was Jerzy Jodłowski, the former director of Legal Education at the Ministry of Justice and a member of the Democratic Party, one of the "decorative" noncommunist parties allowed to exist. A professor of civil law, Jodłowski also headed the Organization of Polish Jurists, the sole state-approved legal association, whose convention in December 1955 had "violated all the canonical scenarios" and turned the tables on attending premier Józef Cyrankiewicz, who was forced to sit by and listen as speakers demanded Gomułka's return to public life. This same legal milieu pushed for the amnesty to be as wide as possible, although its "main purpose was the release of the Underground."[2] But if the amnesty was also intended to gain "social acceptance" for the state and "settle the bill of injustice," as Kubicki put it, then surely the cessation of the August trials was understood by society to be part of the bargain.

CLOSING TIME

It was true that the trials themselves had mostly dried up. In 1955 only 247 people were convicted, of whom 208 received less than ten years and two the death penalty. Altogether, they made up only 4.5 percent of the total caseload of the middle-level Regional Courts, the courts of first instance for August crimes. Nor were many of the more than 20,244 people convicted of August crimes still in prison by 1956; the vast majority had served out their sentences or benefited from some combination of the 1951 law on parole and the 1952 amnesty. Statistics compiled by the ministry showed that as of January 1, 1956, there were only 1,532 persons convicted of "Hitlerite-fascist" crimes and 153 war criminals, presumably Germans, out of a total of 9,307 men and women serving time for "counterrevolutionary" and other nonstandard crimes.[3]

Other administrative steps speeded the process. Beginning in 1954 the General Prosecutor's Office also undertook a more concerted effort to have what it considered meritorious clemency requests reviewed by the Supreme Court and the Council of State, leading to drastic reductions in some cases. In practice, the only people who were likely to serve their full prison term were people who had been sentenced between 1944 and 1951 to terms that ended before 1951, when the parole law mandated that convicts could be released after serving half their term. Thus, someone who was condemned in 1945 to six years in prison would have the misfortune of sitting out the whole term, whereas someone sentenced in 1950 to six years was likely to be released after serving only three or four years. Of all the convicted perpetrators described in this study, none of those sentenced to life, or to ten years or more, or whose sentences straddled 1951 or were issued after that year did the full time allotted to them. They were typically released a year or so after the halfway point of their sentence. With parole being granted virtually automatically, the 1956 amnesty was merely an extra push. For example, a fifteen-year sentence in 1951 that would have led to parole around 1958 was now reduced to ten years with parole possible in 1956.

The 1956 amnesty deliberately excluded those convicted of murder under the August Decree, but that was mostly an empty gesture. As we have seen, virtually all the death sentences issued in 1949 and later were commuted, and a person serving a life sentence was eligible for parole after ten years. Thus, the longest term served by any of the convicted defendants in this study for whom information was available was twelve years—the prisoner in question was Paweł Jaworski, the deputy of Chrzanów fire chief Władysław Ciupak—and only because the lower court had not subtracted from his sentence the time he had served in pretrial detention, a courtesy extended to most other convicts. Adam Grzechowiak, the Blue Policeman who had delighted in shooting Jews in the groin to watch their death agonies, was the runner-up with eleven years, leaving prison in 1961, the same year as Jaworski. More fortunate than Grzechowiak or Jaworski was Antoni Paskudzki who, like them, had had his death sentence for killing Szanjdla Zysman and stuffing her body into a barrel commuted to life imprisonment in 1950. But after the General Prosecutor's Office decided to forward his case to the Supreme Court for review in 1957, a panel of judges headed by Mieczysław Szerer contradicted the court's earlier rulings by finding that because Paskudzki's motive was "not the desire to benefit the occupation authorities, but exclusively ... to steal [Zysman's] property," he should have been convicted of murder under the ordinary Criminal Code, not the August Decree. His life sentence was therefore immediately reduced to twelve years by the terms of the 1952 amnesty and, having served eight years, he was paroled two months later.[4]

The generally mechanical and predictable timing of parole did not stop the constant petitioning of the courts, ministry, and head of state by the defendants and their friends and family. While often formulaic, the requests occasionally let slip flashes of popular opinion. The mother of Krzysztof Tomaszewski, who had captured a Jew at the tender age of sixteen, complained that the "remainders of prewar Sanacja have unfairly buried my son in prison," apparently referring to the continuing service of prewar jurists. Paweł Jaworski's brother-in-law, on the other hand, hinted at the injustice of the Stalinist period when he insisted that his relative had been sentenced "at a time when he could not properly defend himself and could not prove his innocence." Some invoked sentimentality; very rarely were they acerbic. Letters written by children, presumably with adult prompting, were sometimes submitted to plead for imprisoned fathers. The family of Stanisław Wiejak, who was serving a six-year sentence for tracking and capturing Dawid-Henryk Polski, sent a charming hand-drawn postcard to Bolesław Bierut on his sixtieth birthday with an illustration of a little girl fretting over the drafting of birthday wishes. Dr. Józef Syga, the mentally unstable lawyer who had denounced a prewar acquaintance, mailed numerous rants to the authorities well into the 1960s, claiming that he was a victim of "Jewish revenge" and "Jewish criminals," and ridiculing—ironically, since objections to the same awkward wording had been raised within the government years before—the August Decree's phrasing for acting to the benefit of the Germans, literally "going on their hands [*idąc na rękę*]," comparing it to the nonsense phrase "entering upon a Jewish leg."[5]

THE AFTERLIFE OF THE AUGUST DECREE

If there was any popular criticism of the de facto suspension of the August Decree in the heady atmosphere of 1956, no trace of it remains. A 1957 report on the amnesty composed for the newly appointed minister of justice admitted that its "negative side" was the "mechanical embrace" of entire categories of offenders and recommended against the frequent promulgation of amnesties, advocating instead for the path of individual commutation. In an otherwise praiseful article on the amnesty published in the country's main legal periodical in November 1956, the author admitted that certain "paradoxical situations" had arisen with regard to August crimes:

> The perpetrator . . . who is caught and sentenced, benefits only from a reduction in punishment. [But] the perpetrator who has managed to effectively hide up until now benefits from a pardon. This is the reward for cunningly hiding oneself, for the concealment of evidence, and for lack of loyalty to the justice system.
>
> A no less peculiar situation arises in instances when—whether due to the necessity of preparing evidence (in many cases witnesses have to be interviewed on the territory of the USSR) or from other predominantly procedural reasons—a case lasting several years is not completed before the end of April 1956. Criminal proceedings in such instances will be suspended. An analogous case, in which a verdict has been issued before the end of April, puts the perpetrator in a much worse situation.

Only a few cases in my sample retain traces of the paradoxical situations described above, but presumably they must not have been uncommon if the phenomenon merited comment in a national legal magazine. Jan Borkowski, for example, went into hiding in 1948 and escaped the fate of his comrades in the capture, beating, and transport of a young Jew, all of whom were sentenced to five and a half year terms. Living under a false name and working in lumber yards, he had founded a communist youth circle at his place of employment and eventually became the secretary of the local party organization. Hearing of the impending amnesty, he turned himself in to the General Prosecutor's Office in April 1956. Four months later the outstanding charges against him for capture under Article 1 were officially dropped.

Blue Police commander Ignacy Łaganowski did not have to go to quite the same lengths. Freed on his own recognizance before he was convicted of murder in 1947 under Article 1 and sentenced to the minimum of five and a half years, he had spent nine years hiding in, of all places, his own house, before surrendering in May 1956. Although not technically eligible for amnesty—among other things, he had ordered a small Jewish boy to be shot—his lawyer bewailed the "severe penal repression in the period of [Łaganowski's] sentencing, i.e., 1947 and 1948," and argued that "in light of the present interpretation of the rules of the August Decree" his case was "trifling." The Regional Court prosecutor recommended clemency given Łaganowski's "earnest admissions" and the Council of State obliged by commuting his sentence in its entirety.[6]

The exclusion of the crime of murder under Article 1 from the 1956 amnesty was not just a fig leaf—there were still twenty, thirteen, and seven guilty verdicts issued in 1958, 1959, and 1960, respectively, with two death sentences in 1959—and the law, minus the death penalty, remains in force to this day. But for all intents and purposes, 1956, with the mothballing of the August Decree, marked the cessation of postwar retribution in Poland. In the estimation of Leszek Kubicki, the preservation of Article 1 was a "symbolic" gesture intended to contrast with Western reluctance to pursue war criminals in the "continuing ideological conflict" between the Eastern and Western blocs: "Due to political considerations it was not possible in [the 1956] amnesty to do the same that the West was accused of." In 1964, People's Poland passed a law suspending the twenty-year statute of limitations in regard to Article 1, and Poland was also a major supporter of the 1968 UN Convention on the Non-Applicability of Statutory Limitations to War Crimes and Crimes Against Humanity.[7]

THE AUGUST TRIALS IN POST-SOVIET POLAND

For over forty years, the August cases—inconvenient truths and unflattering stories that had been exposed by a branch, however independent, of a state otherwise associated with political co-optation, repression, and doublespeak—disappeared from view, buried beneath more immediate issues and the weight of a national mythology that had no use for them. That would only change in 2000 with the publication of Jan Gross's book *Neighbors,* which drew from newly unsealed case files regarding the 1941 pogrom in the village of Jedwabne.

The likely extent to which the verdicts of the August trials, for those who could remember them, were assumed to have been invalidated by the passage of time is reflected by the requests for rehabilitation that were submitted following the promulgation in postcommunist Poland of a 1991 law, "On Vacating the Convictions of Persons Repressed for Actions on Behalf of Polish Independence." This is not the place for an analysis of the scale of the response to the law, which was intended to clear the records of members of the political and military opposition who had been punished for resisting the communists between 1944 and 1956, or the quality of the judgments in its name. It remains, as Alina Skibińska writes, a topic requiring further and separate investigation.[8] Suffice it to say that it also seems to have attracted a number of former August trial defendants who assumed that, without much effort on their part, any complaint about a ruling from the "Soviet" period would be favorably received. In the four instances I came across in my sample, all from the Lublin area, the petitioners were to be disappointed. The daughter of Michał Gołębiowski, who had ambushed and hacked Ajzyk Wasung with an axe, failed to provide any evidence that her father was a member of a resistance organization. Bronisław Wójtowicz, seeking to have his conviction for convoying thirty Jews overturned, gave conflicting and contradictory statements about when and for how long he was a member of the Underground. In any event, the court ruled in 1999 that "the mere belonging of the petitioner in the designated period to an independence organization, even if that membership had actually existed . . . would not be sufficient to accept a connection between it and [his] punishment."[9]

That same year the court rejected the petition of the daughter of Jan Mazur, who along with his brother the fire chief had captured twenty Jews and sent them to the Germans. In its ruling, the Lublin District Court noted that there was no evidence that the crime of which he had been convicted had been for the benefit of Polish independence as the law demanded, and soberly observed,

> This case may serve as an example justifying the thesis that mere service in the ranks of the Home Army is not equivalent to activity on behalf of Polish independence, since the justified fear of repression by the German occupier [which had been Mazur's defense] was so strong that the accused . . . decided to "provide convoying services on behalf of the Hitlerite authorities."[10]

Most remarkable was the request of Stanisław Taras, who did not claim to have been a member of any resistance group but applied to have his conviction for hacking to death two Jews vacated because it was preventing him from receiving benefits as a decorated combat veteran of the Polish Army on the Eastern Front. Appearing at the Regional Court of Lublin as an eighty-one-year-old in 1996, he remained curiously unselfconscious, admitting his guilt, but arguing that "if he hadn't killed the Jews, they would have escaped." The court, apparently shocked by this matter-of-fact display, opined in the conclusion to its ruling that while the "petitioner committed a crime, whose disgraceful shadow of anti-Semitism has been cast over all of Polish society up until today," one could still take comfort in the knowledge that "incidents such as this one . . . were entirely isolated."[11]

But other courts preferred not to acknowledge any "exceptions" to the rule. As Alina Skibińska noted, "there are many indications that the verdicts in these cases did not have an exclusively meritorious character, but were also political." Indeed, in one case cited by her, the Regional Court in Kielce summarily granted the request of Wincenty Tomasik, a Home Army partisan officer who had been sentenced to ten years in prison for massacres committed by soldiers under his command. At the original trial, Tomasik had not denied that the massacres had happened, merely that they had taken place without his authorization. Without referring to or citing any details of the case other than the incontrovertible fact of Tomasik's wartime service, the court canceled his conviction in a 200-word ruling.[12]

In another series of cases documented by Skibińska, the famed *Wybranieccy* Home Army partisan unit in the Kielce region was implicated in the murder and robbery of multiple Jewish men, women, and children, as well their Polish helpers. Three former unit members, including commander Marian "Barabasz" Sołtysiak, were convicted between 1951 and 1952 of taking part in the killings, given "surprisingly light" sentences, and then released from prison between 1953 and 1957. The convictions of two of the men, Sołtysiak and Władysław Szumielewicz, eventually were overturned under the 1991 law. A third, Edward Skrobot, who became an activist in the state-sponsored veterans' movement in the 1960s and was even awarded a Virtuti Militari, Poland's highest military honor, by the communist government for his wartime service, was found not guilty in a new trial in 1996.

THE LEARNING PROCESS

The year 1956 represented a limited but major victory of the Polish people over their Soviet-imposed leaders. The worst Stalinists, having terrorized society for a decade, were forced from office and the government conceded a degree of freedom in public life that would remain inconceivable for decades afterward in the Soviet Union and even in other neighboring satellites, such as Czechoslovakia and East Germany. But it would be a misunderstanding to view these events as a simple alteration in the balance of power between two supposedly implacable opponents, the communist state and the rebellious society. Through the August trials, the government had learned to respond to its citizens, to mimic their hopes and dreams, and to cater to their less-noble impulses. The state's changing interpretations of the laws and concessions to popular and judicial pressure had helped to conceal the wartime ethnic cleansing of Jews by Poles and obscure its significance. Meanwhile, the deceptions of the public on behalf of the defendants—evaluated, often accepted, and sometimes abetted by the professional judiciary—had exonerated or mitigated the sentences of many offenders while creating a legally codified memory of the occupation from which evidence of Polish participation in the ethnic cleansing of the Jews was excised. Even if the postcommunist state overturned the convictions of Underground members justly accused of capturing and killing Jews, it could not and would not overturn the larger verdict agreed upon by state, society, and judiciary.

CONCLUSION

The Conspiracy of Memory

INSOFAR AS THE Holocaust remains a flashpoint in Polish society—capable of seizing the national conversation and provoking international incidents three-quarters of a century after the end of the Second World War—the August trials are never far beneath the surface of contemporary debate. Their centrality stems from the fact that their proceedings documented, in an incomparably candid manner, wartime conduct at the ground level; reexamined decades later, these cases complicate the purely heroic depiction of the war in Poland. The trial evidence suggests that the involvement of Poles in the ethnic cleansing of their Jewish neighbors, particularly in the countryside, was more enthusiastic, more elaborate, and more widespread than previously believed.

But as we have seen, it was never the intention of the Soviet-backed state, the fiercely independent judiciary, or the recalcitrant society that took part in the trials to create a lasting indictment of wartime behavior. On the contrary, the verdicts they forged together reflected a consensus about the need to excuse much of that wartime conduct and codify a variety of exculpatory myths about the war. The myths they created live on today, but the story of the trials, of their comparative independence and sophistication—and their legacy, the collaborative, tripartite nature of the shaping of memory under communism—have been forgotten or obscured. Successive Polish governments have refused to acknowledge the role of the communist period in shaping modern Polish identity and promoted the idea that 1939 to 1989 was a period of continuous, uncompromising struggle against foreign rule. To this end, hundreds of millions of dollars have been invested in an academic-bureaucratic infrastructure, the Institute of National Remembrance (Instytut Pamięci Narodowej, IPN), whose mission is to uphold the state-sponsored narratives of the past and to combat any scholarship critical of them.

Although the IPN has been controversial since its founding in 1999, it has fluctuated between periods of lesser and greater politicization for most of its history.[1] Its three-year investigation into the 1941 massacre at Jedwabne, which concluded that Polish civilians played the "decisive role in the realization" in the burning alive of several hundred Jews in a barn, is widely accepted as definitive and meticulous. But by 2016, foreshadowing the controversy in 2018, the IPN's duties were expanded by the PiS government to include "popularizing . . . the recent history of Poland as an element of patriotic education" and "counteracting the spread at home and abroad of information and publications with false historical content detrimental to or slanderous of the Polish Republic or Polish Nation."[2]

The IPN is correspondingly led by historians committed to the exculpatory myth of the war. A month after the change to the IPN's mandate, a longtime institute historian who publicly rejected the findings of the IPN's own investigation into Jedwabne, instead accusing the Germans of having committed the crime along with a "small group" of villagers who were forced to take part, was selected by parliament to serve as president of the institute. Reflecting the importance of the IPN reforms to the radical fringe of Polish politics, his candidacy was praised by, among others, a parliamentary deputy who formerly headed the revived extreme right-wing group All-Polish Youth (Młodzież Wszechpolska), best known for its violent attacks on Jewish students in the 1920s and 1930s. In his remarks to the Sejm, he applauded the IPN's new chief for refusing to conduct a "politics of history on the orders of the Federal Republic of Germany or Jewish milieus [środowisk żydowskich] making claims against Poland."[3]

These moves coincided with continuing evidence of the prevalence of anti-Semitism in Polish society; in 2017 a survey by the Department of Psychology at the University of Warsaw revealed that only 27 percent of respondents definitively refuted the medieval anti-Semitic canard that Jews practiced the kidnapping of Christian children, and only 21 percent rejected the suggestion that "Jews strive to rule the world." Conversely, 55 percent agreed that "Jews want to get compensation from the Poles for the things that in fact were done to them by the Germans" and that "it annoys me when today the topic of crimes committed by the Poles on the Jews is still being discussed."[4]

Although the Polish government ultimately agreed to amend the controversial 2018 amendment enabling the IPN to criminally prosecute persons who "slandered" the Polish nation, Israel's Holocaust remembrance authority, Yad Vashem, judged that the revisions left "the gist of the legislation unchanged." It would still be possible to "press [civil] charges for ostensible injury to 'the reputation of the Polish Nation' even if said injury was not committed 'publicly' and 'contrary to the facts.'" Yad Vashem noted that the chairman of the PiS party had cheered the revisions as "'open[ing] the way for an anti-defamation offensive.'"[5]

For their part, the remaining Jewish communities of Poland issued a joint statement decrying the "growing wave of intolerance, xenophobia, and anti-Semitism in Poland" set off by the 2018 amendment. They accused Poland's president, prime minister, and the PiS chairman of "empty words" and equated the state's inaction with "tacit consent for hatred directed against the Jewish community."[6] The controversy died down after the revision of the amendment in June 2018, only to burst into public view again in February 2019 when the Israeli prime minister, during a visit to Warsaw, was misquoted as saying that "the Poles" and not simply "Poles" had "cooperated with Nazis." Following the pronunciation by Israel's acting foreign minister of Yitzhak Shamir's notorious remark that Poles "drink anti-Semitism with their mother's milk," the Polish prime minister canceled his participation in a summit of Eastern European countries meant to be held in Jerusalem. The editorial page of the Israeli newspaper *Haaretz* commented that the new crisis showed that "nothing" had been resolved in the matter of the controversial IPN amendments, while the *Jerusalem Post* warned that these crises were not about "semantics" but would "continue as long as Poland's government insists on whitewashing history."[7]

The furor around the amendment apparently took the IPN by surprise; the head of the institute's governing council lamented that "none of us knew about the huge reserves of anti-Polonism dormant in Jewish milieus."[8] But it was not long before the institute, whose budget in 2018 was more than four times that of the entire Polish Academy of Sciences, ramped up its "counteracting" work, contesting the investigative records of the August trials while simultaneously upholding their exonerating conclusions.[9] Part of its offensive was the debut in February 2019 of a new periodical ostensibly dedicated to "Polish-Jewish Studies." The inaugural publication, whose color scheme conspicuously evokes the dark blue-and-grey used in the publications of the pioneering Center for Holocaust Research at the Polish Academy of Sciences, contained no new research. Entitled "Correcting the Picture?" (*Korekta obrazu?*), it instead consisted entirely of a seventy-four-page rebuttal of *Dalej jest noc* (Night without End), a massive two-volume microhistory of the Holocaust in rural Poland published in 2018 and authored by the leading scholars grouped around the Center for Holocaust Research, including Barbara Engelking, Jan Grabowski, Dariusz Libionka, and Alina Skibińska. Many of the events described in *Dalej jest noc* are reconstructed using the records of the August trials.

The rebuttal takes hairsplitting issue with everything from the definition of the word "strategy" to the number of pages in each chapter, all the while inveighing against "paraliterary" writing, "unscientific practices," and "publicistic deviations."[10] But its main purpose is to repeat the key element of the myth of the war—that insofar as crimes against Jews are concerned, Poles had no agency whatsoever. The author describes the Polish countryside as being under "total German occupation" and the representatives of the village administration—the headmen, watchmen, firemen, and others—as being utterly captive to German orders. The Blue Police, too, were either helpless pawns or treated Poles as badly as they did Jews. The Jews themselves engaged in crimes ranging from theft to denunciation. German policemen and informers lurked everywhere, enforcing total compliance with Nazi regulations. And German crimes or the actions of "hooligan elements" were sometimes mistaken as anti-Jewish crimes committed by Poles.[11]

If many of these arguments are familiar from the August trials, that is because they *are* from the trials. Demonstrating the profound and enduring contradiction of postwar justice in Poland—that the process is written off as "political" justice even as the results are used to underpin the myth of the past—the IPN author alternates between casting suspicion on the trials and citing their acquittals as proof of the innocence of the accused. On the one hand, according to the author, they were "communist trials" produced under the so-called "'justice system' of a totalitarian regime." UB investigators did not "shy from physical violence" against suspects, "occupation realities" were ignored, and testimonies contained "radical contradictions." On the other hand, he accepts acquittals issued by the courts without question and takes to task the contributors to *Dalej jest noc* for not doing the same. In his estimation, the contributors are guilty of "independently making accusations in matters which even a communist court considered unfounded."[12]

The debate about the Holocaust in Poland is inflammatory because it is understood, by extension, to be a debate about the origins of modern Poland. The destruction during and immediately after the Second World War of the Polish aristocracy and Polish Jewry, two minorities disproportionately represented among the country's landowners and business owners, cleared the way for the establishment of an ethnically Polish middle and smallholding class, a development recognized and commented on by observers at the time of the events.

The accompanying fear of Jewish demands for restitution, first aired in the aftermath of the Second World War, still hangs over the public conversation. Significantly, Poland remains the only country in Europe without a law to compensate owners of property confiscated by Nazi or Communist governments.[13] Heightening the Polish government's angst in 2018, the US administration in May of that year signed into law the Justice for Uncompensated Survivors Today (JUST) Act, mandating a report detailing what European countries are doing to return property lost during the Holocaust to owners. Although the law ordered nothing more than an assessment, it was greeted in apocalyptic terms by Polish media and politicians. A former minister of defense who is one of the most prominent figures in the ruling PiS party warned that the JUST Act was a blow to the "honor, pride, and dignity of all Poles," which threatened nothing less than the "ruination of our economy."[14] Polish state television declared that "Jewish organizations are forcing through a law which could cost Poland billions." Two years later, during the Polish presidential elections, the country's main evening news program again warned that "200 billion złotys" in family subsidies were at risk of being diverted to "satisfy the claims of Jewish organizations." After the incumbent swore that he would never agree to compensation for unclaimed property, the chief rabbi of Poland declared that the country's "Jewish community . . . was shocked" by a "statement that specifically appealed to the votes of anti-Semites."[15]

While Polish participation in the Holocaust captures public attention for its legal implications and its potential to disrupt national identity, the debate itself is essentially a dispute about the credibility of the August trials, whose contents have propelled all the major research into the subject since the fall of Communism, even as the story of how they were generated has been forgotten. As this book has documented, the trials themselves do not conform to a postcommunist narrative of Stalinist tyranny and popular resistance. They were not "political justice" in the sense of communist show trials. On the contrary, they were more complex, sophisticated, and democratic than what anyone could have expected.

Polish-on-Jewish crime during the war had fundamentally differed from Polish-on-Polish crime in the degree of sadism, lethality, and public sanction it enjoyed. Whereas Polish-on-Polish crime had been furtive and opportunistic and had exposed the perpetrators to social ostracism, Polish-on-Jewish crime had been overt and programmatic and had mobilized whole communities. These inconvenient truths haunted postwar Poland and drove state, society, and judiciary to create a denialist and exculpatory memory of collaboration by ethnic Poles in the Holocaust, a version of memory that prevails to this day.

In the process, none of the major parties to the trials lived up to the historical stereotype of the Stalinist period. Much of the judiciary that presided over the trials was independent and arguably even nationalistic. Polish witnesses and defendants were not cowed participants in the proceedings, but vigorously, creatively, and successfully defended their actions. And the supposedly omnipotent state increasingly acceded to the popular will, eventually catering to its demands. The verdicts are a testament to both the independence of the trial process and the myth of the war, because a close reading of case files shows that defendants were often convicted on lesser charges or acquitted on highly dubious grounds.

That having been said, the total figure of 1,835 death sentences meted out for all August crimes from 1944 to 1956 is sobering proof that postwar retribution was hardly an empty threat. It is not known how many of the sentences were actually carried out—in my estimation it was certainly fewer than half, of which a significant proportion were for German war criminals and their Volksdeutsche collaborators; however, it is likely that several dozen Poles were executed for denouncing, capturing, and killing their Jewish neighbors during the war. Thousands more had their lives disrupted by arrest, trial, and prison terms of up to ten years.

Ultimately, the problem with criticizing the shortcomings of the August trials for crimes against Jews is the assumption that an alternative was possible in both a legal and a practical sense. A different legal outcome was certainly possible, because, as we have seen, the mechanisms and evidence necessary to prosecute these crimes to the full extent of the law were readily available. What was missing, of course, was the political will—on the part of the government, judiciary, and society, each for its own reasons—to see the majority of these cases through to their logical conclusion.

The trials shed light on both magnificent and shabby aspects of modern Polish history. On the one hand, a vassal state of the world's largest totalitarian empire—in the decade *before* Stalin's demise—was compelled by popular pressure to renegotiate the social contract. On the other hand, appalling crimes were hushed up and many perpetrators were unjustly excused. The trials also illuminate Poland's connection to the rest of Europe. Even though Poland is hardly the only country to believe in its uniqueness, the feeling of national exceptionalism has an especially long genealogy there, dating back to the fifteenth century when the Polish nobility began to cultivate the idea that they were descended from the Sarmatians, ancient Iranian invaders of the Slavic lands.

Today, Polish exceptionalism is characterized by a suspicion of "foreign" social and cultural forces—"LGBT ideology" is frequently invoked, for example—that are believed to have a disintegrating effect on "traditional" values.[16] The cult of martyrdom surrounding the horrific losses that Polish civilians and soldiers incurred battling Nazi Germany from the war's first day to the last has reinforced the feeling of being apart from the rest of Europe, contrasting sharply as it does with the comparative passivity of many European countries under Nazi occupation and the declining role of military glory in the national identity of western Europe. But then as now, Poland is inescapably part of a pan-European continuum. In all the other formerly occupied countries of Europe—France, the Netherlands, Belgium, Norway, Denmark, the Czech lands, Yugoslavia, and the USSR—processes of postwar retribution also foundered to varying degrees on institutional, social, and political resistance. Poland's trials were hardly alone in their susceptibility to political expediency, popular denial, national self-image, and Cold War geopolitics.

A PAN-EUROPEAN CONTINUUM

Where societies had been divided ethnically or politically, there was bound to be disagreement about the purpose, intensity, and targets of postwar retribution. In France, almost the whole of the political establishment had voted to endorse the arguably legal collaborationist regime of Marshal Pétain, whose base of popular support was more or less the entire right wing of the French political spectrum. The anti-Vichy coalition that won the war, on the other hand, was a motley crew—united only by its refusal to accept the capitulation, and divided between those who merely sought a restoration of the prewar system and those who hoped for a renovation or even a revolution. For his part, de Gaulle wanted to "forgive and forget" and admitted privately he would have preferred not to prosecute Pétain.[17]

Similar issues of legitimacy dogged other countries where the occupation had been relatively soft and where the Germans courted the ruling elite. How were German collaborators in Denmark to be judged when the king and government themselves had remained in the country and officially accepted cooperation with the occupiers from their surrender in 1940 until August 1943? Disturbingly, the number of Danes who died as a result of Nazi oppression or fighting for the Allies abroad was roughly equivalent to the number who had died fighting for the Germans on the Eastern Front.[18]

The humiliation of the Czechs, who had been forced to cede their sovereignty without firing a shot, was profound and would manifest itself in the furious "wild purges" of ethnic Germans after the liberation in 1945. But ironically, as a technologically sophisticated, industrialized nation that was essential to the Nazi war effort, the Czechs had enjoyed "living conditions [that] compared favorably even to those in the Reich," with the population experiencing a net gain of over 200,000 during the occupation, presided over by a technocratic cabinet in the so-called Protectorate of Bohemia and Moravia.[19]

The desire of the Belgian king and government-in-exile to restore credibility tarnished by wartime fecklessness coincided with the fact that the middle and upper classes, many of whom had prospered during the occupation, were not interested in pursuing the opportunistic collaboration of major industrialists. Furthermore, the ethnic divide between the Flemish and Walloon halves of the country guaranteed that postwar accounting would be politically charged, especially given the contrast between the relative strength of the anti-German resistance in the former and separatism in the latter.[20]

Where there was no credible collaborationist government to speak of and hatred for the occupiers was undeniable, such as in the Netherlands, economic and administrative collaboration—half of Dutch industry was serving the Germans, and the police participated in the arrests of Dutch Jews—still implicated a broad swath of the population. After the war, the investigative services were swamped by complaints regarding about 5 percent of the population.[21]

And even in the two countries where revolution was a stated priority, the Soviet Union and Yugoslavia, the rooting out of collaborators blended with the combating of all political opposition, undermining the legitimacy of the entire process. In the Ukrainian Soviet Socialist Republic, for example, the focus was on stamping out the nationalist guerrillas who could still pose a threat to Soviet power, rather than documenting crimes against humanity such as the Holocaust, which was a taboo subject in any case. In Yugoslavia, terror was indiscriminately employed, not only against bona fide collaborators, but against much of the prewar political establishment, in the hope of achieving a rapid revolution from above.[22]

Nevertheless, the need for reconciliation was not lost on even the Soviet Union, with its unmatched monopoly on violence and a pervasive security apparatus. As in Poland, the authorities in the reconstituted Estonian Soviet Socialist Republic relied on local "national communists" and other people with dubious ideological credentials, who in turn would exercise a braking influence on Soviet repression.[23]

Traditions of leniency and strict legality in countries like the Netherlands, Norway, and Denmark also meant that, given the right circumstances, even the most hardened war criminals would likely be spared. Although all three countries reinstated the death penalty specifically to address crimes of the occupation after having abolished it years and even decades before, its use would be subject to the vagaries of time and politics.[24]

The search for judicial solutions also led the formerly occupied countries down similar paths. With the exception of Yugoslavia, where a revolution was under way, and the Soviet Union, all of them were, at least initially and in theory, democracies that were committed to restoring the rule of law. To deal with the extraordinary crimes of the occupation, however, most had to find constitutional and legal workarounds to justify the violation of the principles of no retroactive law and no crime without a corresponding law. Gaullist France and the liberated Czech lands pretended that the legal continuity of their prewar states had been abrogated by Pétain's assumption of power and the Munich Agreement, respectively, whereas Belgium, the Netherlands, and Norway benefited from the existence of undisputed governments-in-exile.[25] A variety of special and supplemental laws, justified by states of emergency or legalized ex post facto, were hastily enacted. In France, the Czech lands, and the Netherlands, special courts featuring expedited handling and lay jurors were established, whereas Belgium entrusted its cases to military courts (whose caseloads still demanded the conscription of civilian manpower), and Norway and Denmark relied on their regular criminal courts. Several court systems featured lower tiers—like the Dutch *Tribunalen* or the French *chambres civiques*—to deal with less serious cases of "national indignity," reflecting the gradation necessary to address the nebulous class of offenses that hovered somewhere below the level of a felony but still called out for punishment.[26]

Of course, laws and institutions were not enough to overcome political and social inertia. In France the judicial purge was denounced as a "complete failure" as early as 1945. Occupational purges of the army, judiciary, civil service, and parliament ejected only a small number of officeholders. Some collaborators flew under the radar entirely, only to resurface in the 1980s and 1990s, while some of the German architects of the Final Solution in France were released for political reasons in the 1960s. Successive commutations and amnesties meant that fewer than a third of death sentences were carried out, and by 1956 fewer than 100 collaborators were still behind bars, although more than 2,000 had been sentenced to life imprisonment.[27]

Eager to restore its authority with minimum disruption to the economic elite, the Belgian government so narrowed the definition of economic collaboration that, despite public dissatisfaction, only 2 percent of accusations ever led to a trial; nor was any member of the prewar elite held to account. Only a year after the liberation, the recommended penalties for some categories of local SS and Gestapo members were reduced from death to five years or less. Around one-sixth of all death penalties were carried out, and by 1965 just three people, out of almost 2,000 sentenced to life, remained in prison.[28]

Overwhelmed by the number of denunciations filed with the authorities, the Dutch political and legal establishment recoiled from severity and the death penalty in particular, emphasizing instead the didactic nature of punishment. Of 154 death sentences, only 40 were carried out, and despite "very heavy protests," pardon "waves" beginning in the late 1940s emptied out the prisons, so that by 1964 only four Germans and no Dutch were still incarcerated.[29]

With 700 persons executed, Czech retribution was no trifling matter, but like the Poles and other Europeans, they took an indulgent view of certain offenses, largely exonerating the collaborationist Protectorate ministers and exhibiting reluctance to pursue anti-Jewish crimes.[30]

Only a year after passing its special laws, the Danish government amended them significantly in favor of leniency. Just as in Poland, the courts used the articles for mitigating factors on a "considerably larger scale than primarily intended" to avoid "severe" mandatory sentences. Of 78 death sentences pronounced for collaboration, only 46 were carried out, and none of the seven death sentences pronounced against Germans for war crimes was carried out; the last Dane serving a life sentence was freed in 1956.[31]

In Norway, popular opposition to the death penalty mounted rapidly, and after an early string of forty-five death sentences, most of which were carried out, its use was discontinued in 1947. But bizarre and controversial outcomes were not unknown there either; the chief SS executioner in Norway was released on the grounds that he did not understand that his duties were illegal, and the high-ranking Norwegian police officer who had organized the arrest and deportation of Oslo's Jews was twice acquitted in view of his alleged aid to the Resistance.[32]

Finally, even the Soviet Union adopted a conciliatory approach when called for. Given the extent of collaboration in the Baltics and the more pressing need to fight the anticommunist insurgency, it was decided in 1946 that Balts who had served as enlisted men or NCOs in the German forces would be exempt from the standard punishment applied to other Soviet citizens. The extent of the compromise is demonstrated by the fact that while thirteen to 15,000 political arrests were made in the Estonian Soviet republic from 1944 to 1945, one-third of whom were members of the anticommunist resistance, at least 50,000 Estonian veterans of the German armed forces remained in the country.[33]

NATIONAL ALIBIS

With the collapse of the Soviet Union and the enlargement of the European Union, there has been a search for common narratives integrating East and

West. This has been a history of one of those common threads, albeit a dark one. With or without a quisling, Poland could not help being part of that European mainstream in which Nazi-inspired ethnic cleansing and mass participation in the German project were followed after the war by various "national cleansings" that had to be aborted or abridged as the scale and depth of complicity became clear.

Here too, Louis-Napoléon's fateful words about circumventing legality for the sake of justice held true—except that after 1945, the lawfulness that was being sacrificed was the punishment of individual perpetrators, and the "justice" that was being served was the political will and self-image of majority populations who rapidly lost interest in counting the skeletons in the closet. Like the expulsion of the biblical scapegoat into the wilderness, the postwar retribution across Europe was an act of symbolic contrition, intended not to punish evenly or even all those collaborators who had been captured, but to sound an "all-clear," to signal to the masses that a page had been turned, that justice had been done, and that everyone could return to the pursuits of modern life, unencumbered by the past.

To return to the Polish example—though the same question might be asked of every European country—had justice been done for that most completely vanished of minorities, the Jews? In a philosophical sense, the answer is, clearly, not quite—if not an outright no. But in the eyes of a society that itself had suffered terrible losses under occupation, was eager to move on, and was uninterested in sacrificing citizens who had transgressed against people considered culturally, religiously, and racially alien, then perhaps, sadly, the answer is yes.

ARCHIVAL ABBREVIATIONS

NOTES

ACKNOWLEDGMENTS

INDEX

ARCHIVAL ABBREVIATIONS

Archiwum Akt Nowych (AAN)
—Armia Krajowa 1942–1945 (AK)
—Ministerstwo Sprawiedliwości w Warszawie (MS)
—Polski Komitet Wyzwolenia Narodowego (PKWN)
—Sąd Najwyższy (SN)

Archiwum Instytutu Pamięci Narodowej w Warszawie (AIPN)
—Sąd Wojewódzki dla Województwa Warszawskiego (SWWW)
—Sąd Wojewódzki miasta stołecznego Warszawy (SWmstW)
—Specjalny Sąd Karny w Warszawie (SSKW)

Archiwum Państwowe miasta stołecznego Warszawy—Oddział w Milanówku (APmstW-M)
—Sąd Apelacyjny w Warszawie (SAW)
—Sąd Okręgowy w Warszawie (SOW)

Archiwum Państwowe miasta stołecznego Warszawy—Oddzial w Pułtusku (APmstW-P)
—Sąd Specjalny w Warszawie 1940–1944 (SS)

Archiwum Państwowe miasta stołecznego Warszawy—Stare Miasto (APmstW—SM)

Archiwum Państwowe w Siedlcach (APS)
—Sąd Okręgowy w Siedlcach (SOS)

United States Holocaust Memorial Museum (USHMM)
—Sąd Apelacyjny w Kielcach (SAK)
—Sąd Apelacyjny w Lublinie (SAL)

—Sąd Okręgowy w Kielcach (SOK)
—Sąd Okręgowy w Lublinie (SOL)
—Sąd Okręgowy w Radomiu (SORd)
—Specjalny Sąd Karny w Krakowie (SSKKr)
—Specjalny Sąd Karny w Lublinie (SSKL)

United States National Archives and Records Administration (NARA)

Żydowski Instytut Historyczny (ŻIH)

NOTES

Introduction

Author's note: All translations are those of the author unless otherwise noted.

1. "Struktura ludności: Polska—1970–2050," Główny Urząd Statystyczny, accessed March 16, 2019, http://stat.gov.pl/obszary-tematyczne/ludnosc/ludnosc/ludnosc-piramida/; Aleksandra Wróbel, "Poland's Leaders Barred from White House Meetings over Holocaust Law," *Politico,* March 7, 2018, https://www.politico.eu/article/polands-leaders-barred-from-white-house-meetings-over-holocaust-law/.

2. "Ustawa z dnia 26 stycznia 2018 r. o zmianie ustawy o Instytucie Pamięci Narodowej—Komisji Ścigania Zbrodni przeciwko Narodowi Polskiemu, ustawy o grobach i cmentarzach wojennych, ustawy o muzeach oraz ustawy o odpowiedzialności podmiotów zbiorowych za czyny zabronione pod groźbą kary," *Dziennik Ustaw* 2018, poz. 369.

3. Editorial Board, "Poland Is Sliding into Authoritarianism: Now We See if the E.U. Can Stop the Drift," *Washington Post,* December 21, 2018. In December 2018 the European Court of Justice ordered Poland to suspend a recent law that had lowered the retirement age of Supreme Court judges in an attempt to force out uncompliant judges.

4. Marek Strzelecki, "Exit by Polish Top Brass Guts Command on NATO Front Line," *Bloomberg,* February 23, 2017, https://www.bloomberg.com/news/articles/2017-02-23/exodus-by-polish-top-brass-guts-command-of-front-line-nato-state; Monika Sieradzka, "Is Media Censorship a Coming Threat in Poland?," *Deutsche Welle,* December 10, 2018, https://www.dw.com/en/is-media-censorship-a-coming-threat-in-poland/a-46671328; Derek Scally, "Polish National Broadcaster Turns into Propaganda Machine," *Irish Times,* May 19, 2016, https://www.irishtimes.com/news/world/europe/polish-national-broadcaster-turns-into-propaganda-machine-1.2652527; Natalia Ojewska, "How Did Poland's President Die? It Depends Which Official Version You Believe," *EuroNews,* October 4, 2018, https://www.euronews.com/2018/04/09/how-did-poland-s-president-die-it-depends-which-official-version-you-believe; Joanna Berendt and Marc Santora, "Poland Reverses Supreme Court Purge, Retreating from Conflict with E.U.," *New York Times,* December 17, 2018, https://www.nytimes.com/2018/12/17/world/europe/poland-supreme-court.html.

5. Antony Polonsky and Joanna B. Michlic, eds., *The Neighbors Respond: The Controversy over the Jedwabne Massacre in Poland* (Princeton, NJ: Princeton University Press, 2004), 6–10; Dariusz Stola, "Fighting against the Shadows: The *Anti-Zionist* Campaign of 1968," in *Antisemitism and Its Opponents in Modern Poland*, ed. Robert Blobaum (Ithaca, NY: Cornell University Press, 2005), 293–294; Andrzej Czyżewski, "The Myths of March '68: Conflicts of Memory in Contemporary Poland," in *Unsettled 1968 in the Troubled Present: Revisiting the 50 Years of Discussions from East and Central Europe*, ed. Aleksandra Konarzewska, Anna Nakai, and Michał Przeperski (London: Routledge, 2019), 165.

6. Czyżewski, "The Myths of March '68," 165–166; Joanna Wawrzyniak, *Veterans, Victims, and Memory: The Politics of the Second World War in Communist Poland* (Frankfurt am Main: Peter Lang, 2015), 203–209.

7. Wawrzyniak, *Veterans, Victims, and Memory*, 223–225; Czyżewski, "The Myths of March '68," 163, 172–175; Jo Harper, "Never Mind the Boleks!," in *Poland's Memory Wars: Essays on Illiberalism*, ed. Jo Harper (Budapest: Central European University Press, 2018), 29–33.

8. Harper, "Never Mind the Boleks!," 26; Andrzej Leder, "Sleepwalking the Revolution: An Exercise in Historical Logic," lecture at the Einstein Forum, Berlin, Germany, October 24, 2019. See also Andrzej Leder, *Prześniona rewolucja: Ćwiczenie z logiki historycznej* (Warsaw: Wydawnictwo Krytyki Politycznej, 2014).

9. Neal Pease, "'This Troublesome Question': The United States and the 'Polish Pogroms' of 1918–1919," in *Ideology, Politics and Diplomacy in East Central Europe*, ed. M. B. B. Biskupski (Rochester, NY: University of Rochester Press, 2003), 63, 72; Polonsky and Michlic, *The Neighbors Respond*, 7, 10.

10. AAN, MS, *Uregułowanie prawne wymiaru kary dla faszystowsko-hitlerowskich zbrodniarzy . . .* , syg. 3979, pp. 93–100.

11. Oscar Pinkus, *House of Ashes* (Cleveland: World Publishing Co., 1964), 119.

12. Although contemporary critics may justifiably point out that the use of the terms "Poles" and "Jews" reifies the racist and segregationist distinctions of the occupiers, the reality is that, with the exception of some small liberal corners of Polish society, the term "Pole," then and now, is understood to mean a Catholic citizen of Poland with no Jewish heritage. In the case files of the August trials, Jews were never referred to as "Poles" but as persons or Polish citizens "of Jewish ethnicity" (*żydowskiej narodowości*). In recognition of this reality and for the sake of convenience, the terms "Pole" and "Jew" will be used here.

13. See Alina Skibińska, "'Dostał 10 lat, ale za co?' Analiza motywacji sprawców zbrodni na Żydach na wsi kieleckiej w latach 1942–1944," in *Zarys krajobrazu: Wieś polska wobec Zagłady Żydów 1942–1945*, ed. Barbara Engelking and Jan Grabowski (Warsaw: Centrum Badań nad Zagładą Żydów, 2011), 313–444; Andrzej Pasek, *Przestępstwa okupacyjne w polskim prawie karnym z lat 1944–1956* (Wrocław: Wydawnictwo Uniwersytetu Wrocławskiego, 2002); Leszek Kubicki, *Zbrodnie wojenne w świetle prawa polskiego* (Warsaw: PWN, 1963).

14. Roman Dmowski, *Myśli nowoczesnego Polaka* (Wrocław: Nortom, 2008), 34; Brian Porter-Szücs, *Poland in the Modern World: Beyond Martyrdom* (Chichester: Wiley-Blackwell, 2014), 222, 225; Roman Dmowski, *Przewrót* (Wrocław: Nortom, 2006), 129, 151.

15. Dariusz Libionka, "Polska hierarchia kościelna wobec eksterminacji Żydów— Próba krytycznego ujęcia," *Zagłada Żydów: Studia i materiały* 5 (2009): 20, 25.

16. Szymon Rudnicki, "Anti-Jewish Legislation in Interwar Poland," in Blobaum, *Antisemitism and Its Opponents*, 161.

17. Alina Skibińska and Joanna Tokarska-Bakir, "'Barabasz' i Żydzi: Z historii oddziału AK 'Wybranieccy,'" *Zagłada Żydów: Studia i materiały* 7 (2011): 110; Krzysztof Persak, "Wstęp," in Engelking and Grabowski, *Zarys krajobrazu*, 10, 12. These figures are based on estimates and extrapolations from demographic data and county-level samples, as the exact number of escapees from the deportations will never be known. For further discussion, see Persak, "Wstęp," 26; Barbara Engelking and Jan Grabowski, "Wstęp," in *Dalej jest noc: Losy Żydów w wybranych powiatach okupowanej Poski*, vol. 1, ed. Barbara Engelking and Jan Grabowski (Warsaw: Centrum Badań nad Zagładą Żydów, 2018), 27–31.

1. "There Are Many Cains among Us"

The chapter title quote is from an article about collaboration published in a Poznań newspaper. "Zaufany urzędnik," *Głos Wielkopolski*, March 28, 1947.

1. ŻIH, *Zbiór relacji Żydów ocalałych*, statement of Leon Bukowiński, syg. 301/ 4424, p. 9.

2. Alina Skibińska, "'Dostał 10 lat, ale za co?' Analiza motywacji sprawców zbrodni na Żydach na wsi kieleckiej w latach 1942–1944," in *Zarys krajobrazu: Wieś polska wobec Zagłady Żydów 1942–1945*, ed. Barbara Engelking and Jan Grabowski (Warsaw: Centrum Badań nad Zagładą Żydów, 2011), 315; Jan Grabowski, *Hunt for the Jews: Betrayal and Murder in German-Occupied Poland* (Bloomington: Indiana University Press, 2013), 135; Krzysztof Persak, "Wstęp," in Engelking and Grabowski, *Zarys krajobrazu*, 26–27; Barbara Engelking, "'Po zamordowaniu udaliśmy się do domu': Wydawanie i mordowanie Żydów na wsi polskiej w latach 1942–1945," in Engelking and Grabowski, *Zarys krajobrazu*, 262. Recent studies of the fates of Jews who escaped deportation in nine rural counties found that, on average, 67 percent perished before the war's end. See Barbara Engelking and Jan Grabowski, "Wstęp," in *Dalej jest noc: Losy Żydów w wybranych powiatach okupowanej Poski*, vol. 1, ed. Barbara Engelking and Jan Grabowski (Warsaw: Centrum Badań nad Zagładą Żydów, 2018), 36.

3. Jan Gross, "O kolaboracji," *Zagłada Żydów: Studia i materiały* 2 (2006): 412.

4. Dariusz Libionka, "Zagłada na wsi w optyce polskiej konspiracji (1942–1944)," in Engelking and Grabowski, *Zarys krajobrazu*, 79.

5. Skibińska, "'Dostał 10 lat, ale za co?,'" 321–323.
6. Jan Karski, *Raport Karskiego: Zagadnienie Żydowskie w kraju* (1940), 10, retrieved from www.jankarski.org.
7. APS, SOS, File 734, p. 81 *verte*; ibid., File 744, pp. 52, 128–129 *verte*; ibid., File 729, p. 98; ibid., File 690, p. 3 *verte*; ibid., File 725, pp. 194–203. Author's note: verte is translated as "reverse of." Most Polish files from the archives, even if the pages are double-sided, are only paginated on the front of the page. Thus, in the first work there is a page numbered 81, but the reverse side has no numbering, while the front side of the next page is marked 82, and so on.
8. APS, SOS, File 754, pp. 106, 121–122; ibid., File 595, pp. 71 (investigative files), 271–272 (trial files); ibid., File 687, p. 3; ibid., File 693, pp. 15–18 *verte*; APmstW–M, SOW, File 470, p. 5.
9. APS, SOS, File 562, pp. 13–15 (investigative files); ibid., File 624, p. 162 and *verte*.
10. USHMM, SSKL, File 147, Reel 5, Slides 635–637; APS, SOS, File 648, pp. 202–203; ibid., File 783, pp. 90–94; APmstW–M, SOW, File 183, p. 112; ibid., File 2459, pp. 63–64.
11. APS, SOS, File 560, pp. 3–12 (investigative files); ibid., File 574, pp. 80–81 (investigative files), 68–74, 131–141 (trial files); APmstW–M, SOW, File 228, pp. 98–102 *verte*.
12. APS, SOS, File 663, pp. 51–52.
13. APmstW–SM, Komenda Policji Polskiej m. Warszawy, 1939–1944, File 12, pp. 61, 78, 97, 330 (irregular pagination); AAN, AK, Microfilm 2375 / 17, File 203 / III-123, pp. 6–7.
14. AAN, AK, Microfilm 2375 / 16, File 203 / III-119, Raport 7.VII.42, p. 4. See also APmstW–SM, Komenda Policji Polskiej m. Warszawy, File 12, pp. 2, 203.
15. AAN, AK, Microfilm 2375 / 16, File 203 / III-117, p. 12; ibid., File 203 / III-112, Raport 106 / 76 (no pagination); ibid., File 202 / III-140, p. 4; APmstW–SM, Komenda Powiatowa Policji Polskiej Ostrów Mazowiecka, 1939–1944, Files 1–47.
16. AAN, AK, Microfilm 2375 / 17, File 203 / III-123, Protokół No. 1, p. 1a, Rozkaz No. 100, p. 14; ibid., File 203 / III-127, Meldunek No. 9, pp. 8–9.
17. APmstW–SM, Komenda Policji Polskiej m. Warszawy, File 5, *Fotografie*, pp. 45–46.
18. APmstW–M, SOW, File 2837.
19. See Adam Hempel, *Pogrobowcy klęski: Rzecz o policji "granatowej" w Generalnym Gubernatorstwie, 1939–1945* (Warsaw: PWN, 1990), 218; APmstW–SM, Komenda Policji Polskiej m. Warszawy, File 5, *Fotografie*, p. 46. See examples of policemen shot in reprisal by the Underground in AAN, AK, Microfilm 2375 / 16, File 203 / III-112, Raport 105 / 75 z 1.VI.1944; ibid., File 203 / III-118, pp. 85, 115; APmstW–SM, Komenda Powiatowa Policji Polskiej Ostrów Mazowiecka, 1939–1944, File 13, p. 20.
20. AAN, AK, Microfilm 2375 / 16, File 203 / III-112, Raport 153 / 28 z 17.V.1944.
21. Those accused of denunciation sometimes defended themselves by pointing out that they contacted the Blue Police rather than the Germans, as in APmstW–M,

SOW, File 2450, pp. 2 and *verte*, and File 1914, pp. 3 and *verte*. In at least three instances in my sample, defendants were faulted by the authorities for not having first contacted the Blue Police to resolve their disputes. See APmstW–M, SOW, File 3033, pp. 4 and *verte*; APS, SOS, File 759, p. 116; and ibid., File 647, pp. 69 and *verte*.

22. APmstW–M, SOW, File 1344, pp. 39 *verte* and 40; ibid., File 146, pp. 37 and *verte*; ibid., File 450, pp. 2 *verte*; ibid., File 2514, pp. 6–7; ibid., File 2787, pp. 62–65, 76–77.

23. APmstW–M, SOW, File 210, pp. 114–118.

24. APS, SOS, Files 673, pp. 106–107; ibid., File 717, pp. 112–113 *verte*; ibid., File 732, pp. 10–11 *verte*; ibid., File 742, pp. 42–43, 71–77; APmstW–M, SOW, File 2450, pp. 49–53; ibid., File 2670, pp. 53–54 *verte*; ibid., File 1914, pp 3–4; ibid., File 1832, pp. 3–4, 176–178; ibid., File 1994, p. 2–3; ibid., File 2638, pp. 5–6.

25. APmstW–M, SOW, File 1240, pp. 51–54; ibid., File 261, *Protokół przesłuchania podejrzanego z dnia 1 sierpnia 1945* (pagination unclear). See also the cases of Henryka Kęska and Halina Fedorowicz in SOW, File 269, and USHMM, SSKL, File 281.

26. APmstW–M, SOW, File 199, pp. 87–88 *verte*, 110 *verte*; ibid., File 284, pp. 56–58; ibid., File 2822, pp. 4–5; APS, SOS, File 779, pp. 5 and *verte*; ibid., File 639, pp. 3–4 *verte*; ibid., File 197, p. 58; ibid., File 2612, pp. 5–7.

27. APmstW–M, SOW, File 3512, pp. 28–31; ibid., File 2280, pp. 168–172 *verte*; APS, SOS, File 616, p. 42.

28. APS, SOS, File 712, pp. 1–2; APmstW–M, SOW, File 573, p. 148 *verte* (this file is divided into three separate folders—trial files, second investigation, first investigation—each with its own pagination; this is from the trial files), pp. 18 and *verte* (from second investigation), p. 3 *verte* (from first investigation).

2. Crowdsourcing Genocide

1. Samuel Moyn, *A Holocaust Controversy: The Treblinka Affair in Postwar France* (Waltham, MA: Brandeis University Press, 2005), 46–47.

2. For a review of the history, see Henry Rousso, *The Vichy Syndrome: History and Memory in France since 1944*, trans. Arthur Goldhammer (Cambridge, MA: Harvard University Press, 1991).

3. David Engel, "Poland since 1939," *The YIVO Encyclopedia of Jews in Eastern Europe*, http://www.yivoencyclopedia.org/article.aspx/Poland/Poland_since_1939.

4. Marta Tychmanowicz, "Domy płonęły, walka trwała, a przed murem grała karuzela," *WP Wiadomości*, April 29, 2011, https://wiadomosci.wp.pl/domy-plonely -walka-trwala-a-przed-murem-grala-karuzela-6036804608434817a.

5. "L. Żebrowski: Gdy prawdziwych świadków historii pozostało niewielu, obowiązuje narracja narzucona przez J. T. Grossa, J. Grabowskiego czy B. Enkelking," *RadioMaryja.pl*, July 6, 2018, http://www.radiomaryja.pl/informacje/tylko-u -nas-l-zebrowski-gdy-prawdziwych-swiadkow-historii-pozostalo-niewielu-obo

wiazuje-narracja-narzucona-przez-j-t-grossa-j-grabowskiego-czy-b-enkelking/; "Nowe fałsze Grossa," *RadioMaryja.pl,* August 7, 2006, http://www.radiomaryja.pl /informacje/nowe-falsze-grossa-4/.

6. Dariusz Libionka, "Zagłada na wsi w optyce polskiej konspiracji (1942–1944)," in *Zarys krajobrazu: Wieś polska wobec Zagłady Żydów 1942–1945,* ed. Barbara Engelking and Jan Grabowski (Warsaw: Centrum Badań nad Zagładą Żydów, 2011), 88; Jan Grabowski, *Hunt for the Jews: Betrayal and Murder in German-Occupied Poland* (Bloomington: Indiana University Press, 2013), 101.

7. Grabowski, *Hunt for the Jews,* 58.

8. Dariusz Libionka, "Polska hierarchia kościelna wobec eksterminacji Żydów—Próba krytycznego ujęcia," *Zagłada Żydów: Studia i materiały* 5 (2009): 27, 40–44. Although the church archives are not open to researchers, a church report sent to the Government-in-Exile and covering the period of June to July 1941 stated that it was a sign of "God's providence" that the Germans had "showed the possibility of liberating Polish society from the Jewish plague." See ibid., 59.

9. The CSS KWC are not to be confused with the Special Courts of the postwar communist state. Libionka, "Zagłada na wsi," 64–65, 104–105, 111, 114, 128; Dariusz Libionka, "ZWZ-AK i Delegatura Rządu wobec eksterminacji Żydów Polskich," in *Polacy i Żydzi pod okupacją niemiecką 1939–1945: Studia i materiały,* ed. Andrzej Żbikowski (Warsaw: IPN, 2006), 35.

10. Libionka, "ZWZ-AK i Delegatura Rządu," 67–68, 114–116; Libionka, "Zagłada na wsi," 126, 131.

11. Libionka, "ZWZ-AK i Delegatura Rządu," 116.

12. Ibid., 115–116.

13. Aleksandra Bańkowska, "Partyzantka polska lat 1942–1944 w relacjach żydowskich," *Zagłada Żydów: Studia i materiały* 1 (2005): 153–154; Libionka, "Zagłada na wsi," 58. See also Libionka's discussion of the issue of Jews in the AK in Libionka, "ZWZ-AK i Delegatura Rządu," 107–113. The assassinations of the two highly assimilated Jews—Jerzy Mazowiecki and Ludwik Widerszal—who ran the Delegatura's Press Bureau, on the orders of their superior, are another tragic example, albeit in the city of Warsaw. See Libionka, "ZWZ-AK i Delegatura Rządu," 136.

14. Grabowski, *Hunt for the Jews,* 82.

15. See Andrzej Leder, *Prześniona rewolucja: Ćwiczenie z logiki historycznej* (Warsaw: Wydawnictwo Krytyki Politycznej, 2014).

16. Alina Skibińska, "'Dostał 10 lat, ale za co?' Analiza motywacji sprawców zbrodni na Żydach na wsi kieleckiej w latach 1942–1944," in Engelking and Jan Grabowski, *Zarys krajobrazu,* 377; Dagmara Swałtek, "Dla płaszcza, walizki i jabłka: Zbrodnie na Żydach ukrywających się we wsiach Falkowa, Wieniec i Janowice w świetle powojennych dokumentów procesowych," *Zagłada Żydów: Studia i materiały* 4 (2008): 436.

17. Dariusz Libionka, "Narodowa Organizacja Wojskowa i Narodowe Siły Zbrojne wobec Żydów pod Kraśnikiem—Korekta obrazu," *Zagłada Żydów: Studia i materiały* 7 (2011): 58; Grabowski, *Hunt for the Jews*, 163.

18. As Jan Gross observes, Jewish communists greeted the Soviets out of ideological sympathy, whereas other Jews viewed them as deliverers from the threat of Nazi violence; see Jan Gross, *Revolution from Abroad: The Soviet Conquest of Poland's Western Ukraine and Western Belorussia* (Princeton, NJ: Princeton University Press, 2002), 32. Jan Karski, on pages 5–7 of his famous report, in the section entitled "Sytuacja Żydów na terenach zajętych przez ZSRR," described the Jewish community as divided, with communists, small traders, artisans, and workers embracing Soviet rule as an opportunity for advancement and liberation from anti-Semitic Polish harassment and persecution, while Jewish businessmen, white-collar professionals, and intelligentsia suffered from the same "restrictions" and "pressure" as other nationalities. See Jan Karski, *Raport Karskiego: Zagadnienie Żydowskie w kraju* (1940), 5–7, retrieved from www.jankarski.org.

19. Joanna Michlic, *Poland's Threatening Other: The Image of the Jew from 1880 to the Present* (Lincoln: University of Nebraska Press, 2006), 154.

20. Joshua D. Zimmerman, *The Polish Underground and the Jews, 1939–1945* (Cambridge: Cambridge University Press, 2015), 99–100.

21. Ibid., 132.

22. Libionka, "Zagłada na wsi," 86.

23. Libionka, "ZWZ-AK i Delegatura Rządu," 130.

24. Libionka, "Zagłada na wsi," 87.

25. Ibid., 89.

26. Zimmerman, *The Polish Underground*, 188.

27. Libionka, "ZWZ-AK i Delegatura Rządu," 130.

28. Ibid.

29. Libionka, "Zagłada na wsi," 93.

30. Zimmerman, *The Polish Underground*, 353–354.

31. Libionka, "ZWZ-AK i Delegatura Rządu," 131.

32. Michlic, *Poland's Threatening Other*, 154.

33. Zimmerman, *The Polish Underground*, 296.

34. Skibińska, "'Dostał 10 lat, ale za co?,'" 356–357; Grabowski, *Hunt for the Jews*, 82, 103.

35. Grabowski, *Hunt for the Jews*, 64. For examples of wartime elections in the vicinity of the towns of Kraśnik, Siedlce, and Chełm, see USHMM, SAL, File 34, Reel 7, Slide 254; APS, SOS, File 734, p. 21 *verte*; USHMM, SOL, File 17, Reel 1, Slide 253. In the latter case, the village's "militiamen" were also elected by popular vote in 1942.

36. Grabowski, *Hunt for the Jews*, 106.

37. USHMM, SAL, File 54, Reel 10, Slide 764.

38. APS, SOS, File 652, *Protokół rozprawy głównej z dnia 27 maja 1948*, pp. 21–23 (original pagination; file has not been completely paginated by archives).

39. Ibid., pp. 54 *verte*–55 *verte*, p. 188 (archival pagination); APS, SOS, File 653, p. 162 *verte*.

40. APS, SOS, File 653, p. 163.

41. APS, SOS, File 695, pp. 3, 11, 14 *verte*, 15 *verte*, 17 *verte*, 38 *verte*–40, 113 *verte*. Andrew Kornbluth, "The Holocaust and Postwar Justice in Poland in Three Acts," in *Microhistories of the Holocaust*, ed. Claire Zalc and Tal Bruttmann (New York: Berghahn Books, 2017), 274.

42. USHMM, SAL, File 7, Reel 1, Slide 780.

43. USHMM, SOL, File 142, Reel 5, Slide 632.

44. USHMM, SAL, File 114, Reel 23, Slides 631–689; ibid., File 96, Reel 17, Slide 904.

45. APS, SOS, File 694, p. 7.

46. Grabowski, *Hunt for the Jews*, 66.

47. USHMM, SSKKr, File 91, Reel 3, Slides 462–485.

48. USHMM, SORd, File 189, Reel 10, Slides 352–464; APmstw–M, SOW, File 3442, pp. 138, 143; APS, SOS, File 734, pp. 63 *verte*, 66 *verte*.

49. USHMM, SAL, File 5, Reel 1, Slides 306–323, 497–504; ibid., File 109, Reel 21, Slides 1047–1050; ibid., File 146, Reel 30, Slides 616–621; ibid., File 165, Reel 34, Slides 421–429; APmstW–M, SOW, File 3266, pp. 54–56.

50. APmstW–M, SAW, File 100, pp. 3 and *verte*, 12–13; APmstW–M, SOW, File 900, pp. 2 and 12 *verte*; USHMM, SAL, File 94, Reel 17, Slides 168–173.

51. USHMM, SAL, Files 83, Reel 15, Slides 558–560, 694–699; ibid., File 70, Reel 12, Slides 529–623, 770–805; ibid., File 158, Reel 33, Slides 12–37, 321–325.

52. USHMM, SAL, File 164, Reel 34, Slide 126.

53. USHMM, SSKL, File 172, Reel 6, Slides 258, 310.

54. USHMM, SOK, File 325, Reel 3, Slide 927, Reel 4, Slides 17–25, 111–115; USHMM, SAL, File 101, Reel 20, Slides 7–10; USHMM, SORd, File 136, Reel 7, Slide 762.

55. APmstW–P, SS, File 507/281, p. 7.

56. APmstW–P, SS, File 602/509; ibid., File 462/398; APmstW–P, Sąd Niemiecki w Warszawie, 1940–1944, File 1067, p. 3; ibid., File 2176.

57. APmstW–P, SS, File 753/913, pp. 28–31; ibid., File 446/390, p. 13; ibid., File 711/536, pp. 2–49.

58. APmstW–SM, Komenda Policji Polskiej m. Warszawy, 1939–1944, File 10, pp. 1, 4, 11; File 16, p. 91. Evidence of the shoot-to-kill order can be found in AAN, Delegatura Rządu RP na Kraj 1940–1945, Microfilm 2225/8, File 202/II/44, p.112, and AAN, AK, Microfilm 2375/17, File 203/III-129, p. 25.

59. AIPN, SWmstW, File 94, pp. 182–184; USHMM, SOK, File 332, Reel 1, Slide 197; AIPN, SWWW, File 131, p. 537; AIPN, SSKW, File 205, p. 25; APS, SOS, File 663, p. 85 *verte*.

60. AIPN, SWmstW, File 38, pp. 36, 54–56; APmstW–M, SOW, File 582, pp. 74, 191.

61. AIPN, SWmstW, Files 298–300, pp. 145–162, 199–209; USHMM, SSKL, File 47, Slides 787–788; APmstW–M, SAW, File 271, p. 70 *verte*; APS, SOS, File 550, p. 19; USHMM, SAL, File 91, Reel 16, Slides 848–858.

62. USHMM, SOL, File 22, Reel 16, Slide 756.
63. USHMM, SSKKr, File 448, Reel 10, 1099–1100, Reel 11, Slides 257–269; APS, SOS, File 663, pp. 51–52, 68 verte, 155 and verte.
64. Libionka, "ZWZ-AK i Delegatura Rządu," 116; USHMM, SAL, File 148, Reel 31, Slide 168.
65. See, for example, Mielniczuk's testimony, USHMM, SAL 148, Reel 31, Slide 140.
66. Skibińska, "'Dostał 10 lat, ale za co?,'" 409.
67. Alina Skibińska and Joanna Tokarska-Bakir, "'Barabasz' i Żydzi: Z historii oddziału AK 'Wybranieccy,'" *Zagłada Żydów: Studia i materiały* 7 (2011): 63–122; Jan Grabowski, "Chcę nadmienić, że nie byłem uświadomiony i wykonywałem zadanie jako żołnierz Armii Krajowej," *Zagłada Żydów: Studia i materiały* 6 (2010): 214–215; Jerzy Mazurek and Alina Skibińska, "'Barwy Białe' w drodze na pomoc walczącej Warszawie: Zbrodnie AK na Żydach," *Zagłada Żydów: Studia i materiały* 7 (2011): 428; Libionka, "Narodowa Organizacja Wojskowa," 47; Jacek Andrzej Młynarczyk, "Pomiędzy współpracą a zdradą: Problem kolaboracji w Generalnym Gubernatorstwie—Próba syntezy," *Pamięć i Sprawiedliwość* 1, no. 14 (2009): 109; Joanna Tokarska-Bakir, "Proces Tadeusza Maja: Z dziejów oddziału AL 'Świt' na Kielecczyźnie,'" *Zagłada Żydów: Studia i materiały* 7 (2011): 170–209.
68. USHMM, SAL, File 148, Reel 30, Slide 952; ibid., Reel 31, Slides 113, 164–165, 172.
69. Skibińska, "'Dostał 10 lat, ale za co?,'" 431; USHMM, SOK, File 171, Reel 5, Slides 427, 429.
70. USHMM, SAK, File 233, Reel 37, Slides 436–437, 552–554.
71. USHMM, SAK, Files 260–267.
72. APmstW-M, SOW, File 3451, pp. 74–78.
73. USHMM, SORd, File 90, Reel 3, Slides 805–807. Arrested and released by the Gestapo in 1943, Chojnacki joined a Peasant Battalions partisan unit in 1943, then the Socialist Party partisan unit of Kazimierz "Huragan" Aleksandrowicz, which saw heavy combat against regular units of the Wehrmacht in the summer and fall of 1944, then in the "forest gendarmerie" of the Home Army.

3. Hearts Grown Brutal

1. Dariusz Libionka, "Zagłada na wsi w optyce polskiej konspiracji (1942–1944)," in *Zarys krajobrazu: Wieś polska wobec Zagłady Żydów, 1942–1945*, ed. Barbara Engelking and Jan Grabowski (Warsaw: Centrum Badań nad Zagładą Żydów, 2011), 79.
2. Joanna Michlic, *Poland's Threatening Other: The Image of the Jew from 1880 to the Present* (Lincoln: University of Nebraska Press, 2006), 183.
3. Ibid., 184.
4. Marcin Zaremba, *Wielka trwoga: Polska 1944–1947—Ludowa reakcja na kryzys* (Warsaw: Znak, 2012), 555.
5. Ibid., 556.

6. AAN, MS, syg. 5559, p. 393.

7. Primo Levi, *The Reawakening* (New York: Touchstone, 1995), 55–56.

8. Igor Rakowski-Kłos, "IPN: Romuald Rajs, ps. 'Bury' odpowiada za zbrodnie noszące znamiona ludobójstwa," *Gazeta Wyborcza,* February 23, 2019, http://wyborcza.pl/alehistoria/7,121681,24486433,ipn-romuald-rajs-ps-bury-odpowiada-za-zbrodnie-noszace.html.

9. Better known as "Operation Vistula" (Akcja Wisła).

10. AAN, MS, syg. 186, pp. 57–58, 68.

11. AAN, MS, syg. 187, pp. 231–289, 74, 109.

12. AAN, PKWN, syg. XI / 6, Microfilm 24269, pp. 2, 17, 25, 29; ibid., syg. I / 4, p. 246.

13. NARA, RG-84, M1945, General Records of the American Embassy in Warsaw, 1945–1947, Roll 4, "Report of Lt. William Tonesk on Visit to Krakow," September 1945, pp. 3–4.

14. NARA, RG-84, M1945, Roll 12, "Memorandum on Jewish Emigration from Poland," March 7, 1946, pp. 3–4.

15. NARA, RG-84, M1945, Roll 12, "Impressions of a Trip through the Country," February 12, 1946, pp. 1–8.

16. NARA, RG-84, M1945, Roll 12, "Factors Affecting Migration of Jewish DPs into the United States Zone," February 8, 1946, pp. 1–2.

17. AAN, PKWN, syg. IX / 10, p. 53.

18. AAN, MS, syg. 1104, p. 60.

19. NARA, "Impressions of a Trip," p. 3.

20. David Engel, "Emil Sommerstein," *The YIVO Encyclopedia of Jews in Eastern Europe,* http://www.yivoencyclopedia.org/article.aspx/Sommerstein_Emil.

21. AAN, PKWN, syg. I / 4, pp. 124, 245–248.

22. NARA, "Impressions of a Trip," pp. 3–4.

23. NARA, RG-84, M1945, Roll 4, "Airgram Warsaw-A-397," undated; NARA, RG-84, M1945, Roll 12, "Factors Affecting Migration," p. 1; ibid., "Jewish Refugees from Poland," January 1, 1946, p. 2.

24. NARA, RG-84, M1945, Roll 12, "Report to the Ambassador: POLISH REFUGEES," January 25, 1946, p. 2.

25. AAN, MS, syg. 4549, pp. 55–56.

26. Zaremba, *Wielka Trwoga,* 96. He also mentions a maximum of probably 300,000 high school graduates.

27. "Manifest Polskiego Komitetu Wyzwolenia Narodowego," republished in *Rocznik Lubelski* (1959), 7–14, http://bazhum.muzhp.pl/media//files/Rocznik_Lubelski/Rocznik_Lubelski-r1959-t2/Rocznik_Lubelski-r1959-t2-s7-14/Rocznik_Lubelski-r1959-t2-s7-14.pdf. Secondary and postsecondary education had been fee-based in the interwar Polish Republic; see "Polska. Oświata: Druga Rzeczpospolita," *Encyklopedia PWN,* https://encyklopedia.pwn.pl/haslo/Polska-Oswiata-Druga-Rzeczpospolita;4575098.html.

28. *Dziennik Ustaw* 1944 (*DzU*), no. 4, poz. 17.

29. Andrzej Leder, *Prześniona rewolucja: Ćwiczenie z logiki historycznej* (Warsaw: Wydawnictwo Krytyki Politycznej, 2014), 135.

30. See Leder, *Prześniona rewolucja*, 26, 99; and Czesław Miłosz, *Wypraw w dwudziestolecie* (Kraków: Wydawnictwo Literackie, 1999), 267, 395.

31. Waldemar Kowalski, "Reforma rolna—mit założycielski Polski Ludowej," Muzeum Historii Polski, September 4, 2014, http://muzhp.pl/pl/c/1380/reforma-rolna-mit-zaoycielski-polski-ludowej.

32. Leszek Kubicki, personal interview, November 28, 2012.

33. Leon Chajn, *Kiedy Lublin byl Warszawą* (Warsaw: Czytelnik, 1964), 16, 19, 26.

34. Andrzej Rzepliński, "Ten jest ojczyny mojej? Sprawy karne oskarżonych o wymordowanie Żydów w Jedwabnem w świetle zasady rzetelnego procesu," in *Wokół Jedwabnego*, vol. 1, ed. Paweł Machcewicz and Krzysztof Persak (Warsaw: IPN, 2002).

35. *DzU* 1944, no. 4, poz. 16.

36. According to art. 15 of the Decree of January 22, 1946, which established the Supreme National Tribunal (Najwyższy Trybunał Narodowy) for major German war criminals, the Chief Prosecutor of the Tribunal could appeal any Special Court verdict within three months of its issuance. *DzU* 1946, no. 5, poz. 45.

37. For the full text, see https://ru.wikisource.org/wiki/Указ_Президиума_ВС_СССР_от_19.04.1943_№_39.

38. Andrzej Wesołowski, *W cieniu wojny i polityki: Sądownictwo Wojska Polskiego na froncie wschodnim w latach 1943–1945* (Toruń: Adam Marszałek, 2003), 31–32.

39. Engel, "Emil Sommerstein."

40. Wesołowski, *W cieniu wojny*, 32–34.

41. Centralne Archiwum Wojskowe, III-23/301, *Dekret Rady Wojennej PSZ i Rozporządzenie*, 1944.

42. AAN, PKWN, syg. I/136, "O wymiarze kary dla niemiecko_faszystowskich zloczyncow winnych zabojstw i znecan sie nad polska ludnoscia cywilna i jencami wojennymi, dla szpiegow i zdrajcow Narodu Polskiego sposrod obywateli polskich i dla ich poplecznikow" [sic], pp. 71–72; ibid., "Dekret Polskiego Komitetu Wyzwolenia Narodowego z dnia.... o wymiarze kary za dokonanie zabójstw i działania na szkodę Państwa Polskiego, jego obywateli i osób przebywających na jego terenie," unnumbered; AAN, PKWN, syg. I/81, p. 1, 3; AAN, PKWN, syg. I/4, pp. 118, 163. Although the PKWN was ultimately a vehicle for Soviet interests, its leadership was hardly undivided in its commitment to legality. Dr. Sommerstein protested after Stanisław Radkiewicz arbitrarily amended several laws just before their publication in the *Dziennik Ustaw* and demanded that they be rescinded. See Chajn, *Kiedy Lublin byl Warszawą*, 37–38.

43. *DzU* 1944, no. 6, poz. 27, Articles 85–103; *DzU* 1944, no. 10, poz. 50.

44. Grzegorz Jakubowski, *Sądownictwo powszechne w Polsce w latach 1944–1950* (Warsaw: IPN, 2002), 52. For more about Tarnowski, see Krzysztof Szwagrzyk, "Oficerowie sowieccy w strukturach wymiaru sprawiedliwości Wojska Polskiego," *Aparat Represji w Polsce Ludowej* 1, no. 2 (2005): 9–23; and Jerzy Poksiński, "Sędziowie wojskowi w latach 1944–1956: Próba zarysowania problemu," in *Niepodległość i Pamięć* 4, no. 1(7) (1997): 35–49.

45. Adam Lityński, *Historia Prawa Polski Ludowej* (Warsaw: Wydawnictwo prawnicze LexisNexis, 2005), 19–20. See also Adam Lityński, "Administracja, Polityka i Sąd Tajny w Polsce Ludowej, 1950–1954," *Roczniki Administracji i Prawa* 10 (2010): 21–37. For the mistaken assumption that the Special Courts tried persons for crimes against the "new order," see Elżbieta Romanowska, "Przekształcenia w powszechnym wymiarze sprawiedliwości w Polsce w latach 1944–1956," *Czasopismo prawno-historyczne* 68, no. 2 (2016): 33–62.

46. Adam Wendel, "Odrodzone sądownictwo polskie," in *Wymiar sprawiedliwości w odrodzonej Polsce* (Warsaw: Ministerstwo Sprawiedliwości, 1945), 84; AAN, PKWN, syg. IX/8, "Pismo z dnia 23 sierpnia 1944 do Prezesa Sądu Apelacyjnego ob. Jana Prokopowicza," p. 15 or 439 (pagination unclear); AAN, MS, syg. 7087, p. 88.

47. "Martyrologia sądownictwa lubelskiego," in *Wymiar sprawiedliwości*, 101; Ewa Mędrzycka, "Sądownik polski ma głos," in *Wymiar sprawiedliwości*, 97–99.

48. "Zagadnienia Resortu Sprawiedliwości w obradach X sesji krajowej Rady Narodowej," *Demokratyczny Przegląd Prawniczy* 2, no. 5–6 (1946): 51.

49. Chajn, *Kiedy Lublin był Warszawą*, 20; "Zagadnienia Resortu Sprawiedliwości," 52; AAN, PKWN, syg. I/71, p. 1.

50. Arkadiusz Bereza and Witold Okniński, *Sądownictwo siedleckie: Tradycje i współczesność* (Warsaw: Wolters Kluwer, 2010), 160, 169.

51. Leon Chajn, "Próba bilansu," in *Wymiar sprawiedliwości*, 20.

52. In the Poland of this period, the term "democratic" served as a euphemism to describe communists and fellow travelers. AAN, MS, syg. 7087, p. 87.

53. Chajn, "Próba bilansu," 21.

54. AAN, PKWN, syg. IX/8, p. 16; Władysław Grzymała, "Wspomnienia rozpoczęte w dniu 17 kwietnia 1982" (unpublished autobiographical manuscript in author's possession), 53–54.

55. Wendel, "Odrodzone sądownictwo polskie," 85–89; Mędrzycka, "Sądownik polski ma głos," 96–98.

56. Bereza and Okniński, *Sądownictwo siedleckie*, 137–144.

57. AAN, MS, Aleksander Chrościcki, Spis zdawczo-odbiorczy no. 13, poz. 421, syg. 13/2055, p. 121.

58. Grzymała, *Wspomnienia*, 3–4, 23.

59. Wacław Barcikowski, *W kręgu prawa i polityki: Wspomnienia z lat 1919–1956* (Katowice: Krajowa Agencja Wydawnicza, 1988), 78, 90–91.

60. Marek Kornat, "Rafał Lemkin's Formative Years and the Beginning of International Career in Inter-war Poland," in *Rafał Lemkin: A Hero of Humankind*, ed. Agnieszka Bieńczyk-Missala and Sławomir Dębski (Warsaw: PISM, 2010), 63.

61. Andrzej Pilch, *Studencki Ruch Polityczny w Polsce w latach 1932–1939* (Warsaw: PWN, 1972), 149, 151.

62. Grzymała, *Wspomnienia*, 84.

63. Jacek Misztal, "Działalność Związku Akademickiego Młodzież Wszechpolska na terenie miasta Warszawy w okresie międzywojennym—zarys problematyki," in *Organizacje młodzieżowe w XX wieku: Struktury, ideologia, działalność*, ed. Patryk Tomaszewski and Mariusz Wołos (Toruń: Adam Marszałek, 2008).

64. This left the appointment of new lawyers up to the minister, who could thus effectively control the flow of ethnic Jews into the profession. See Stanisław Gross, "Adwokatura," in *Wymiar sprawiedliwości w odrodzonej Polsce*, 79; Alina Cała, *Żyd—wróg odwieczny? Antysemitizm w Polsce i jego źródła* (Warsaw: Wydawnictwo Nisza, 2012), 382n134.

65. Grzymała, *Wspomnienia*, 23.

66. Cała, *Żyd—wróg odwieczny?*, 374–375.

67. Kubicki, personal interview, November 23, 2012; AAN, PKWN, syg. I / 4, p. 246.

4. The Special Courts

1. AAN, MS, syg. 1413, pp. 92–93. The theater today seats around 300 people (https://teatr-rzeszow.pl/article/plan-widowni?m=12).

2. Marcin Zaremba, *Wielka trwoga: Polska, 1944–1947: Ludowa reakcja na kryzys* (Warsaw: Znak, 2012), 565; Leon Chajn, *Kiedy Lublin byl Warszawą* (Warsaw: Czytelnik, 1964), 52.

3. Marek Gotard, "200 tys. gapiów oglądało egzekucję zbrodniarzy ze Stutthofu," *Trojmiasto.pl*, July 15, 2009, http://www.trojmiasto.pl/wiadomosci/200-tys-gapiow-ogladalo-egzekucje-zbrodniarzy-ze-Stutthofu-n33749.html; Zaremba, *Wielka Trwoga*, 567–568; Adam Kryński, "Egzekucje publiczne," *Tygodnik Powszechny* 2, no. 25 / 66, June 23, 1946.

4. Gabriel N. Finder and Alexander V. Prusin, *Justice behind the Iron Curtain: Nazis on Trial in Communist Poland* (Toronto: University of Toronto Press, 2018), 26.

5. Adam Lityński, *O prawie i sądach początków Polski Ludowej* (Białystok: Temida 2, 1999), 72; Leszek Kubicki, personal interview, November 28, 2012.

6. For more on the NTN, see Patrycja Grzebyk, "The Role of the Polish Supreme National Tribunal in the Development of Principles of International Criminal Law," in *Historical Origins of International Criminal Law*, vol. 2, ed. Morten Bergsmo,

Cheah Wui Ling, and Yi Ping (Brussels: Torkel Opsahl Academic EPublisher, 2014), 603–630.

7. Finder and Prusin, *Justice behind the Iron Curtain*, 51; see also 110, 126.
8. AAN, MS, syg. 962, pp. 19–21; AAN, PKWN, syg. IX/10, pp. 18–19.
9. AAN, MS, syg. 1413, pp. 33–42.
10. AAN, MS, syg. 7087, pp. 92, 100.
11. Ibid., p. 95.
12. Ibid., pp. 95 and *verte*. See also AAN, MS, syg. 892, p. 109.
13. AAN, MS, syg. 6821, p. 66.
14. See Art. 4.2, *Dziennik Ustaw (DzU)* 1944, no. 4, poz. 21, and Art. 7, *DzU* 1945, no. 53, poz. 303.
15. AAN, MS, syg. 1484, p. 9.
16. AAN, MS, syg. 1436, p. 167.
17. Kubicki, personal interview, November 28, 2012.
18. AAN, MS, syg. 1413, "Uwagi o zagadnieniach chwili obecnej," pp. 60–79.
19. AAN, MS, syg. 7087, p. 82.
20. Władysław Grzymała, "Wspomnienia rozpoczęte w dniu 17 kwietnia 1982" (unpublished autobiographical manuscript in author's possession), 54–60. Although the military courts were responsible for judging crimes with "anti-state" intent, civilian courts were empowered by a November 1945 Decree (*DzU* 1945, no. 53, poz. 301) to apply the death penalty to a wide range of regular crimes, including murders, robberies, and abuse of office, in "summary" [*doraźne*] proceedings heard by special sections of the civilian courts. The "hooded courts" described by Grzymała appear to refer to these special sections, which appear to have existed only on paper at his court. See also Grzegorz Jakubowski, *Sądownictwo powszechne w Polsce w latach 1944–1950* (Warsaw: IPN, 2002), 39–40.
21. AAN, PKWN, syg. IX/9a, p. 22.
22. AAN, MS, syg. 892, pp. 106–108.
23. AAN, MS, syg. 6821, pp. 65–66.
24. AAN, MS, syg. 8903, p. 2; AAN, MS, syg. 8670, p. 15.
25. AAN, MS, syg. 6821, pp. 64–66 *verte*.
26. AAN, MS, syg. 7087, p. 100.
27. AAN, MS, syg. 859, p. 25.
28. Alina Skibińska, "'Dostał 10 lat, ale za co?' Analiza motywacji sprawców zbrodni na Żydach na wsi kieleckiej w latach 1942–1944," in *Zarys krajobrazu: Wieś polska wobec Zagłady Żydów, 1942–1945*, ed. Barbara Engelking and Jan Grabowski (Warsaw: Centrum Badań nad Zagładą Żydów, 2011), 319n14.
29. Chajn, *Kiedy Lublin był Warszawą*, 51; AAN, MS, syg. 7087, p. 100; AAN, MS, syg. 892, p. 109.
30. AAN, MS, syg. 1436, pp. 126–127.
31. AAN, MS, syg. 7087, p. 92.

32. AAN, MS, syg. 1436, p. 126.
33. AAN, MS, syg. 6821, pp. 65 verte-66.
34. AAN, MS, syg. 7087, pp. 92 verte, 99.
35. Chajn, *Kiedy Lublin byl Warszawą*, 55-56.
36. AAN, MS, syg. 1436, p. 127; AAN, MS, syg. 7087, pp. 93-94 verte, 99.
37. Leszek Kubicki and Sylwester Zawadzki, *Udział ławników w postepowaniu karnym: Opinie a rzeczywistość* (Warsaw: Wydawnictwo Prawnicze, 1970).
38. Zaremba, *Wielka Trwoga*, 263; W. Dubiański, A. Dziuba, and A. Dziurok, *Kadra bezpieki, 1945-1990: Obsada stanowisk kierowniczych aparatu bezpecieństwa w województwach śląskim/katowickim, bielskim i częstochowskim* (Katowice: IPN, 2009), 20; Henryk Dominiczak, *Organy bezpieciéństwa PRL, 1944-1990* (Warsaw: Bellona, 1997), 27, 36.
39. AAN, MS, syg. 6821, pp. 65 and verte.
40. Wacław Barcikowski, "Ważniejsze zagadnienia ustawodawcze," *Demokratyczny Przegląd Prawniczy (DPP)* 2, no. 2 (1946): 2.
41. Ewa Mędrzycka, "Sądownik polski ma głos," in *Wymiar sprawiedliwości w odrodzonej Polsce* (Warsaw: Ministerstwo Sprawiedliwości, 1945), 99.
42. AAN, MS, syg. 892, p. 107.
43. AAN, MS, syg. 7087, p. 85; AAN, PKWN, syg. IX/6, p. 241.
44. AAN, PKWN, syg. IX/9a, p. 17.
45. AAN, MS, syg. 1661, p. 1.
46. Adam Kopciowski, "Zajścia antyżydowskie na Lubelszczyźnie w pierwszych latach po drugiej wojnie światowej," *Zagłada Żydów: Studia i materiały* 3 (2007): 183; Krzysztof Szwagrzyk, ed., *Aparat bezpieczeństwa w Polsce: Kadra kierownicza*, vol. 1, *1944-1956* (Warsaw: IPN, 2005), 63; Dubiański, Dziuba, and Dziurok, *Kadra bezpieki, 1945-1990*, 17-18; Tomasz Rochatka, *Urzad Bezpiecienstwa w Gnieźnie w latach 1945-1956* (Poznań: Wydawnictwo Poznańskie, 2010), 78.
47. Zaremba, *Wielka Trwoga*, 266, 269; AAN, PKWN, syg. XI/6, p. 35; Skibińska, "'Dostał 10 lat, ale za co?,'" 380; USHMM, SSKKr, File 193, Reel 4, Slide 687; NARA, RG84, M1945, Roll 12, "Jewish Refugees in Poland," January 1, 1946, p. 2.
48. Lawrence Douglas, *The Memory of Judgment: Making Law and History in the Trials of the Holocaust* (New Haven, CT: Yale University Press, 2005), 65.
49. There is some uncertainty about the number of death sentences issued by the Special Courts. Leszek Kubicki, in his 1963 monograph *Zbrodnie wojenne w świetle prawa polskiego*, quotes a figure of 631 death sentences, but this appears to be based on an incomplete estimate published in the July 1946 issue of *Demokratyczny Przegląd Prawniczy*, before the Special Courts completed their work. A complete accounting from 1948 (see AAN, MS, syg. 859, p. 19) contains the 721 figure. A more recent study counted 759 individual clemency requests and estimated a total of 780 based on the number of requests for clemency to Bierut's office; see Zdzisław Biegański, "Kara śmierci w orzecznictwie Specjalnych Sądów Karnych

w Polsce (1944–1946)," *Echa Przeszłości* 5 (2004): 194. Because the discrepancy does not materially alter the conclusions of this book, I have stuck to the official figures from the Ministry of Justice. The French number comes from Peter Novick, *The Resistance versus Vichy: The Purge of Collaborators in Liberated France* (New York: Columbia University Press, 1968), 186. Keep in mind that there were about 10,000 extrajudicial executions in France.

50. AAN, PKWN, syg. IX/8, p. 76.

51. See Rozdział XVIII, Kodeks Karny, *DzU* 1932, no. 60, poz. 571; AAN, PKWN, syg. IX/8, pp. 76–77.

52. Zygmunt Kapitaniak, "Nadzór sądowy a niezawisłość sędziowska," *DPP* 2, no. 2 (1946): 4.

53. Antoni Landau, "Omówienia: Zbiór przepisów specjalnych przeciwko zbrodniarzom hitlerowskim i zdrajcom narodu," *DPP* 2, no. 3–4 (1946): 92.

54. Antoni Pyszkowski, "Bilans działalności sądów specjalnych," *DPP* 2, no. 11–12 (1946): 37.

55. Jerzy Sawicki, "O prawie sądów specjalnych," in *Wymiar sprawiedliwości w odrodzonej Polsce,* 55.

56. Ibid., 60; Landau, "Omówienia," 92; Wacław Barcikowski, *W kręgu prawa i polityki: Wspomnienia z lat 1919–1956* (Katowice: Krajowa Agencja Wydawnicza, 1988), 146.

57. Stanisław Podemski, "Stryczek i kula: Historia kary śmierci w PRL," *Gazeta Wyborcza,* January 13, 2001; Chajn, *Kiedy Lublin byl Warszawą,* 53–59. For evidence that Bierut carefully considered opinions on commutation and went against some that had very powerful backers, see Zdzisław Biegański, "Kara śmierci," 197.

58. Chajn, *Kiedy Lublin byl Warszawą,* 137.

59. AAN, PKWN, syg. IX/10, pp. 133–134.

60. AAN, MS, syg. 7087, p. 93.

61. Czesława Żuławska, "Dekret sierpniowy widziany okiem sędziego," *Forum Żydzi-Chrześcijanie-Muzułmanie,* June 9, 2011, https://www.znak.org.pl/?lang1=pl&page1=viewpoint&subpage1=viewpoint00&infopassid1=299&scrt1=sn.

62. AAN, MS, syg. 3979, pp. 17–18 (documents may not be properly paginated).

63. *DzU* 1945, no. 7, poz. 29.

64. AAN, MS, syg. 1436, p. 127.

65. Chajn, *Kiedy Lublin byl Warszawą,* 41; AAN, PKWN, syg. IX/10, pp. 62–63.

66. Pyszkowski, "Bilans działalności sądów specjalnych," 37.

67. Antoni Landau, "Omówienia," 92–93.

68. Judith Shklar, *Legalism: Law, Morals, and Political Trials* (Cambridge, MA: Harvard University Press, 1986), 8–9, 111.

69. Ibid., 143, 118.

70. Ibid., 112, 147, 192.

71. Ibid., 167.

72. Ibid., 192.

5. Rewriting the Narrative of the Past

1. Elżbieta Romanowska, "Przekształcenia w powszechnym wymiarze sprawiedliwości w Polsce w latach 1944–1956," *Czasopismo prawno-historyczne* 68, no. 2 (2016): 37, 39.

2. Special Courts were created in the Warsaw, Lublin, Kraków, Łódź, Toruń, Katowice, Wrocław, Poznań, and Gdańsk appellate areas. The few existing studies of the work of the Special Courts have not uncovered any examples of politically motivated prosecutions of anticommunists. Dariusz Burczyk, who studied the Special Court in Gdańsk, cites a witness to the trial of Carl Maria Splett, the German bishop of occupied Gdańsk, who condemned it as a "typical Stalinist show trial." However, the eagerness to convict Splett, who spent ten years in prison and in detention in a monastery before being deported to Germany, is clearly not of a piece with the repression of the nationalist Polish Underground, which is what "political trials" are generally understood to refer to in postwar Poland. Overall, Burczyk notes that the court in Gdańsk strove for objectivity in its verdicts. See Dariusz Burczyk, "Specjalny Sąd Karny w Gdańsku (1945–1946): Przyczynek do monografii," *Przegląd Archiwalny Instytutu Pamięci Narodowej* 7 (2014): 306, 308.

3. See Adam Lityński, "Administracja, Polityka i Sąd Tajny w Polsce Ludowej, 1950–1954," *Roczniki Administracji i Prawa* 10 (2010): 21–37. Also see Maria Stanowska and Adam Strzembosz, *Sędziowie warszawscy w czasie próby, 1981–1988* (Warsaw: IPN, 2005), 23–32.

4. Donald Bloxham, *Genocide on Trial: War Crimes Trials and the Formation of Holocaust History and Memory* (Oxford: Oxford University Press, 2010), 10.

5. From September 1944 to October 17, 1946, death penalties made up 18.2 percent of all guilty verdicts. From October 17, 1946, to the end of 1947, they made up 5.5 percent of all guilty verdicts. For the years 1948 to 1956, death penalties made up the following percentages of all guilty verdicts: 1948, 7.9 percent; 1949, 13.7 percent; 1950, 10.7 percent; 1951, 4.1 percent; 1952, 1.6 percent; 1953, 1.7 percent; 1954, 0.8 percent; 1955, 0.8 percent; 1956, 0 percent. These data can be found in: AAN, MS, syg. 859, pp. 19, 25; AAN, MS, syg. 1510, p. 34; AAN, MS, syg. 854, p. 129; Leszek Kubicki, *Zbrodnie wojenne w świetle prawa polskiego* (Warsaw: PWN, 1963), 182.

6. "Zjazd w Krakowie, 9–10.ii.1946," *Demokratyczny Przegląd Prawniczy* 2, no. 2 (1946): 41.

7. These statistics are based on a search of the IPN's electronic records in Warsaw, conducted in the fall of 2011.

8. Regarding the conviction rates of the Lublin and Kraków Special Courts, it is important to note that these are approximations because the archival collections of the Special Courts may not contain all the cases actually heard by those courts. For example, the case file of Tadeusz Chojnacki (see Chapter 7) was removed from the collection of the Lublin Special Court, where Chojnacki was initially acquitted, and transferred to the Radom District Court, where it became part of their archival

collection, when he was retried on appeal and acquitted three years later. It has not, however, been possible to establish why other case files were moved. For example, the cases of the village policeman from Cholerzyn and Edward S. (see Chapter 6), both of whom were tried and convicted by the Kraków Special Court under lesser articles of the August Decree before prosecutors appealed their sentences to the Supreme Court, are missing from the collection of the Kraków Special Court. In their cases, the Supreme Court rejected the prosecutorial appeals and no new trial was held, but their files do not appear to have been returned to the archive of the Kraków Special Court.

9. Kamiński, who was from the Slovak town of Rimavská Sobota, is the only defendant in my case sample who was not identified as an ethnic Pole. However, I feel it is legitimate to include him in this study given his close and enduring identification with Poland: he fought in Polish partisan units, worked as a postwar Polish state employee, was misidentified as a Pole by the security services, attracted interest at the highest levels of government, and appears to still have been living in Poland as of 1965 (see USHMM, SSKL, File 34, Reel, 2, Slides 244 and 402). More information about him is provided below.

10. USHMM, SSKL, File 34, Reel 2, Slide 353; USHMM, SSKKr, File 59, Reel 2, Slide 719.

11. USHMM, SSKL, File 56, Reel 3, Slides 3, 12–15, 68, 74–76, 135–138, 143, 147, 152.

12. USHMM, SSKL, File 34, Reel 2, Slides 229–231.

13. Although the Supreme National Tribunal technically had oversight responsibility, the actual appeals filed by the Tribunal prosecutor were heard by the Supreme Court, from which the Tribunal judges were drawn. I have not been able to find the reason for this bureaucratic discrepancy, although the Supreme Court had a wider pool of judges to draw from and was therefore the more practical appeals venue.

14. The Lublin Special Court was the first in the country to begin operations and, according to the USHMM's database, Obarzanek's was the first such case to be tried by the court.

15. USHMM, SSKL 9, Reel 1, Slides 496, 524, 529–533, 543–544, 556, 559–560. The archival number of the Supreme Court decision is K 2463 / 46 (Judges Bzowski, Jamontt, Petrusewicz). From January 1946 to October 1946, the judges and prosecutors of the Supreme National Tribunal had oversight responsibility for the Special Courts. The chief prosecutor of the Tribunal could appeal Special Court verdicts by cassation to the NTN within three months of issuance. See *Dziennik Ustaw* 1946, no. 5, poz. 45, Articles 15–16.

16. USHMM, SSKL, File 15, Reel 1, Slides 575, 578, 613–620, 630–633. The archival number of the Supreme Court decision is K 2459 / 46 (Judges Giżycki, Sokalski, Szerer).

17. USHMM, SSKL, File 98, Reel 4, Slides 269, 286, 290, 294, 300, 318–321, 325, 332, 350–353. The archival number of the Supreme Court case is K 2505 / 46 (Judges

Bzowski, Schwakopf, Petrusewicz). Andrew Kornbluth, "The Holocaust and Postwar Justice in Poland in Three Acts," in *Microhistories of the Holocaust,* ed. Claire Zalc and Tal Bruttmann (New York: Berghahn Books, 2017), 271–272.

18. USHMM, SSKKr, File 193, Reel 4, Slides 656–657, 849, 856.
19. USHMM, SSKL, File 77, Reel 3, Slides 770–772, 790, 793–795, 819–821, 825, 829.
20. USHMM, SSKL, File 172, Reel 6, Slides 333, 464, 467, 498.
21. USHMM, SSKKr, File 91, Reel 3, Slides 462, 464, 468, 479, 548, 583–587.
22. USHMM, SSKKr, File 447, Reel 11, Slide 1062.
23. USHMM, SSKKr, File 157, Reel 4, Slides 409–415, 423–424, 471.
24. USHMM, SSKKr, File 156, Reel 4, Slide 321.
25. USHMM, SSKKr, File 288, Reel 7, Slides 726–727.
26. USHMM, SSKKr, File 383, Reel 9, Slide 844.
27. Ibid., Slides 911–915.
28. AIPN, SWmstW, Files 145–146, pp. 29, 43, 47.
29. Stanisław Król, already a doctor of laws, had been promoted from assessor to municipal court judge in March 1929. See the official register in *Ruch Służbowy: Dodatek do Dziennik Urzędowego Ministerstwa Sprawiedliwości,* no. 14 (1929): 99, https://jbc.bj.uj.edu.pl/Content/357107/PDF/NDIGCZAS016651_1929_dod__014.pdf. The NKVD assumed that the functioning of municipal courts in the war meant that judicial personnel had collaborated. He was released and became a Special Court judge. See *Tarnów: Wielki przewodnik,* vol. 10 (Tarnów: Tarnowskie Towarzystwo Kulturalne, 2003), 86.
30. USHMM, SSKKr, File 288, Reel 7, Slides 709–710.
31. USHMM, SSKKr, File 69, Reel 2, Slides 1039–1041, 1044, 1047.
32. USHMM, SSKKr, File 288, Reel 7, Slide 714.
33. Ibid., Slides 623, 700.
34. USHMM, SSKKr, File 60, Reel 2, Slides 841–846, 856, 870–878, 880. The archival number of the Supreme Court decision is K 2532 / 46 (Judges Bzowski, Korsak, Kirst).

6. Between Politics and Retribution

1. Judith Shklar, *Legalism: Law, Morals, and Political Trials* (Cambridge, MA: Harvard University Press, 1986), 9, 107–108.
2. Ibid., 112.
3. For the duration of the existence of the Special Courts, from October 1944 to November 17, 1946, there were 55,354 August cases that reached Special Court prosecutors, 12,529 indictments issued, and 17,021 cases suspended. A total of 7,364 August cases were actually adjudicated by the Special Courts, and 3,954 criminal sentences were issued, of which 2,690 were sentences of less than 10 years (68 percent of the total), 543 were of more than 10 years (13.7 percent of the total), and 721 were death sentences (18.2 percent of the total). See AAN, MS, syg. 859, pp. 19, 25.

4. From September 12, 1944, to October 17, 1946, the courts heard 7,364 August cases and issued 3,954 guilty verdicts (53.6 percent). From October 17, 1946, through 1947, there were 9,765 cases heard and 5,463 guilty verdicts (55.9 percent). In 1948 an unknown number of cases were heard and 3,227 guilty verdicts were issued. In the first half of 1949, there were 1,552 cases heard and 825 guilty verdicts (53.2 percent). See AAN, MS, syg. 859, pp. 19, 25; AAN, MS, syg. 1510, p. 34; AAN, MS, syg. 854, p. 129.

5. These conviction rates must be taken as approximations because of the possibility that some case files may have been transferred elsewhere. Although I have found no evidence of missing District Court records, as opposed to Special Court records, the possibility cannot be excluded. Based on a count of the collections held by the Warsaw city archive (APmstW), the Siedlce city archive (APS), and the United States Holocaust Memorial Museum (USHMM), I estimate that the rates of conviction from 1946 to 1949 for anti-Jewish crimes were 38 percent in Warsaw (111 cases, 141 defendants, 54 convictions, 6 acquitted on appeal, and 2 convicted on appeal); 19 percent in Siedlce (25 cases, 36 defendants, 7 convictions); 32 percent in Radom (22 cases, 28 defendants, 9 convictions, 2 more acquitted at retrial); 15 percent in Kielce (30 cases, 53 defendants, 8 convictions); and 71 percent in Lublin (16 cases, 32 defendants, 23 convictions).

6. Chajn was referring to the practice in the Generalgouvernement whereby German courts were responsible for political offenses and felonies, while Polish courts continued to hear contractual and inheritance disputes, as well as misdemeanors.

7. Leon Chajn, "Sądy a społeczeństwo," *Demokratyczny Przegląd Prawniczy (DPP)* 1, no. 2 (1945): 7–9.

8. Zygmunt Kapitaniak, "Nadzór sądowy a niezawisłość sędziowska," *DPP* 2, no. 2 (1946): 4, 7; AAN, MS, syg. 582, pp. 6, 22.

9. Stefan Bancerz, "Wymiar sprawiedliwości w świetle narady krajowej prawników PPR," *DPP* 2, no. 9–10 (1946): 29–30.

10. Leon Chajn, "Trzeci rok," *DPP* 2, no. 7 (1946): 6–7.

11. Jerzy Jodłowski, "Przemówienia na otwarciu szkoły prawniczej w Łodzi," *DPP* 2, no. 5–6 (1946): 54; AAN, MS, syg. 582, pp. 35–36.

12. AAN, MS, syg. 3979, pp. 13, 30, 50–53. The revised decree is registered under *Dziennik Ustaw (DzU)* 1946, no. 69, poz. 377.

13. AAN, MS, syg. 5702, pp. 2, 53, 56, 105 *verte*, 106, 107 *verte*.

14. Wacław Barcikowski, *W kręgu prawa i polityki: Wspomnienia z lat 1919–1956* (Katowice: Krajowa Agencja Wydawnicza, 1988), 158.

15. Władysław Grzymała, "Wspomnienia rozpoczęte w dniu 17 kwietnia 1982" (unpublished autobiographical manuscript in author's possession), 60–61, 66–69.

16. AAN, MS, syg. 5703, pp. 108 *verte* and 109, 167, 170–171.

17. Grzymała, *Wspomnienia*, 62–63.

18. Barcikowski, *W kręgu prawa i polityki*, 137, 142–144, 156.
19. Wacław Barcikowski, "Ważniejsze zagadnienia ustawodawcze," *DPP* 2, no. 2 (1946): 3; Kapitaniak, "Nadzór sądowy," 7.
20. Barcikowski, *W kręgu prawa i polityki*, 153, 158, 165–166.
21. Leon Chajn, *Kiedy Lublin byl Warszawą* (Czytelnik: Warsaw, 1964), 45.
22. Leszek Kubicki, personal interview, November 28, 2012.
23. "Sawicki, Jerzy," in *Polski słownik biograficzny*, ed. Henryk Markiewicz, vol. 35, book 3/146 (Wrocław: PAN, 1994), 319–320; Leszek Kubicki, personal interview, November 23, 2012.
24. Michał Fajst, "Leszek Lernell, Stanisław Batawia i Warszawska szkoła kryminologiczna w latach pięćdziesiątych XX wieku," *Studia Iuridica* 46 (2006): 63; Kubicki, personal interview, November 28, 2012.
25. Lech Falandysz, "Arnold Gubiński (1916–1997)," *Studia Iuridica* 34 (1997): 219–221; Kubicki, personal interview, November 23, 2012.
26. Kubicki, personal interview, November 28, 2012. See also Arkadiusz Bereza, "Prokuratura Sądu Najwyższego w latach 1945–1950," in *Regnare Gubernare Administrare: Z dziejów administracji, sądownictwa, i nauki prawa*, ed. Stanisław Grodziski and Andrzej Dziadzio (Kraków: Akademia Frycza Modrzewskiego, 2012), 139–152; Jerzy Szenfeld and Józef Szarek, "Fenomen Uniwersytetu Woldenberskiego," in *Dawna medycyna i weterynaria militarna*, ed. Mariusz Felsmann, Józef Szarek, and Mirosława Felsmann (Chełmno: Towarzystwo Przyjaciół Dolnej Wisły, 2009), 175.
27. Marcin Kwiecień, "Przyczynek do dziejów Komisji powołanej w związku z wynikiem kampanii wojennej 1939 roku: Sprawa Tadeusza Cypriana przeciwko Jerzemu Giertychowi," in *Krakowskie Studia z Historii Państwa i Prawa*, 5/2012, ed. Wacław Uruszczak, Dorota Malec, and Maciej Mikuła (Kraków: Wydawnictwo Uniwersytetu Jagiellońskiego, 2013), 332n12; "Obiektyw w kamaszu," *Profotografia.pl*, November 12, 2018, https://www.profotografia.pl/portal/rozmowy-opinie/obiektyw-w-kamaszu-2/; "Notatki jeńca," *Profotografia.pl*, November 13, 2018, https://www.profotografia.pl/portal/publikacje/notatki-jenca-tadeusz-cyprian-na-i-wojnie-swiatowej/; Violetta Szostak, "Życie żołnierzy poza frontem na reporterskich zdjęciach sprzed stu lat," *Tygodnik Poznań, Wyborcza.pl*, March 15, 2019, https://poznan.wyborcza.pl/poznan/7,105531,24548228,wieczorem-wezuwiusz-jest-bardzo-ozywiony.html.
28. Kubicki, personal interviews, November 23 and 28, 2012.
29. Juliusz Makarewicz, "Prawo karne w Katowicach," *Gazeta sądowna warszawska* 64, no. 6 (February 8, 1937): 81–85, 87.
30. AAN, MS, syg. 142, pp. 8–9.
31. Leon Chajn, "Na przełomie dwóch lat," *DPP* 4, no. 1 (1948): 5–6.
32. Antoni Pyszkowski, "Bilans działalności sądów specjalnych," *DPP* 2, no. 11–12 (1946): 38.

33. Leszek Kubicki, *Zbrodnie wojenne w świetle prawa polskiego* (Warsaw: PWN, 1963), 79–80.

34. Arkadiusz Bereza, *Sąd Najwyższy w latach 1945-1962: Organizacja i działalność* (Warsaw: C. H. Beck, 2012), 54.

35. Kubicki, *Zbrodnie wojenne*, 93–94.

36. Jerzy Sawicki and Arnold Gubiński, "Logika celowości czy logika werbalizmu: Rzecz o orzecznictwie Sądu Najwyższego w sprawach z Dekretu z dnia 31. VIII.1944," *DPP* 3, no. 26 (1947): 17; "Wyrok z 10 marca 1947 (K. 2485 / 46)," *Państwo i Prawo* (*PiP*) 2, no. 29 (1947): 176. The presiding judges were Bzowski, Schwakopf, and Petrusewicz.

37. Kubicki, *Zbrodnie wojenne*, 103, 114–115.

38. "Wyrok z dnia 8 lutego 1947 r. (K. 2451 / 46)," *Zbiór orzeczeń Sądu Najwyższego: Orzeczenia Izby Karnej* 2 (1947): 99–101; Kubicki, *Zbrodnie wojenne*, 115.

39. "Wyrok z 20 marca 1947 r. (K. 2509 / 46)," *PiP* 2, no. 9 (1947): 175.

40. These three cases are mentioned in Kubicki, *Zbrodnie wojenne*, 104 and n42.

41. "Wyrok z 10 marca 1947 r. (K 2506 / 46)," *PiP* 2, no. 9 (1947): 176.

42. Kubicki, *Zbrodnie wojenne*, 106, 109.

43. Sawicki and Gubiński, "Logika celowości," 16–24.

44. USHMM, SSKKr, File 256, Reel 6, Slides 183, 426–429.

45. Sawicki and Gubiński, "Logika celowości," 24–27.

46. Arkadiusz Bereza, *Sąd Najwyższy*, 54.

47. AAN, MS, syg. 4852, p. 1.

48. "Do orzeczenia Sądu Najwyższego w sprawie Nr K 1771 / 47," *PiP* 2, no. 12 (1947): 143–145.

49. AAN, MS, syg. 5503, p. 2 (original pagination, documents in file not numbered consecutively).

50. Barcikowski, *W kręgu prawa i polityki*, 178; Bereza, *Sąd Najwyższy*, 55–57, 59.

51. *DzU* 1948, no. 18, poz. 124; AAN, MS, syg. 582, pp. 35–36; Kubicki, personal interviews, November 23 and 28, 2012; Piotr Kładoczny, "Kształcenie prawników w Polsce w latach 1944–1989," *Studia Iuridica*, 35 (1998): 100; Grzymała, *Wspomnienia*, 66, 69. For further discussion of the influence of universities on the development of communism in East Central Europe, see John Connelly, *Captive University: The Sovietization of East German, Czech, and Polish Higher Education, 1945–1956* (Chapel Hill: University of North Carolina Press, 2000).

7. The District Courts

1. APS, SOS, File 652, pp. 3, 9 and *verte*, 12 and *verte*, 15, 101–103, 187 and *verte*, *Protokół rozprawy głównej z dnia 27 maja 1948*, pp. 18 *verte*, 19, 30 *verte*–32 (this is the original pagination—the file is lacking archival pagination); APS, SOS, File 653, pp. 158, 167 *verte*, 168, 230 *verte*, 231.

2. The original complainant in the case, MO officer Wiktor Kopyść, believed that the boy's executioner was a local Blue Policeman who was a defendant in an earlier case.

3. APS, SOS, File 695, pp. 128–129. Andrew Kornbluth, "The Holocaust and Postwar Justice in Poland in Three Acts," in *Microhistories of the Holocaust,* ed. Claire Zalc and Tal Bruttmann (New York: Berghahn Books, 2017), 275.

4. APS, SOS, File 694, pp. 6–7, 13 and *verte,* 16–17 *verte,* 45, 47 *verte*–48, 113 *verte,* 117, 112–118 *verte,* 126–128.

5. USHMM, SORd, File 90, Reel 3, Slides 857, 862, 893–896, 1095–1100, 1113–1114. "Comanche" was identified by a witness as one Tadeusz Pogorzelski.

6. USHMM, SSKL, File 9, Reel 1, Slide 530; USHMM, SOL, File 142, Reel 6, Slide 118; USHMM, SORd, File 74, Reel 3, Slide 763.

7. USHMM, SORd, File 220, Reel 11, Slides 1033–1034, 1041, 1048–1052, 1090–1097.

8. Although responsibility for trying August crimes was transferred from the District Courts to the Appellate Courts in 1949, for unknown reasons the Warsaw District Court still tried this case in 1950. According to the reorganization of the court system in 1949, Appellate Courts became responsible for hearing appeals from District Courts, which is why the appeal in Siedlecki's case went to the Warsaw Appellate Court and not the Supreme Court. See Grzegorz Jakubowski, *Sądownictwo powszechne w Polsce w latach 1944–1950* (Warsaw: IPN, 2002), 166.

9. APmstW–M, SOW, File 3948, pp. 26 *verte*–28 *verte,* 48 *verte*–49, 78.

10. APmstW–M, SOW, File 2814, pp. 99 *verte*–100.

11. USHMM, SOK, Files 121–122, Reel 1, Slides 397, 506, 695, 721–722, 725. The victim is also referred to in the documents by a Polonized version of her name and by her maiden name as Wólowa and Topielowa.

12. USHMM, SORd, File 59, Reel 2, Slides 916, 920, 925–926; APmstW–M, SOW, File 900, pp. 58–59 *verte;* USHMM, SORd, File 136, Reel 7, Slides 762–763, 839. The device of the "dropped" evidence was used in more than one case. Blue Policeman Stanisław Witkowski fended off claims that he had shot a Jewish woman by insisting that he had let her go after checking her papers, only for her real IDs to "fall out" as she was walking away, whereupon a Ukrainian shot her. USHMM, SOL, File 2, Reel 17, Slides 366–367.

13. APmstW–M, SOW, File 3216; USHMM, SORd, File 206, Reel 11, Slides 170, 173; APmstW–M, SOW, File 2455, pp. 111–113; APmstW–M, SOW, File 3344, pp. 255 *verte*–257, 371 *verte.* For unknown reasons the Jankowska case is bundled with APmstW–M, SOW, File 3344, and lacks a unique Warsaw city archive number. The file is marked with its original docket number, Kspec No. 1216 / 46, and period inventory number, V Sn. 352 / 46.

14. From 1946 to 1949, six death sentences were issued by the Warsaw court, representing 11 percent of all guilty verdicts; two were commuted and one was

overturned on appeal. In Kielce, three death sentences were issued, representing 37 percent of all guilty verdicts; three were commuted. In Radom, three death sentences were issued, representing 33 percent of all guilty verdicts; two were commuted. In Lublin, eight death sentences were issued, representing 34 percent of all guilty verdicts; five were commuted. It Siedlce, no death sentences were issued. These figures are based on a count of the collections held by the Warsaw city archive (APmstW), the Siedlce city archive (APS), and the United States Holocaust Memorial Museum (USHMM). However, as noted previously, these conviction rates must be taken as approximations because of the possibility that some case files may have been transferred elsewhere. Although I have found no evidence of missing District Court records, as opposed to Special Court records, the possibility cannot be excluded.

15. APmstW-M, SOW, File 582, pp. 102 and *verte,* 104-105; USHMM, SOL, File 142, Reel 6, Slides 166-174; USHMM, SOL, File 46, Reel 17, Slide 752; USHMM, SOL, File 17, Reel 1, Slides 267, 480; USHMM, SORd, File 39, Reel 1, Slide 521; USHMM, SOK, File 325, Reel 4, Slides 136-137.

16. USHMM, SOK, File 248, Reel 9, Slide 283; USHMM, SOL, File 46, Reel 17, Slides 543, 546; USHMM, SORd, File 167, Reel 9, Slide 601; USHMM, SOK, File 171, Reel 5, Slide 449; APmstW-M, SOW, File 3143, p. 165 *verte;* USHMM, SORd, Files 111-112, Reel 5, slides 562, 596, 1004.

17. USHMM, SORd, File 39, Reel 1, Slides 505, 508; USHMM, SOL, File 17, Reel 1, Slides 451-455.

18. SOS, APS, File 695, pp. 143-144 *verte;* USHMM, SAL, File 179, Reel 37, Slide 137.

19. Władysław Grzymała, "Wspomnienia rozpoczęte w dniu 17 kwietnia 1982" (unpublished autobiographical manuscript in author's possession), 58; USHMM, SORd, File 39, Reel 1, Slides 408-409.

20. APS, SOS, File 550, pp. 1-21 (investigative files), pp. 162 *verte*-163, 243 *verte* (trial files).

21. USHMM, SORd, File 74, Reel 3, Slides 759-765.

22. USHMM, SOK, File 65, Reel 5, Slides 10, 53-55.

23. Janusz Bardach and Kathleen Gleeson, *Surviving Freedom: After the Gulag* (Berkeley: University of California Press, 2003), 20.

24. Oscar Pinkus, letter to the author, June 27, 2013.

25. USHMM, SSKL, File 98, Reel 4, Slide 319; APS, SOS, File 652, p. 32. This is the original document pagination; the file has not been fully paginated by the archive.

26. ŻIH, Zbiór relacji Żydów ocalałych, statement of Abram Rozenman, syg. 301/5609, privately translated from the Yiddish by Anna Szyba, translation, pp. 5-7; APS, SOS, file 663, pp. 29-30, 64 *verte.*

27. Wacław Sławiński (APS, SOS, File 709) and Władysław Kozioł (APS, SOS, File 629) were acquitted. Zdzisław Kędzierski (APS, SOS, File 694) and Franciszek Kuś (APS, SOS, File 663) were sentenced to three and eight years, respectively.

8. Cold War Considerations

1. Brian Porter-Szücs, *Poland in the Modern World: Beyond Martyrdom* (Chichester: Wiley-Blackwell, 2014), 208.

2. AAN, MS, syg. 450, p. 122.

3. From October 17, 1946, through 1947, there were 9,765 cases adjudicated and 5,463 guilty verdicts, of which there were 4,733 sentences of less than 10 years, 425 of more than 10 years, and 305 death sentences (5.5 percent of total sentences). In 1948 an unknown number of cases were adjudicated and 3,227 guilty verdicts were issued, of which there were 2,576 sentences of less than 10 years, 301 of more than 10 years, 92 life sentences, and 258 death sentences (7.9 percent of total sentences). In 1949 there were 2,964 cases adjudicated and 1,667 guilty verdicts, of which there were 520 sentences of less than 3 years, 494 of from 3 to 6 years, 380 of more than 6 years, 43 life sentences, and 230 death sentences (13.7 percent of total sentences). See AAN, MS, syg. 859, pp. 19, 25; AAN, MS, syg. 1510, p. 34; AAN, MS, syg. 854, p. 129; Leszek Kubicki, *Zbrodnie wojenne w świetle prawa polskiego* (Warsaw: PWN, 1963), 182.

4. "Ustawa z dnia 27 kwietnia 1949 o zmianie przepisów postępowania karnego," *Dziennik Ustaw (DzU)* 1949 no. 32, poz. 238; APmstW–SM, Inwentarz archiwalny, vol. 257, Sąd Apelacyjny w Warszawie, 1945–1950, p. 11.

5. In the fourth quarter of 1949, August crimes made up the following percentages of the caseloads of selected Appellate Court prosecutors: Białystok, 56 percent; Kielce, 57.5 percent; Kraków, 51.5 percent; Lublin, 38.5 percent; Łódź, 64 percent; Poznań, 37.5 percent; Rzeszów, 59.4 percent; Warsaw, 61.5 percent. See AAN, MS, syg. 1576, pp. 1, 67, 82, 101, 115, 143, 169, 200.

6. AAN, MS, syg. 854, p. 42, 129; AAN, MS, syg. 455, p. 214; AAN, MS, syg. 450, p. 208.

7. AAN, SN, syg. 1/4, p. 38.

8. AAN, MS, syg. 372, pp. 136–139. What he did not mention, although many in the audience must have known, was that his brother Włodzimierz, a landowner who had been a deputy in the Sejm from 1930 to 1935, had perished in Uzbekistan in 1942 after being arrested and deported by the NKVD in 1939.

9. AAN, MS, syg. 372, pp. 136–139; AAN, SN, syg. 1/4, p. 39.

10. Arkadiusz Bereza, *Sąd Najwyższy w latach 1945–1962: Organizacja i działalność* (Warsaw: C. H. Beck, 2012), 55–56; Agnieszka Watola, "Problem niezawisłości w świetle obsady kadr Sądu Najwyższego i Naywyższego Sądu Wojskowego w początkach Polski Ludowej," *Z Dziejów Prawa* 4, no. 12 (2011): 241.

11. "Wyrok z dnia 13 lutego 1948 r. (Kr. K. 33/48)," *Zbiór orzeczeń Sądu Najwyższego: Orzeczenia Izby Karnej (Zb O)* 2 (1948): 98–100; "Wyrok z dnia 20 lutego 1948 (To. K. 362/47)," *Zb O* 4 (1948): 211–213; "Wyrok z dnia 19 maja 1948 r. (Kr K 393/48)," *Zb O* 3 (1948): 173–175; "Wyrok z dnia 28 września 1948 r. (Lu K 345/48)," *Zb O* 1 (1949): 45–46.

12. See, for example, "Wyrok z 10 października 1947 r. (K 1172/47)," *Państwo i Prawo* (*PiP*) 3, no. 3 (1948): 187. Also see verdicts referenced in Kubicki, *Zbrodnie wojenne*, 105n43, 109n51, 110n32.

13. "Wyrok z dnia 16 września 1947 r. (916/47)," *Zb O* 2 (1948): 102–103; "Wyrok z dnia 28 stycznia 1948 r. (Kr K 32/47)," *Zb O* 2 (1948): 100–101; Kubicki, *Zbrodnie wojenne*, 115, 116n63.

14. Kubicki, *Zbrodnie wojenne*, 115n60; "Tezy z orzeczeń Izby Karnej Sądu Najwyższego," *PiP* 5, no. 1 (1950): 137–138. The original verdict is to be found in AAN, SN, syg. 2/8695, pp. 6–10 (K 1519/49).

15. "Wyrok z dnia 8 lutego 1947 r. (K 2451/46)," *Zb O* 2 (1947): 98–102; "Tezy z orzeczeń Izby Karnej Sądu Najwyższego," *PiP* 5, no. 1 (1950): 138–139.

16. The seven judges were Rappaport, Sokalski, Potępa, Szerer, Eimer, Sitnicki, and Dorsz. Szerer, Sitnicki, and Dorsz later sat on the secret section of the Supreme Court.

17. Leszek Kubicki, personal interview, November 23, 2012.

18. For more on the secret section, see Adam Lityński, *Historia Prawa Polski Ludowej* (Warsaw: Wydawnictwo prawnicze LexisNexis, 2005), 19–20; Lityński, "Administracja, Polityka i Sąd Tajny w Polsce Ludowej, 1950–1954," *Roczniki Administracji i Prawa* 10 (2010): 21–37; Maria Stanowska and Adam Strzembosz, *Sędziowie warszawscy w czasie próby, 1981–1988* (Warsaw: IPN, 2005), 23–32.

19. The judges were Zygmunt Kapitaniak, Aleksander Bachrach, and Tadeusz Gdowski. AAN, SN, syg. 2/11793, K. 1076/50, p. 23. The General Prosecutor's Office was created in July 1950, following the Soviet practice, as an entirely separate government organization distinct from the Ministry of Justice.

20. "Uchwała całej Izby Karnej Sądu Najwyższego z dnia 2 lutego 1951 r. Nr K 1076/50," *PiP* 6, no. 4 (1951): 779–780. A month later, the sentences of the four perpetrators were reduced from 8 years to 3 years and from 5½ years to 1 year. The original rulings are in AAN, SN, syg. 2/11793, K. 1076/50, pp. 52–56 *verte*.

21. For a list of the judges involved in the secret section, see Stanowska and Strzembosz, *Sędziowie warszawscy*, 23–32. The judges involved in the 1951 decision were Bzowski, Rybczyński, Potępa, Szerer, Sitnicki, Kapitaniak, Bachrach, Merz, Haber, Czajkowski, and Kurowski. Only Potępa, Rybczyński, Haber, and Kapitaniak did not serve on the secret section.

22. AAN, MS, syg. 1972, pp. 13–15. Andrew Kornbluth, "The Holocaust and Postwar Justice in Poland in Three Acts," in *Microhistories of the Holocaust*, ed. Claire Zalc and Tal Bruttmann (New York: Berghahn Books, 2017), 280.

23. From 1950 to 1954, the sentencing breakdown for August crimes was as follows. 1950: 2,059 sentences, 1,633 for less than 10 years (79 percent of total), 169 for more than 10 years, 35 for life, and 222 for death (10.8 percent of total sentences). 1951: 1,596 sentences, 1,368 for less than 10 years (86 percent of total), 131 for more than 10 years, 30 for life, and 67 for death (4.2 percent). 1952: 782 sentences, 693 for less than 10 years (89 percent of total), 61 for more than 10 years, 15 for life, and 13

for death (1.7 percent). 1953: 744 sentences, 619 for less than 10 years (83 percent of total), 84 for more than 10 years, 28 for life, and 13 for death (1.7 percent). 1954: 454 sentences, 393 for less than 10 years (87 percent), 35 for more than 10 years, 22 for life, and 4 for death (0.9 percent). See Kubicki, *Zbrodnie wojenne*, 182.

24. AAN, MS, syg. 456, pp. 183–185, 187, 191; Kubicki, *Zbrodnie wojenne*, 183.

25. AAN, MS, syg. 7127, *Analiza i ocena orzecznictwa sądów województwa białostockiego w roku 1952 i w I kwartale 1953 r.*, p. 1 (original pagination); Leszek Kubicki, personal interview, November 28, 2012.

26. AAN, SN, syg. 1/9, pp. 40–41.

27. "Postanowienie składu siedmiu sędziów Izby Karnej Sądu Najwyższego z dnia 22 sierpnia 1951 r. (II K 128/50)," *Zb O* 2 (1952): 51; "Orzecznictwo Karne," *PiP* 6, no. 10 (1951): 646–647.

28. AAN, MS, syg. 450, p. 30; AAN, MS, syg. 2058; *DzU* 1951, no. 58, poz. 399; *DzU* 1952, no. 46, poz. 309; Henryk Podlaski, "Ustawa o amnestii—Wyrazem wielkoduszności i siły Polski Ludowej," *PiP* 8, no. 1 (1953): 70.

29. AAN, MS, syg. 1510, p. 72; AAN, MS, syg. 450, p. 59–60; AAN, MS, syg. 455, pp. 214, 219; AAN, MS, syg. 456, pp. 89, 91.

30. AAN, MS, syg. 456, pp. 92–96.

31. AAN, MS, syg. 450, p. 122. Kubicki, personal interview, November 28, 2012; Stanowska and Strzembosz, *Sędziowie warszawscy*, 24–25.

32. AAN, MS, syg. 456, p. 91; AAN, MS, syg. 450, pp. 152, 207–208; AAN, MS, syg. 7127, p. 22.

33. AAN, MS, syg. 450, pp. 180–182; AAN, MS, syg. 7127, p. 27; AAN, MS, 1508, p. 3.

34. AAN, MS, syg. 1510, pp. 66–68, 74, 77; AAN, MS, syg. 457, p. 231.

35. Władysław Grzymała, "Wspomnienia rozpoczęte w dniu 17 kwietnia 1982" (unpublished autobiographical manuscript in author's possession), 70, 74–77, 84–87.

9. The Principles of Socialist Humanism

1. APS, SOS, File 695, p. 152. Andrew Kornbluth, "The Holocaust and Postwar Justice in Poland in Three Acts," in *Microhistories of the Holocaust*, ed. Claire Zalc and Tal Bruttmann (New York: Berghahn Books, 2017), 281.

2. USHMM, SAL, File 54, Reel 10, Slides 908–909, 947.

3. USHMM, SAL, File 3, Reel 1, Slides 140–143.

4. USHMM, SAL, File 5, Reel 1, Slides 501, 504.

5. USHMM, SAL, File 112, Reel 23, Slides 147–148, 259–262.

6. USHMM, SAL, File 132, Reel 27, Slides 761, 765; USHMM, SAL, File 70, Reel 12, Slide 775.

7. USHMM, SAL, File 126, Reel 26, Slides 605–608.

8. USHMM, SAL, File 54, Reel 10, Slide 1014.

9. USHMM, SAL, File 91, Reel 16, Slide 904.
10. USHMM, SAL, File 119, Reel 24, Slides 948–949.
11. USHMM, SAL, File 103, Reel 20, Slide 639.
12. See, for example, USHMM, SAL, File 97, Reel 18, Slides 402, 443; USHMM, SAL, File 132, Reel 27, Slides 793–794; USHMM, SAL, File 45, Reel 10, Slide 36; USHMM, SAL, File 107, Reel 21, Slides 856–857.
13. USHMM, SAL, File 161, Reel 33, Slide 656, 668.
14. USHMM, SAL, File 147, Reel 30, Slide 805, 894.
15. USHMM, SAL, File 169, Reel 34, Slide 1076; ibid., File 114, Reel 23, Slide 864; ibid., File 163, Reel 33, Slides 997–999; ibid., File 154, Reel 32, Slide 1141.
16. USHMM, SAL, File 165, Reel 34, Slide 458; USHMM, SAL, File 158, Reel 33, Slide 359; USHMM, SAL, File 145, Reel 30, Slide 470.
17. USHMM, SAL, Files 148–149, Reel 31, Slides 188, 302, 550, 567–576. Jan Pawelec, the defendant in military court, was sentenced to fifteen years in prison.
18. USHMM, SAL, File 168, Reel 34, Slides 706, 796, 866.

10. The Math of Amnesty

1. *Dziennik Ustaw (DzU)* 1956, no. 11, poz. 57; Leszek Kubicki, personal interviews, November 23 and 28, 2012; AAN, MS, syg. 2075, pp. 6–7; AAN, MS, syg. 2074, p. 20.
2. AAN, MS, syg. 2070; Kubicki interview, November 28, 2012.
3. Leszek Kubicki, *Zbrodnie wojenne w świetle prawa polskiego* (Warsaw: PWN, 1963), 182; AAN, MS, syg. 9441, p. 53; AAN, MS, syg. 2074, p. 39.
4. USHMM, SAL, File 3, Reel 1, Slides 262, 292.
5. APS, SOS, File 734, p. 103; USHMM, SAL, File 54, Reel 10, Slide 1155; USHMM, SAL, File 55, Reel 11, Slide 415; USHMM, SSKKr, File 256, Reel 6, Slide 506.
6. AAN, MS, file 2075, pp. 6–8; Leo Hochberg, "Amnestia 1956 roku," *Państwo i Prawo (PiP)* 11, no. 10 (1956): 651; USHMM, SOL, File 149, Reel 9, Slides 951–962; USHMM, SOK, File 98, Reel 6, Slides 829, 831–833, 835.
7. Kubicki, *Zbrodnie wojenne,* 182; *DzU* 1997, no. 88, poz. 554; Kubicki interview, November 28, 2012; *DzU* 1964, no. 15, poz. 86.
8. *DzU* 1991, no. 34, poz. 149; Alina Skibińska, "'Dostał 10 lat, ale za co?' Analiza motywacji sprawców zbrodni na Żydach na wsi kieleckiej w latach 1942–1944," in *Zarys krajobrazu: Wieś polska wobec Zagłady Żydów, 1942–1945,* ed. Barbara Engelking and Jan Grabowski (Warsaw: Centrum Badań nad Zagładą Żydów, 2011), 326.
9. USHMM, SAL, File 114, Reel 23, Slide 880; USHMM, SAL, File 158, Reel 33, Slides 431–433.
10. USHMM, SAL, File 7, Reel 2, Slide 210.
11. USHMM, SOL, File 142, Reel 6, Slides 358–359.

12. Skibińska, "'Dostał 10 lat, ale za co?,'" 326, 436; USHMM, SAK, File 233, Reel 37, Slides 1060–1061.

Conclusion

1. Florian Peters, "Remaking Polish National History: Reenactment over Reflection," trans. David Burnett, October 3, 2016, paper presented at the *Cultures of History Forum,* University of Jena, Germany, http://www.cultures-of-history.uni-jena.de/politics/poland/remaking-polish-national-history-reenactment-over-reflection/.

2. Instytut Pamięci Narodowej, Postanowienie o umorzeniu śledztwa z dnia 30 czerwca 2003, June 30, 2003, https://ipn.gov.pl/pl/dla-mediow/komunikaty/10057,Komunikat-dot-postanowienia-o-umorzeniu-sledztwa-w-sprawie-zabojstwa-obywateli-p.html; *Dziennik Ustaw,* 2016, poz. 749.

3. Polska Agencja Prasowa, "Kandydat na szefa IPN o Jedwabnem: Wykonawcami zbrodni byli Niemcy, którzy wykorzystali Polaków," July 19, 2016, https://wiadomosci.dziennik.pl/polityka/artykuly/526800,kandydat-na-szefa-ipn-o-jedwabnem-wykonawcami-zbrodni-byli-niemcy-ktorzy-wykorzystali-polakow.html; Jacek Harłukowicz, "Robert Winnicki: 'Niech lewaki i pedały się boją': Oto nowy poseł z Dolnego Śląska," *Wyborcza.pl Wrocław,* November 5, 2015, http://wroclaw.wyborcza.pl/wroclaw/1,35771,19140220,niech-lewaki-i-pedaly-sie-boja-oto-nowy-posel-dolnego-slaska.html; Piotr Forecki, "Zabójcy pamięci i testowanie Jedwabnem: Rewizjonizm Holokaustu w IPN," *OKO.press,* October 10, 2017, https://oko.press/zabojcy-pamieci-testowanie-jedwabnem-rewizjonizm-holokaustu-ipn/.

4. Dominika Bulska and Mikołaj Winiewski, *Antisemitism in Poland: Results of Polish Prejudice Survey 3,* Center for Research on Prejudice, Department of Psychology, University of Warsaw, Poland, 2018, pp. 4–5, http://cbu.psychologia.pl/uploads/PPS3_raporty/Antisemitism_PPS3_DB_MHW_fin.pdf.

5. David Silberklang, Dan Michman, and Havi Dreifuss, *Yad Vashem Historians Respond to the Joint Statement of the Governments of Poland and Israel concerning the Revision of the January 26, 2018, Amendment to Poland's Act on the Institute of National Remembrance* (Jerusalem: World Holocaust Remembrance Center, 2018), https://www.yadvashem.org/research/historians-reaction.html.

6. Tomek Jędrczak, *Open Statement of Polish Jewish Organizations to the Public Opinion,* Union of Jewish Communities in Poland, February 19, 2018, http://jewish.org.pl/wiadomosci/oswiadczenie-organizacji-zydowskich-do-opinii-publicznej-open-statement-of-polish-jewish-organizations-to-the-public-opinion/.

7. Editorial Board, "Poland's 'Holocaust Law': The Wound Is Still Open," *Haaretz,* February 16, 2019, https://www.haaretz.com/opinion/editorial/poland-s-holocaust-law-the-wound-is-still-open-1.6939484; Editorial Board, "Poland, Face Facts," *Je-*

rusalem Post, February 18, 2019, https://www.jpost.com/Opinion/Poland-face-facts-580956.

8. Michał Zaręba, "Prof. Wojciech Polak o nowelizacji ustawy o IPN: 'To krok w tył,'" *Radio PiK*, June 27, 2018, http://www.radiopik.pl/2,70140,prof-wojciech-polak-o-nowelizacji-ustawy-o-ipn-t.

9. Bartosz Kocejko, "Przeliczamy budżet państwa na IPN-y: Ilu prawicowych historyków trzeba, by ochronić polską przyrodę?," *OKO.press*, January 12, 2018, https://oko.press/przeliczamy-budzet-panstwa-ipny-ilu-prawicowych-historykow-trzeba-by-ochronic-polska-przyrode/; *Plan finansowy na 2018 rok w części 67—Polska Akademia Nauk na podstawie ustawy budżetowej na rok 2018 z dnia 11 stycznia 2018 r., podpisanej przez Prezydenta RP dnia 29 stycznia 2018 r. (Dz.U. z 2018 r. poz. 291)*, Ministerstwo Nauki i Szkolnictwa Wyższego, Biuletyn Informacji Publicznej, http://www.bip.nauka.gov.pl/g2/oryginal/2018_02/3b4f024f166743f3af6b0b531251465b.pdf.

10. Tomasz Domański, "Korekta Obrazu? Refleksje źródłoznawcze wokół książki Dalej jest noc. Losy Żydów w wybranych powiatach okupowanej Polski, t. 1–2, red. Barbara Engelking, Jan Grabowski, Warszawa 2018," *Polish-Jewish Studies* 1 (February 2019): 3–72, https://ipn.gov.pl/pl/aktualnosci/65746,Korekta-obrazu-Refleksje-zrodloznawcze-wokol-ksiazki-Dalej-jest-noc-Losy-Zydow-w.html.

11. Ibid., 33–34.

12. Ibid., 38, 40, 44.

13. Joanna Berendt, "In Poland, 'a Narrow Window to Do Justice' for Those Robbed by Nazis," *New York Times*, June 10, 2018, https://www.nytimes.com/2018/06/10/world/europe/poland-holocaust-nazis-restitution.html.

14. Adam Leszczyński, "Politycy PiS kontra amerykańska ustawa 447: 'Żydzi przychodzą po nasze'; Sprawdzamy," *OKO.press*, May 13, 2018, https://oko.press/politycy-pis-kontra-amerykanska-ustawa-447-zydzi-przychodza-po-nasze-sprawdzamy/.

15. "Organizacje żydowskie przepychają ustawę, która może kosztować Polskę miliardy," *TVP Info*, January 22, 2018, https://www.tvp.info/35700355/organizacje-zydowskie-przepychaja-ustawe-ktora-moze-kosztowac-polske-miliardy; "Trzaskowski odbierze Polakom 200 miliardów?," *TVP Wiadomości*, June 15, 2020, https://wiadomosci.tvp.pl/48538765/trzaskowski-odbierze-polakom-200-miliardow; "'Wiadomości' krytykowane za tezę, że Trzaskowski pieniądze z 500+ mógłby przeznaczyć na roszczenia żydowskie," *Wirtualnemedia.pl*, June 16, 2020, https://www.wirtualnemedia.pl/artykul/rafal-trzaskowski-wybory-prezydenckie-wiadomosci-tvp-lacza-go-z-tematem-roszczenia-zydowski; "Polish Presidential Election Managed Well Despite Legal Uncertainties, But Intolerance and Public Media Bias Tarnished Campaign, International Observers Say," Organization for Security and Cooperation in Europe, Office for Democratic Institutions and Human Rights (OSCE ODIHR), June 29, 2020, https://www.osce.org/odihr/elections/poland/455731; "Andrzej Duda: Nie zgodzę się na odszkodowania za mienie bezspadkowe,"

RMF24.pl, July 9, 2020, https://www.rmf24.pl/raporty/raport-wybory-prezydenc kie2020/najnowsze-fakty/news-andrzej-duda-nie-zgodze-sie-na-odszkodowania -za-mienie-bezsp,nId,4601956; Tovah Lazaroff, "Duda's Fateful Polish Victory a Mixed Bag for Israel, Jews," *Jerusalem Post,* July 14, 2020, https://www.jpost .com/international/dudas-fateful-polish-victory-a-mixed-blessing-for-israel-jews -analysis-634937.

16. Joanna Podgórska and Łukasz Wójcik, "Obcy Zachód?," *Polityka,* July 11, 2017; Monika Pronczuk, "Polish Towns That Declared Themselves 'L.G.B.T. Free' Are Denied E.U. Funds," *New York Times,* July 30, 2020; Jo Harper, "Illiberal, Aliberal, Anti-liberal?," in *Poland's Memory Wars: Essays on Illiberalism,* ed. Jo Harper (Budapest: Central European University Press, 2018), 21–22.

17. Peter Novick, *The Resistance versus Vichy: The Purge of Collaborators in Liberated France* (New York: Columbia University Press, 1968), 5, 10, 13, 92, 99, 157, 173.

18. Claus Bundgård Christensen, Niels Bo Poulsen, and Peter Scharff Smith, "The Danish Volunteers in the Waffen SS and German Warfare at the Eastern Front," *Contemporary European History* 8, no. 1 (1999): 94.

19. Benjamin Frommer, *National Cleansing: Retribution against Nazi Collaborators in Postwar Czechoslovakia* (Cambridge: Cambridge University Press, 2004), 26–27.

20. Martin Conway, "Justice in Postwar Belgium: Popular Passions and Political Realities," in *The Politics of Retribution in Europe: World War II and Its Aftermath,* ed. István Deák, Jan Gross, and Tony Judt (Princeton, NJ: Princeton University Press, 2000), 135–140, 144–146, 150; Luc Huyse, "Belgian and Dutch Purges after World War II Compared," in *Retribution and Reparation in the Transition to Democracy,* ed. Jon Elster (New York: Cambridge University Press, 2006), 175.

21. Gerhard Hirschfeld and Peter Romijn, "Die Ahndung der Kollaboration in der Niederlanden," in *Politische Säuberung in Europa: Die Abrechnung mit Faschismus und Kollaboration nach dem Zweiten Weltkrieg,* ed. Klaus-Dietmar Henke and Hans Woller (Munich: Deutscher Taschenbuch Verlag, 1991), 283–287, 294.

22. Tanja Penter, "Local Collaborators on Trial: Soviet War Crimes Trials under Stalin (1943–1953)," *Cahiers du Monde russe* 49, no. 2/3 (2008): 341–364; Srđan Cvetković, *Između srpa i čekića: Represija u Srbiji, 1944–1953* (Belgrade: Institut za savremenu istoriju, 2006), 168, 173–188.

23. Olaf Mertelsmann and Aigi Rahi-Tamm, "Cleansing and Compromise: The Estonian SSR in 1944–1945," *Cahiers du Monde russe* 49, no. 2/3 (2008): 334, 337–339.

24. Henry L. Mason, *The Purge of Dutch Quislings: Emergency Justice in the Netherlands* (The Hague: Martinus Nijhoff, 1952), 64; Hans Fredrik Dahl, "Dealing with the Past in Scandinavia: Legal Purges and Popular Memories of Nazism and World War II in Denmark," in Elster, *Retribution and Reparation,* 153–154; Stein U. Larsen, "Die Ausschaltung der Quislinge in Norwegen," in Henke and

Woller, *Politische Säuberung in Europa*, 262–264; Huyse, "Belgian and Dutch Purges," 176; Hirschfeld and Romijn, "Die Ahndung der Kollaboration," 298–299.

25. Novick, *The Resistance versus Vichy*, 147; Frommer, *National Cleansing*, 79.

26. Frommer, *National Cleansing*, chap. 3; Novick, *The Resistance versus Vichy*, 151–154; Luc Huyse, "The Criminal Justice System as a Political Actor in Regime Transitions: The Case of Belgium, 1944–1950," in Deák, Gross, and Judt, *The Politics of Retribution in Europe*, 164; J. M. Van Bemmelen, "The Treatment of Political Delinquents in Some European Countries," *Journal of Criminal Science* 1 (1948): 114–119; Carl Christian Givskov, "The Danish Purge-Laws," *Journal of Criminal Law and Criminology* 39, no. 4 (1949): 454; Hans Fredrik Dahl, "Dealing with the Past," 161; Mason, *The Purge*, 60–62, 69–70.

27. Novick, *The Resistance versus Vichy*, 79–87, 158, 188; Henry Rousso, *The Vichy Syndrome: History and Memory in France since 1944*, trans. Arthur Goldhammer (Cambridge, MA: Harvard University Press, 1991), 61–62; Rousso, "The Purge in France: An Incomplete Story," in Elster, *Retribution and Reparation*, 103, 108.

28. Conway, "Justice in Postwar Belgium," 138, 140, 146, 152; Huyse, "The Criminal Justice System," 163; Van Bemmelen, "The Treatment of Political Delinquents," 113; Steven Dhondt and Luc Huyse, *La répression des collaborations, 1942–1952: Un passé toujours present* (Brussels: CRISP, 1993), 28; Huyse, "Belgian and Dutch Purges," 172.

29. Ido de Haan, "Failures and Mistakes: Images of Collaboration in Post-War Dutch Society," in *Collaboration with the Nazis: Public Discourse after the Holocaust*, ed. Roni Stauber (London: Routledge, 2010), 74–78; Hirschfeld and Romijn, "Die Ahndung der Kollaboration," 294, 298–299; Huyse, "The Criminal Justice System," 171. For major works on the purge in the Netherlands, see Peter Romijn, *Snel, streng en rechtvaardig: Politiek beleid inzake de bestraffing en reclassering van "foute" Nederlanders, 1945–1955* (Houten: De Haan, 1989); Harald Fühner, *Nachspiel: Die niederländische Politik und die Verfolgung von Kollaborateuren und NS-Verbrechern, 1945–1989* (Münster: Waxmann, 2005); Helen Grevers, *Van landverraders tot goede vaderlanders: De opsluiting van collaborateurs in Nederland en België, 1944–1950* (Amsterdam: Balans, 2013).

30. Frommer, *National Cleansing*, 3, 133–134, 297; Benjamin Frommer, "How Postwar Czech Courts Exposed and Exonerated Perpetrators of Crimes against Bohemian and Moravian Jews," paper presented at the ASEEES Annual Convention, New Orleans, November 15, 2012.

31. Givskov, "The Danish Purge-Laws," 451, 458; Dahl, "Dealing with the Past," 154; Ciara Damgaard, *Individual Criminal Responsibility for Core International Crimes* (Berlin: Springer Verlag, 2008), 108nn407–408. For other major works on the purge in Denmark, see Ditlev Tamm, *Retsopgøret efter besættelsen* (Copenhagen: Udgiverselskab for Danmarks nyeste historie, 1984); Jesper Nissen, *Den strengeste straf: Dødsstraffens genindførelse i Danmark, 1945* (Frederiksberg: Roskilde Universitetsforlag, 2001).

32. Damgaard, *Individual Criminal Responsibility*, 109nn409–410; Dahl, "Dealing with the Past," 155; United Nations War Crimes Commission, "Trial of Hauptsturmführer Oscar Hans, Eidsivating Lagmannsrett, January 1947 and Supreme Court of Norway," *Law Reports of Trials of War Criminals* 5 (1948): 82–93; Christopher Harper, "Landssvikoppgjørets behandling av jøderforfølgelsen i Norge, 1940–1945," *Lov og rett* 49, no. 8 (2010): 469–489. For the major work on the purge in Norway, see Johannes Andenæs, *Det vanskelige oppgjøret: Rettsoppgjøret etter okkupasjonen* (Oslo: Tanum-Norli, 1979).

33. Mertelsmann and Rahi-Tamm, "Cleansing and Compromise," 333, 339.

ACKNOWLEDGMENTS

As with every work of history, there is a lot of credit (or maybe blame) to go around. I owe my interest in the discipline to my high school history teacher, Michael Rowe of the International School of Geneva. István Deák of Columbia University introduced me to the countries between Germany and Russia. John Connelly of the University of California, Berkeley, saw this project to completion. Jan Grabowski of the University of Ottawa provided much of the inspiration with his own pioneering work, as did Alina Skibińska of the Center for Holocaust Research at the Polish Academy of Sciences. Yuri Slezkine and Jason Wittenberg of Berkeley patiently read the manuscript. Samuel Moyn of Yale University listened to me complain for twenty years.

In no particular order, I thank my colleagues for their support and friendship over the years: Christopher Casey, Adam Wolkoff, James Skee, Tomasz Frydel, Luca Fenoglio, Erica Lee, Eric Johnson, Jason Morton, Sarah Cramsey, Mark Keck-Szajbel, Michael Dean, Andrej Milivojević, Charles Shaw, Nicolas Patin, Dorota Nowak, John Bigham, Noah Kaye, and Johannes Hoyos.

This project would not have been possible without material and archival support from the American Council of Learned Societies, the Saul Kagan Fellowship in Advanced Shoah Study, the Takiff Family Foundation, and the Emerging Scholars Program of the Jack, Joseph and Morton Mandel Center for Advanced Holocaust Studies at the United States Holocaust Memorial Museum. The views expressed herein are those of the author and are not intended to reflect the views of any other entity.

In particular, I owe tremendous thanks to Steven Feldman of the Holocaust Memorial Museum for not letting me drag my feet on the publication of this book and to my editor at Harvard University Press, Kathleen McDermott, for seeing potential in it. Additionally, I am grateful to John Donohue and Wendy Nelson at Westchester Publishing Services for their careful copyediting.

I would also like to single out for special thanks Leszek Kubicki, Polish minister of justice from 1996 to 1997 and one of the last surviving eyewitnesses to the process of postwar retribution in Poland. The recollections he shared, and the candor and humor with which he did so, were some of the most memorable moments in the creation of this book.

Finally, thanks go to my family, for putting up with me.

INDEX

Abramowski, Aleksander, 60–61
Abramowski, Bolesław, 60–61
Adamów, 70, 100
Af, Rubin, 51
Ajchel, Kazimierz, 201
Ajchel, Wincenty, 52–53, 200–202, 224
Ajzenberg, Chaim, 58, 203–205, 211
All-Polish Youth. *See* Młodzież Wszechpolska
Amnesty of 1952, 240, 262–263
Amnesty of 1956, 258–265; criticism of, 264
Annopol, 61
Anti-Semitism: 1968 anti-Zionist campaign, 2–3, 37; during occupation, 19, 44–47; postcommunist Poland, 270–271, 273, 290n8; postwar expressions of, 78–79, 82–88, 168, 170; postwar violence, 82–84, 221; prewar Poland, 3, 12–13, 40, 104; prewar universities, 102–103. *See also* Judiciary
Araczewski, Jan, 23
Arbeitsamt. *See* Nazi German institutions
August Decree: amendments to, 128, 165–166, 183, 193, 197; criticism of, 124–130, 195, 235–238; genesis of, 90–96; interpretation of, 180–194, 227, 230–235, 239–240; number of cases, convictions, and death sentences, 7, 124, 135, 227, 238, 262, 274, 299–300n49, 301n5, 303n3, 304n4, 307–308n14, 309n3, 309n5, 310–311n23; postcommunist rehabilitation, 266–268; proposed revision of, 236–237; rate of conviction, 7–8, 161–162, 304n5; retroactivity, 129–130; use against postwar anticommunist resistance, 96, 132, 217, 233, 301n2

Bancerz, Stefan, 163–164, 173
Bandau, Henryk, 22
Barcikowski, Wacław, 102, 120, 125–127, 167, 170–176, 196, 228
Bardach, Janusz, 223
Barglik, Franciszek, 154
Bartkowiak, Lidia, 34
Bartnik, Adam, 211
Barwy Białe partisan unit. *See* Home Army
Baudienst. *See* Nazi German institutions
Belarusian minority, 11, 12, 80, 246
Belgium, 275–278
Belniak, Aleksander, 21
Bełzów, 76
Berkowicz, Pola, 218
Berling, Zygmunt, 86, 93
Berman, Jakub, 90, 95, 99
Betiuk, Stanisław, 215
Bezek-Kolonia, 146
Białystok, 46, 72, 97, 98, 168, 238, 243–245

Bierut, Bolesław, 99, 171, 243, 260; role in commutations, 127, 135, 138–140, 157, 214–215, 249, 252–254, 299–300n49
Błędowski, Mieczysław, 76, 218
Błoński, Jan, 37–38
Bloxham, Donald, 133
Blue Police, 17–20, 22, 31, 33, 45, 50, 52, 59, 66–72, 76, 136, 149–150, 154–159, 183, 192–193, 201–203, 210–212, 214, 217–218, 221, 224, 229, 232, 234, 252, 256, 263, 265, 272; autonomy to kill Jews, 39, 47–48, 66, 68–69; infiltration by Underground, 29; morale and corruption, 25–29; reemployment in postwar police, 123. See also Kriminalpolizei
Bogucice, 75
Borkowski, Jan, 264
Brenner, Chil, 61–62
Bryła, Stanisław, 101
Brześć Trial, 102, 125
Budnicki, Wacław, 213
Burzec, 53
Bytom, 82
Bzowski, Kazimierz, 140, 143, 148, 158–159, 196, 228–229, 233, 235–236, 239, 309n8

Camps, concentration and extermination: Auschwitz, 22, 80, 107, 123, 148, 219, 245; Bełżec, 13; HASAG, 73; Majdanek, 106, 126, 174, 254; Sobibór, 14; Stutthof, 106; Treblinka, 14, 52, 210
Catholic Church, 13, 40, 81, 290n8
Center for Holocaust Research. See Centrum Badań nad Zagładą Żydów
Central Committee of Polish Jewry, 83, 86–88

Centrum Badań nad Zagładą Żydów (Center for Holocaust Research), 9, 271–272
Chaciński, Władysław, 62, 212
Chajn, Leon, 90, 98–99, 101, 105, 118, 127, 129, 138–139, 162, 164, 171–177, 179–180
Chamit, Sława, 51, 249–250
Charlejów, 71
Chełm, 64, 146
Chmielewski, Henryk, 242
Chojecka, Marianna, 59
Chojnacki, Tadeusz, 77, 205–206, 218, 293n73
Chojnacki, Walenty, 69–70, 214
Chojnowski, Bronisław, 75
Chojnowski, Władysław, 110, 113–114, 119
Cholerzyn, 192
Chrościcki, Aleksander, 101
Chruściel, Antoni, 61–62, 250, 252
Chruszczyna, 76
Chrzanów, 51, 249, 263
Cieślak, Eugeniusz, 213
Cieśluk, Henryk, 114
Ciupak, Władysław, 51, 249–250, 252, 263
Communist party, Polish, 2, 37, 80, 88, 90, 98–99, 106, 109, 119, 163, 170, 174–175, 205, 226, 229, 233, 243, 245, 260–261; cases involving members of, 57, 61, 64, 151, 154–155, 213, 215
Council of State. See Rada Narodowa
Courts, Appellate: rulings of, 248–254; transfer of jurisdiction to, 227–228. See also August Decree: number of cases, convictions, and death sentences; Judiciary; Supreme Court
Courts, District: rulings of, 199–225; sentencing of, 161–162; transfer of jurisdiction to, 165–167. See also

August Decree: number of cases, convictions, and death sentences; Judiciary; Supreme Court
Courts, military, 93, 96, 132, 164, 217, 219, 257, 278
Courts, Regional: renaming of Appellate Courts as, 228; rulings of, 255–259. *See also* August Decree: number of cases, convictions, and death sentences; Judiciary; Supreme Court
Courts, Special: abolition of, 165–166; composition and procedure of, 92; functioning and reception of, 105–131; number of cases and convictions, 134–135, 299n49, 303n3; public executions, 106; rulings of, 132–159. *See also* August Decree: number of cases, convictions, and death sentences; Judiciary; Supreme Court
Courts, summary, 113, 132, 298n20
Courts, underground. *See* Cywilne Sądy Specjalne Kierownictwa Walki Cywilnej
Cybulski, Jan, 30
Cyprian, Tadeusz, 143, 145, 147–148, 165, 176
Cyrankiewicz, Józef, 261
Cywilne Sądy Specjalne Kierownictwa Walki Cywilnej (CSS KWC) (Civilian Special Courts of the Directorate of Civil Resistance), 41
Czaja, Franciszek, 155, 157–158
Czechoslovakia, 85, 105, 261, 268, 275–279; ethnic minority in Poland, 81
Czechowski, Jan, 90

Dąb, Adolf, 176, 178–179
Dąbrowa Tarnowska, 39

Death penalty. *See* August Decree; Bierut, Bolesław; Supreme Court
Dębica, 155
Delegatura (underground state), 4, 46, 72, 78–79, 90, 166, 219, 257. *See also* Home Army; Poland: government-in-exile
Democratic Legal Review, 162–163, 167, 175, 179–180, 185
Democratic Party (Poland). *See* Stronnictwo Demokratyczne
Denmark, 275–279, 316n31
Długosz, Edward, 216
Dmowski, Roman, 12, 169
Doliński, Jan, 21
Dorosiewicz, Stanisław, 219
Douglas, Lawrence, 124
Dudek, Helena, 31

Endecja. *See* Narodowa Demokracja
Engelking, Barbara, 9, 16, 272
Estonia / Estonian Soviet Socialist Republic, 277, 279
Evangelical-Augsburg Church, 82, 189

Fabian, Alina, 68
Faliszewski, Jan, 69
Feldman, Fela, 221
Feldman, Guta, 221
Fieldorf, Emil, 233
Fijoł, Józef, 215, 221
Firemen. *See* Village administration
Firlej, 149
First Polish Army. *See* Poland: army in the East
First World War, 11–12, 15, 23–24, 40, 69, 101–102, 127, 141
Fischer, Ludwig, 106, 187, 194
Flaga, Ignacy, 52, 201
Flechtman, Hersz, 64, 150–151, 216

France, 24, 37, 79, 105, 123–124, 168, 210, 275–278
Furgała, Antoni, 145, 215

Gałecki, Franciszek, 155
Gansiniec, Stefan, 254–255
Garncarek, Jan, 30
Garwolin, 113
Gaulle, Charles de, 276
Gdańsk, 243, 301n2
Gendarmerie. *See* Nazi German institutions
Generalgouvernement, 9, 13, 16, 39–40, 43, 72–73, 83, 98, 108, 132, 182, 188, 304n6
General Prosecutor's Office, 174, 234, 237, 244, 249, 258, 262–263, 265, 310n19
Gestapo. *See* Nazi German institutions
Ghettos, 13, 36, 38, 42, 51–53, 60–61, 66–68, 70, 76–77, 97, 153, 158–159, 173, 187, 201–202, 206–207, 209, 211, 225. *See also* Warsaw: Ghetto
Giebułtowski, Kazimierz, 214
Giedroyc, Jerzy, 173
Głaz, Jan, 55, 57
Głogowski, Mieczysław, 154
Gmur, Karol, 204
Godziszów, 54
Goławski, Leon, 21
Gołębiów, 148
Gołębiowski, Michał, 57, 266
Gombrowicz, Janusz, 207–209
Gomułka, Władysław, 99, 171, 174, 226, 259–261
Góra, Moszek-Mendel, 52, 201–202, 224
Górski, Józef, 24
Górski, Mieczysław, 209–210
Grabowski, Jan, 6, 9, 16, 42, 272
Grabuszyński, Marian, 222–223
Gregoruk, Michał, 146

Greiser, Arthur, 106–107, 187, 194
Grójec, 46
Gross, Jan, 1–3, 9, 16, 266
Gross, Stanisław, 103
Grynbaum, Ignacy, 221
Grzechowiak, Adam, 70, 252–253, 263
Grzymała, Władysław, 100–102, 104, 112–113, 168–170, 174, 198, 200, 202–203, 205, 220–221, 233, 245–248
Gubiński, Arnold, 175, 180, 185–186, 188–194, 196, 208, 232, 255
Güntner, Mieczysław, 99, 112
Gutman, Abram, 69

Hałaj, Feliks, 55
Handzel, Józef, 151–154
Headmen. *See* Village administration
Herling-Grudziński, Maurycy, 194, 237, 242
Hlond, August, 13, 40
Holocaust: commentary on property transfer, 43–47, 78–79, 83; memory of, 3–4, 37–38; Nazi German implementation of, 13–14; property restitution, 83, 270, 273; survivors as witnesses, 52, 59–60, 123, 134, 145–147, 155, 191, 194, 201–202, 209–210, 213, 221–225, 246–247, 249–251; wartime opinion regarding, 44–46, 78–79. *See also* Anti-Semitism
Home Army, 4, 25, 27–29, 39, 68, 84, 96, 100, 168, 176, 189, 205, 219, 224; analysis of public opinion regarding Holocaust, 19, 44–47, 78–79; cases involving members of, 46–47, 54, 71, 73–77, 205–207, 218–219, 257–258, 266–267; postwar threats against Jews, 84; suspicion of Jews as bandits, 41–42, 72
Hot, Lejba, 250–251

Huczkowski, Dobromil-Emilian, 25
Hungary, 261; Jewish refugees from, 84; 1956 uprising, 260

Ilczuk, Franciszek, 66
Institute of National Remembrance. *See* Instytut Pamięci Narodowej
Instytut Pamięci Narodowej (IPN) (Institute of National Remembrance), 10, 269–272; law on, 1, 270–271
IPN. *See* Instytut Pamięci Narodowej

Jagnicki, Aleksander, 55
Janczuk, Henryk, 64, 150–151, 216
Jankowska, Anna, 213
Jasionowski, Henryk, 137, 148, 150
Jaworski, Paweł, 263
Jęczmien, Jankel, 246–247
Jędruś partisan unit. *See* Home Army
Jedwab, Samuel, 168
Jedwabne, 9, 247, 266, 270
Jehovah's Witnesses, 81
Jeruchem, Artur, 67
Jezierski, Władysław, 144
Jodłowski, Jerzy, 164, 261
Judiciary: anti-Semitism in, 102–104, 167–170, 229, 245–246; collusion between prosecutors and judges, 168–169, 245–247; criticism of, 99, 160–164, 178–180, 219–220, 226, 229, 244–245; influence of prewar cadre, 197–198, 228, 240–243, 245; new legal schools, 164–165, 167, 170, 197–198, 228, 241–243, 245; party affiliation, 169–170, 243–245; postwar rebuilding of, 89, 97–102; role of universities, 101–103, 164–165, 197, 241, 243, 245
Juny, Adam, 148, 193–194, 255

Kac, Chena, 66
Kądziela, Mieczysław, 148
Kałuszyn, 61
Kamieniec, 31
Kamiński, Jan, 136, 138–139, 302n9
Kania, Stanisław, 221–222
Kania, Wacław, 143–145
Kapitaniak, Zygmunt, 162–163, 172, 176
Karski, Jan, 19, 291n18
Karwowski, Józef, 101
Kaszów, 155
Katowice, 80, 177
Katra, Józef, 211
Kąty, 25
Kędzierski, Zdzisław, 58, 203–205, 211
Kęsicki, Szczepan, 24
Khrushchev, Nikita, 247, 260
Kielce, 16, 18, 73–74, 83, 100, 123, 161, 216–218, 223, 267
Kilanowicz, Stefan, 256
Kliszko, Zenon, 99
Kłos, Edward, 25
Kłyza, Piotr, 253
Kock, 204
Komorowski, Tadeusz, 41–42
Kondera, Natalia, 223
Konstantynów, 81
Kopyść, Stanisław, 203
Korsak, Bohdan, 206
Kosiński, Czesław, 200, 203
Kossak-Szczucka, Zofia, 17, 78
Koszalin, 79
Kotarski, Stanisław, 141–142
Kott, Jan, 106
Kozioł, Józef, 218
Krajowa Rada Narodowa (KRN) (State National Council), 90, 92, 106, 110, 127
Kraków, 24, 45, 73, 80, 82–83, 97, 99–100, 103, 105, 108–109, 112–113, 115–118, 121, 123, 127, 132–133, 135–136, 148, 154–155, 158, 170, 182, 191–192, 259

Kraśnik, 74
Krasnystaw, 218
Krawczyk, Mieczysław, 71
Krawczyk, Urszula, 21
Kriminalpolizei (Kripo), 18, 28–29, 67–69, 123, 148, 184, 188, 193, 250, 255
Kripo. *See* Kriminalpolizei
KRN. *See* Krajowa Rada Narodowa
Król, Bronisław, 62
Król, Stanisław, 157–158, 303n29
Kubicki, Leszek, 89, 99, 102, 104, 106–107, 111, 118, 173–177, 182, 197, 233, 238, 260–261, 265
Kuciak, Jan, 211–212
Kuczyński, Stanisław, 158–159
Kupczyński, Franciszek, 250–251
Kurek, Stanisław, 57
Kuś, Franciszek, 71
Kwaśniowski, Stanisław, 58–59, 151–153
Kwiatkowski, Stanisław, 59–60

Łaganowski, Ignacy, 265
Landau, Antoni, 123, 125–126, 130, 165, 194, 196
Landau, Leib, 173
Lane, Arthur Bliss, 87
Law and Justice Party. *See* Prawo i Sprawiedliwość
Lay judges, 92, 95, 108–111, 118, 125–127, 129, 132–134, 140, 143–144, 146–148, 150, 160, 165, 240, 243–244, 246, 278
League for the Defense of the Rights of Man and Citizen, 127, 176
Lech, Franciszek, 218
Leder, Andrzej, 3
Lejb, Chana, 55
Lemkin, Rafał, 102–103
Lernell, Leszek, 174–176, 226, 236
Leśniowice, 55

Levi, Primo, 80
Lewandowski, Stanisław, 215
Libionka, Dariusz, 9, 272
Lieberfreund, Rozalia, 194
Liebeskind, Adolf, 191
Lis, Irena, 34
Liszki, 192
Łódź, 44, 81, 165, 167, 221
Łopiennik Górny, 74–75
Lubartów, 57
Lublin, 5, 45–46, 70, 74, 89, 94, 97, 100–101, 106, 116, 122, 124, 129, 132–133, 135, 138, 141, 143, 148, 162, 171, 173–174, 184, 205, 216, 221, 234, 248–249, 251, 253, 255, 266–267
Łuków, 22, 36, 225
Lustman, Berek, 75
Lviv. *See* Lwów
Lwów, 34, 45, 173, 175

Maciejowice, 138
Maj, Tadeusz, 74
Majdan Leśniowski, 55
Majewski, Włodzimierz, 21–22
Makarewicz, Juliusz, 177, 180
Makowski, Julian, 166
Maksym, Paweł, 65, 212
Makuła, Zygmunt, 203
Margoshes, Samuel, 83, 85–86
Margules, Hanna, 213
Marzęcin, 75, 218
Mazur, Jan, 266
Mazur, Marian, 237
Międzyrzec Podlaski, 203
Mielec, 83
Mielniczuk, Kazimierz, 75
Mikołajczyk, Stanisław, 226
Milicja Obywatelska (MO) (Citizens' Militia): creation of, 118–119; criticism of, 115, 118–123, 168, 246; involvement

of members in crimes against Jews, 57, 64, 122–123, 138, 151, 154–156, 217–218
Miłosz, Czesław, 38, 89
Minc, Hilary, 246
Ministry of Justice: criticism of, 170–172, 177–180, 245; internal debate about August trials, 235–238; Jews in, 170–171, 173–176; offices of judicial and prosecutorial oversight, 162, 172, 174–176, 178, 220, 242, 244–245; rebuilding of, 89–90, 98, 170–173. *See also* General Prosecutor's Office; Judiciary
Mińsk Mazowiecki, 27, 46
Miśkiwa, Aleksandr, 105
Miszczuk, Marceli, 62
Młodzież Wszechpolska (All-Polish Youth), 103, 270
Mniszewski, Witold, 111–112
MO. *See* Milicja Obywatelska
Moczar, Mieczysław, 138
Molęda, Wojciech, 148–150
Moyn, Samuel, 37
Mrozowska, Aleksandra, 145–147

Najwyższy Trybunał Narodowy (NTN) (Supreme National Tribunal), 107, 112, 140, 143, 158, 174, 176, 187, 189, 194
Narodowa Demokracja (Endecja) (National Democracy), 12, 103–104, 169
Narodowe Siły Zbrojne (NSZ) (National Armed Forces), 41–42, 72–74, 84, 251
Narutowicz, Gabriel, 12
Nasielsk, 24
Natalin, 144
National Armed Forces. *See* Narodowe Siły Zbrojne

National Democracy movement. *See* Narodowa Demokracja
National Military Organization. *See* Narodowe Siły Zbrojne
Nazi German institutions: Arbeitsamt, 22–23, 27, 35, 246; Baudienst, 23, 28, 185, 230; Gendarmerie, 6, 18, 27, 30, 33, 35, 39, 45, 48, 64–65, 136–138, 152–153, 168, 202, 204, 221; Gestapo, 17, 25, 30, 32–36, 69, 74, 85, 120, 136, 166, 184–185, 190–191, 220, 252, 278; Ordnungspolizei, 26; Sicherheitsdienst (SD), 68, 136, 166, 212; SS, 27, 67, 136, 138–139, 141, 166, 254, 278–279
Netherlands, 275–278, 316n29
Nieć, Wiktor, 152–154
Niemójki, 61
NKVD. *See* Soviet Union
Norway, 275, 277–279, 317n32
Nowak, Zygmunt, 213
NSZ. *See* Narodowe Siły Zbrojne
NTN. *See* Najwyższy Trybunał Narodowy
Nuremberg Trials, 107, 126, 131, 133, 143, 158, 161, 166, 174, 176, 186–187, 189, 194

Obarzanek, Aleksander, 141–143, 145
Office of Public Security. *See* Urząd Bezpieczeństwa Publicznego
Okulus, Władysław, 52–53
Okuniew, 69
Olchownik, Kazimierz, 74
Old Catholic Church, 81
Omelański, Wincenty, 157–158
Opatów, 212
Osiemborów, 59
Osmólski, Edward, 242–243
Osóbka-Morawski, Edward, 86, 90, 98, 106
Ostrów Mazowiecka, 27

Oszust, Franciszek, 55, 57
Otwock, 100

Parole, law on, 240, 253, 258, 262
Paskudzki, Antoni, 250, 252, 263
Paszkot, Józef, 155
Patoleta, Aleksander, 31
Pawelec, Henryk, 47
Pawelec, Jan, 75, 257
Peasant Battalions, 41–42, 65, 72, 75–76, 212, 257–258
Penner, Leon, 237
People's Army (communist partisan unit), 23, 28–29, 41–42, 57, 61, 63, 73, 138, 189, 215, 217; cases involving members of, 63, 74
People's Guard. *See* People's Army (communist partisan unit)
Pétain, Henri, 276
Pietrasik, Józef, 31, 33
Piłatowicz, Marian, 24
Piłsudski, Józef, 11–12, 101–102, 177
Pińczów, 39, 45
Pinkus, Oscar, 5–6, 17, 223–224
Pionki, 77, 207, 211, 218
Piotrawin, 144
PiS. *See* Prawo i Sprawiedliwość
PKWN. *See* Polski Komitet Wyzwolenia Narodowego
Podlaski, Henryk, 173–174, 220, 238, 240
Poland: army in the East, 40, 56, 90, 93, 171, 173, 215, 267; government-in-exile, 3–4, 41, 44, 46, 90, 93, 99, 112, 164, 176; Sanacja government, 12, 102, 177, 263; social change under communism, 2–3, 43, 45, 88–89; Thaw of 1956, 259–261
Police, Nazi German. *See* Nazi German institutions

Police, postwar Polish. *See* Milicja Obywatelska
Police, postwar Polish political. *See* Urząd Bezpieczeństwa Publicznego
Police, village. *See* Village administration: watchmen
Police, wartime Polish. *See* Blue Police; Kriminalpolizei
Polish Armed Forces. *See* Poland: army in the East
Polish Committee of National Liberation. *See* Polski Komitet Wyzwolenia Narodowego
Polish Peasant Party. *See* Polskie Stronnictwo Ludowe
Polish People's Army (socialist partisan unit). *See* Polska Partia Socjalistyczna: underground organizations
Polish Socialist Party. *See* Polska Partia Socjalistyczna
Polish-Soviet War, 40, 53, 101, 149, 153, 176
Polish United Workers' Party. *See* Communist party, Polish
Polish Workers' Party. *See* Communist party, Polish
Polody, Ignacy, 36
Polska Partia Robotnicza. *See* Communist party, Polish
Polska Partia Socjalistyczna (PPS) (Polish Socialist Party), 11, 40, 44, 53, 76, 80, 109, 172, 176, 205, 226; underground organizations, 42, 69, 71, 76, 205, 218
Polska Zjednoczona Partia Robotnicza. *See* Communist party, Polish
Polski, Dawid-Henryk, 263
Polski Komitet Wyzwolenia Narodowego (PKWN) (Polish Committee of National Liberation), 82, 85–86,

88–91, 93–100, 104, 118–119, 121, 124, 127–129, 164, 173
Polskie Siły Zbrojne. *See* Poland: army in the East
Polskie Stronnictwo Ludowe (PSL) (Polish Peasant Party), 65, 80, 88, 169, 212, 226
Powrózek, Józef, 54
Poznań, 100, 122, 207, 245, 260
PPR. *See* Communist party, Polish
Prawo i Sprawiedliwość (PiS) (Law and Justice Party), 2–3, 270–271, 273
Provisional Government of National Unity. *See* Tymczasowy Rząd Jedności Narodowej
Przybysławice, 63
Przymusiński, Franciszek, 28
PSL. *See* Polskie Stronnictwo Ludowe
PSZ. *See* Poland: army in the East
Pszczoła, Jan, 75
Pudzianowski, Józef, 148–150
PZPR. *See* Communist party, Polish

Rada Narodowa (Council of State), 248, 258, 262, 265
Radkiewicz, Stanisław, 96, 259, 295n42
Radomsko, 27, 69
Radzymin, 35
Rappaport, Emil Stanisław, 102–103, 127, 194–195, 233, 238
Ratuszniak, Zygmunt, 241
Reszczyński, Aleksander, 26–27, 29
Romania, 261
Rowecki, Stefan, 44
Rozen, Majer, 218
Rozenberg, Dawid, 217
Rozenman, Abram, 205, 224–225
Ruda Opalin, 70
Rusiniak, Sylwester, 67
Rzepa, Władysław, 136
Rzeszów, 105, 122
Rzymowski, Wincenty, 84

Sady, Edward, 203
Sanacja. *See* Poland: Sanacja government
Sawicki, Jerzy, 126, 129–130, 158–159, 165, 173–176, 180, 185–186, 188–194, 196, 208, 232, 255
Sciborowski, Franciszek, 210–211
SD. *See* Nazi German institutions
Secret Section of the Warsaw City Court, 96, 132, 233, 235, 237, 239, 243, 258
Sekutowicz, Bolesław, 101
Serokomla, 58, 225
Shklar, Judith, 130–131, 161
Sicherheitsdienst. *See* Nazi German institutions
Siedlce, 23, 33, 68–69, 100–101, 121, 161, 168–169, 198, 200, 204, 220, 223–224, 245, 248
Siedlecki, Piotr, 209–210
Sielec, 55
Siemiatycze, 168, 247
Silesia, 40, 100, 122, 254
Skawa, 154
Skibińska, Alina, 9, 18, 115, 266–267, 272
Skrobot, Edward, 268
Skrzeszewski, Stanisław, 104
Skwara, Wacław, 68
Ślezak, Witold, 28, 212
Sliwiński, Antoni, 23
Śliwiński, Stanisław, 165, 196
Sliz, Jędrzej, 59
Słomiński, Ludwik, 71
Smietanko, Czesław, 70, 221–222
Socha, Józef, 256
Sokołowski, Apolinary, 53–54, 58, 202–203, 220, 248, 256

Sołtysiak, Marian, 47, 73, 268
Sommerstein, Emil, 13, 86–87, 93–94, 295n42
Sot, Stanisław, 136–138
Soviet Union: NKVD, 83, 112, 157; occupation of eastern Poland in 1939–1941, 13, 44–45, 64, 151, 246–247; postwar retribution, 277–279; Thaw of 1956, 259–260
Spiechowicz, Stanisław, 217
SS. *See* Nazi German institutions
Stalin, Joseph, 7, 89–90, 93, 175, 243, 259–260, 275
Starachowice, 74, 76
State National Council. *See* Krajowa Rada Narodowa
Steinlauf, Michael, 38
Strojna, Aniela, 71
Stronnictwo Demokratyczne (Democratic Party), 80, 170, 175–176, 261
Strożek, Władysław, 30
Supreme Court: criticism of, 180–181, 185–194, 228–229, 237, 244; criticism of appeals process, 194–196; revising mitigating circumstances, 239–240; role in appeasing public opinion, 235–237, 239–240, 253–255, 258; rulings on Special Court appeals, 140, 143, 145, 147–148, 157–159. *See* August Decree: interpretation of; August Decree: proposed revision of; Secret Section of the Warsaw City Court
Supreme National Tribunal. *See* Najwyższy Trybunał Narodowy
Surowiec, Piotr, 31, 33
Świątkowski, Henryk, 106, 127, 172, 195, 229, 237, 242
Światło, Józef, 170, 259
Świderska, Anna, 33
Syga, Józef, 191, 263

Szczecin, 222
Szczerbówka, 76
Szejnberg, Chil, 201–202
Szerer, Mieczysław, 194–195, 197, 233, 263
Szewczuk, Bronisław, 258
Szmajcer, Berek, 212
Szumielewicz, Władysław, 268
Szwarcberg, Szymon, 59–60
Szymański, Stefan, 22

Taras, Stanisław, 55–57, 215, 267
Tarnów, 83, 158, 231
Tarnowski, Aleksander, 96
Tomasik, Wincenty, 76, 267
Tomaszewski, Hieronim, 61
Tomaszewski, Krzysztof, 61, 263
Toruń, 23, 111, 127
TRJN. *See* Tymczasowy Rząd Jedności Narodowej
Trzciniec, 57
Turowski, Aleksander, 258
Tygodnik Powszechny, 106, 174
Tymczasowy Rząd Jedności Narodowej (TRJN) (Provisional Government of National Unity), 86–87

UB. *See* Urząd Bezpieczeństwa Publicznego
Ukraine, 11–12, 46, 79, 81–82, 98, 167, 209; Ukrainian collaborators, 105, 108, 135, 141, 145–146, 188, 208; Ukrainian Insurgent Army, 12, 80; Ukrainian Soviet Socialist Republic, 277; war with, 40, 69, 101
Underground: infiltration of Blue Police, 29; position on Holocaust, 40–42, 52; punishment of Polish collaborators, 15, 21–22, 25, 29–31, 34–36, 41. *See also* Home Army;

Narodowe Siły Zbrojne; Peasant Battalions; People's Army; Polska Partia Socjalistyczna: underground organizations
Underground state. *See* Delegatura
Union of Polish Patriots. *See* Związek Patriotów Polskich
Urząd Bezpieczeństwa Publicznego (UB) (Office of Public Security), 36, 93, 96, 136, 141, 148, 165, 169, 215, 219, 245–247, 251, 259, 272; cases involving members, 40, 57, 71–72, 122–123, 155–157, 215, 217–218; criticism of, 83, 113, 115, 118–123, 170; Jews in, 83, 122, 168, 170; reluctance to support legislation against anti-Semitism, 88
USSR. *See* Soviet Union

Village administration: firemen, 19, 47–48, 50–54, 66, 154–155, 201–202, 211, 249–250, 272; headmen, 17, 19–21, 47–48, 50, 53–55, 57–61, 63–64, 66, 71, 76, 137–138, 146–147, 149–150, 155, 158, 192, 203, 206, 210, 217, 219–221, 231–232, 234, 256, 272; wartime elections to village office, 20–21, 48, 55, 61, 146, 291n35; watchmen, 19, 47–48, 50, 55–59, 64, 66, 145, 149, 151, 156, 192, 204, 215, 217, 232, 253, 256, 272
Vistula River, 62, 68, 100, 169
Volksdeutsche, 78, 107–109, 113, 117–118, 130, 135, 141, 152, 196, 213, 274

Wadowice Górne, 154
Warsaw, 16, 24, 26–29, 33–36, 46, 60, 66, 68, 70, 72, 74, 83, 97, 100, 103, 106, 108, 110–111, 113–114, 121, 132, 135, 158, 161, 165, 169, 171, 174–176, 187, 196, 210, 213–214, 218, 221, 223, 233, 241–242, 245, 247, 271; Ghetto, 38, 60, 66–67, 97, 209; Uprising, 22–23, 30, 68, 73, 76, 176, 215
Wąsala, Andrzej, 64, 216
Wasung, Ajzyk, 57, 266
Watchmen. *See* Village administration
Węgrów, 25, 51–53, 201, 224
Welo, Jan, 62
Welo, Paulina, 256
Wendel, Adam, 171
Wiącek, Józef, 219
Wiejak, Stanisław, 263
Wielebski, Jan, 70
Wiesenfeld, Gustawa, 83
Wiewiorka, Stanisław, 36
Winerowicz, Marian, 33
Witak, Stanisław, 29
Witosińska, Bronisława, 69
Włoszczowa, 217
Wojciechowski, Jan, 156
Wojcieszków, 53
Wójtowicz, Bronisław, 266
Wola Bukowska, 21
Wola Przybysławska, 63, 256
Wola Wielka, 158
Wólka Serokomlska, 58
Wróblewski, Lucjan, 213
Wrocław, 24, 201
Wrona, Lucjan, 216
Wybranieccy partisan unit. *See* Home Army
Wysocki, Ireneusz, 30

Yad Vashem, 271
Yugoslavia, 275, 277

Zabornia, 151
Zamość, 167, 187

Zaremba, Marcin, 79
Zbrozek, Stanisław, 201
Zdun, Władysław, 215, 217–218
Żelizer, Chana, 201–202, 224
Zimnowłodzki, Jerzy, 23
Ziserman, Szloma, 145–147, 224

ZPP. *See* Związek Patriotów Polskich
Żuławska, Czesława, 128
Żuziak, Andrzej, 158
Związek Patriotów Polskich (ZPP) (Union of Polish Patriots), 93–94, 96
Zysman, Szajndla, 250, 263